ADVANCES IN QUALITY-OF-LIFE THEORY AND RESEARCH

Social Indicators Research Series

Volume 20

This new series aims to provide a public forum for single treatises and collections of papers on social indicators research that are too long to be published in our journal *Social Indicators Research*. Like the journal, the book series deals with statistical assessments of the quality of life from a broad perspective. It welcomes the research on a wide variety of substantive areas, including health, crime, housing, education, family life, leisure activities, transportation, mobility, economics, work, religion and environmental issues. These areas of research will focus on the impact of key issues such as health on the overall quality of life and vice versa. An international review board, consisting of Ruut Veenhoven, Joachim Vogel, Ed Diener, Torbjorn Moum, Mirjam A.G. Sprangers and Wolfgang Glatzer, will ensure the high quality of the series as a whole.

ADVANCES IN QUALITY-OF-LIFE THEORY AND RESEARCH

Edited by

M. JOSEPH SIRGY

Virginia Polytechnic Institute and State University, U.S.A.

DON RAHTZ

The College of William and Mary, U.S.A.

and

A. COSKUN SAMLI

University of North Florida, U.S.A.

KLUWER ACADEMIC PUBLISHERS

DORDRECHT / BOSTON / LONDON

A C.I.P. Catalogue record for this book is available from the Library of Congress.

ISBN 1-4020-1474-0

Published by Kluwer Academic Publishers,
P.O. Box 17, 3300 AA Dordrecht, The Netherlands.

Sold and distributed in North, Central and South America
by Kluwer Academic Publishers,
101 Philip Drive, Norwell, MA 02061, U.S.A.

In all other countries, sold and distributed
by Kluwer Academic Publishers,
P.O. Box 322, 3300 AH Dordrecht, The Netherlands.

Printed on acid-free paper

Printed in the Netherlands.

This book is dedicated to all quality-of-life researchers worldwide.

LIFE IS LIKE
AN ARTICHOKE.
YOU STRIP AWAY
A FEW YEARS.
YOU PEEL OFF
AN ILLUSION OR TWO,
AND WHAT REMAINS
IS ESSENTIAL . . .
THE HEART.

ANONYMOUS

ACKNOWLEDGEMENTS

There are many people who helped us directly and indirectly develop this volume. The authors who made a contribution to this volume deserve the greatest credit. Those who helped us directly by assembling the papers and putting the volume in the right format and book template include Wanda Nolley (secretary to Joe Sirgy) and Carolyn Gavin (secretary to Josh Samli). Our acknowledgements extend to Alex Michalos, the editor of the Social Indicators Research Book Series, for approving this volume as part of the book series. Finally, we like to express our appreciation to the management and editorial staff at Kluwer Academic Publishers. They include Myriam Poort, Renee de Boo, Peter de Liefde, Susan Jones, Welmoed Spahr, and Yan Yan Chan. We owe them our gratitude and deep appreciation for their caring attitude and helpfulness.

TABLE OF CONTENTS

PREFACE

I am honored to be invited to write this preface. A few years ago when we started ISQOLS, I certainly did not dream of writing a preface of this magnitude.

This book has 14 chapters. These are very important culmination of very intense research efforts. They reiterate my conviction that quality of life research is a very broad multidisciplinary topic that needs to be explored in a multidisciplinary manner. The chapters of this book not only reiterate the conviction of QOL as a multidisciplinary area of investigation, but also each chapter offers an aspect of exploration of this all-encompassing discipline. Each chapter not only offers some profound findings in different areas of QOL research but also makes a contribution to understand that under similar circumstances the methodologies utilized in each chapter can be further utilized in other cultures, geographic areas, different socioeconomic and demographic groups as well as in different QOL domains.

I truly consider this volume a treasure of research and exploration. Chosen from numerous and valuable other submissions, the chapters of this volume have some major claims to make. First, they reiterate the need of knowledge and creativity to undertake QOL related research. Second, they identify the difficulties and impediments in undertaking social research. Third, each chapter makes a concrete contribution to the aspect QOL research it set out to do. Fourth, the more laborious and time consuming the research efforts, the greater the importance of findings and profundity of the conclusions. Finally, and perhaps most importantly, we, in different disciplines of social and behavioral sciences, all have a major contribution to make to the knowledge pool therefore we must interact and communicate more through interdisciplinary activities such as the development of this volume.

I would like to congratulate ISQOLS putting together such a path breaking volume. I certainly hope that such an effort is not just going to be a one-time activity but a continuing tradition.

Young, serious minded, ambitious and devoted colleagues will have a picnic with this book. All I can say is "may the force by with you." We need more and even better efforts so help us.

A. Coskun Samli, Ph.D.
Research Professor
University of North Florida

PART I:

HAPPINESS, OLD AGE, AND INCOME

One of the most important indicators of Quality of Life is happiness. Happiness, among other variables, is connected to old age and income. As populations in different societies become older, the question of happiness and its connection to aging becomes more and more critical.

In this section four important chapters deal with these areas. Lengyel, Zello, Berenbaum, Henry and Whiting explore the food intake and adequate nutrition for the elderly residing in long-term care facilities. In order to enhance food quality and delivery the authors construct a new framework.

Easterlin explores happiness in later life in the form of a gender study. Among other important issues, he points out that if men and women are in the same work and marital circumstances, women are happier than men. He makes important suggestions regarding future research.

Prince and Manolis examine income and happiness. They take this relationship to a higher plateau by introducing self-esteem and optimism as they relate to income. They demonstrate further the relationship between income and happiness further by casual modeling.

Suthers, Saito and Crimms look at emotional well-being among older persons by comparing Japanese and American elderly. They found out that the overall levels of negative emotions of the elderly are the same in both countries.

Christina O. Lengyel, Gordon A. Zello, Shawna L. Berenbaum, Carol J. Henry, Susan J. Whiting

1. A MODEL FOR FOOD SERVICE DELIVERY AND QUALITY OF LIFE IN LONG-TERM CARE FACILITIES

ABSTRACT: For groups of elderly who reside in long-term care (LTC) facilities, eating is one of the most important aspects of their daily lives. Inadequate nutrition, which results in increased morbidity and mortality, may be fostered by poor quality diets, as well as issues related to quality of life. Therefore, food service delivery to elderly should be provided in an environment that promotes autonomy, interpersonal relations, and security. We surveyed food service and quality of life issues related to eating in LTC facilities in Saskatoon, Saskatchewan as part of an evaluation of food services. Questionnaires were administered to both residents and administrative staff in LTC facilities. Residents were satisfied with most areas of food service delivery, however, relative dissatisfaction was associated with food variety, quality, taste, appearance, and the posting of menus. Quality of life issues related to eating also were found to be positive, however, issues related to autonomy such as food choice and snack availability were less positive. Administrative surveys examined practices, standards, philosophies, and policies of the LTC facilities. We propose a framework, based on the systems theory, to show how the various components of food services are linked together. This framework considers six components: resources, transformation, outcomes, controlling factors, potential change indicators, and the environment. These components are interactive and are required to produce an effective and efficient food service system, while enhancing the quality of life of LTC residents. This framework can assist health care professionals in understanding how quality of life is affected by food service delivery outcomes in a LTC environment.

KEY WORDS: long-term care, elderly, quality of life, food services, framework

1.1. Introduction

Mealtimes are significant for elderly residents living in long-term care (LTC) facilities (American Dietetic Association, 2000). Meals contribute to a resident's daily sense of security, order, meaning, structure, independence and control over his/her environment (Amarantos, Martinez, and Dwyer, 2001). Moreover, meals provide the opportunity for residents to make food choices and interact with others socially. Mealtime enjoyment and nutritional well-being contribute to improved health status and increased quality of life. The consequences of poor nutritional status include malnutrition, and subsequent morbidity and mortality.

Quality of life has become a critically important concept in health care in recent years (Mitchell and Kemp, 2000). Quality of life refers to the assessment of subjective importance and perceived availability of autonomy, interpersonal relations, and security in a LTC environment (Lind, 1983). Quality of life must be considered in the overall care of individuals residing in LTC facilities to ensure that residents' are provided with the best possible care in a home-like environment (Mitchell and Kemp, 2000). Residents' ability to exercise choice in a LTC setting is important as some control over personal care and routines are lost once admitted

M. Joseph Sirgy et al. (eds.), Advances in Quality-of-Life Theory and Research, 3–12, 2003.

into a LTC facility. The ability to control some aspect of their lives is a critical determinant of their perceived quality of life (Forbes, Jackson, and Kraus, 1987).

1.1.1. *Resident Food Service Satisfaction*

Customer satisfaction surveys are necessary tools in assessing products and services provided to consumers and for measuring health care (Owens and Batchelor, 1996; Scott and Smith, 1994). Satisfaction surveys have been widely used in hospital settings to monitor patient care (Ehnfors and Smedby, 1993) and less commonly used for assessing food service satisfaction (Dube, Trudeau, and Belanger, 1994). When food service satisfaction surveys are conducted, subjects 65 years of age and older are generally excluded because of the notion that it can be difficult selecting a cognitively non-impaired sample and collecting information via face-to-face or written surveys (Simmons et al., 1997).

Dissatisfaction with food services provided by LTC facilities may influence an individual's dietary intake and perceived quality of life. Decreased food intakes among LTC residents may be influenced by the monotony of institutionalized food, failure of food service staff to recognize cultural and geographic food preferences, and food presentation (Chambers, 1996; Morley, 1997). Resident satisfaction to the meal delivery system also may influence an individual's food intake (Lambert et al., 1999).

1.1.2. *General Systems Theory*

The theoretical framework used to explain and guide this paper was adapted from the literature on the General Systems Theory (GST) as it applies to the field of organizational development and management (Mink et al., 1994; Spears, 2000). The GST provides a framework to explain the interactions and the interrelationships that occur between specific components within an organization and within its environment. It assists in identifying the factors that influence the functioning of an organization from both an internal and external perspective.

The GST has evolved over time and can be traced back to ancient philosophers. It was in the mid 1900s that the ideas on the GST were developed by an Austrian biologist, Ludwig von Bertalanffy. He promoted the view that systems not only interact as separate whole entities, but also interact with their external environments (Barker, Sturdivant, and Smith, 2000). GST later emerged in the late 1950s and early 1960s in response to the compartmentalization of scientific disciplines (Mink et al., 1994). The terms "systems theory", "systems thinking", "systems approach", and "systems perspective" are used frequently and interchangeably in contemporary organizational development literature (Mink et al., 1994). Systems thinking de-emphasizes the separate parts of a structure as the basis for an organization (Mink et al., 1994) by adopting an emphasis of understanding organizations that does not focus on the separation and study of constituent parts (Barker,

Sturdivant, and Smith, 2000). A systems perspective focuses on the totality of the entire organization and how processes link parts together.

There are many assumptions of the systems perspective such as: it is a holistic entity; all parts of the system are interdependent; all parts of the system work together to create synergy; the system is composed of many subsystems which function within the larger system and within its surrounding environment; the extent of interaction of a system with its environment is determined by its degree of openness; the parts of a system respond dynamically; the system attempts to maintain a current state in response to changes; the system has a goal; the system has a purpose; the system has the ability to achieve the same end using different means; feedback mechanisms are in operation to correct changes in a system's overall performance; and the system contains an input-output device which allows for a continuous flow of resources (e.g., materials, ideas, and personnel) through the system Mink et al., 1994). Although a systems approach has considerable heuristic and practical value for understanding organizations, it does have a few limitations. It lacks the ability to adapt to change as determined by growth and intraorganizational conflict since the system is considered a whole entity Peery, 1975). Even though this is a weakness, the primary limitation to the application and use of this theory lies with those using it Peery, 1975), as the assumptions of the theory may not be understood or applied appropriately.

General Systems theory has been applied to organizations across a wide variety of disciplines in the physical, biological, and social science arenas (Kast and Rosenzweig, 1973; Barker, Sturdivant, and Smith, 2000). Various models for the systems approach also have been developed to meet the goals and objectives of the various disciplines (e.g., physics, biology, technology, sociology, food service organizations, etc.). By the mid 1960s, the systems theory became known as a useful tool in managing food service operations. The general systems theory has provided a guiding framework for managers of food service organizations to facilitate problem solving and decision making (Spears, 2000). A major example is the Food Service Systems Model proposed by Vaden (1980).

The Vaden Food Service Systems Model consists of six components: input, transformation, output, internal and external controls, memory, and feedback (Vaden, 1980; Spears, 2000). All of these components are subject to influence by both internal (e.g., food experiences) and external (e.g., the environment in which the system operates) environmental factors. Vaden showed that a food service system is affected by and impacts its environmental context. The two-way arrows represent the unspecified bi-directional relationship between a systems model and the environment in which it operates. Input refers to the resources that are incorporated into the system to assist and contribute to the production of goods and services for the organization. These resources include human (e.g., labour and skills), physical (e.g., materials and facilities) and operational (e.g., money, time, utilities and information) sources. Transformation involves the process of changing inputs into outputs (e.g., activities involved in food production). The process involves management functions (e.g., planning, organizing, leading), functional subsystems (e.g., procurement, production, distribution), and linking processes (e.g., decision making, communication). Within the transformation stage, controls are set. Internal and external controls provide direction to organizations to ensure that their resources are used effectively and efficiently to accomplish their goals and objectives within legal and regulatory guidelines. Internal controls refer to the goals, objectives, standards, policies, and procedures of the organization. External controls consist of local, provincial, and federal laws, regulations, and guidelines (e.g., diet manual, food guides, nutrient recommendations). The output is the product of the transformation process. In food services this relates to the quality and quantity of meals provided, customer satisfaction, employee satisfaction, and financial accountability. Memory includes stored information (e.g., inventory, financial, personnel, master menu cycles, forecasting) pertaining to the operation of an organization. The feedback component refers to the process by which information in a system is received from its internal and external environments. Feedback may be expressed as positive or negative. The feedback loop is essential in this model as it enables food service organizations to recognize where adjustments or changes need to be made. If the food served to residents of a LTC facility is unacceptable, corrective action may be taken in the input stage, such as purchasing quality food items, training staff, or in the transformation stage, such as the improving the food preparation techniques.

The Vaden Food Service Systems Model was constructed in the late 1970s to illustrate applications of the systems theory to the management of food service organizations. With the changing approaches to the healthcare industry, the terms used in this model do not reflect the current themes in health promotion and evaluation. Moreover, findings and applications from the field since its development suggest that a revision of both terminology and refinement of predicted processes may be warranted. We therefore set out to revise this model based on our studies of food services and quality of life issues related to eating in LTC facilities (Lengyel, 2002).

1.2. Food Service Studies Conducted

Our studies involved 18 LTC facilities in a health district in Saskatoon, Saskatchewan. Briefly, our research examined four food service areas in the LTC facilities in Saskatoon: 1) menus, 2) practices, 3) dietary intakes, and 4) residents' food service satisfaction (Lengyel, 2002). For menus, we determined nutrient composition of foods offered; under practices, we looked at food service delivery system, staffing, policies and procedures, facility demographics; and dietary intakes were measured in selected facilities. These are described in full elsewhere (Lengyel, 2002; Lengyel et al., 2002a, b). The satisfaction part of this research involved questionnaire development and administration by interview to a large sample of elderly residents (205 completed the survey). Residents were eligible to participate if they met the following selection criteria: 1) 65 years of age and older; 2) cognitively able to answer simple, easy to understand questions, verbally or non-verbally, as determined by the food service representatives of each LTC facility; and 3) residing in the facility for at least two months. Ethical approval was obtained from the University of Saskatchewan Advisory Committee on Ethics in Human Experimentation, and site specific ethics committees where they existed.

The questions selected for the questionnaire were based on two domains: quality of life and food services; the quality of life domain was further subdivided into *autonomy*, *interpersonal relations*, and *security* (Dube, Trudeau, and Belanger, 1994; O'Hara et al., 1997; Forgan Morle, 1984; Zinn, Lavizzo-Mourey, and Taylor, 1993). The questions addressing food service areas are listed in Table 1.1; those which we found to be answered in the positive are in the upper panel, while those receiving less positive responses are in the lower panel. The questions addressing quality of life issues are listed in Table 1.2; those which we found to be answered in the positive are in the upper panel, while those receiving less positive responses are in the lower panel. From our previous work we found that scores from the food services and quality of life domains were positively correlated ® = 0.451, $p < 0.001$) indicating that high scores on food services were associated with high quality of life scores.

1.3. MODEL FOR FOOD SERVICE AND QUALITY OF LIFE

Food service delivery provided to LTC residents is complex and involves many aspects. To understand how quality of life is affected by food service delivery outcomes in a LTC environment, the food service systems model developed by Vaden (1980) was modified as the PROTEC Food Service Systems Model (Figure 1.1). The PROTEC model was developed as a result of our research examining four

Table 1.1. Food Service Items in the Questionnaire.[a]

	Food Service Item
A.[b]	Are your meals served on time?
	Do you like the foods that are served for holidays or special occasions?
	Are you satisfied with the amount of food given to you?
	Is the cold food cold?
	Are you happy with the service you receive at mealtimes?
B.[c]	Do you know ahead of time what foods will be served at meals by a menu board, staff, or a menu?
	Do you like the types of foods that are served?
	Is the food served to you tasty?
	Is the hot food hot?
	Does the food look appealing?
	Is there a wide assortment of foods served to you?

[a] Lengyel (2002).
[b] Positive response items.
[c] Less positive response items.

Table 1.2. Quality of Life Items in the Questionnaire.[a]

	Quality of life item
A.[b]	Are you satisfied with the meals that you receive? (Autonomy)[c]
	Would you like to have more choice in whom you eat with? (Autonomy)
	If you had any concerns or problems about the food would they be taken seriously by staff? (Interpersonal Relations)
	Do you enjoy mealtimes? (Autonomy)
	Do you feel free to express your concerns or complaints about the food given to you? (Interpersonal Relations)
	Do you like where you eat your meals? (Security)
B.[d]	Would you like to be given more choice in what you eat? (Autonomy)
	Can you have a snack when you what to? (Autonomy)
	Are different meals served for holidays or special occasions? (Autonomy)

[a] Lengyel (2002).
[b] Positive response items.
[c] Quality of life determinant category in parenthesis.
[d] Less positive response items.

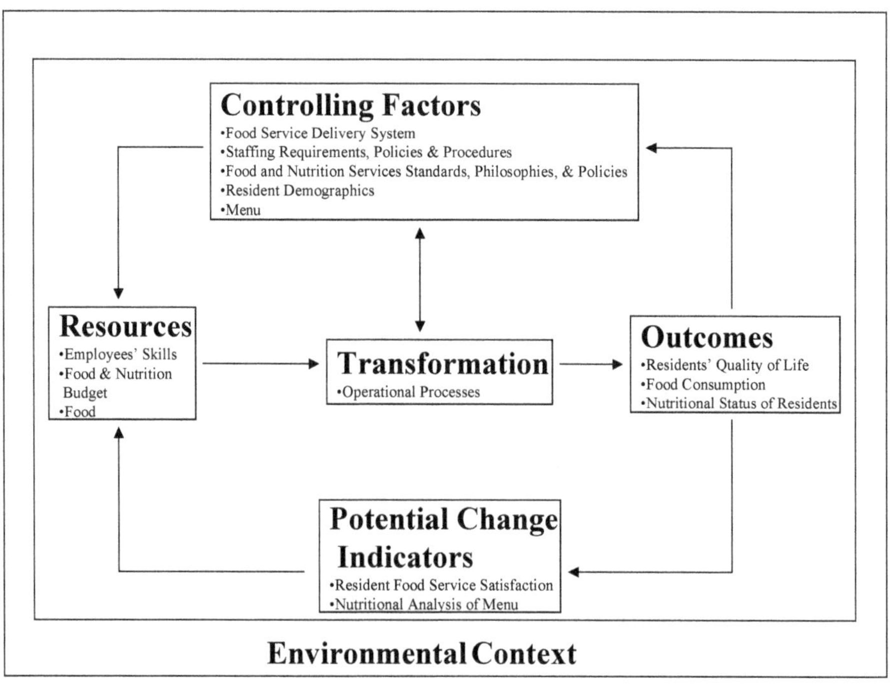

Figure 1.1. PROTEC Food Service Systems Model.

key areas of food service in LTC facilities, i.e., menus, satisfaction, practices, and nutrient intakes (Lengyel, 2002). In the PROTEC model, each letter denotes an important element in this systems model: Potential change indicators, Resources, Outcomes, Transformation, Environmental context, and Controlling factors.

Resources refer to the necessary entities needed to produce quality food service delivery and nutritional care. These include human labour and skills (e.g., registered dietitians), financial resources, food, supplies, and operational space (facility design and utilities). In order to produce a desired outcome, the resources require transformation. The transformation component is inherent to the model as this is the stage that drives the model's processes. It consists of managerial functions that work interdependently at all levels of the food service operation such as food procurement, production, distribution, sanitation, and safety. At this stage, the entire process is enhanced with the use of computerized systems that make menu planning efficient based on the needs of the specific resident population. Computerized systems aid in menu planning, recipe production, product forecasting, food production, analyzing trends, and menu changes. Transformation leads to outcomes. Outcomes are the products and services that are developed as a result of the transformation stage which expresses the goals and objectives of the food service organization. Nutrition and food service related outcomes developed from this research were residents' quality of life, food consumption (quality and quantity), and nutritional analysis of menus. In order to produce desired outcomes that coincide with the organizations goals, controlling factors must be in place. Controlling factors of a system include standards, policies and procedures, and programs of a food service organization. In this study the factors were: the type of food service delivery system (e.g., conventional, ready prepared, commissary, assembly serve) staffing requirements, policies and procedures; food and nutrition service standards, philosophies and policies; resident demographics, and the menu. To link all of the components together and maintain the dynamic nature of the model, a feedback mechanism is needed. Potential change indicators are critical to this model as they provide information about the effectiveness of the entire food service system in terms of evaluation and control. A food service satisfaction survey was used in this research to evaluate the quality of the food and food services delivered to LTC elderly residents. Furthermore, each component is affected by the environmental context. These factors include physiological changes due to aging, personal beliefs and perceptions, food experiences, medical conditions, medication usage, and the environment in which the system operates (e.g., LTC facility vs. a full service restaurant).

The main emphasis of this framework is the inclusion of nutrition related quality-of-life outcomes. These outcomes include residents' food consumption and nutritional status, which ultimately affects the residents' overall quality of life. Nutrition directly impacts on the quality of life of older adults as good nutrition may prevent nutrient deficiencies, malnutrition, and complications associated with medical conditions and medication usage (Amarantos, Martinez, and Dwyer, 2001). In this context, quality of life refers to the following three specific dimensions: autonomy, interpersonal relations, and security (Lind, 1983). Each dimension plays an integral role in residents' perception of their quality of life, thus influencing their satisfaction of food services and their eating behavior. Autonomy emphasizes individuality, physical independence, and control over aspects of daily life. For example the choice residents have over the amount and type of food offered, and the time their meals are served. The aspect of choice in food and food service delivery serves to prevent boredom and encourage participation in the mealtime experience. Interpersonal relations refers to expression, relationships with LTC staff, respect/privacy, and friendship. These components are important in the social aspects of eating. In LTC facilities, the prevalence of widowhood, and decreased social networks often is associated with poor mealtime enjoyment, decreased appetite, and weight loss (Rosenbloom and Whittington, 1993). The third dimension of quality of life is security. Security encompasses physical comfort, safety, services, routine, and structure. Since residents now reside in an environment different than their own private homes in which they previously resided, it is important to try to provide a homelike environment to prevent any transitional problems (i.e., relocation syndrome). A secure mealtime environment should consist of good heating and lighting, safe, and pleasant surroundings (i.e., quiet, clean and easily accessible facilities). The interactions that may occur as a result of this framework may affect resident food consumption and their quality of life either negatively or positively. For example, when food service delivery is unsatisfactory, food consumption may decrease, and thus, may make LTC residents susceptible to adverse health effects. Therefore, the feedback loop is an important control mechanism for the model.

The model reinforces the understanding that a food service system continually interacts with its environment. Therefore, it is viewed as a whole entity rather than the accumulation of individual parts. The model illustrates the dynamic relationship that exists between all of the external and internal components of a LTC food service system and provides insight into how food services in LTC facilities operate and also may be used in other food service operations. Quality of life is an outcome that is dependent *on resources* as well as *factors that control* the facility situation. Residents' satisfaction is a potential change indicator, i.e., if they are dissatisfied with food services, this must be determined and action taken. Satisfaction can therefore affect quality of life. Therefore, the PROTEC Food Service Systems Model is here to "protect" LTC residents' quality of life.

1.4. Future Research

The PROTEC Food Service Systems Model presents a framework for exploring the quality and effectiveness of a food service delivery system in relation to quality of life issues. The model identifies a set of interrelated internal and external factors that are critical to food service delivery. Applications of the model need to be tested to further define the components and the relationships between and among the model's components. The PROTEC model has potential to become a promising way to explore food service systems and its impact on the quality of life of elderly LTC residents.

1.5. REFERENCES

Amarantos, E., Martinez A., and Dwyer, J. (2001). Nutrition and quality of life of older adults. *Journals of Gerontology: SERIES A*, **56A**(Special Issue II), 54–64.

American Dietetic Association. (2000). Nutrition, aging, and the continuum of care. *Journal of the American Dietetic Association*, **100**(5), 580–595.

Barker, T. S., Sturdivant, V. A., and Smith, H. W. (2000). The systems approach to the university: Integrating technology. *Information Analyses*, 1–19.

Chambers, J. (1996). Food can make the resident feel at home. *Provider*, **22**(3), 36–38.

Dube, L., Trudeau, E., and Belanger, M. C. (1994). Determining the complexity of patient satisfaction with foodservices. *Journal of the American Dietetic Association*, **94**(4), 394–401.

Ehnfors, M. and Smedby, B. (1993). Patient satisfaction surveys subsequent to hospital care: Problems of sampling, non-response and other losses. *Quality Assurance in Health Care*, **5**(1), 19–32.

Forgan Morle, K. M. (1984). Patient satisfaction: care of the elderly. *Journal of Advanced Nursing*, **9**, 71–76.

Forbes, W. F., Jackson, J. A., and Kraus, A. S. (1987). A demographic profile of the institutionalized elderly. In W. F. Forbes, J. A. Jackson, and A. S. Kraus (eds.), *Institutionalization of the Elderly in Canada* (pp. 37–45). Toronto: Butterworths.

Kast, F. E. and Rosenzweig, J. E. (1973). *Contingency Views of Organization and Management.* Chicago: Science Research Associates, Inc.

Lambert, L. G., Bondreaux, J., Conklin, M., and Yadrick, K. (1999). Are new meal distribution systems worth the effort for improving patient satisfaction with foodservice? *Journal of the American Dietetic Association*, **99**(9), 1112–1114.

Lengyel, C. O. (2002). *Assessment of food service delivery to elderly residents in long term care facilities.* Unpublished doctoral dissertation, University of Saskatchewan, Saskatoon, Saskatchewan.

Lengyel, C. O., Zello, G. A., Smith, J. T., and Whiting, S. J. (2002a). *Food satisfaction of elderly residents in long-term care facilities in a health district in Saskatchewan.* Manuscript submitted for publication.

Lengyel, C. O., Zello, G. A., Smith, J. T., and Whiting, S. J. (2002b). Evaluation of menu and food service practices of long-term care facilities of a health district in Canada. *Journal of Nutrition for the Elderly* (In Press).

Lind, S. D. (1983). *Quality of Life Assessment: A Profile of Resident Satisfaction.* Washington, D.C.: American Association of Homes for the Aging.

Mink, O. G., Mink, B. P., Downes, E. A., and Owen, K. Q. (1994). *Open Organizations: A Model for Effectiveness, Renewal, and Intelligent Change.* San Francisco: Jossey-Bass Publishers.

Mitchell, J. M. and Kemp, B. J. (2000). Quality of life in assisted living homes: A multidimensional analysis. *Journal of Gerontology: Psychological Sciences*, **55B**(2), P117–P127.

Morley, J. E. (1997). Anorexia of aging: physiologic and pathologic. *American Journal of Clinical Nutrition*, **66**, 760–773.

O'Hara, P. A., Harper, D. W., Kangas, M., Dubeau, J., Borsutzky, C., and Lemire, N. (1997). Taste, temperature, and presentation predict satisfaction with foodservices in a Canadian continuing-care hospital. *Journal of the American Dietetic Association*, **97**, 401–405.

Owens, D. J. and Batchelor, C. (1996). Patient satisfaction and the elderly. *Social Sciences Medicine*, **42**(11), 1483–1491.

Peery, N. S., Jr. (1975). General systems theory approaches to organizations: Some problems in application. *The Journal of Management Studies*, **12**(3), 266–275.

Rosenbloom, C. A. and Whittington, F. J. (1993). The effects of bereavement on eating behaviours and nutrient intakes in elderly widowed persons. *Journal of Gerontology*, **48**, S223–S229.

Scott, A. and Smith, R. D. (1994). Keeping the customer satisfied: Issues in the interpretation and use of patient satisfaction surveys. *International Journal for Quality in Health Care*, **6**(4), 353–359.

Simmons, S. F., Schnelle, J. F., Uman, G. C., Kulvicki, A. D., Lee, K. H., and Ouslander, J. G. (1997). Selecting nursing home residents for satisfaction surveys. *The Gerontologist*, **37**(4), 543–550.

Spears, M. C. (2000). Foodservice Organizations. *A Managerial and Systems Approach* (4th ed). Upper Saddle River: Prentice Hall.

Vaden, A. G. A. (1980). *Model for evaluating the foodservice system.* Manhattan: Kansas State University.

Zinn, J. S., Lavizzo-Mourey, R., and Taylor, L. (1993). Measuring satisfaction with care in the nursing home setting: The nursing home resident satisfaction scale. *The Journal of Applied Gerontology*, **12**(4), 452–465.

1.6. AFFILIATIONS AND ACKNOWLEDGEMNT

Christina O Lengyel, Ph.d., RD., Department of Nutrition, The University of North Carolina at Greensboro, 318 Stone Building, Greensboro, NC 27402-6170. Gordon A. Zello, Ph.D., Shawna L. Berenbaum, Ph.D., Carol J. Henry, MSC., MED., RD, and Susan J. Whiting, Ph.D., College of Pharmacy and Nutrition, University of Saskatchewan, 110 Science Place, Saskatoon, SK, S7N 5C9, Canada.

This study was supported by grants from the University of Saskatchewan and the Canadian Association on Gerontology. Correspondence should be addressed: Christina O. Lengyel, Ph.D., RD., Department of Nutrition, The University of North Carolina at Greensboro, 318 Stone Building, Greensboro, NC 27402-6170; E-mail: colengye@uncg.edu

Richard A. Easterlin

2. HAPPINESS OF WOMEN AND MEN IN LATER LIFE: NATURE, DETERMINANTS, AND PROSPECTS

ABSTRACT: As they move into and through the retirement years women's advantage over men in happiness is reversed. Although the happiness of both sexes is affected similarly by retirement from work, marital disruption, and changes in income and health, the difference between men and women in the life cycle occurrence of retirement and widowhood results in different trends in happiness. Men who survive to older age benefit disproportionately from the positive effect on happiness of retirement, while women suffer disproportionately from the adverse effect of widowhood. For women and men in the same work and marital circumstances, women continue to be happier than men. In the future, the turnaround in the relative happiness of women and men in later life is likely to continue, but the shift will be somewhat smaller in magnitude.

2.1. Introduction

Who are happier, women or men? Does the gender difference, if any, vary over the life cycle? The answers to these questions are a puzzle. A survey by Argyle (1987) concludes that there is little gender difference in satisfaction with life as a whole. A more recent review leads Mrocek and Kolarz (1998) to the view that "women appear to be less happy, and this seems to persist across all age groups" (p. 1336). In contrast, Nolen-Hoeksema and Rusting (1999) report that "a number of studies have found that women report experiencing greater happiness and more intense positive emotions than men" (p. 333). Recent statistical analyses by economists of large data sets for the United States, United Kingdom, and a number of continental European nations also find that women are happier (Blanchflower and Oswald, 2001; DiTella, MacCulloch, and Oswald, 2001; Oswald, 1997).

The mixed results in the literature arise from several sources. Generalizations are not always based on a nationally representative sample. Also, the possibility is seldom considered that the gender differential might differ at various points in the life cycle. Of the studies cited above, Mrocez and Kolarz are the exception. In addition, a clear distinction is not always made between the simple bivariate gender differential and the gender differential when circumstances such as marital and work status are held constant.

Another possible source of conflicting results is the use of point-of-time associations with age to infer change over the life cycle. If, for example, older persons are found to be happier than younger in the year 1990, it is sometimes inferred that happiness tends to increase over the life cycle. But those ages 65 to 74 in 1990 were born in the period 1916–25; those ages 25 to 34, in 1956–65. Clearly the two age groups have quite different histories. To line up these and the intervening age groups to infer life cycle change is to jumble together people that are different in many ways (cf. also George, 1992).[1]

In this study I compare the happiness of women and men with and without

M. Joseph Sirgy et al. (eds.), Advances in Quality-of-Life Theory and Research, 13–25, 2003.

controls for various circumstances, as they age from their fifties onward. I use a nationally representative data set, the General Social Survey (GSS) and the demographers' technique of cohort analysis, sometimes called a "synthetic panel," to follow essentially the same people as they age.

A previous paper using this technique found that for both sexes taken together, happiness remains essentially constant over the life course (Easterlin and Schaeffer, 1999; see also Easterlin 2001). Here, I find that, despite this overall constancy, a reversal takes place in the relative well-being of women and men as they age from around 60 years old onward. Before this age, women are typically happier than men, but during their sixties, men's subjective well-being becomes greater than women's, and this differential persists as women and men progress through their seventies and eighties. The principal reason for this shift is gender differences in the changing composition of the older population. Men who survive to older age benefit disproportionately from the positive effect on subjective well-being of retirement, while women suffer disproportionately from the adverse effect of widowhood. When differences in work and marital status are controlled, the happiness differential is reversed – women are typically happier than men.

2.1.1. Data and Methods

For most years from 1972 to 1998 the GSS includes the following question: "Taken all together, how would you say things are these days – would you say that you are very happy, pretty happy, or not too happy?" (National Opinion Research Center, 1999, p. 171). In the present analysis, I have coded the responses 3, 2, and 1, respectively; the mean happiness of a cohort at any given date is a simple average of the individual numerical responses thus coded.

As previously indicated, the life cycle pattern of happiness is obtained by following a ten-year birth cohort through the adult ages, linking appropriate age data for successive calendar years. Thus to trace the life cycle pattern of subjective well-being of the cohort born, say, in the decade 1911 to 1920, I link the mean happiness of those ages 52–61 in 1972 (the first survey year) to that of those ages 53–62 in 1973, 54–63 in 1974, and so on through ages 78–87 in 1998 (the last survey year). The happiness data span a 26 year period, so I am able to follow a given birth cohort for only that segment of its life cycle. But because I have cohorts starting in 1972 at younger as well as older ages, it is possible to form an impression of experience throughout most of the adult life cycle by bringing together the various segments of life cycle experience represented by the different birth cohorts. The youngest cohort included in the present analysis is that of 1931–40, which ages from 32–41 to 58–67; the oldest is that of 1891–1900, which starts at ages 72–81 and can be followed through ages 79–88 (the shorter time span is due to the fact that single-year-of-age data are available in the GSS only through age 88). Throughout the analysis a five year moving average is calculated from the annual data for a cohort to reduce the variability arising from small sample sizes.[2] Five year averages are dated at the midpoint of the average; thus, the average for 1972–76 is dated at

1974. In some cases, a five item average is computed for a time span exceeding five years, because no GSS survey was conducted in 1979, 1981, 1992, 1995, and 1997, and the average is dated at the mid-point of the longer span.

Life cycle patterns of work status, marital status, self-reported health, and real household income per capita are obtained like those for happiness as five-item moving averages of annual data for each cohort by gender. Work status is a six category variable (full-time, part-time, unemployed, retired, keeping house, and other). Marital status is a four category variable (married, widowed, divorced or separated, and never-married). Self-reported health is four categories (excellent, good, fair, poor). Household income per capita for each respondent is obtained as the quotient of household income and household size. Income in the GSS is reported in categories ranging in number from 12 in 1972 to 23 in 1998. Each respondent is assigned the midpoint value of the category reported; for those reporting in the open-ended top income category, the bottom income of the category is multiplied by factors increasing from 1.1 in 1972 to 1.166 in 1998; for those reporting in the open-ended bottom category, the top income of the category is multiplied by 0.5. Money income in each year is converted to 1994 dollars using the Consumer Price Index of the Bureau of Labor Statistics. In preliminary analyses, age (in 5 year groupings) was included as an independent variable, but it was subsequently deleted because of multicollinearity problems. The mean and standard deviation of each variable are given in Appendix Table A.1, columns 1 and 2.

The relationship of happiness to the four independent variables – work status, marital status, health, and income – is estimated for each gender by an ordered logit regression, pooling data for all persons 50 and over in the survey years 1972 through 1998 for which observations on all variables are available. (The question on self-reported health was not asked in 1978, 1983, and 1986 and was asked of two-thirds of the sample from 1988 through 1994.) The logit regression for each gender is used to obtain predicted values of happiness for each cohort for dates corresponding to those for actual happiness by substituting in the regression equation each cohort's actual (5 year average) value for each independent variable in a given year.

2.2. RESULTS

2.2.1. *Gender Differentials in Life Cycle Happiness*

As women and men go through the life cycle a shift occurs in their relative happiness. In the younger and middle adult years women are typically happier than men; at older ages the opposite is true. For example, among persons born between 1911 and 1920, who were aging from 54–63 to 74–83 in the time period covered here, females were happier than males at every age up to 58–67; thereafter, males were consistently happier (see Figure 2.1, curve labeled c. 1911–20). This pattern is repeated by other cohorts. Note that at older ages, the right side of Figure 2.1, the curves lie above the zero axis; at younger ages, the curves tend to

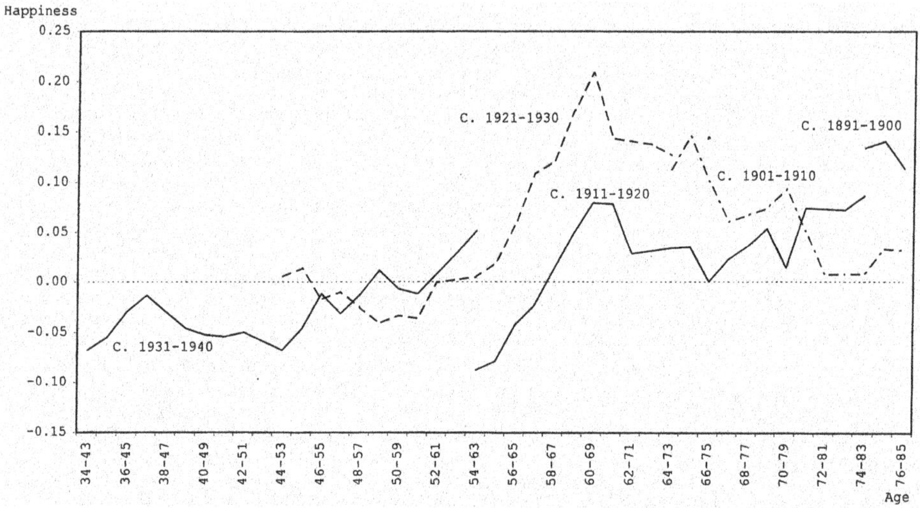

Figure 2.1. Excess of Male over Female Actual Happiness at Specified Age, by Cohort.

be below. The turnaround in the gender differential appears to be due chiefly to an increase in the absolute level of happiness of males, although there is also a slight decline in the average happiness of females from before to after the crossover.

The typical size of the shift within a cohort in the relative happiness of men and women is hard to pinpoint because of data limitations, but it seems to be considerable. Based on rough impressions from Figure 2.1, the overall shift is roughly 0.2 on our 1–3 scale of happiness – from an excess at ages under 60 of female over male happiness of 0.05 to an excess at older ages in favor of males of nearly 0.15. This is equivalent to shifting one-fifth of the male population into the next higher happiness category – say from "pretty happy" to "very happy" – holding the female distribution constant.

There is a hint that among younger cohorts the crossover from excess female to excess male happiness is occurring earlier than in the past. In the two youngest cohorts, those of 1921–30 and 1931–40, the shift to a male excess occurs around ages 52–61. For the cohort born in 1911–20 the shift occurs at ages 59–68.

2.2.2. *The Relation of Happiness to Life Circumstances*

Older persons, both women and men, are happiest if retired, currently married, in excellent health, and high income. They are least happy if unemployed; widowed, divorced, or separated; in poor health, and low income (Appendix Table A-1, column 3). These relationships, found in an ordered logit regression of GSS data 1972–98 for the population 50 and older, are consistent with those typically observed (cf. Blanchflower and Oswald 1999; Frey and Stutzer 2001; Gallie and Russell, 1998; Michalos, Zumbo, and Hubley, 2000; Wortman, Silver, and Kessler, 1993).

Regressions derived from ordinary least squares give results for the signs and significance of coefficients quite similar to those obtained with ordered logit (Table A-1, column 4).

The happiness of men and women is affected quite similarly by changes in their work or marital status, health, and income. For married persons in good health with median income, retirement from full-time job, adds 0.10, on a 1–3 scale, to the happiness of women, and 0.14 to the happiness of men (Table 2.1, panel A, columns 1 and 2). For married persons with a full-time job, good health and median income, becoming widowed reduces happiness by 0.32 among women, and 0.42 among men (panel B, columns 3 and 4). Variations in health also have a noticeable impact – downward shifts between adjacent categories reduce happiness by almost 0.2 (panel C). In contrast, income differences of the magnitude typically found between men and women – on the order of 25 percent – have only a slight impact on happiness (panel D). This small effect is, in part, because a 25 percent difference in income is a fairly small change relative to the income distribution as a whole. It is also due to the fact that the income effect in Table 2.1 is after employment, marital status, and health are controlled; the bivariate effect of income

Table 2.1. Predicted Happiness by Work Status, Marital Status, Health, and Income, Persons Aged 50 and Older, by Gendera.[a]

		Female	Male
A. Work status	☐ Retired	2.66	2.67
	☐ Keeping house	2.62	2.63
	☐ Full-time worker	2.56	2.53
	☐ Part-time worker	2.59	2.49
	☐ Other	2.48	2.54
	☐ Unemployed	2.17	2.35
B. Marital status	☐ Married	2.56	2.53
	☐ Never-married	2.36	2.19
	☐ Divorced or separated	2.20	2.15
	☐ Widowed	2.24	2.11
C. Self-reported health	☐ Excellent	2.77	2.71
	☐ Good	2.56	2.53
	☐ Fair	2.40	2.40
	☐ Poor	2.22	2.14
D. Household income per capita	☐ 1.25 median	2.57	2.54
	☐ Median	2.56	2.53
	☐ 0.75 median	2.55	2.52

[a] Estimated from ordered logit regressions in Appendix Table A-1. Reference groups are 'full-time worker,' 'married,' 'good health,' and 'median income.' Thus, for work status above, the panel A, column (1) entries give the predicted happiness of married women in good health with median income whose work status varies from retired to unemployed; panel B, column 3 gives the predicted happiness for women of each marital status who are employed full time; in good health with median income; and so on.

on happiness would include as well the adverse effects of unemployment and poor health on income, and be considerably larger than the multivariate effect.

2.2.3. *Predicted Gender Differentials in Life Cycle Happiness*

The similarity in the regression results by gender implies that if women and men had the same changes in life cycle circumstances as they move into older age, their happiness would change in a similar way. As we have seen, however, their happiness changes differently. The principal reason for this is the difference in their life cycle patterns of work and marital status. Typically, at any given age a larger proportion of men are retired, boosting their happiness, and a larger proportion of women are widowed, lowering their happiness.

Consider, again, for example, the cohort of 1911–20, whose changing life cycle circumstances are fairly typical of the cohorts generally. At ages 54–63, the proportion of men retired exceeds that of women by about 11 percentage points (Figure 2.2, panel C). Over the next eight to nine years as the cohort ages, this excess rises to a peak of about 35 percentage points, and then levels off and drifts gradually downward. Thus, as the cohort moves from its fifties to its sixties, retirement is giving a disproportionate lift to the happiness of men relative to women.

In contrast, widowhood is acting on the happiness differential within the cohort to lower the happiness of women relative to men. At ages 54–63, the proportion of women widowed exceeds that of men by about 13 percentage points (Figure 2.2, panel D). In the next eight to nine years the excess proportion of women that are widowed rises to about 30 percentage points, and eventually, by ages 72–81, to about 44 percentage points, after which it levels off. This sustained rise in the excess of women widowed has a continuing adverse impact on the happiness of women relative to men.

Unlike work and marital status, the male-female differences in health and income have little impact on the trend in the happiness differential. This is because they do not move consistently up or down (panels E and F). In contrast, the excess percentage of men retired and the excess percentage of women widowed both trace paths in later life that are rather similar to that of the gender differential in happiness (panels A, C, D).

The differential in male-female happiness in the cohort of 1911–20 predicted by these differing life cycle patterns of work and marital status in fact approximates closely the actual differential in happiness (Figure 2.2, panels A and B). Not only is the turnaround in the male-female differential predicted, but the timing of the crossover is also approximated fairly closely. The predicted values here are obtained by substituting in the regression equation for each gender the absolute values at each age of work status, marital status, health, and income (Appendix Table A-1, column 3).

Taking all of the cohorts together, the predicted differentials in happiness over the life cycle look quite similar to the actual differentials (compare Figure 2.3 with Figure 2.1). At older ages men are consistently happier than women; at younger

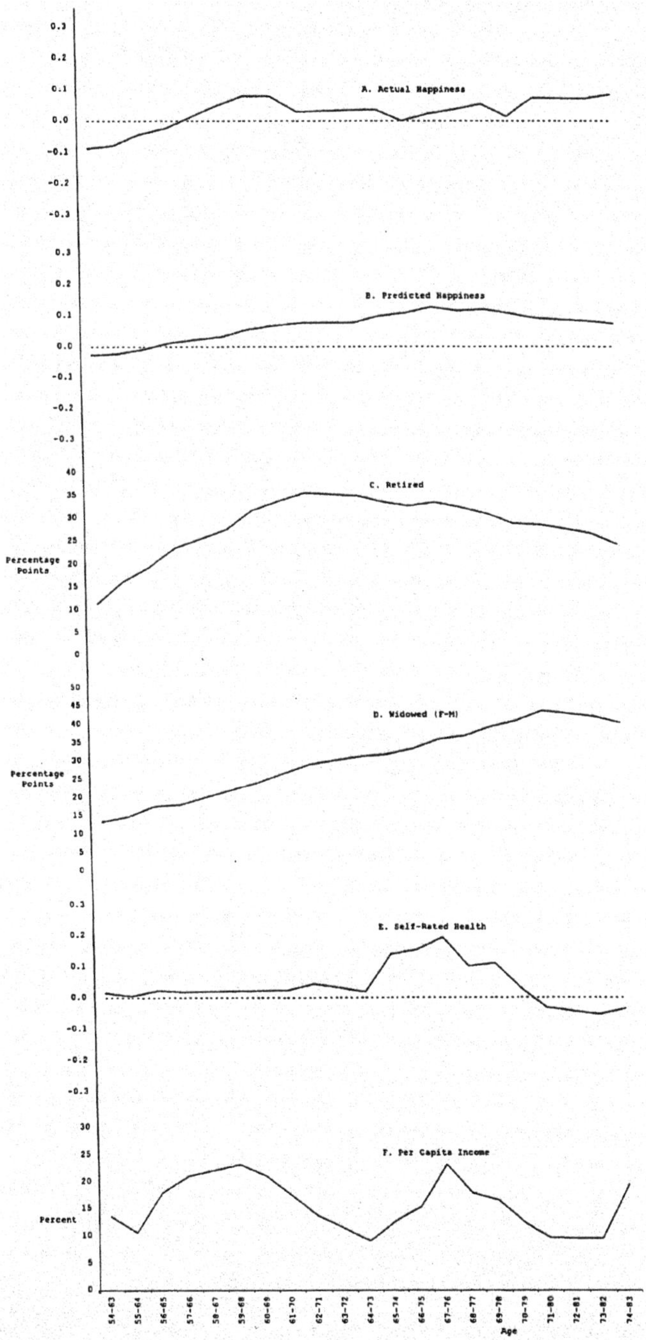

Figure 2.2. Excess of Men Over Women in Specified Characteristics, Cohort of 1911–1920 from Ages 54–63 to 74–83 (5-Year Moving Average).

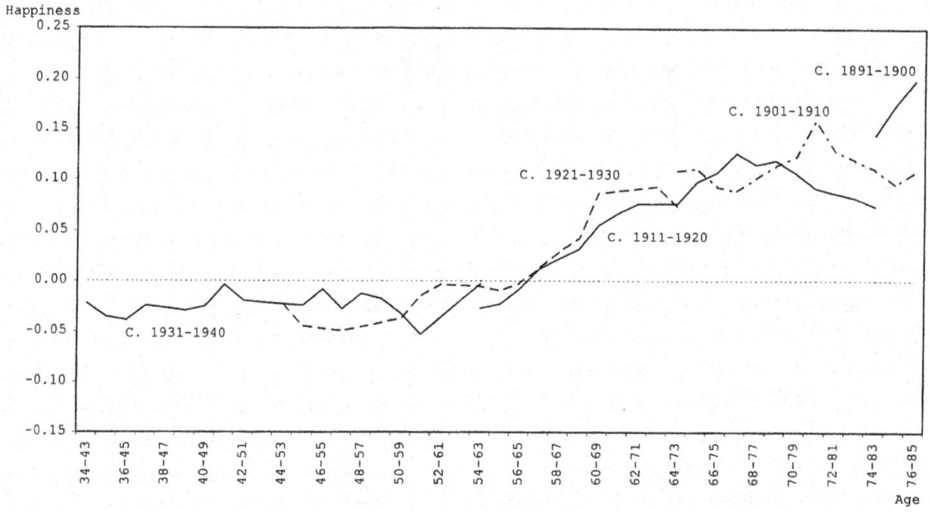

Figure 2.3. Excess of Male over Female Predicted Happiness at Specified Age, by Cohort.

ages, the opposite is true; and the magnitude of the shift approaches 0.2 on a 1–3 scale. The turnaround in the differential occurs as cohorts age from their fifties to their sixties, and the crossover occurs a little earlier among the youngest cohorts. Thus, in its main features, the predicted pattern of the happiness differential replicates well the actual pattern.

2.3.4. *Gender Differentials When Life Circumstances are the Same*

Happiness differences between women and men in later life depend to an important extent on differences in their work and marital circumstances. But what about women and men in the same situation? Perhaps the happiness difference at older ages is reversed when circumstances are alike. Note that in the limited number of same-circumstance comparisons in Table 2.1, women are typically happier than men.

A more general test confirms that for those in like situations in the population 50 and over women are, on average, happier than men. In a regression run on pooled data for both sexes in which work status, marital status, health, and income are controlled, females are significantly happier (Table A-2). The overall happiness differential in favor of males at older ages thus means that the effect on happiness of gender differences in work and marriage status overrides the tendency for women to be happier than men in like conditions.

2.3.5. *Implications for the Future*

The older population here is persons born between 1890 and 1940. What of those born after 1940 who will be reaching their sixties in this century – will the same turnaround in the gender differential occur? The answer appears to be yes, because the gender differentials in work and marital status will persist. However, the magnitude of the shift is likely to be smaller, because of a narrowing in the gender differential in full-time work.

The narrowing of the gender differential in work status is suggested by comparing younger with older cohorts at the same age. For example, when the cohort of 1931–40 was 34 to 43 years old the percentage of men with full-time jobs was 54 percentage points higher than that of women. The differential at this age span for the next two younger cohorts, those of 1941–50 and 1951–60, is only about half as great, 30 and 25 percentage points. In the future, while men will continue to benefit more than women from the impact on happiness of retirement from full-time work, the differential magnitude of the impact will be less.

In the case of widowhood, the gender differential is unlikely to change. Given below (Table 2.2) is the excess percentage of women widowed relative to men for different birth cohorts at the same age:

A vertical reading of the tabulation gives little indication that the widowhood differential is smaller for cohorts born later in the century. For example, in each of the three cohorts that can be compared at ages 54–63, the differential is an identical 14 percent. A slight exception to the similarity in the gender differential across cohorts at a given age is at ages 44–53, but in the context of the results for the other age groups, this is too slim a basis for inferring a trend toward a narrowing of the widowhood differential.

Thus, the adverse impact of widowhood on the happiness of women relative to men is likely to persist in the future. So too will the beneficial effect on men of retirement from full-time work, although the differential benefit for men will be lessened. Overall, the shift in the gender differential in later ages is likely to continue, but to be somewhat smaller in magnitude.

2.3. SUMMARY

In speculating on the sources of gender differences in well-being, Nolen-Hoeksema and Rusting (1999) suggest that "males are socialized not to experience or express affect as intensely as females . . ." (p. 344) There is nothing here to contradict this speculation, but, as the authors recognize, other circumstances may also affect

Table 2.2. Excess Percentage of Women Widowed Relative to Men for Different Birth Cohorts at the Same Age.

	Ages 34–43	44–53	54–63	64–73
Birth cohort 1951–60	2	–	–	–
1941–50	2	3	–	–
1931–40	2	7	14	–
1921–30	–	7	14	30
1911–20	–	–	14	31
1901–10	–	–	–	29

the relative happiness of women and men. Among older persons of both sexes, retirement and income have positive effects on well-being, and widowhood and poor health, negative effects. As women and men age from their fifties onward, the incidence of retirement and widowhood differs markedly by gender. Men benefit disproportionately from the positive effect of retirement, while women suffer disproportionately from the negative effect of widowhood. Because of this, the excess of female over male happiness is gradually reversed as the two sexes age from their fifties onward. For men and women in the same work and marital circumstances, however, females remain happier than men, as a result perhaps of the difference in socialization experience emphasized by Nolen-Hoeksema and Rusting.

In the future, the differential benefit from retirement that men experience will lessen somewhat, because of the increased proportion of full-time workers among women in more recent birth cohorts. But the widowhood differential is likely to persist both in direction and magnitude. The reversal from excess female to excess male happiness in later life is therefore likely to continue, although the magnitude of the shift will be more moderate.

2.4. NOTES

[1] Mrocek and Kolarz are characteristically careful on this point, saying "that we could not tell from these cross-sectional data whether there was an aging or cohort effect" (ibid., p. 1338).

[2] The lowest '*n*' for a single five-year average for a given gender is 127; in most cases '*n*' is 300 or more.

2.5. APPENDIX

Table A-1. Regression Statistics: Happiness on Specified Variables, Population Ages 50 and Over, by Gender, 1972–1998.

Variable	(1) Mean	(2) Standard deviation	(3) Ordered logit coefficient	(4) Ordinary least squares coefficient
		A. FEMALES		
1. Happiness	2.209	0.657	–	–
2. Work status				
a. Full-time workera	0.209	0.407	–	–
b. Retired	0.235	0.424	0.338***	0.104***
c. Keeping house	0.419	0.493	0.205**	0.062**
d. Part-time worker	0.089	0.284	0.104	0.037
e. Other	0.042	0.200	–0.267*	–0.088*
f. Unemployed	0.007	0.080	–1.094**	–0.357**
3. Marital status				
a. Marrieda	0.478	0.500	–	–
b. Never-married	0.045	0.207	–0.608***	–0.184***
c. Divorced, separated	0.128	0.334	–1.015***	–0.319***
d. Widowed	0.349	0.477	–0.911***	–0.287***

Table A-1. (Continued).

Variable	(1) Mean	(2) Standard deviation	(3) Ordered logit coefficient	(4) Ordinary least squares coefficient
4. Self-reported health				
a. Excellent	0.209	0.407	0.829***	0.237***
b. Gooda	0.397	0.489	–	–
c. Fair	0.277	0.448	–0.475***	–0.154***
d. Poor	0.117	0.321	–0.949***	–0.299***
5. Ln hh income p.c., (1994 dollars)	16,279	13,494	8.08e^{-6}***	2.52e–6***
Number of observations			5277	5277
R^2 or pseudo R^2			0.0767	0.1365
Prob > F			0.0000	0.0000
		B. MALES		
1. Happiness	2.249	0.656	–	–
2. Work status				
a. Full-time workera	0.421	0.494	–	–
b. Retired	0.433	0.496	0.458***	0.143***
c. Keeping house	0.010	0.098	0.322	0.089
d. Part-time worker	0.062	0.241	–0.135	–0.051
e. Other	0.049	0.216	0.004	0.001
f. Unemployed	0.026	0.158	–0.517*	–0.174**
3. Marital status				
a. Married[a]	0.724	0.447	–	–
b. Never-married	0.060	0.238	–0.935***	–0.298***
c. Divorced, separated	0.116	0.320	–1.039***	–0.326***
d. Widowed	0.100	0.300	–1.130***	–0.359***
4. Self-reported health				
a. Excellent	0.231	0.421	0.658***	0.195***
b. Gooda	0.403	0.491	–	–
c. Fair	0.258	0.438	–0.389***	–0.126***
d. Poor	0.108	0.310	–1.057***	–0.333***
5. Ln hh income p.c., (1994 dollars)	19,037	15,059	8.82e^{-6}***	2.79e^{6}***
Number of observations			4155	4155
R^2 or pseudo R^2			0.0674	0.1241
Prob > F			0.0000	0.0000

[a] Omitted group in regression.
Significance levels: * 0.01 < p < 0.10; ** 0.001 < p < 0.01; *** p < 0.001.
Note: Happiness is measured on a three point scale (very happy = 3, pretty happy = 2, not too happy = 1).
Source: National Opinion Research Center, 1999.

Table A-2. Regression Statistics: Happiness on Specified Variables, both Sexes Combined, Ages 50 and Over, 1972–98.

Variable	(1) Mean	(2) Standard deviation	(3) Ordered logit coefficient	(4) Ordinary least squares coefficient
1. Happiness	2.226	0.656	–	–
2. Gender				
a. Male[a]	0.420	0.494	–	–
b. Female	0.580	0.560	0.155**	0.049**
3. Work status				
a. Full-time worker[a]	0.298	0.457	–	–
b. Retired	0.318	0.466	0.407***	0.126***
c. Keeping house	0.247	0.431	0.212**	0.064**
d. Part-time worker	0.077	0.267	0.021	0.007
e. Other	0.045	0.207	–0.128	–0.043
f. Unemployed	0.015	0.120	–0.694***	–0.226***
4. Marital status				
a. Married[a]	0.581	0.493	–	–
b. Never-married	0.051	0.221	–0.783***	–0.244***
c. Divorced, separated	0.123	0.328	–1.034***	–0.326***
d. Widowed	0.245	0.430	–0.982***	–0.311***
5. Self-reported health				
a. Excellent	0.218	0.413	0.752***	0.219***
b. Good[a]	0.400	0.490	–	–
c. Fair	0.269	0.443	–0.436***	–0.142***
d. Poor	0.113	0.316	–0.990***	–0.312***
6. Ln hh income p.c., (1994 dollars)	17,483	14,264	$8.22e^{-6}$***	$2.59e^{-6}$***
Number of observations			9432	9432
R^2 or pseudo R^2			0.0721	0.1299
Prob > F			0.0000	0.0000

[a] Omitted group in regression.
Significance levels: ** $0.001 < p < 0.01$; *** $p < 0.001$.
Note: Happiness is measured on a three point scale (very happy = 3, pretty happy = 2, not too happy = 1).
Source: National Opinion Research Center (1999).

2.6. REFERENCES

Argyle, M. (1987). *The psychology of happiness.* London: Routledge.

Blanchflower, D. G. and Oswald, A.J. (2001, October). Well-being over time in Britain and the USA. Unpublished manuscript. Warwick: Warwick University.

Di Tella, R., MacCulloch, R. J., and Oswald, A. J. (2001, March). Preferences over inflation and unemployment: evidence from surveys of happiness. *American Economic Review*, **91**(1), 335–341.

Easterlin, R. A. (2001, July). Income and happiness: towards a unified theory. *The Economic Journal*, **111**(473), 465–484.

Easterlin, R. A. and Schaeffer, C. M. (1999). Income and subjective well-being over the life cycle. In C. D. Ryff and V. W. Marshall (eds.), *The self and society in aging processes* (pp. 279–302). New York: Springer.

Frey, B. S. and Stutzer, A. (1999). Measuring preferences by subjective well-being. *Journal of Institutional and Theoretical Economics*, **155**, 1–24.

Gallie, D. and Russell, H. (1998). Unemployment and life satisfaction: A cross-cultural comparison. *Archives Europeennes de Sociologie*, **XXXIX**(2), 248–280.

George, L. K. (1992). Economic status and subjective well-being: a review of the literature and an agenda for future research. In N. E. Cutter, D. W. Grigg, and M. P. Lawton (eds.), *Aging, money, and life satisfaction: aspects of financial gerontology*. New York: Springer Publishing Co.

Michalos, A. C., Zumbo, B. D., and Hubley, A. (2000). Health and the quality of life. *Social Indicators Research*, **51**, 245–286.

Mrozek, D. K. and Kolarz, C. M. (1998). The effect of age on positive and negative affect: A developmental perspective on happiness. *Journal of Personality and Social Psychology* **75**(5), 1333–1349.

National Opinion Research Center (1999). General social surveys, 1972–1998: Cumulative codebook. Chicago: National Opinion Research Center.

Nolen-Hoeksema, S. and Rusting, C. L. (1999). Gender differences in well-being. In D. Kahneman, E. Diener, and N. Schwarz (eds.), *Well-being: the foundations of hedonic psychology* (pp. 330–350). New York: Russell Sage Foundation.

Oswald, A. J. (1997, November). Happiness and economic performance. *Economic Journal*, **107**(445), 1815–1831.

Wortman, C. B., Silver, R. C., and Kessler, R. C. (1993). The meaning of loss and adjustment to bereavement. In M. S. Stroebe, W. Stroebe, and R. O. Hansson (eds.), *Handbook of bereavement: Theory, research, and intervention* (pp. 349–366). New York: Cambridge University Press.

2.7. ACKNOWLEDGEMENTS

I am grateful for the excellent assistance of Donna H. Ebata and Paul Rivera, and for helpful comments to Rivera, Kenneth Land, Leonard Schiffman, Elaine Sherman, and Kristen Suthers.

Financial support was provided by the University of Southern California.

Mel Prince and Chris Manolis

3. CONSUMER INCOME AND BELIEFS AFFECTING HAPPINESS

ABSTRACT: Recent syntheses of empirical studies have clearly demonstrated a consistently positive relationship between income and happiness. Research is needed to reduce uncertainty and disentangle such relationships, which have been found to be quite modest, but significant in the aggregate. The present study contributes to this end, in that it investigates the moderating effect of income on the relationship between beliefs that serve as internal buffers and happiness. We go beyond simple associations of income and happiness to examine relationships between income and self-esteem and between income and optimism. Finally, causal modeling is employed to demonstrate that, under varying income levels, these beliefs affect happiness by the same process – with distinct yet predictable outcomes.

KEY WORDS: money, happiness, beliefs, income, causal model

3.1. Introduction

Evidence from extensive empirical studies demonstrates the general positive relationship between income and happiness. However, the influence of income on specific processes that directly affect happiness has not been well established and is the focus of this study. Thus, this study advances the literature on quality of life by showing the extent to which specific dispositional factors are linked to income, as a system that strongly affects the quality of life

A variety of ad hoc and anecdotal reasons have been advanced to explain complexities of the relation between income and happiness. Income is viewed as a resource for self-validating activities and a sense of mastery, goal attainment, for gratifying leisure pursuits, work satisfaction tracing from personal autonomy and skill utilization. It serves as a basis of life chances, social status determination, and participation in social networks.

The lack of income is seen as frustrating individuals from meeting universal human needs, constraining fulfillment of material aspirations, allocation of satisfying discretionary time, the consumption of necessaries, and being associated with a higher incidence of unemployment. Higher levels of income may also be seen as having negative utilities, such as increased occupational tensions, theft and damage to valued possessions, and complexity of existence. (Ahuvia and Friedman, 1998; Cummins, 2000a; Diener et al., 1993; Easterlin, 2001; Marks and Fleming, 1999; Mullis, 1992; Staats and Horner, 1999; Veenhoven, 1996; Weston, 1999).

3.1.1. *Formal Theories of Happiness*

Set-point theory states that there are individual levels of happiness that are relatively fixed, but subject to some fluctuation around this fixed point over time. In other

M. Joseph Sirgy et al. (eds.), Advances in Quality-of-Life Theory and Research, 27–39, 2003.

words, happiness is a homeostatic process, where individual levels generally are maintained within a narrow range. The process depends, in part on first order determinants, based on such personality factors as extroversion and neuroticism. These personality factors, in turn, influence sociability and interpersonal warmth. These traits are associated with enjoyment of leisure and extensive friendships (Headey and Wearing, 1992). Experience with the environment also impacts the system, but internal buffers attenuate it. Internal buffers include such beliefs as self-esteem, where the self is seen as praiseworthy and competent, and optimism, or the view that tomorrow will be better than its today (Cummins, 1998).

However, the environment may prove to be sufficiently aversive so as to exceed adaptational capacities for maintaining happiness. The set-point value below which homeostasis has been defeated for a majority of group members has been estimated at 70% of scale maximum. The distribution of happiness is leptokurtic and studies of its parameters suggest that this 70% score is the cutoff for a line of resistance representing a homeostatic lower bound. One example among environmental factors that can defeat the homeostasis is the lack of money to buy needed commodities (Cummins, 2000a, 2001).

A hierarchical model of well-being has been advanced as an omnibus theoretical framework.. The hierarchy includes, in order of presentation, social background, personality, social networks, domain satisfaction and well-being (Headey and Wearing, 1992).

3.2. LITERATURE REVIEW AND HYPOTHESES

3.2.1. *Optimism, Self-Esteem and Happiness*

Dispositional optimism has been defined as "positive outcome expectancy." Optimists have been found to be more adaptive under stressful encounters. This type of individual more frequently employs problem-focused strategies. Extroversion, which is positively related to happiness, is also positively related to optimism (Lai, 1997). Dispositional optimism, together with self-esteem, act as buffers to minimize stress effects. Self-esteem is positively associated with optimism. Specific buffer mechanisms tracing from optimism and self-esteem beliefs are "breathers", which introduce breaks in coping activity (Scheier and Carver, 1985). Social network activities are known to favorably affect happiness. Self-esteem, in particular, is positively associated with such networking factors as volunteerism and civic participation. Optimism is also important for the broader social dynamic complex of social trust, civic engagement and life satisfaction (Scheufele and Shah, 2000). Happy people tend to be cooperative, conservative in risk-taking, more logical and imaginative, exhibiting more competence and self-esteem (Lane, 1999).

Perceived psychological wellness is strongly associated with optimism and self-esteem. People with these traits tend to be happier with themselves, expecting positive outcomes, regardless of what they encounter (Adams et al., 1998; Veenhoven, 1996). Both optimism and self-esteem have also been positively linked to higher levels of intimacy, health and subjective quality of life (Cummins and McCabe, 1994). In one study, self-esteem was found to be the best predictor of life satisfaction, followed by optimism (Lewinsohn, Redner, and Seeley, 1991). The relationship between optimism, self-esteem and happiness is reasonably well established (Myers, 1993; Myers and Diener, 1997). In fact, optimism and selfr-esteem beliefs were selected to successfully demonstrate the convergent validity of the happiness scale employed in this research (Lyubomirsky and Lepper, 1999).

Therefore, it is hypothesized that:

H1: optimism and self-esteem beliefs generate happiness.

3.2.2. *Income and Happiness*

A modest relationship between income and happiness has been confirmed by many researchers (Ahuvia, 1999; Ahuvia and Friedman, 1998; Cummins, 2000a; Diener et al., 1993; Lewinsohn, Redner, and Seeley, 1991; Marks and Fleming, 1999; Mullis, 1992; Schor, 1999). It is generally reported that a positive effect of income on happiness is found at all income segments. Some researchers, however, have indicated that positive effects of income on happiness on income may be stronger among lower income segments (Ahuvia and Friedman, 1998; Cummins, 2000a).

Therefore, it is hypothesized that:

H2: happiness is lower for the lower income group compared with the upper income group

3.2.3. *Optimism, Self-Esteem and Income*

Possessions enhance self-image. Social status and respectability, which reinforce self-esteem, are indicated by wealth, while poverty may be stigmatizing. Higher incomes are associated with less job insecurity, which may strengthen feelings of optimism (Marmot and Wilkinson, 2001). Environmental factors, such as money available to buy needed commodities, impinge on beliefs. Income directly affects optimism and self-esteem (Cummins, 2000b).

Therefore, it is hypothesized that:

H3: beliefs affecting happiness – optimism and self-esteem – are lower for the lower income groups compared with the upper income group

3.2.4. *Causal Paths from Beliefs to Happiness for Income Groups*

Reported sources of happiness are different between wealthy and non-wealthy people. The former cite self-esteem and self-actualization more frequently as sources. The latter are more likely to attribute happiness to psychological and security needs (Diener, Horwitz, and Emmons, 1985).

As noted by Lu (1999), to understand happiness it is necessary to take into account both environmental and personal variables, including self-esteem, optimism.

Personality variables, such as self-esteem and optimism, relate to both income and happiness. Income is positively related to interpersonal trust and confidence in one's leadership and interpersonal influence (Scheufele and Shah, 2000). In one study, self-esteem was isolated as the most important predictor of happiness. Self-esteem inoculates against negative experiences and helps to ensure a positive outlook (Hong and Giannakopoulos, 1994). Higher income occupations offer greater job autonomy and skill utilization with resulting greater job satisfaction. In turn, a link exists between job satisfaction and life satisfaction (Ahuvia and Friedman, 1998). Education, which is positively related to income, provides personal "stocks" which aid in coping with adverse experiences, thus maintaining happiness. Income also enables location in favorable areas. The result of this is a lower incidence of unemployment and personal assault for higher income individuals. Higher stock levels provide psychic income and, thereby, positively affect happiness (Headey and Wearing, 1991).

Wealth generates a sense of self-esteem, and a belief that the environment is under personal control. Rich people are less likely to experience situations that compromise happiness. Money is only one of a variety of ways to acquire resources and, thus, the relationship between money and happiness is indirect, since money explains little variance in happiness after that accounted for by subjective variables (Cummins, 2000a).

Personal dispositions such as optimism and self-esteem influence happiness. These dispositions modify, rather than overshadow, the impact of external environmental effects. Income and a constellation of beliefs, including self-esteem and optimism may be construed as individual "life chances," affecting the likelihood of happiness (Veenhoven, 1996, 2000).

Therefore, it is hypothesized that:

> *H4:* causal paths from optimism and self-esteem beliefs to happiness are invariant across the lower and upper income groups

3.2.5. *Methodology Procedure and Sample*

In order to test the hypotheses noted above, we secured a sample of some 137 adults. The procedure whereby these data were collected was as follows. First, students from four different marketing classes at two small, private universities (two classes from each university) in the northeastern United States were asked to deliver a survey (to be discussed shortly) to one of their parents. Half of the students were directed to have their mother fill-out the survey, and half were asked to have to their father complete the survey. In addition to the survey, students were provided with a self-addressed envelope (addressed to the researchers). The students were instructed to have their parent complete the survey and return it via the self-addressed envelope. Students were also instructed to either deliver the survey to their parent in-person, or to mail the survey directly to their parent. To provide necessary information for the parent-respondents, an instruction sheet accompanied the survey. Parents were assured that the sons and/or daughters would not be privy to the information provided in the survey, and that all surveys would be completely anonymous. In order to secure adequate participation in the study, students were given extra-credit in the course if their parent returned a questionnaire. Some 180 parent questionnaires were dispensed yielding an approximate 76 percent response-rate.

Some 58 percent of the sample were female, and 76 percent were married. Approximately 26 percent were under the age of 44, 28 percent were between the ages of 45 and 49, 29 percent were between the ages of 50 and 54, and 17 percent were over 55 years of age. Approximately 44 percent of the sample graduated from college and/or had a postgraduate degree. Just under 70 percent worked full-time, and over half held professional- and/or business executive/managerial-type positions.

3.2.6. *Measures and their Psychometric Properties*

Each of the scales utilized in the study are established scales. In order to demonstrate satisfactory degrees of reliability and validity for the measures, a series of psychometric tests were conducted. Specifically, we utilized both Cronbach's coefficient alpha (α) and confirmatory factor analysis (*CFA*).

Self-esteem was measured using Rosenberg's (1965) scale of self-esteem. This ten-item scale utilized four-point Likert-type items (*1 = strongly disagree; 4 = strong agree*).

Higher scores are indicative of more self-esteem, and α for the scale was satisfactory at 0.83. Next, we estimated a single-factor measurement model (*CFA*). Although the χ^2 value was significant (20.91, $df = 9$, $p < 0.013$; χ^2 for the null model was 295.20, $df = 15$), high values for fit indices suggest a well-fitting model (CFI = 0.96; *IFI* = 0.96; *RMSEA* = 0.099). In addition, all of the items loaded significantly and positively on to the latent variable or factor (p's < 0.05; average standardized loading = 0.69).

Optimism was operationalized via Scheier and Carver's (1985) Life Orientation Test. Cronbach's alpha for the eight, five-point Likert-type items (*1 = strongly disagree; 5 = strong agree*) was 0.79, and higher scores are indicative of more optimism. To verify further the reliability of this measure, we again conducted a single-factor *CFA*. Although Scheier and Carver (1985) indicate that it is likely most reasonable to treat the scale as unidimensional, they also suggest that there is evidence for a two factor model. Accordingly, we allowed various error terms in the model to covary according to Scheier and Carver's (1985) two factor solution. A significant χ^2 value (29.69, $df = 14$, $p < 0.008$; χ^2 for the null was 352.85, $df = 28$) was offset by high values for fit indices (*CFI* = 0.95; *IFI* = 0.95; *RMSEA* = 0.091), ultimately indicating a well-fitting model. All of the items loaded significantly and positively on to the factor (p's < 0.05; average standardized loading = 0.51), and each of the correlations between the various error terms was significant (p's < 0.05).

The last scale we analyzed was the happiness measure. To operationalize the happiness construct we utilized Lyubomirsky and Lepper's (1999) measure of subjective happiness. Higher scores on the four, seven-point Likert-type items (*1 = not a very happy person; 7 = a very happy person*) are associated with higher levels of subjective happiness. Responses to the scale yielded an α of 0.76. As the scale was intended to have one underlying factor in common across all the items, a single-factor *CFA* was conducted. Overall, results were satisfactory and suggest that the scale is psychometrically sound: $\chi^2 = 14.93$, $df = 2$, $p < 0.001$; $CFI = 0.93$; $IFI = 0.93$; $RMSEA = 0.219$ (the χ^2 for the null was 189.09, $df = 6$). Further, all items loaded significantly and positively on to the factor (p's < 0.05; average standardized loading = 0.71).

3.2.7. *A Measure of Income*

A single, nine-point measure of yearly family income was employed where higher scores are indicative of more income (*1 = under $20,000; 2 = $20,000 to $24,999; 3 = $25,000 to $34,999; 4 = $35,000 to $49,999; 5 = $50,000 to $74,999; 6 = $75,000 to $99,999; 7 = $100,000 to $149,999; 8 = $150,000 to $199,999; 9 = $200,000 and above*). This item was used to, among other things, divide the sample into two groups: a lower income group ($N = 70$) and an upper income group ($N = 65$). Specifically, the sample was divided according to the median of the income variable (*median* = 5; $M = 5.1$; $SD = 2.2$). In support of this strategy, there is evidence to suggest that the income variable is fairly normally distributed as 74 percent of the scores on this variable ($N = 100$) fall within one standard deviation of the mean, and all scores are within two standard deviations of the mean. The mean income for the lower income group is 3.4 (roughly between $30,000 and $47,000), and 7 for the upper income group (between approximately $100,000 and $149,999).

3.3. RESULTS

In an effort to test Cummins's homeostatic theory of subjective well-being or normative life satisfaction, the analysis strategy coincides with the four hypotheses discussed earlier. In accord with Cummins's (2000a) homeostatic theory of subjective well-being, *H1* states that optimism and self-esteem beliefs will generate happiness. To test this hypothesis we ran a simple (*OLS*) regression model wherein optimism and self-esteem served as independent (exogenous) variables and happiness served as the dependent (endogenous) variable. The overall model was significant ($F = 40.20$; $p < 0.000$), and the two independent variables accounted for 38 percent of the variance in the subjective happiness measure (*adjusted* $R^2 = 0.38$). Accordingly, we examined the individual path coefficients (β's) to assess specifically the research predictions. Before examining these coefficients, however, we evaluated the models for multicollinearity. The effects of multicollinearity were assessed through a set of statistics as proposed by Freund and Littell (2000), and include variance inflation factors and principle component analysis. The results of these assessments indicate that multicollinearity is not present in the model.

The model tests the effects of the self-esteem and optimism dimensions on the subjective measure of happiness. Findings indicated that both self-esteem and optimism have a significant effect on happiness (standardized β's = 0.22 and 0.47, respectively; p's < 0.01). Thus, *H1* is supported.

Hypothesis 2 states that the happiness mean of the lower income group will be significantly lower than the corresponding mean for the upper income group. This hypothesis was tested via a two-way (income) analysis of variance (*ANOVA*). A significant main effect of income was obtained for the subjective measure of happiness ($F = 5.61$; $p < 0.02$). This finding indicates that the upper income group was significantly happier compared with the lower income group (see Table 3.1).

Hypothesis 3 states that the variable means for the beliefs affecting happiness – namely optimism and self-esteem – will be significantly lower for the lower income group compared with the corresponding means for the upper income group. This hypothesis was also tested via a series of two-way (income) *ANOVA*'s. A significant main effect of income was obtained for optimism ($F = 4.30$; $p < 0.04$). The

Table 3.1. Variable Means and Correlations.

Group variable	Higher Income	Lower Income
Subjective happiness		
M	5.44	5.05
SD	1.02	0.91
Optimism		
M	3.82	3.61
SD	0.59	0.52
Self-esteem		
M	3.44	3.32
SD	0.50	0.41

Dimension	1.	2.	3.
Factor Intercorrelations – Entire Sample			
1. Happiness	1.00		
2. Self-Esteem	0.52	1.00	
3. Optimism	0.61	0.61	1.00
Factor Intercorrelations – Lower Income Group			
1. Happiness	1.00		
2. Self-Esteem	0.33	1.00	
3. Optimism	0.43	0.40	1.00
Factor Intercorrelations – Higher Income Group			
1. Happiness	1.00		
2. Self-Esteem	0.49	1.00	
3. Optimism	0.54	0.74	1.00

Note: All parameter estimates differing significantly from zero are underscored.

result indicates that the upper income group is significantly more optimistic compared with the lower income group (see Table 3.1). There was no significant effect of income on self-esteem ($p > 0.13$). In sum, *H3* is partially supported.

The final hypothesis to be tested, H4, predicts that the identified causal paths from optimism and self-esteem to happiness will be invariant across the lower and upper income groups. That is, the effects of optimism and self-esteem are predicted to be the same for the two income groups. To test this prediction we conducted a multi-sample, path analysis and compared paths across the two income groups. The estimated model is essentially the same model tested earlier except that the analysis is conducted with two samples or groups (the two income groups) as opposed to one, and we constrained the paths from self-esteem to happiness and from optimism to happiness to be equal across the two groups. It is worth noting that a multi-sample analysis technique was employed as our primary interest is to statistically compare paths across the two sets of data (i.e., two different income groups) versus maximizing the fit of any one particular model *per se*. The significant χ^2 value (23.27, $df = 4$, $p < 0.001$) for the two-sample model was not surprising given the relatively small sizes of the two samples and the use of a multi-sample technique. (The χ^2 for the null was 131.46, $df = 6$). Moderate yet acceptable values for fit indices ($CFI = 0.85$; $IFI = 0.85$; $RMSEA = 0.191$), however, suggests a satisfactorily fitting model across both sets of responses, and all paths were significant and positive (p's < 0.05). Of particular interest, we found that the equality constraints across the two sets of responses were correctly imposed (p's > 0.30) thereby confirming that the effects of optimism and self-esteem on happiness are in fact invariant (i.e., statistically equal) across the two income groups (see Figure 3.1). In sum, *H4* is supported.

3.4. DISCUSSION

The present research was conducted to validate and to disentangle relationships between income and happiness. In so doing, the present study tests significant aspects of the homeostatic theory of happiness. The theory states that happiness levels of individuals tend to be maintained at relatively high levels, with variations within a fairly narrow range. The operation of buffer variables represented by specific beliefs is posited to account for homeostasis. However, environmental variables, such as income, may affect levels of happiness despite the trend toward normative levels of happiness.

The theory-driven model of internal buffering by self-esteem and optimism beliefs affects happiness levels, regardless of income grouping. However, income directly affects levels of these internal buffers and thereby indirectly drives happiness in expected directions. Higher income leads to greater happiness than does lower income. That is to say, beliefs may be viewed as the *engine* of happiness, and income as the *operator*. Figure 3.2 illustrates this process as a formal causal model.

Results confirm the theory that income may provide maintenance of subjective well-being, i.e., homeostasis of happiness levels is more likely when income is

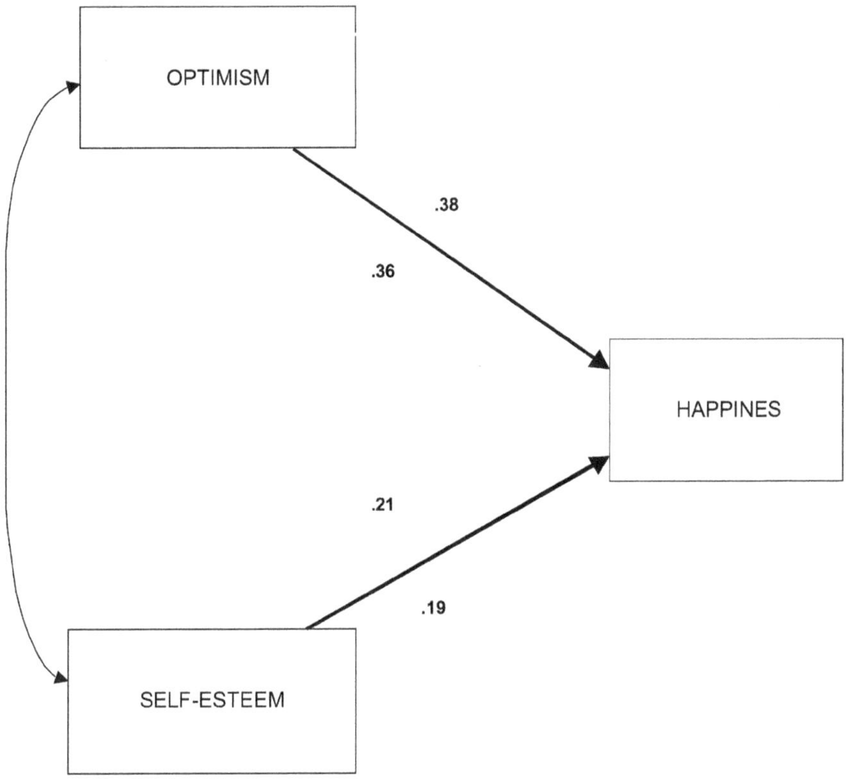

Figure 3.1. Path Model.

sufficient to make the environment less stressful. This is amply supported by corroboration of hypotheses of positive relationships between beliefs and happiness, income and happiness, income and beliefs (significant for optimism), and equivalent causal influences of beliefs on happiness for upper and lower income groups.

Thus, it is concluded that resulting happiness scores of the causal model show that income effects are mediated in the appropriate direction by the belief buffering variables, as predicted by Cummins' homeostatic model (2000a). This is to say, higher income is generates levels of self-esteem and optimism that promote higher levels of happiness.

3.5. FURTHER RESEARCH

These results were based on a sample of middle-aged American adults who had offspring enrolled in universities. This population controls for possible demographic confounding factors such as age, family size, and family life stage to get at estimates of the impact of income. Nevertheless, the model should be replicated for other populations.

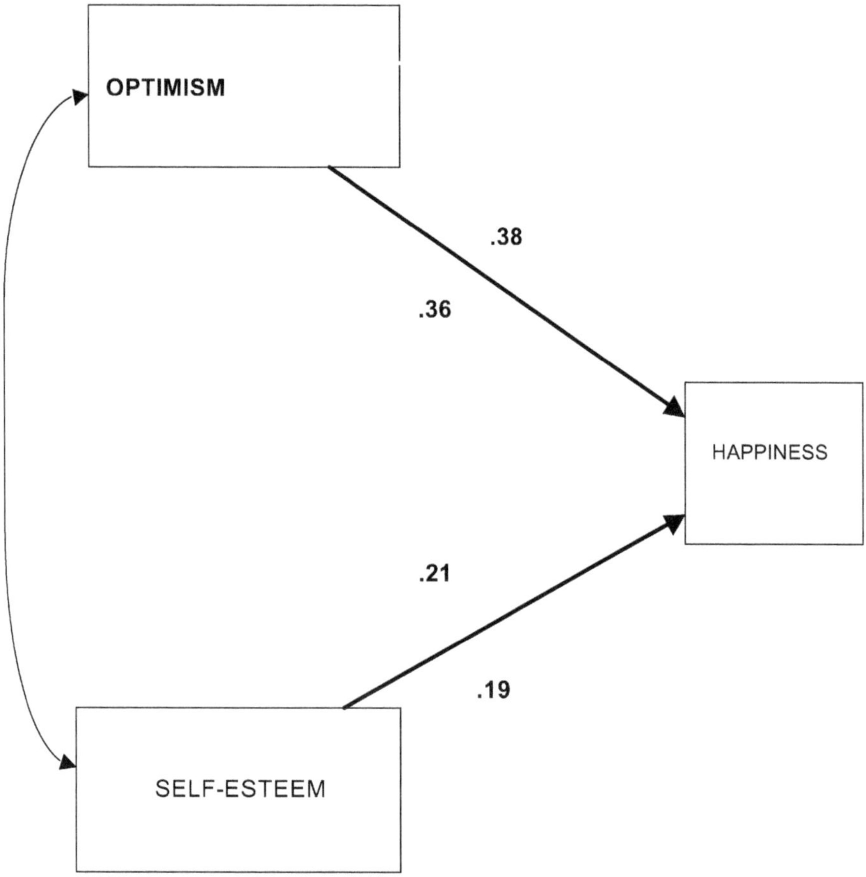

Figure 3.2. Conceptual Model: Moderating Effect of Personal Income.

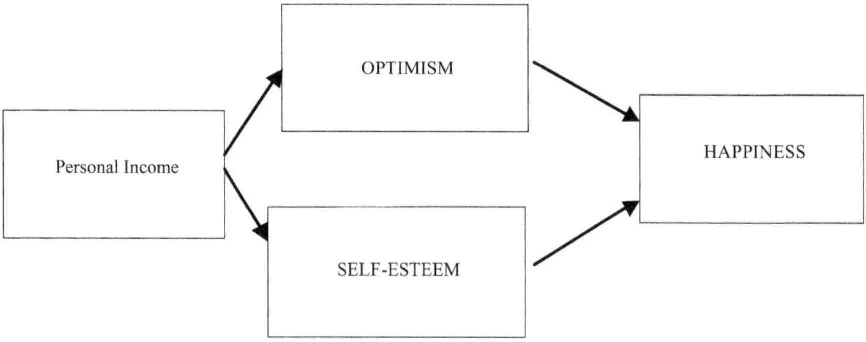

Figure 3.3. Consumer Income and Beliefs Affecting Happiness.

This study addressed the impact of optimism and self-esteem as buffering variables mediating the income-happiness relationship. Income has been found to have a positive relationship with other buffer variables known to affect happiness, including control (Cummins, 2000a; Lewinsohn, Redner, and Seeley, 1991). Therefore, a second priority for future research is to enlarge the structure of the homeostatic model to include more buffer variables. Also, more theory-building and methodological research is needed to explore the nature of non-linear relationships between variables. It is this particular roadblock that constrains us to use of the analysis of variance and makes structural equation modeling especially problematic.

Easterlin (2001) suggested that a reason why income is not more strongly associated with happiness is that income is a proxy for an interrelated set of socio-economic circumstances. Indeed, composite or index measures that include income have been found slightly stronger in explaining subjective well-being (Mullis, 1992). Income may be viewed as one indicator of important latent constructs, such as economic well-being or social status. This approach might importantly advance theory building and address measurement error concerns.

Finally, domain satisfaction has been found to be strongly associated with subjective well-being (Headey and Wearing, 1992). Consequently, future research might incorporate the linkages between objective income and subjective satisfaction in models explaining homeostatic levels of happiness.

3.6. REFERENCES

Adams, T., Bezner, J., Garner, L., and Woodruff, S. (1998). Construct validation of the perceived wellness survey. *American Journal of Health Studies*, **14**, 212–220.

Ahuvia A. (1999). Honor versus hedonism: A cross-cultural analysis of the missing link between income and subjective well-being. *Proceedings of the Seventh Symposium on Cross-Cultural and Business Studies.*

Ahuvia, A. and Friedman, D. (1998). Income, consumption, and subjective well-being: Toward a composite macromarketing model, *Journal of Macromarketing*, **18**, 153–169.

Burke, K., Joyner, B. A., Czech, D. R., and Wilson, M. J. (2000). An investigation of concurrent validity between two optimism/pessimism questionnaires: The life orientation test-revised and the optimisin/pessimism scale. *Current Psychology*, **19**, 129–137.

Cileli, M. and Tezer, E. (1998). Life and value orientations of Turkish university students. *Adolescence*, **33**, 219–229.

Cummins, R. A. and McCabe, M. P. (1994). The comprehensive quality of life scale (COMQOL): Instrument development and psychometric evaluation on college staff and students. *Educational and Psychological Measurement*, **54**, 372–383.

Cummins, R. A. (1995). On the trail of the gold standard for subjective well-being. *Social Indicators Research*, **35**, 179–200.

Cummins, R. A. (1996). The domains of life satisfaction: An attempt to order chaos. *Social Indicators Research*, **38**, 303–328

Cummins, R.A. (1998). The second approximation to an international standard for life satisfaction. *Social Indicators Research*, **43**, 307–334.

Cummins, R.A. (2000a). Personal income and subjective well-being: A review. *Journal of Happiness Studies*, **1**, 133–158.

Cummins, R. A. (2000b). Objective and subjective quality of life: An interactive model. *Social Indicators Research*, **52**, 55–73.

Cummins, R. A. (2001). Normative life satisfaction: Measurement issues and a homeostatic model, in 13. In Zumbo (ed.), *Methodological Developments and Issues in Quality of Life Research* (in press).

Diener, E., Horwitz, J., and Emmons, R. A. (1985). Happiness of the very wealthy. *Social Indicators Research*, **16**, 263–274.

Diener, E., Sandvik, E., Seidlitz, L., and Diener, M. (1993). The relationship between income and subjective well-being: Relative or absolute? *Social Indicators Research*, **28**, 195–223.

Easterlin, R. A. (2001). Income and happiness: Towards a unified theory. *Economic Journal*, **111** (in press).

Esmer, Y. (2000). Human development and social integration: The case of Turkey. A *Paper Presented at the Second Global Forum on Human Development.*

Freund, R. J. and Littell, R. C. (2000). *SAS System for Regression*, 3rd ed., North Carolina: SAS Institute Inc.

Frey, B. S. and Stutzer, A. (2000). Happiness, economy and institutions. *Economic Journal*, **110**, 918–938.

Gardyn, R. (2001). Happiness grows on trees. *American Demographics*, **23**, 18–21.

Hermans, H. J. M. (1992). Unhappy self-esteem: A meaningful exception to the rule. *Journal of Psychology*, **126**, 557–571.

Hsieh, C. (1997). Financial Well-Being and Happiness Among Middle-Age and Old-Age Americans. *Doctoral Dissertation in Social Welfare* (University of Pennsylvania, Philadelphia).

Graham, J. F. (1999). Materialism and consumer behavior: Toward a clearer understanding. *Journal of Social Behavior and Personality*, **14**, 241–259.

Headey, B. and Wearing, A. (1991). Subjective well-being: A stocks and flows framework. In F. Strack, M. Argyle and N. Schwarz (eds.), *Subjective Well. Being: An. Interdisciplinary Perspective* (pp. 49–71). New York: Plenum Press.

Headey, B. and Wearing, A. (1992). *Understanding Happiness: A Theory of Subjective Well-Being.* Melbourne: Longman Cheshire.

Hong, S. M. and Giannakopoulos, E. (1994). The relationship of satisfaction with life to personality characteristics. *Journal of Psychology*, **128**, 547–559.

Kasser, T. (2000). Two versions of the American dream: Which goals and values make for a high quality of life? In E. Diener and D. R. Rahtz (eds.), *Advances in Quality of Life Theory and Research* (pp. 3–12). UK: Kluwer Academic Publishers.

Krause, N. (1995). Religiosity and self-esteem among older adults. *Journal of Gerontology*, **50**, 236–253.

Lai, J. C. L. (1997). Relative predictive power of the optimism vs. the pessimism index of a Chinese version of the life orientation test. *Psychological Record*, **47**, 399–411.

Lane, R. E. (1999). Diminishing returns to income, companionship and happiness. *Journal of Happiness Studies*, 103–119.

Lewinsohn, P. M.,.Redner, J. E., and Seeley, J. R. (1991). The relationship between life satisfaction and psychosocial variables: New perspective. In F. Strack, M. Argyle and N. Schwarz (eds.), *Subjective Well-Being: An Interdisciplinary Perspective* (pp. 141–169). New York: Plenum Press.

Lu, L. (1995). The relationship between subjective well-being and psychosocial variables in Taiwan. *Journal of Social Psychology*, **135**, 351–358.

Lu, L and Shih, J.B. (1997). Sources of happiness: A qualitative approach. *Journal of Social Psychology*, **137**, 181–188.

Lu, L. (1999). Personal or environmental causes of happiness: A longitudinal analysis. *Journal of Social Psychology*, **139**, 79–90.

Lyubomirsky, S. and Lepper, H. S. (1999). A measure of subjective happiness: Preliminary reliability and construct validation. *Social Indicators Research*, **46**, 137–155.

Marks, G. N. and Fleming, N. (1999). Influences and consequences of well-being among Australian young people. *Social Indicators Research*, **46**, 301–323.

Marmot, M. and Wilkinson, R. G. (2001). Psychosocial and material pathways in the relation between income and health. British Medical Journal, **322**, 1233–1237.
Mookherjee, H. N. (1994). Effects of religiosity and selected variables on the perception of well-being. *Social Psychology*, **134**, 403–406.
Mullis, R. E. (1992). Measures of economic well-being as predictors of psychological well-being. *Social Indicators Research*, **26**, 119–135.
Myers, D. G. (1993). Pursuing happiness. *Psychology Today*, **26**, 32–38.
Myers, D. G. and Diener, E. (1997). The science of happiness. *Futurist*, **31**, 1–7.
Rogers, S. J. and Bebor, D. D. (2001). Changes in wives' income: Effects on marital happiness, psychological well-being and the risk of divorce. *Journal of Marriage and the Family*, **63**, 458–473.
Rosenberg, M. (1965). *Society and the Adolescent Self Image*. Princeton: Princeton University Press.
Saris, W. E. (2001). The relationship between income and satisfaction. *Social Indicators Research*, **53**, 117–136.
Scheier, M. F. and Carver, C. S. (1985). Optimism, coping, and health: Assessment and implications of generalized outcome expectancies. *Health Psychology*, 219–247.
Scherpenzeel, A. and Saris, W. (1996). Causal direction in a model of life satisfaction: The top-down/bottom-up controversy. *Social Indicators Research*, **38**, 161–180.
Scheufele, D. A. and Shah, D. V. (2000). Personality strength and social capital. *Communication Research*, **27**, 107–132.
Scheufele, D. A. and Shah, D. V. (2001). The relationship between income and satisfaction. *Social Indicators Research*, **53**, 117–136.
Schor, J. B. (1999). *The Overspent American American*. New York: Basic Books.
Sirgy, J. M. (1998). Materialism and quality of life. *Social Indicators Research*, **43**, 227–260.
Staats, S. and Horner, K. (1999). Allocating time to people and pets: Correlates with income and well-being in a Midwest community sample. *Journal of Psychology*, **133**, 541–553.
Veenhoven, R. (1996). Developments in satisfaction research. *Social Indicators Research*, **37**, 1–46.
Veenhoven, R. (2000). The four qualities of life. *Journal of Happiness Studies*, **1**, 1–39.
Weston, R. (1999). Factors contributing to personal well-being. *Fammily Matters*, **52**, 54–61.

3.7. AFFILIATIONS

Mel Prince, Marketing Department, Southern Connecticut State University, 501 Crescent Street, New Haven, CT 06515, USA; E-mail: MelDarien@cs.com

Chris Manolis, Marketing Department, Xavier University, Cincinnati, Ohio, USA.

KRISTEN SUTHERS, YASUHIKO SAITO, AND EILEEN CRIMMENS

4. EMOTIONAL WELL-BEING AMONG OLDER PERSONS: A COMPARATIVE ANALYSIS OF THE 70+ POPULATION IN JAPAN AND THE UNITED STATES

ABSTRACT: The purpose of this analysis is to identify differences in the level of positive and negative emotions among older adults in Japan and the United States. Further, the relationships between positive and negative emotional states and socioeconomic, demographic, and health conditions are explored. Two nationally representative samples of adults aged 70 and over are used for this analysis: the Nihon University Japanese Longitudinal Study of Aging (N = 3,276) and the Assets and Health Dynamics of the Oldest Old survey in the United States (N = 7,443). OLS regression models are used to determine the relationship between positive and negative emotions and socioeconomic, demographic, and health indicators in each country. Overall, the level of negative emotions among older adults in both countries is similar. However, Americans report more positive emotions compared to their Japanese counterparts. The relationships between socioeconomic, demographic, health factors and emotional states are similar in each country, however, the magnitude of the effect of these factors is greater on negative emotions, compared to positive emotions.

4.1. INTRODUCTION

Emotional well-being is essential to maintaining an optimal quality of life. Among adults, the challenges to emotional well-being are likely to multiply as age increases; for example, loved ones may die, social roles may change, income may decline, and health may deteriorate. These life changes associated with aging are universal. Therefore, in order to understand quality of life at the oldest ages, it is useful to explore the relationship between emotional well-being and life circumstances. Further, examining these relationships in different cultures can elucidate whether the *effects* of these life changes are universal. The purpose of this paper is to examine the level of positive and negative emotion expressed by the older population in two culturally divergent countries: Japan and the United States. We will also compare the association between socioeconomic, demographic and health factors and the expression of positive and negative emotions in old age in each of these countries.

4.2. BACKGROUND

In his landmark analysis, Powell Lawton described four components in which social scientists may measure quality of life: behavioral competence, environmental quality, domain specific satisfaction, and subjective well-being (1997). The measures of emotional states in this paper fall under the domain of subjective well-being. Studies of subjective well-being in old age have focused primarily on differentiating positive and negative emotional states, and determining whether differences in well-being exist between younger and older age groups. No clear pattern of findings on increasing age and subjective well-being has been demonstrated across studies (Costa et al., 1987; Herzog and Rogers, 1981; Stacey and Gatz,

M. Joseph Sirgy et al. (eds.), Advances in Quality-of-Life Theory and Research, 41–50, 2003.

1991). Diener and Suh (1997) conducted a multi-national review of quality of life studies and found that in multiple countries throughout the world, age was not related to diminished life satisfaction, measured as positive and negative affect. Although the level of positive emotions was lower in older age groups, the authors point out that this may be the result of cohort differences, rather than aging related differences (Diener and Suh, 1997). In a longitudinal analysis of older adults ranging in age from 70–103, Kuntzmann, Little and Smith (2000) found that it was not aging which was a cause of decline in subjective well-being, but rather health constraints.

Diener and Diener (1996) also explored the relationship between subjective well-being and external conditions. The results of these analyses indicated that even under conditions that may be deemed undesirable by most, such as low income or physical disabilities, people still reported positive levels of subjective well-being. Older adults who are married report higher levels of subjective well-being (Diener and Suh, 1997). However, the authors note that this may not necessarily be due to the intrinsic value of marriage in improving quality of life; rather, at the older ages when many people are widowed, a person may consider him or herself fortunate to still have a spouse.

Cross-cultural studies of depression in Japanese and American peoples can elucidate patterns of emotional well-being across these two countries (Baron and Matsuyama, 1988; Krause and Liang, 1992; Marsella, 1987; Zung, 1977). Asian populations generally have lower levels of depression when compared to Western populations, regardless of age (Baron and Matsuyama, 1988; Krause and Liang, 1992; Marsella, 1987; Zung, 1977). This discrepancy is likely a result of differences in levels of both positive and negative emotions. For example, older Asian adults report higher positive emotion scores, lower negative emotion scores, lower depressed affect scores and fewer interpersonal difficulties than their American counterparts (Krause and Liang, 1992). Therefore, lower levels of depression among Asians could be attributed to fewer negative emotions and higher levels of positive emotions (Krause and Liang, 1992).

There are a number of advantages to the current analysis. Previous research studies still have not clarified the relationship between external conditions and emotional well-being, specifically in older adults. Further, the advantage of the current analysis is the nationally representative samples of older adults in Japan and the United States, which allows us to extrapolate our findings to older adults in each country. There are compelling reasons to explore the relationship between emotional well-being and socio-demographic and health characteristics among older adults in different cultures. Cross-cultural analyses contribute to the understanding of how emotional well-being in old age differs across cultures. Findings from these analyses may contribute to improvements in international policy approaches to mental health among older adults. Differentiating relationships between emotional states and individual characteristics between cultures enables identification of unique risk factors based on cultural background.

The study of positive and negative emotional states as separate entities is important because each is thought to have different etiologies and be relatively independent of the other (Baker et al., 1992; Diener and Suh, 1997). Therefore, elucidating the relationships between positive and negative emotional states and socio-demographic and health characteristics among the current generation of older adults will inform understanding about the health and well-being of future cohorts of older adults.

4.3. METHODS

4.3.1. *Data Sources*

In order to compare older adults in Japan and the United States, results from two nationally representative surveys are utilized: the Nihon University Japanese Longitudinal Study of Aging, (NUJLSOA), and the Assets and Health Dynamics of the Oldest Old (AHEAD) dataset. In Japan, 4,499 self respondents over the age of 65 were interviewed in 1999 during the first wave of data collection for the NUJLSOA. Since the US sample is representative of adults over 70, only those 3,276 NUJLSOA participants 70 years of age and over are included in the Japanese sample. The AHEAD study in the United States began in 1993, with interviews of 7,443 community-dwelling older Americans over the age of 70. Data from the first wave of this nationally representative survey are used for these analyses. Mean respondent age for Japan is 76; 59% of the sample is female. The mean age for the American sample is 77; 63% of the sample is female. Both data sets are weighted to adjust for the probability of sample selection.

In each data set, some respondents were eliminated from the analysis because they did not provide answers to every question. In Japan there were 214 respondents missing on the positive index and 181 missing on the negative index. Compared to responders, Japanese adults with missing data were slightly older, had a significantly lower income, slightly less education, and more difficulty in physical functioning. With the exception of income, none of these differences are statistically significant. In the US, we found that non-responders were significantly older, had lower income, and they reported significantly more difficulty with physical functioning than responders. Because of the larger sample size, smaller differences are significant in the United States.

4.3.2. *Measurement*

Indicators of positive and negative emotions are derived from items included in scales designed to measure depression. The CES-D is a scale developed by the Center for Epidemiological Studies to screen for depressive symptoms in community sample populations (Radloff, 1977). The entire CES-D scale consists of items designed to represent three domains: positive and negative emotional states and depressive symptoms. Various forms of this scale have been used extensively in epidemiological studies of depression in many countries and many age groups (Kessler et al., 1992; Blazer et al., 1991). A CES-D was administered in both countries but in slightly different formats.

AHEAD respondents are asked to answer yes or no to eight CES-D items. Five of the items asking about positive and negative emotional states during the past week are included in these analyses (Table 4.1). The yes/no response format used in AHEAD differs from the original construction of the scale that asks respondents to gauge their symptoms along a continuum of severity by using more response categories. Factor analyses of the revised AHEAD CES-D8 binary response scale indicate that the revised scale is comparable to the original (Turvey, Wallace, and Herzog, 1999). In order to indicate levels of positive and negative emotional well-being, two separate scores are calculated. A positive emotion indicator is calculated by summing the two CES-D positive items, with a resulting score range of 0–2. Likewise, a negative emotion indicator is calculated by summing the three CES-D negative items, with a resulting score range of 0–3.

In Japan, twelve CES-D items are administered in the NUJLSOA survey. In order to maintain comparability between countries, only the items that assess emotional states and are comparable to the AHEAD items are used in the current analysis (Table 4.1). These items also ask the subject to report on emotional states over the past week. The original response format to the CES-D in Japan consisted of three responses: rarely, sometimes, and often. To compare Japan with the US, this response format is recoded so that, "sometimes" and "often" became a "yes" response, while "rarely" became a "no" response. The two indicators of emotional well-being are determined by summing the positive items for a positive emotion indicator ranging from 0–2, and a total negative emotion indicator on a scale of 0–3.

Independent variables representing socioeconomic conditions, health conditions, work status, and family circumstances are derived from responses to similar questions in each country and coded into similar response categories when necessary. Education is coded as a categorical measure, using the same categories in both countries. Income is also coded as similar categorical measures in both coun-

Table 4.1. Positive and Negative Emotion Items Analyzed in Each Country. Respondents Answered Questions Based on Week Prior to Interview.

Japan	% endorsing item	USA	% endorsing item
Negative Emotion Indicator		*Negative Emotion Indicator*	
I felt depressed	16.9	I felt depressed	20.0
I felt lonely	21.8	I felt lonely	20.6
I felt sad	17.5	I felt sad	19.5
Mean Score: NEG = 0.55 (range: 0–3)		*Mean Score: NEG = 0.59 (range: 0–3)*	
Positive Emotion Indicator		*Positive Emotion Indicator*	
I was happy	51.6	I was happy	87.9
I enjoyed life	48.3	I enjoyed life	93.1
Mean Score: POS = 0.99 (range: 0–2)		*Mean Score: POS = 1.81 (range: 0–2)*	

tries. However, in Japan, for the 21% of respondents who did not answer questions about income, the value of income is set at the mean. A dummy variable that identifies respondents with missing income is included to control for this effect while retaining these sample members. On the other hand, since 31% of American respondents did not provide exact estimates of their total household income, a set of unfolding questions were administered to determine the range of the respondent's income and were used by the AHEAD staff to impute income for American respondents with missing data. Functioning ability is indicated by the total number out of eleven of "Activities of Daily Living" and "Independent Activities of Daily Living" which the person is unable to perform. Health variables are indicators of the presence or absence of disease. The conditions included in this analysis are highly prevalent diseases for the older adult population worldwide: stroke, arthritis, heart disease, diabetes and cancer. They are either major causes of mortality or morbidity or both.

Table 4.2 presents the mean sample characteristics for each of the independent variables included in the models, by country. *T*-tests indicate that Japanese and American respondents differed significantly on all independent variables. On average, older Americans had more years of education, more living children and slightly higher incomes. Americans reported worse physical functioning and a higher proportion of the population had these diseases than Japanese older adults. A greater proportion of Japanese than American older adults are married and working.

Table 4.2. Mean Score and Standard Deviation of Independent Variables for 70+ Population by Country

	Japan		US	
Age	76.18	(4.56)	77.50	(5.87)
Education[a]	1.55	(0.94)	2.38	(1.49)
# Children	2.43	(1.25)	2.70	(2.08)
Married	0.57	(0.47)	0.50	(0.50)
Income[b]	$24,259	($20,599)	$25,960	($33,228)
# ADL/IADL Problems	0.43	(1.35)	1.26	(2.28)
Working	0.21	(0.38)	0.09	(0.28)
Stroke	0.07	(0.25)	0.09	(0.28)
High Blood Pressure	0.34	(0.45)	0.50	(0.50)
Arthritis	0.18	(0.36)	0.25	(0.43)
Heart Condition	0.18	(0.36)	0.32	(0.46)
Diabetes	0.09	(0.28)	0.13	(0.33)
Cancer	0.04	(0.18)	0.14	(0.34)

[a] Education is coded as categorical: 1 = less than or equal to 9 yrs., 2 = 10–12 yrs, 3 = 13 yrs, 4 = 14 yrs., 5 = 15–16 yrs., 6 = 17+ yrs.

[b] Mean value of US income adjusted for CPI change between 1993 and 1999. Income in regression is coded into thirteen categories ranging from 1 to 13 for each country.

4.3.3. *Statistical Analyses*

Ordinary Least Squares (OLS) regression models are evaluated to determine the relationship between positive and negative emotion scores and age, marital status, number of living children, education level, income level, labor force participation, number of ADL/IADL difficulties, and medical conditions. Two separate models are calculated for each country; one model specifies the negative emotional indicator as the dependent variable, while the second model specifies the positive emotional indicator as the dependent variable.

4.4. RESULTS

Table 4.1 gives the proportion of respondents endorsing each of the positive and negative emotion indicators. Responses of Japanese adults to negative emotion items are fairly similar to those in the US; however, responses to positive items are quite different between countries. Japanese sample members were almost equally likely to choose between "yes" and "no" responses on the positive indicators, meaning that only about 50% of persons endorse the positive items. This is in contrast to the Americans who overwhelmingly reported feeling happy and enjoying life.

Table 4.1 also shows the means for positive and negative emotion scores in both countries. There is no significant difference between Japan and the US in the average negative emotion score. On the other hand, the average positive score is about twice as high in the United States. Americans almost unanimously endorse the positive items as the average of 1.8 is only slightly below the theoretical maximum of 2.0.

Table 4.3 presents the regression coefficients for the OLS models relating independent variables to the positive and negative emotions indicators. The clearest finding is that there is a strong relationship between the number of physical functioning difficulties and emotional states in both countries. More physical functioning difficulties are associated with fewer positive emotions among both Japanese and American older adults. Physical functioning appears to play a more consistent role in determining emotions than the presence of disease. Although older Americans with heart disease or arthritis are likely to have fewer positive emotions, and the size of the effect of either of these diseases is similar to that of having one more IADL or ADL impairment, in Japan, no health conditions are associated with positive emotions.

In both countries, people with higher SES in old age are likely to report more positive emotions. In both Japan and the United States, higher income is found to be related to higher positive emotion scores. Higher education is associated with higher positive emotion scores in Japan, however, not in the United States.

No other factors are related consistently to the expression of positive emotions in the two countries. When other factors are controlled, older age is associated with more positive emotions among Americans; this pattern is not observed among Japanese older adults. One could argue that once health, marital status and income

Table 4.3. Coefficients from OLS Regression Models for Adults aged 70 and Over in Japan and the US.

	Dependent Variable: Positive Emotion Indicator		Dependent Variable: Negative Emotion Indicator	
	Japan	USA	Japan	USA
Intercept	0.574	0.409	1.019	0.814
Age	–0.002	0.003**	–0.004	–0.001
Female	0.187**	–0.017	0.031	0.035
Education	0.092**	0.0006	–0.005	–0.054**
Married	0.028	0.023	–0.171**	–0.310**
# Children	0.021	0.002	–0.023	–0.004
Income	0.020*	0.008**	–0.024**	0.011
Missing Income	–0.094*	–	–0.044	–
Working	–0.050	0.037	–0.097*	–0.075
# ADL/IADL	–0.033**	0.056**	0.073**	0.107**
Stroke	0.036	0.001	0.227**	0.063
High Blood Pressure	–0.023	0.011	0.003	0.031
Arthritis	0.082	–0.046**	0.147**	0.114**
Heart Condition	–0.002	–0.042**	0.107*	0.094**
Diabetes	0.051	0.001	–0.010	0.039
Cancer	0.004	–0.010	0.236**	0.018
N	3,026	6,609	3,095	6,631
Adj. R2	0.021	0.117	0.052	0.051

* $p < 0.05$; ** $p < 0.01$.
Emotional Well-Being Among Older Persons.

are controlled, older persons in the US feel better simply for having attained an additional year. An association is found between female gender and higher positive emotion scores in Japan. Being female is not associated with more positive emotions in the United States.

More of these factors affect negative emotions than positive emotions. In each country the proportion of variance explained is negative emotions is about twice that of the variance in positive emotions. In both countries health states, marital status, and socioeconomic status affect the level of negative emotional state. Among both Japanese and American older adults, not being married, which generally means being widowed, is strongly associated with increased negative emotions. Given that being married is not associated with higher positive emotion scores, marital status appears to have negative but not positive consequences.

Higher socioeconomic status is related to lower expression of negative emotions in both countries. Higher education is associated with lower negative emotions among older adults in the United States; in Japan higher income is associated with fewer negative emotions. This is similar to the results reported above indicating a relationship between higher socioeconomic status and more positive emotions in both countries but with the significant indicator differing between countries. This means that in both countries higher socioeconomic status appears to result in higher positive emotions and lower negative emotions.

Increased negative emotions are associated with more physical functioning difficulties in both countries. This variable has the most consistent effect on emotional states across countries in both a positive and negative direction.

The presence of diseases increases negative emotions in both countries. Among the Japanese, having had a stroke or cancer increased negative well-being by about a quarter of a point. The presence of a heart condition or arthritis also increases negative emotions in Japan but the size of the effects are about half of those for stroke and cancer. In the US the increase in negative emotions with arthritis and heart disease is very similar in size to that in Japan. This means that these two disease states are the most likely to influence emotional state. In Japan the only influence is to increase negative emotions; in the US the presence of disease works in both ways, to decrease positive as well as to increase negative emotions.

With these controls, no relationship between age and negative emotions is found in either country; nor is there a relationship between negative emotions and gender in either country once other factors were controlled. Having children is not associated with higher positive or negative scores among older adults in either country. Working only reduces negative emotions in Japan; it does not affect emotional state in the United States.

4.5. DISCUSSION

Japanese and Americans over the age of 70 report relatively similar levels of negative emotions. Within each population, individual expression of negative emotion is affected by similar factors. In both countries, people in worse health or who are not married or who were of lower socioeconomic status, report feeling more negative emotions. In contrast, the level of expression of positive emotions in the two countries is quite different. Our results show that older Americans report, or are willing to express, more positive emotions than older Japanese. This finding differs from that in other studies (Krause and Liang, 1992) and may be an important consideration in future cross-cultural work in depression and emotions.

Even though older Japanese report fewer positive emotions, the factors predicting their expression are fairly similar in the two countries. Not surprisingly, in both countries, older people of high socioeconomic status and in good health feel more positive about life. As Diener and colleagues have hypothesized, this does not necessarily indicate the absence of positive feelings among those of low socioeconomic status, rather it is likely an indicator of greater resources equating with increased pleasure (Basabe et al., 2002) The magnitude of these effects on positive emotions is relatively small compared to negative emotions. However, given the small amount of variance in the responses in the United States, these findings are not surprising.

We found little effect of age on expressions of positive and negative emotions among those over seventy once other factors were controlled. Given that Diener and Suh's (1997) longitudinal analyses failed to find a relationship between age and positive emotions, it is likely that the higher level of positive emotions among older Americans is likely a cross-sectional artifact of this analysis (i.e. a survivor's effect). Were we to follow these older adults longitudinally, we may find that positive emotions do not necessarily increase with age, but rather, those persons with more positive emotions over the entire lifespan may have a survival advantage.

The effect of physical functioning difficulties was strongly related to both positive and negative emotions in both countries, indicating the centrality of health to emotional state in old age. This is consistent with previous research that found declines in subjective well-being were a result of health constraints, rather than age (Kuntzmann, Little, and Smith, 2000). Our findings support the conclusion that emotional well-being in old age, in both Japan and the United States, is closely tied to physical functioning abilities, which may also be indicative of ability to provide self care and to live independently.

As in previous studies (Diener and Diener, 1996), we find that being married is a major determinant of emotional well-being in old age in both countries. As Diener and Diener (1996) point out, marriage may reflect a sense of relative rather than absolute well-being, in that those older adults who still have a living spouse may simply consider themselves more fortunate than widowed spouses, resulting in a greater number of positive emotions. Our finding of the lack of an effect of the number of children on positive emotions in two very different familial cultures further supports Diener and Diener's hypothesis. It suggests that the number of children is not the critical mechanism in determining the advantage of marriage. Future research is essential to determine whether it is the quality of the marriage, rather than simply the existence of a living spouse, which is the mechanism for greater positive emotions in old age. It would also be useful to examine the relationship between quality of parent/child interaction and well-being.

Overall, these findings indicate that although the relationships between positive and negative emotions and life circumstances are similar between the United States and Japan, there are notable differences. Although cultural differences may be the explanatory mechanism in some cases, such as the relationship between work status and negative emotions, there are clearly factors, such as difficulties in physical functioning, which transcend borders and have universal effects on positive and negative emotions. Future research is essential to clarify the explanatory mechanisms that exist in the relationship between those socio-demographic significant and positive and negative emotional states in older adults.

4.6. REFERENCES

Baker, L. A., Cesa, I. L., Gatz, M., and Mellins, C. (1992). Genetic and environmental influences on positive and negative affect: Support for a two-factor theory. *Psychology and Aging*, **7**, 158–163.

Baron, M. and Matsuyama, Y. (1988). Symptoms of depression in Japanese and American college students. *Journal of Social Psychology*, **128**, 803–816.

Basabe, N., Paez, D., Valencia, J., Gonzalez, J., Rime, B., and Diener, E. (2002). Cultural Dimensions, socioeconomic development, climate, and emotional hedonic level. *Cognition and Emotion*, **16**, 103–125.

Blazer, D., Burchett, B., Service, C., and George, L. (1991). The association of age and depression among the elderly: an epidemiologic exploration. *Journals of Gerontology*, **46**, M210–M215.

Costa, P. T., Zonderman, A. B., McCrae, R. R., Cornoni-Huntley, J., Locke, B. Z., and Barbano, H. E. (1987). Longitudinal analysis of psychological well-being in a national sample: Stability of mean levels. *Journals of Gerontology*, **42**, 50–55.

Diener, E. and Diener, C. (1996). Most people are happy. *Psychological Science*, **7**, 181–185.

Diener, M. and Suh, M. (1997). Subjective well-being and age: an international analysis. In: K. W. Schaie and M. P. Lawton (eds.). *Focus on Affect and Adult Development.* New York, NY: Springer Publishing.

Herzog, A. R. and Rogers, W. L. (1981). Age and satisfaction: Data from several large surveys. *Research on Aging*, **3**, 142–165.

Kessler, R., Foster, C., Webster, P., and House, J. (1992). Relationship between age and depressive symptoms in two national surveys. *Psychology and Aging*, **7**, 119–126.

Krause N. and Liang J. (1992). Cross-cultural variations in depressive symptoms in later life. *International Psychogeriatrics*, **4**, 185–202.

Kuntzmann, U., Little, T., and Smith, J. (2000). Is age-related stability of subjective well-being a paradox? Cross-sectional and longitudinal evidence for the Berlin Aging Study. *Psychology and Aging*, **15**, 511–526.

Lawton, M. P. (1997). Measures of Quality of Life and subjective well-being. *Generations* (Spring), 45–47.

Marsella, A. (1987) The measurement of depressive experience and disorder across cultures. In A. Marsella, R. Hirschfield, and M. Katz (eds.), *The Measurement of Depression*. New York: Guilford Press.

Radloff, L. (1977). The CES-D Scale: A self-report depression scale for research in the general population. *Applied Psychological Measurement*, **1**, 385–401.

Stacey, C. A. and Gatz, M. (1991). Cross-sectional age differences and longitudinal change on the Bradburn Affect Balance Scale. *Journals of Gerontology: Psychological Sciences*, **46**, 76–78.

Turvey, C., Wallace, R., and Herzog, R. (1999). A Revised CES-D Measure of Depressive Symptoms and a DSM-Based Measure of Major Depressive Episodes in the Elderly. *International Psychogeriatrics*, **11**, 139–148.

Zung, W. (1977). Operational diagnosis and diagnostic categories of depressive disorder. In W. Fann (ed.), *Phenomenology and Treatment of Depression*. New York: Spectrum Publishing.

4.7. ACKNOWLEDGEMENTS AND AFFILIATIONS

The authors wish to acknowledge grants R03-AG021656, T32-A60037 and P30-A17265 from the US National Institute on Aging. The Japanese data for this study were provided by the Center for Information Networking, Nihon University, Tokyo, Japan.

Kristen Suthers, Andrus Gerontology Center, University of Southern California, Los Angeles, CA 90089-0191, USA.

Yasuhiko Saito, Center for Information Networking, Nihon University, Japan.

Eileen Crimmins, Andres Gerontology Center, University of Southern California, Los Angles, CA 90089-0191, USA.

PART II:

SOCIOECONOMIC, CULTURAL, AND CLIMATE DIFFERENCES IN QUALITY OF LIFE

Socioeconomic issues and growing up in different cultures lead to important differences in quality of life in different countries. In this section different aspects of quality of life are brought out in four different countries: South Africa, Italy, Great Britain and Canada. All four chapters deal with varying aspects of socioeconomic conditions and resultant quality of life.

Moller has determined that in South Africa overall life satisfaction is a key indicator of success in youth development. However, such attitudes as optimism may be more valid as a reference indicator than current subjective well-being measurement.

Nuvolati deals with socioeconomic development as it relates to quality of life in Italy. He uses social indicators and survey data in order to compare QOL during the last 12 years in the ex-industrial and metropolitan regions of Northwest.

Deutsch, Ramos and Silber explore existing inequality of quality of life in Great Britain. They estimate standard of living by measuring resources that develop individual's capabilities. They measure quality of life by analyzing individual functioning. They attempt to compare the relationship between standard of living and quality of life by using an input-output orientation.

Brown examines the impact of abuse and neglect on disabled and nondisabled children so that the quality of life for children can be enhanced. He particularly emphasizes neglect as a common practice in maltreatment of children. The study states the need for child functioning and maltreatment of children with intellectual disability to be examined more closely for improvement of children's quality of life.

Peterson examines how a country's climate contributes to objective QOL. His study investigates the relationship of climate favorableness for the world's countries with other objective QOL indicators previously researched. The group of higher-QOL countries is compared with the group of lower-QOL countries on climate favorableness and other dimensions of objective QOL.

Valerie Møller

5. QUALITY OF LIFE AND POSITIVE YOUTH DEVELOPMENT IN GRAHAMSTOWN EAST, SOUTH AFRICA

ABSTRACT: Quality-of-life studies are ideally suited to fulfilling the new international youth research agenda, which focuses on 'positive youth development' to make recommendations for policy and practice. The paper reports a South African case study conducted among disadvantaged youth for this purpose. A sample survey of close on 900 African youth, aged 15–24 years, sought to identify indicators of positive development to serve as goals of youth and community work in Grahamstown East/Rini, in the Eastern Cape province of South Africa. The setting is unique. This mainly rural province is among the poorest, least developed, and has one of highest unemployment rates. Nevertheless, Grahamstown may offer special development opportunities for local youth due to the proximity of the city centre and diverse extension projects for youth. The survey found that development opportunities were unequally distributed with the materially advantaged youth being more exposed to development opportunities through their schools, spare time activities, and community contacts. They were more ambitious than others and more aware of risks facing contemporary youth. Advantaged youth also reported higher levels of subjective well-being and optimism, findings consistent with earlier studies conducted among adult populations, which report remarkable congruence between material and subjective well-being among South Africans. The analysis used overall life satisfaction as key indicator of successful youth development to learn more about major youth aspirations and goals. In conclusion, the study was able to identify a youth development initiative based on the aspirations of the youth, which might be pursued as a researcher-practitioner partnership project in line with the new international youth research agenda.

5.1. Introduction

5.1.1. *A New Role for Quality-of-Life Studies in Youth Research*

In the last century, the problematic aspects of growing up dominated the youth research literature (Furstenberg, 2000). A new trend in youth research is the focus on 'positive youth development' which seeks to make recommendations for policy and practice (Zeldin, 2000). The new approach emphasises the promotion of human development. Youth empowerment, competence and mastery, emotional well-being, compassion, community connections and belonging, and civic participation are regarded as indicators of positive development, which serve as the new goals of youth and community work. To gain a more complete understanding of development options, adolescence is studied in the community setting and in multiple rather than single contexts. Youth researchers are urged to make their research relevant to policy and practice and even to extend action research to engagement in partnership projects. Ideally, development-oriented youth research involves researchers, practitioners and the youth as co-learners, each group bringing its own expertise to discourse and action over the course of the development initiative (Zeldin, 2000).

M. Joseph Sirgy et al. (eds.), Advances in Quality-of-Life Theory and Research, 53–79, 2003.

Quality-of-life studies, which typically cover multiple domains, are ideally suited to fulfilling the new youth research agenda. Given the nature of their chosen topic of inquiry, quality-of-life researchers are also well placed to advance youth development through an interactive approach which engages practitioners.

South Africa has a long history of promoting applied research in the social sciences. A quality-of-life study conducted in 1999 among youth in Grahamstown East serves as a case study. The study employed quality-of-life indicators as a tool to identify a youth development initiative which could be pursued as a researcher-practitioner partnership project. Although the indicators were collected in a conventional baseline multi-purpose survey, the instrument was specifically designed to inform policy makers and practitioners of the development options for youth in their jurisdiction. Significantly, the survey followed on a community mapping exercise which identified all development agencies in the area and their services to the youth (van Hees, 2000a). The researchers received inputs from youth practitioners which were incorporated in the survey design. Results from the study were later fed back to practitioners and the larger community. A partnership project was proposed based on the survey findings.

The paper is divided in three parts. The first part introduces the background, rationale and method. The second part reviews survey findings. The third part reports on a special analysis of life satisfaction as an outcome indicator of successful youth development. The discussion and conclusions suggest the way forward for initiating an integrated research-and-practice youth development project.

5.1.2. *Background to the Study*

Eastern Cape in South Africa is among the poorest of South Africa's provinces. What opportunities does it offer to young people growing up in the new South Africa? The study conducted among 862 youth resident in Grahamstown East, Makana Municipality, in the Eastern Cape, examined personal and collective development opportunities for young Africans growing up in depressed economic circumstances. The aim was to produce baseline data for youth workers, planners and policy makers, as well as for academics with an interest in youth development. In line with the new positive youth development research agenda, it was hoped that the research would lead to a development initiative involving the youth themselves in collaboration with local development organisations and the researchers.

5.1.3. *The Study Context*

The Eastern Cape comprises two former 'homelands' whose development was neglected under the previous government. The vast majority of the population is African and rural. The standard of living is low and jobs are scarce. Global trends have decreased the profitability of gold mining. Eastern Cape men, who were formerly employed as migrant workers on the mines near Johannesburg, are out of work. The unemployment rate (strict definition) is 35.2% against South Africa's

28.3% (SAIRR, 2000). Those who are employed earn lower wages than in other parts of the country. Major sources of household income are remittances from members of households who work in South Africa's industrial and commercial centres and government transfers in the form of old-age pensions.

Although the economic situation in the Eastern Cape is depressed, the city of Grahamstown nevertheless offers some unique and exciting development opportunities for young people. Grahamstown is a leading educational centre, known for its excellent secondary education institutions. It is home to Rhodes University which sponsors a number of local students from disadvantaged backgrounds. Technical training is available at college-level and through a number of development agencies which encourage young people to improve their employment skills or to start their own businesses. Local organisations are eager to reach out to the underprivileged and have launched a number of development initiatives. Grahamstown is also known as South Africa's premier arts, science and business festival centre. Local schools are encouraged to participate in festivals which open up a window on the world and stimulate personal development. The town centre and university campus are within sight of Grahamstown East and even within walking distance so local youth have access to many of these development openings. The question remains, however, whether Grahamstown East youth are aware of and make use of the opportunities available in the city to get ahead. An important task for the research was to assess participation in existing Grahamstown development initiatives and to identify the obstacles which prevent local youth from making optimal use of opportunities at their fingertips.

5.2. LITERATURE

Youth were in the vanguard of the movement which led to South Africa's adoption of democratic rule in 1994. In the new era, the National Youth Commission was given the task of addressing major youth issues and shaping a development policy for post-apartheid youth whose education and welfare was neglected in the past. The youth of the Eastern Cape were badly affected. A study conducted on behalf of the commission in the mid-1990s found that Eastern Cape youth were disadvantaged due to high levels of poverty and unemployment and lack of basic services in homes and schools. A higher than average percentage of Eastern Cape youth were defined as 'hard to reach' youth in the sense that they were alienated and frustrated. Four-fifths of Eastern Cape youth were unemployed. The main perceived problems of Eastern Cape youth included poverty, inadequate education and unemployment. The young people described themselves as frustrated but ambitious. Nevertheless, the majority was positive about the future (Everatt and Jennings, undated).

Similarly, earlier studies which focused on the youth of Grahamstown East reported mainly negative prospects for development. An inquiry conducted by Manona (1994) for the South African Youth research programme (Slabbert et al., 1994) in the early 1990s found that due to the political unrest of the 1980s some 98% of the schoolgoing youth surveyed had a backlog in their education and 70%

of the school leavers were unemployed. However, the youth were overwhelmingly positive about themselves and keen to improve their situation. A second study conducted for the same research programme found that Grahamstown East matriculants had raised expectations for finding good jobs. The majority stated that they would not be prepared to work as manual labourers and saw self-employment as a last resort. (Haines and Wood, 1994).

5.3. THE YOUTH DEVELOPMENT CONCEPT

Unlike the earlier studies cited above, which focused on youth problems, this study had identified positive youth development and well-being as key concepts. The operationalisation of youth development presented a number of methodological problems. Development can be regarded as both ongoing process and outcome. In the case of the youth, the development process may have hardly begun. Similarly, measuring satisfaction among youth is fraught with problems as young people are inexperienced and lack the type of reference standards which underlie Michalos' multiple discrepancy theory (1985). Noteworthy is that congruence between life goals and perceived achievements in life feature prominently in Neugarten's classical life satisfaction measure developed for use among the elderly (Neugarten et al., 1961). This type of congruence cannot be measured among the youth due to their lack of experience and position in the life-course. Therefore, prospective measures of quality of life might be considered more indicative as proxy outcome measures.

The concept of youth development is used in a fairly broad sense in this study. In the first instance, it refers to young people's personal development which will earn them fulfilment as a person and a place in society. Personal development is a process but one which is oriented towards a specific outcome. Youth have ambitions in life which shape their chosen development paths. Furthermore, youth are part of a web of social circumstances and conditions which will enhance or curtail their development potential.

Alternatively, youth development refers to the institutionalisation of the socialisation process whereby youth become adults who conform to contemporary norms and values in society. Thus, the institution of youth development seeks to assist and guide youth to fulfil their potential while adhering to the accepted norms and values of society.

In their key policy document drawn up for the democratic era, the National Youth Commission defines youth development as a process whereby young men and women are able to improve their skills, talents and abilities to extend their intellectual, physical and emotional capabilities to express themselves and live full lives. Youth development also refers to engaging youth in development activities as participants in the decision-making processes and as beneficiaries (NYC, 1997: 70 in van Hees, 2000b).

A related concept refers to youth empowerment. The National Youth Commission describes youth empowerment as the process of increasing personal, interpersonal and political power to enable young women and men or groups of young people to improve their life situation. Empowerment requires full participation of young men and women in the formulation, implementation and evaluation of decisions impacting on the functioning and well-being of the society. Participation in organisations is seen as a vehicle for promoting youth participation in society (NYC, 1997: 70 in van Hees, 2000b: 20–21).

An assumption adopted for the Grahamstown East project is that society would like to see its youth socialised in a 'pro-social' manner. Pro-social attitudes and behaviours on the part of youth reflect acceptance of dominant norms and values in society. Thus, criminal and anti-social youth might be regarded as an indication of failure on the part of society to provide appropriate development opportunities for youth or failure to ensure that the prescribed route to becoming an upright citizen is sufficiently attractive to youth. Similarly, marginalised youth or 'drop-outs' could be taken as an indication of failure on the part of society to administer to the development needs of all segments of the youth population.

5.4. METHODS

5.4.1. *The Survey Site*

The largest concentration of youth in Grahamstown is in Rini, as the township of Grahamstown East is known to local people. The township is home mainly to the African population of Grahamstown. According to the household survey conducted in tandem to the youth survey reported here, an estimated population of 53,000 lived in Grahamstown East in 1999. However, the city engineers adopted a population figure of 97,210 for servicing Grahamstown East in 1999/2000 (Møller, 2001: 14). Unlike other African townships, Grahamstown East was never removed to a 'homeland' under the previous government so that Grahamstown East and West are contiguous areas. Although divided by a stream and the railway line, a major road connects the two sides of town. Since the redrawing of local government boundaries to reduce the number of South Africa's municipalities from 843 to 284, Grahamstown falls under the Municipality of Makana.

5.4.2. *The Target Population*

The target population was defined as youth resident in Grahamstown East/Rini over 14 years of age and under 25 years of age. In South Africa, the official definition of youth used by the National Youth Commission is young people between the ages of 15 and 35 years. However, as the Grahamstown study sought to inquire primarily into development potential, there was a strong incentive to select a narrower age band than the official one in order to focus on young people whose life careers are still by and large unformed. Even within this narrow band, the target group was expected to include both in-school and out-of-school youth and a wide range of different life circumstances and experiences linked to age.

Another reason for opting for precisely the 15–24 year age band was to be able to match the census age cohorts. According to the 1996 census, youth in the 15–24 year age group comprised 50.2% of the total population of Grahamstown East/Rini and 20,638 individuals (Møller, 2001: 14). The household survey, which was conducted in tandem with the youth survey reported here, estimated that youth in the target age group made up some 53.1% of the total population of Grahamstown East/Rini in 1999 and accounted for some 28 836 individuals (ibid: 14).

5.4.3. *The Instrument*

The study aimed to provide insights into the local opportunities for personal or collective youth development as well as the constraints that retard access to development opportunities. The study was informed by a number of earlier studies. Policy research conducted in the early 1990s was designed to brief the new democratic government in waiting on the situation of the South African youth (Everattt, 1994; Slabbert et al., 1994). Research updates by CASE (2000) and Everatt (2000) evaluate youth policy formation in the democratic era. The National Youth Commission (1997, 1998), established soon after the first democratic elections of 1994, provided development guidelines. More focussed research undertaken by the author and colleagues examine the spare-time use of township youth, family influences on educational achievement, and the role of youth clubs, youth centres and community service in youth development (Leggett, Møller and Richards, 1997; Leggett, Møller, and Sotshongaye, 1997; Møller, 1991, 1992, 1993, 1994a, b; 1995, 1996; Møller, Mthembu, and Richards, 1994; Møller and Richards, 1990).

As the study was exploratory, the survey covered a large number of topics which might impinge on development. Briefly, the topics reviewed in this paper and the rationale for their inclusion in the survey are as follows.

It can be argued that development potential is shaped by *family and schooling background.* Earlier studies of three-generation township households in South Africa showed that school and family advantages are intimately interwoven. Family and educational background may also be breeding grounds for positive dispositions of youth. The education literature speaks of educational advantages being transmitted over generations. The three-generation household study referred to above found that self-confidence was similar among all three generations of township households suggesting that some traits and dispositions might be passed on from one generation to the next (Møller, 1994b).

From a practical perspective, school performances and even school attendance, are made easier for youth from better appointed homes that can feed, clothe and supervise learners, pay their school fees on time and generally encourage their participation in development opportunities in schools, clubs, churches and events in the wider community.

The study probed *life goals and concerns* as the reference standard against which young people might measure their well-being and achievements in life.

Access to development opportunities was examined using a number of items:

Social integration in clubs, church life, knowledge and contact with community organisations that cater to the youth, job skills in preparation for work life and self-employment, aspirations to participate in collective development, and participation in festival.

Leisure, the domain that allows for greater freedom of individual expression and pursuit of interests (Kelly, 1983), was seen as the arena for gaining personal development opportunities. It was assumed that youth who are socially integrated in the community through their memberships and activities in churches, clubs and other organisations might have a headstart in using their spare time to develop their skills and talents.

There is growing interest in the youth research literature in the developmental benefits of unpaid or volunteer jobs (Furstenberg, 2000). A specific item attempted to probe the appeal of the National Youth Commission's *community service* programme to gain better insight into motivations to participate in collective development.

Young people in their teens and early twenties are particularly susceptible to both good and bad influences that may promote or compromise life chances and personal development. It is assumed that youth who engage in *risk behaviour* will be distracted and prevented from shaping their careers along the 'pro-social' development path. A section of the questionnaire explored exposure to risks.

Measures of *subjective well-being*, including self-confidence, overall subjective well-being and satisfaction with various domains in life, were applied as outcome measures. It was anticipated that if youth development as institution were successful, young people should have confidence in themselves, be contented, and be positive about life chances in future. In turn, satisfied young citizens are expected to be proud of their neighbourhood, city and the nation and to be prepared to accept adult responsibilities including exercising their voting rights.

5.4.4. *Research Method*

In total, 862 youth from Grahamstown East were interviewed for the study. The sample used area probability sampling methods to cover the whole township divided into 27 neighbourhoods according to tenure and housing (Manona, 1987). The oldest and largest plots in Grahamstown East had been offered to members of the Mfengu tribe as freehold property in recognition of their assistance in the frontier wars of the 1820s. The newest neighbourhoods established in the 1990s feature core-housing units subsidised by the new democratic government's Reconstruction and Development Programme (RDP). A self-weighting sample design was used: Within each neighbourhood, target households were selected randomly in proportion to the total number of plots. Within households, a target youth was selected randomly. The sample design allowed for replacement of households that did not include a young person.

The fieldwork was carried out in May 1999. Trained local interviewers administered a standard questionnaire to respondents. The interviews were conducted in the young persons' home in the local African language, Xhosa. The questionnaire was divided in two parts. The first part of the interview dealing with youth issues was administered to the young person; the second section on household characteristics was administered to a responsible and knowledgeable person in the youth household. In very few cases the young target person doubled as the household informant. The questionnaire contained mainly closed-ended items. However, response options were based on knowledge gained from earlier youth studies. The questionnaire schedule included over 112 items in the youth and household sections. The analysis worked with some 140 variables and constructs.

5.5. FINDINGS

5.5.1. *Sample Characteristics*

Approximately 30% of the sample were 15 and 16 year olds, almost one-third were in the 17 to 20 age bracket (31%) and the remainder over 20 years of age. Young women accounted for 55% of the sample. Three-quarters of the youth were still at high school (73%). Only 1.5% were studying further.

The vast majority (96%) identified themselves as dependents, that is persons with no regular income. Household heads, income earners, and homemakers accounted for less than 5% of the sample. In the 21–24 year age cohort, some 10% were household heads, earners or homemakers. Approximately half of the economically dependent youth (48%) were in a steady relationship with a boy or girlfriend. Less than 2% of the sample were living together with a partner or married. One person was already widowed. Just over one in ten youth in the sample (12%) had given birth to or fathered a child. The youth in the survey were for the most part raised by their parents, either by their mother (39%) or both parents (33%). Grandmothers played the main parenting role in 20% of cases. Three in four birth mothers (74%) had a full presence in youth households compared to only 37% of birth fathers. Some 28% of youth lived under the same roof with a grandparent.

Grahamstown East youth live in youthful households. The median age of household members is 22 years and some 30% are under 15 years of age. The estimated average household size is some 5.6 persons. Just under 6% of all household members have a matriculation level education and a further 5% have received some education beyond matriculation level at a teacher's training college, technikon or university.

The majority of youth in the survey were raised in Grahamstown. Some 45% of households had stayed in the same area for over 11 years or had never moved. If given a choice, most households would not wish to move from their present location. Potential movers stated they would prefer Grahamstown East to Grahamstown West with the better-appointed neighbourhoods of Grahamstown East, Extensions 4 and 5, among the most popular options.

5.5.2. *Living Conditions*

In 1999, youth households were housed in brick or cement block dwellings (48%) or else in homes built of mud in the traditional style (35%) or with cement plaster applied (16%). The majority (71%) of householders stated they are homeowners. One-fifth of dwellings were built as part of the post-1994 Reconstruction and Development housing programme. The majority of youth households had access to electricity (76%) and amenities including radio (85%), television (74%), and refrigerator (55%). A substantial proportion had either a telephone or cellular phone (40%). While some 13% of youth households had a car in working order, only 1% had access to a personal computer in the home. Most households relied on the bucket system and pit latrines for sanitation; only 16% of households had access to a flush toilet. Some 5% of youth households had piped water in the home; a further 60% had piped water on site, 25% on the street and 9% had to make do without piped water. Since the survey was taken, access to sanitation and piped water has been upgraded in many neighbourhoods.

5.5.3. *Household Income*

Major sources of household income were formal jobs (59% of households), the state old-age pension (41%), and to a lesser extent casual jobs (33%). The largest proportion of youth described the economic situation of their household as one 'of making ends meet (44%). One-quarter (25%) were reportedly 'scraping a living or poor'. The majority of the households described as 'poor' or 'scraping a living' earned up to Rand 500 per month, roughly the equivalent of state old-age pension for one person. Households 'living comfortably' or 'well-off' were in the minority and usually earned no more than Rand 3,000 per month.

5.5.4. *School and Work Life*

One-third of the youth in the sample had attended a pre-school. Although youth identified many problems in schools such as poor facilities and overcrowded classrooms, the majority gave their high school a good quality rating and described their school experience as 'rewarding' rather than 'frustrating'. Some 35% of youth over 17 years were not on-track with their education in the sense that they were two years behind the right class for their age.

The majority of youth were either still at school or planned to continue with education or training. Only 11% had ever had a job of any kind, mainly a casual job. The out-of-school youth in the sample appeared to be at a loss as how to approach the job search. They reported there were no jobs available, they lacked job skills, and the right connections. Youth had few job skills. Some 6% had received training in arts and crafts, the highest in any skill category ranging from typing, computer literacy to a driver's licence. Although training in arts and crafts are sought after in Grahamstown's premier arts festival city, it is not a job requisite in most cases.

5.5.5. *Social Integration*

Almost all youth belonged to a church and four in five youth were members of a club or organisation. Most popular clubs included church youth groups, social youth clubs, and sports clubs. Attending church or religious services, watching and playing sport were among the most popular spare time activities. Youth estimated they watched television for over 3 hours on an average weekday. Sports, films and soap operas were among the favourite programmes. Only 19% of youth, mainly those from homes without television, reported they did not watch TV.

5.5.6. *Concerns*

The most common ambition in life, endorsed by 59% in the sample, was to find a job. The two top concerns for young people were teenage pregnancy (59%), followed by lack of job opportunities (38%). HIV/AIDS, a concern for only 17% of youth, figured at the bottom of the list of 7 options put to respondents. Three in four reported that classmates had dropped out of school because they were pregnant. The most important motivations for engaging in spare time activities were to learn skills and develop talents (38%), ahead of the need to 'belong' or to 'have fun'.

5.5.7. *Access to Development Opportunities*

Between two-thirds and four-fifths had firsthand knowledge of facilities and popular destinations in and around their town. However, only one-fifth had ever visited a nature reserve some 15 km outside of Grahamstown. Up to one-third had been to a Grahamstown festival. The Science Festival followed by the National Arts Festival – the latter celebrated its 25th anniversary in the year of the survey – were among the most popular.

Although the majority had knowledge of eleven community organisations (van Hees, 2000a) serving the youth and the community, less than one in ten had ever had contact with any of these organisations with the exception of an arts centre. Only one quarter had heard of the National Youth Commission. Nevertheless, most youth were keen to participate as volunteers in a hypothetical community service programme under the auspices of the National Youth Commission that offered only pocket money as payment. The opportunity to learn life skills was the most attractive incentive to participate in the programme, far ahead of the opportunity to serve the community or to learn self-discipline.

5.5.8. *Political Participation*

The majority of youth who were eligible had voted in the first democratic elections in 1994 and were registered to vote in the forthcoming national elections in 1999.

5.5.9. *Risk Exposure*

Projective items were used to sound out risks to which youth are exposed in their social environment. Items that attributed risk behaviours to age-peers, friends and young people in the area were used to invite honest disclosure while protecting the integrity of the respondents interviewed at home. Youth were asked what proportion of their age-peers, from 'most' or 'many' to 'some' or 'none', were engaged in a variety of risk behaviours including smoking cigarettes and dagga (cannabis), taking drugs, engaging in unprotected sexual intercourse, and engaging in anti-social and criminal activities. Older youth, particularly young men, were more likely to be exposed to the most common risks of cigarettes, dagga, and unprotected sex. Educationally off-track youth, who are more than two years behind in their schooling, were particularly vulnerable.

Youth reported that young people in their ken were most likely to be exposed to risks associated with cigarette smoking and unprotected sex. In contrast, three-quarters reported that none of their friends take drugs or sniff glue. Generally, youth reported less anti-social behaviour among their friends. Just under two-thirds stated they knew of no one in their circle of friends who is involved in criminal or gang activities. However, the incidence of anti-social and gang behaviours in the neighourhood was higher, suggesting that a substantial proportion of youth live in tough areas although their own circle of friends is somewhat removed from anti-social activities.

In 1999, Grahamstown East youth were almost three times as likely to state they knew of persons who had become fatal victims of violence (65%) and road accidents (64%) than victims of illnesses such as tuberculosis or AIDS. While 35% knew of a person who had died of tuberculosis – a common illness in the Grahamstown area – only 22% knew of a person who had died of AIDS.

Approximately four in ten reported a female friend who had had personal experience as a rape victim. Just under three-quarters (73%) had a classmate who had dropped out of school when she fell pregnant.

All risk behaviours under study were clearly associated with knowledge of other youth becoming fatal victims of risk behaviours, with unsatisfactory educational experience, and with unfulfilled leisure. For example, the association between reporting drug users among age peers and knowledge of AIDS and TB deaths was particularly strong. Knowledge of deaths due to stabbing was more evident in the case of one's age peers reportedly engaging in housebreaking. Youth who gave their high school a poor rating and described school life as not rewarding were consistently at risk. Youth, who complained of too much spare time and that their days drag on without enough to occupy their time, were more at risk than others.

5.5.10. *Self-Esteem*

Over four in five youth in the survey indicated they felt confident about their abilities and achievements in life and equal to their peers. A slightly lower percentage expressed confidence in reaching their goals in life, which may be partly a reflection of the format of the statement, which was posed in the negative. Self-esteem was boosted by the good start in life provided by one's family and school. Noteworthy is that a slightly higher percentage of youth attributed a good start in life to their family than to their school. Educationally on-track youth were more likely than others to say their school had given them a good head start in life.

An index of self-esteem was created, composed of the four attitudes items: confident of abilities, feeling as good as others, confident of achieving goals, and perceptions of having done well in life so far. The fifth item, taken from the quality of life section of the interview, referred to satisfaction with the self. The sample was divided into three roughly equal-sized groups according to their overall score on the five items.

A sense of disillusionment was detected among the older youth. Self-esteem was found to decrease systematically with age. For example, the oldest cohort of youth (21–24 years) was least likely to feel equal to others, to perceive they had made progress in life and to be confident in their goal achievement capabilities. Youth from economically weak households were significantly more likely to produce low scores on the self-esteem index. For example, youth whose households were 'scraping a living' were less likely than others to say they had done well in life or that their family or school had given them a headstart in life. Youth in this group were also least likely to be proud of their neighbourhood.

5.5.11. *Subjective Well-Being*

Towards the end of the interview respondents were asked to evaluate their lives. The global measures of life satisfaction and happiness and all but one of the domain-level satisfaction items used in the Grahamstown survey were based on earlier South African studies conducted among the national population. All items were personalised so that they would have direct meaning to young people. For example, respondents were asked to rate their own education, their own job opportunities, the food they eat, their right to vote, the loyalty of their friends and their own intimate relationships with a person of the opposite sex. Given the personal nature of such assessments, youth were asked only to rate issues of importance to them. Non-important responses were removed from totals. Most items were considered important by more than 95% of respondents. Only 6 items were 'not important' for more than 4% of youth. These included 'your most intimate relationship with a man/woman' (not important = 11.1%), 'your personal possessions – the things you have been able to buy' (7.0%), 'the distance of shops, schools, transport and other services to your dwelling' (6.4%), 'your right to vote' (5.7%), 'the fun you get in life' (4.8%), and 'your job opportunities' (4.5%).

Results on life satisfaction, happiness and domain satisfactions are shown in Table 5.1 below.

Table 5.1. Satisfaction, Happiness and Domain Satisfactions.

"Here are some aspects of people's lives. I would like you to tell me how satisfied you are with each aspect. If you are very satisfied, satisfied, dissatisfied or very dissatisfied. (If the aspect I mention is not important enough to be concerned about, say: not important)."

Percentages	Very[a] satisfied	Not important
GLOBAL[b]		
Life-as-a-whole	69	
Happiness	65	
LIFE DOMAINS		
Health, family, food:		
– Health	95	0
– Family's happiness	88	0
– The food you eat	84	2
Political:		
– Freedom of movement	88	3
– Voting rights	77	6
Education:		
– Education	75	0
– Assistance with career guidance	70	4
Housing:		
– Size of dwelling	50	3
– Security of tenure in area	51	3
Community facilities:		
– Distance to shops, schools, transport etc.	66	6
– Public services in your community	48	3
Safety and security:		
– Your security from crime	39	2
Financial:		
– Personal possessions	57	7
– Family income	33	1
– Job opportunities	19	5
Personal:		
– Yourself as a person	91	1
– Leisure time activities	90	2
– Peer group integration	89	3
– Respect from the community	82	2
– Loyalty of friends	80	3
– The fun you get in life	79	5
– Trust relations in areas	72	3
– Intimate relationship	56	11

Description of items paraphrased, see questionnaire in appendix for exact wording.

[a] The first column gives the percentages 'very satisfied' and 'satisfied' based on the total of respondents for whom the concern was a salient or an 'important' one.

[b] The items read: "Taking all things together, how satisfied are you with your life as a whole these days? Generally speaking would you say you are very satisfied, satisfied, dissatisfied, or very dissatisfied?" "Taking all things together in your life, how would you say things are these days? Would you say you are very happy, fairly happy, fairly unhappy or very unhappy?"

5.5.12. *Overall Subjective Well-Being*

Some two-thirds of youth in Grahamstown East indicated they are satisfied with life (69%) and happy (65%) in 1999. The percentage satisfied is significantly higher than the national average of 53% among all South African adults and 47% among black adults in 1999 (Møller and Dickow, 2002) or the 51% satisfied among township youth in a nationwide 1989 youth study (Møller, 1992). Some 53% of Grahamstown East youth thought life was getting better rather than worse. Youth were mainly optimistic for the future. Some 60% thought life would be better for young people like themselves in five years' time, 9% thought life would be about the same, while only 6% thought life would be worse. However, one in four (26%) were unable to project into the future.

All three subjective well-being items in the survey referring to the present time, satisfaction with life-as-a-whole, happiness, and life getting better rather than worse, are significantly positively associated. In turn, these three indicators are also positively linked to social and personal advantages including self-rated household affluence, a rewarding school experience, being educationally on-track, and self-esteem. Youth from the better-off neighbourhoods, Extensions 4 and 5, were more likely to express life satisfaction, happiness and net optimism (calculated as the percentage perceiving life to be getting better less the percentage perceiving life to be getting worse).

Age is clearly related to decreases in life satisfaction, happiness and feelings that life is getting better rather than worse. This finding suggests that youth shed their rosy view of the world as they grow older and become more disillusioned with life chances as they mature. Self-esteem, which is closely associated with subjective well-being, is also less evident among the older youth cohorts.

5.5.13. *Spare Time Use for Youth Development and Well-Being*

What youth do in their spare time may have an impact on feelings of well-being. The study found that a higher proportion of youth from the better-rated schools and privileged socio-economic backgrounds tended to pursue more active and 'go-to' activities which might be referred to as 'pro-social activities', best defined as youth activities that meet general social approval. Examples from the present survey might include watching and playing sport, participating in dance or drama, singing in choirs, reading newspapers, going to the cinema, going to town, and visiting rural relatives. In contrast, youth from the schools which attracted a less favourable quality rating did less of these activities but were more likely than others to pursue 'kill-time' activities such as hanging out with friends in the streets and visiting shebeens (neighbourhood taverns) in their spare time. Important in the context of a study of youth development is that many of the 'pro-social' spare time activities tend to go hand in hand with positive feelings of well-being. For example, spectator sport, active sport, dance, and cinema attendance were closely associated with both overall life satisfaction and happiness. Interestingly, what might be regarded as two of the most pro-social spare time activities, church attendance and choir singing, did not register significant differences between participants and non-participants possibly because these popular activities are so common among Grahamstown East youth. On the other hand, visiting relatives in town, which might detract from other active leisure, and 'kill-time' leisure, such as spending time in shebeens, and sleeping away from home with girl- or boyfriends, more common among older youth, were negatively associated with life satisfaction and happiness.

5.5.14. *Domain Satisfactions*

Grahamstown East youth rated 23 life domains approximately in the following order according to satisfaction: health, personal and family life, food, education, housing, community facilities, safety and security, income and jobs (see Table 5.1).

As is usually the case, the surveyed youth tended to be more satisfied with the central concerns of life than with the peripheral ones. Issues close to the self under the 'personal' heading attracted higher satisfaction ratings than peripheral issues including housing and community services. As might be expected, given their young ages, the health domain scored highest on the satisfaction scale. Youth also gave above-average satisfaction ratings to family life and the food on the table. The domain of education figured fairly high on the list of satisfied concerns. Youth appear to be mainly satisfied with the education they had received or were still acquiring, a result consistent with positive assessments of their high schools and perceptions that school life was 'rewarding'. Youth were also mainly satisfied with career guidance.

Satisfaction with 'yourself as a person" topped the list of personal satisfactions. Under the same heading, substantial majorities were satisfied with their leisure time – generally regarded as an important dimension for self-development and actualisation –, the fun they get in life and a range of interpersonal relations which generate feelings of belonging in one's peer group, respect, trust, and loyalty among friends. However, youth appeared to be more ambivalent about their sex life, which may be attributed to the wide age span represented in the survey. A substantial group (11%) dismissed their sex life as a non-concern and a further quarter (26%) indicated ambivalence.

Youth were mainly satisfied with issues under the 'political' heading including their voting rights and their freedom of movement. Although the latter item was originally devised as a political indicator in the early eighties, it is possible that youth in the survey may have regarded freedom of movement as personal freedom to come and go and do as they please without parental or adult supervision.

Grahamstown East youth were mainly discontented with safety and security issues, family income and their own job opportunities. Most South Africans are dissatisfied with safety and security issues and Grahamstown East youth are no exception. The results on material possessions and income come as no surprise. Household incomes in Grahamstown East are low by national standards. Moreover, worldwide, income and finance issues tend to attract the lowest satisfaction scores. A more important finding is the overwhelming dissatisfaction with job opportunities for youth. The bleak prospect of finding work is a dominant theme throughout the study elicited in response to spontaneous as well as closed-ended items in the survey. Other research has showed that township youth regard education mainly as a means to an end (Møller, 1991). The study highlights the mismatch between education that mainly satisfies but is not seen to lead to a job after leaving school. While Grahamstown East youth expressed satisfaction with their education they are mainly dissatisfied with their job prospects.

5.5.15. *Differential Domain Satisfactions*

Youth who scored higher on self-esteem were more likely to be satisfied with the personal domain, with aspects of life related to the self and interpersonal relations including fun in life, integration with age-peers, loyalty and trust relations. Area differences seemed to reflect objective differences in living conditions in Grahamstown East. Youth living in shack areas tended to be most dissatisfied with housing and services issues including size of dwelling and community services, and distance of shops in the case of the former only. Economic hardship appeared to colour perceived well-being among Grahamstown youth. Material as well as less tangible concerns were affected. Youth from households reportedly 'scraping a living' were significantly more dissatisfied than others with family happiness, the food they eat, their education, job opportunities, family income, and the size of their dwelling.

The most striking finding to emerge is that older youth were less satisfied with life overall. Signs of age-related disillusionment among Grahamstown East youth are also evident in domain satisfactions. Dissatisfaction among older youth is concentrated on aspects of life which block advancement. Examples include below-average satisfaction with education, assistance with career guidance, job opportunities, and family income. Dissatisfaction in the more personal areas of life is also observed. Progressively lower levels of satisfaction are found with each age cohort for freedom of movement and trust in people. In contrast, progressive satisfaction with age is found in areas of life where age and maturity is an advantage. Significantly higher percentages of older (89% among 21–24 year olds) than younger (62% among 15–16 year olds) cohorts are satisfied with their right to vote. Similarly, 67% of the oldest age cohort compared to 44% in the youngest age cohort, are satisfied with their most intimate relationships.

5.5.16. *National and Local Pride*

In the last section of the interview Grahamstown East youth were invited to discuss civic pride issues. Feelings of national pride surpassed feelings of local pride by far. Although the majority (81%) of youth considered Grahamstown or Grahamstown East to be their 'real home', and 72% wished to settle in Grahamstown in the longer term, local pride was less pronounced than national pride. While 73% of youth stated they were 'very often' and 'often' proud to be South African only 56% felt proud to be a person from Grahamstown. However, an above-average 71% of youth who expressed national pride also took pride in being from Grahamstown. Local pride was most pronounced among youth whose pride was self-evident or rooted in diffuse affective notions of love and attachment to one's hometown.

Factors which inspired pride in Grahamstown were mainly self-evident love of one's birthplace and hometown. A fairly substantial group of youth expressed pride in the Festival City which provided extra income for the household and excitement in the air once a year. Youth who were not proud of Grahamstown tended to associate their hometown with underdevelopment, poverty and boredom.

Youth were able to identify several achievements which inspire national pride. South Africa's Reconstruction and Development Programme (RDP) headed the list. The single largest group, and 33% of the sample, gave this response. Earlier in the interview youth named housing development as one of the key areas in which they had seen substantial progress since the first democratic elections of 1994. Some 20% of houses occupied by youth in 1999 are 'RDP' houses.

Life satisfaction, happiness and perceptions of 'life getting better' are all highly significantly positively associated. In turn, all three indicators of positive subjective well-being are related to strong feelings of national pride. This finding is consistent with trends observed in earlier national studies (Møller, Dickow, and Harris, 1999; Møller and Dickow, 2002).

Survey categories which are associated with more pronounced feelings of national pride include higher self-rated socio-economic status, educational advantages including a rewarding school experience and being educationally on-track for one's age, and membership in a club.

5.5.17. *Youth Initiatives*

To end the interview session youth were invited to think how young people themselves could make Grahamstown a better place for the youth, that is a place that would make young people proud of their home town. The overwhelming response focussed on the need for a concerted effort to promote youth clubs and youth centres. Over one in two respondents thought youth clubs and centres where youth can grow and develop their talents would make a big difference to Grahamstown youth. Along similar lines, respondents supported voluntary work for youth in the community. Other ideas for making Grahamstown a youth-friendly city concentrated on the creation of jobs for youth and providing the requisite education and skills training to allow youth to enter the world of work. A substantial number of youth made specific mention of life skills training and moral guidance as a more general preparation for youth to succeed in life.

5.6. Subjective Well-Being and Youth Development

Overall life satisfaction was designated to be a key indicator of success in positive youth development. However, it was argued at the outset that given the open-endedness of the development process and the early stage of development in the lives of young people, future projections of well-being embodied, for example, in indicators of optimism might be the more valid reference standard than current subjective well-being.

A more systematic analysis was made to explore the association between feelings of well-being and prospects for youth development spanning all the topics included in the study.

5.6.1. *Three Steps were Undertaken for this Purpose*

First, the intercorrelations between life satisfaction and other outcome measures of subjective well-being and national and local pride were examined. As intercorrelations were all highly statistically significant at the 0.001 level according to Spearman's rho (see Table 5.2), life satisfaction was adopted as the dependent variable for the analysis. Life satisfaction was the indicator of choice for several reasons. Firstly, satisfaction scores are generally assumed to be more cognitive and rational judgements and therefore appropriate measures for informing policy decisions. Secondly, the 23 domain indicators were based on satisfaction measures. Thirdly, the life satisfaction indicator has a long history of use as outcome measure in South African quality of life research.

In the next step, select variables covering all topics were correlated with satisfaction with life-as-a-whole. This step was taken to get a better feel of the relationship between predictors and the outcome variable in advance of exploratory regression analysis. Along the lines argued by Cummins (2000: 135) in favour of zero-order correlations, it was reasoned that background factors such as income might be crowded out by subjective indicators, particularly if subjective indicators are measured on the same type of scale as is the case for life satisfaction and domain satisfactions in this study. Findings discussed above show that personal development outcomes and obstacles to development tend to surface only among youth in their late teens. Examples are knowledge of community and national youth organisations, and access to job skills training. Regarding obstacles to development, risk behaviours appeared to become relevant around 17 years of age. Several indicators included under the risk of social exclusion heading only applied to youth over 18 years such as being on-track in one's education and voter participation. Similarly, signs of disillusionment which show up in depressed scores on the subjective well-being measures only become evident in the intermediate age cohort of 17–20 years. Therefore a decision was taken to include in the analysis only the two older age cohorts, 17–20 year olds and 21–24 year olds. Some 115 variables, dummy variables and constructs were entered into the analysis.

The third step was application of exploratory regression analysis using satis-

Table 5.2. Correlation Matrix: Subjective Well-Being Indicators.

	2	3	4	5	6
1. Satisfaction with life-as-a-whole	0.517	0.209	0.527	0.229	0.161
2. Life getting better/worse		0.261	0.474	0.279	0.157
3. Life in 5 years' time: better/worse			0.394	0.256	0.138
4. Global happiness				0.261	0.157
5. Proud to be South African					0.503
6. Proud to be from Grahamstown					

Spearman's rho/Pearson's *r*.

faction with life-as-whole as dependent variable. Indicators were entered in batches simultaneously in 6 regressions. The batches grouped indicators under the topics of 1) household and educational background, 2) subjective well-being indicators, 3) domain satisfactions, 4) risk of social exclusion constructs, 5) spare time activities and development opportunities. The 6th regression combined background and domain satisfactions, the 7th background factors and spare-time items.

Table 5.2 shows the correlation matrix with all subjective well-being items as well as national and local pride for youth 17 years and older. As might be expected, the most closely associated variables of global happiness and life getting better rather than worse were included in the regression solution with an R square of 0.368.

Essentially, Table 5.3 outlines the profile of satisfied Grahamstown East youth in terms of their development prospects. The second column following the descriptor gives the proportion of 17–24 year olds with this characteristic, the third column indicates the proportion in the survey category that is satisfied with life. Column three should be compared against the subsample average of 66.7%. The fourth and fifth columns cite the correlation values according to Spearman's rho and the level of significance. The sixth column identifies the regressions on life satisfaction into which the variable was entered and whether it figured in the solution. As the analysis was exploratory, it was expected that many indicators would overlap or would not discriminate between satisfied and dissatisfied youth. To save space and provide a better overview of results, only indicators with a value of 0.050 or higher for Spearman's rho are included.

The constructs calculated for risk of social exclusion, that is, risk of exclusion from the youth development process, were expected to correlate negatively with life satisfaction. They are shown on a separate table (see Table 5.4).

5.7. DISCUSSION

The profile of satisfied youth underscores the importance of youth development through leisure. Although excess of leisure or boredom did not discriminate well between satisfied and dissatisfied youth in Table 5.3 it did feature in one of the regression solutions. Only select items under the leisure heading were included in the table. Pro-social leisure activities discriminated well. Above-average satisfied

Table 5.3. Profile of Satisfied Youth: 17–24 Year Olds.

Descriptor, survey category[1]	%[2] in category	%[3] satisfied	Rho[4]	Sign[5]	Batch[6]
SAMPLE AVERAGE		66.7			
Background variables					
17–20 years	55.8	69.1	0.058	–	1, 6, 7
Female	53.3	69.6	0.064	–	1, 6, 7
Schoolgoer	62.6	70.9	0.115	b	1, 6, 7
Single (no steady boy/girlfriend)	41.7	73.0	0.113	b	1, 6, 7
No children of own	83.6	68.1	0.067	–	1, 6, 7
Co-resident birth mother	73.0	68.9	0.077	–	1, 6, 7
Co-resident birth father	35.8	70.4	0.065	–	1, 6, 7
Live comfortably/well-off (youth assessment)	28.8	69.5	0.116	b	1, 6, 7
Smaller household size: 1–5 persons	51.2	68.5	0.041	–	1, 6, 7
Did not attend pre-primary school	73.7	68.3	0.057	–	1, 6, 7
School life rewarding	83.6	69.8	0.086	a	1, 6, 7
Sees introduction of student councils as positive	53.7	71.3	0.089	a	1, 6, 7
Never had a job	85.3	68.5	0.093	a	1, 6, 7
Currently not working in a job	93.5	67.4	0.057	–	1, 6, 7
On-track in education	64.9	70.7	0.114	b	1, 6, 7
Spare time					
Has 1 or more job qualifications	19.7	72.3	0.058	–	5, 7
Does 4 hours or more housework weekdays	30.5	71.2	0.063	–	5, 7
Western/ national African Independent church	74.0	68.5	0.054	–	5, 7
Watches sport	89.4	68.7	0.112	b	5, 7
Plays sport, takes exercise	66.2	70.0	0.097	a	5, 7
Does dance/drama	27.0	76.1	0.121	b	5, 7
Does not frequent taverns	79.8	69.2	0.108	b	5, 7
Goes to cinema	36.8	79.3	0.208	c	5, 7
Does not visit relatives in town	37.6	71.8	0.084	a	5, 7
Visits relatives on farm	39.1	70.8	0.069	–	5, 7
Does not sleep over with boy/girlfriend	56.0	71.3	0.110	b	5, 7
Hangs out in streets with friends	63.6	69.5	0.079	–	5, 7
Uses taxi, private car rather than walking	70.0	77.5	0.346	c	5, 7
Exposure to development opportunities					
Has visited nature reserve near Grahamstown	29.4	72.4	0.060	–	5, 7
Heard of National Youth Commission	27.4	72.1	0.068	–	5, 7
Life skills is motivator to do community service	45.0	72.8	0.117	b	5, 7
Has participated in a Grahamstown festival	46.5	69.0	0.045	–	5, 7
Lifestyle					
Has classmates who are pregnancy dropouts	30.1	69.2	0.063	–	5, 7
Has friends who are rape victims	13.2	75.0	0.93	a	5, 7
Neighbourhood youth involved in crime	19.4	76.9	0.082	a	5, 7
Attitudes					
Proud of neighbourhood	87.9	69.1	0.137	b	5, 7
Disagrees: my vote makes no difference	62.1	69.3	0.071	–	5, 7
Disagrees: if cannot find job, must look beyond Grahamstown	9.3	75.0	0.056	–	5, 7

Table 5.3. (Continued).

Descriptor, survey category[1]	%[2] in category	%[3] satisfied	Rho[4]	Sign[5]	Batch[6]
Domain satisfactions					
Education	70.5	73.7	0.229	c	3, 6
Health	94.2	68.7	0.171	c	3, 6
Family happiness	88.4	69.9	0.183	c	3, 6
Food you eat	84.3	70.5	0.187	c	3, 6
Public services	47.0	70.8	0.081	a	3, 6
Right to vote	79.6	68.6	0.079	–	3, 6
Security from crime	36.8	73.9	0.116	b	3, 6
Most intimate relationship with man, woman*	54.1	62.7	0.093	a	3, 6
Assistance with career guidance	65.4	71.6	0.144	c	3, 6
Distance of shops, schools etc.	62.4	69.2	0.069	c	3, 6
Personal possessions	54.0	76.1	0.215	c	3, 6
Security of tenure	49.2	69.4	0.055	–	3, 6
Trust in people	68.5	69.3	0.082	a	3, 6
Fun in life*	74.8	64.4	0.086	a	3, 6
Subjective well-being					
Higher self-esteem (index)	51.8	69.3	0.123	c	5, 7
Life getting better	51.5	90.4	0.517	c	2
Life better in five year's time	60.3	74.7	0.209	c	2
Happy	63.7	85.5	0.527	c	2
Often proud to be South African	71.4	73.5	0.229	c	2
Often proud to be from Grahamstown	55.1	73.6	0.161	c	2

1 Most survey categories were regrouped into 2 categories. Descriptor indicates emphasis that correlates positively with life satisfaction. Exceptions are marked with an asterisk (*).
2 Percentage of subsample (n = 604 youth 17–24 years) that fits the descriptor.
3 Percentage of youth in survey category that state they are very satisfied or satisfied with life.
4 Only variables with a rho value over .050 were included in the table with exception of 'festival participation'. Signs are omitted as the descriptors indicate positive emphasis/correlation with life satisfaction.
5 Spearman's rho significant at the (a) 0.05, (b) 0.01, and (c) 0.001 level. Dash (–) indicates not statistically significant at the 0.05 level.
6 Batch of items entered into regression on life satisfaction. Items which feature in regression solutions are underlined. R squares were 0.080 for batch 1 (6 variables in solution), 0.368 for batch 2 (2), 0.148 for batch 3 (8), 0.186 for batch 5 (8), 0.183 for batch 6 (11), and 0.209 for batch 7 (8).
* Youth in survey category exhibit below-average satisfaction.

youth were ones who watched and played sport or took exercise, did dance or drama and went to the cinema. Cinema might duplicate as a social status advantage as going to 'the movies' involves expenditure.

Higher age is associated with lower life satisfaction even though the age band was reduced by two years for the analysis. Although age itself was not significantly correlated, many proxy indicators of age were. These include the survey categories of schoolgoer, single with no steady boy or girlfriend, and never had a job, which correlated positively with life satisfaction.

Table 5.4. Profile of Dissatisfied Youth 17–24 Years at Risk of Social Exclusion.

Descriptor, survey category[1]	%[2] in category	%[3] satisfied	Rho[4]	Sign[5]	Batch[6]
SAMPLE AVERAGE		66.7			
Risk of social exclusion					
Poor school (self-rated)	32.9	60.3	0.096	a	4
School life frustrating	14.9	58.9	0.070	–	4
No ambition to continue education	5.0	50.0	0.081	a	4
Too much spare time*	20.2	73.0	0.067	–	4
Pocket money comes from theft	0.5	33.3	0.050	–	4
Spend pocket money on drinking with friends	2.2	46.2	0.065	–	4
Over 18 years and non-voter in 1994*	32.9	70.9	0.061	–	4
Friends smoke dagga (cannabis)	27.8	54.8	0.158	c	4
Friends have unprotected sex	27.5	59.0	0.100	a	4
Friends do housebreaking	16.2	58.2	0.080	a	4
Friends steal	16.1	53.6	0.122	b	4
Friends involved in anti-social gangs	16.2	53.1	0.128	b	4
Classmates are pregnancy drop-outs*	30.1	69.2	0.035	–	4
Youth in neighbourhood involved in crime*	19.4	76.9	0.106	b	4
Low self-esteem (index)	20.2	45.9	0.222	c	4
Off-track in education	35.1	59.4	0.114	b	4
Belong to high-risk group (scores 4–11 risks)	58.8	64.5	0.056	–	–

[1] Dummy variables with exception of the last three items that were regrouped into two categories. Descriptor indicates emphasis or pole that correlates negatively with life satisfaction. Exceptions are marked with an asterisk (*).
[2] Percentage of subsample (n = 604 youth 17–24 years) that fits the descriptor.
[3] Percentage of youth in survey category that state they are very satisfied or satisfied with life.
[4] Only variables with a Spearman's rho value over 0.050 were included in the table. Signs are omitted as the descriptors indicate negative emphasis/correlation with life satisfaction.
[5] Spearman's rho significant at the (a) 0.05, (b) 0.01, and (c) 0.001 level. Dash (–) indicates not statistically significant at the 0.05 level.
[6] Items entered into regression on life satisfaction in batch 4. Items which feature in the regression solution are bolded and underlined. R square is 0.123 for batch 4 (6 variables in solution).
* Youth in survey category exhibit above-average satisfaction.

Satisfied youth tended to be better equipped to grasp development opportunities with a definite headstart in life through family and educational background. On the other hand, youth at risk of social exclusion tended to be among the dissatisfied or disillusioned minority.

Family and household headstart factors associated with life satisfaction included perceptions of the household living comfortably or being well-off, a strong presence of the birth mother and particularly the birth father in the home, and a proxy indicator of affluence, access to transport, which is included under spare-time pursuits. Interestingly, youth affiliated to western or nationally organised Christian churches, whose members enjoyed socio-economic and educational advantages over youth affiliated to locally organised churches, scored higher on life satisfaction.

Educational headstart associated with life satisfaction included perceptions of school life being rewarding, positive perception of the Student Representative Councils improving school life, and being on track in one's education. The negative impact of educational disadvantages was also picked up in the risk assessment.

Domain satisfactions underscore the importance of socio-economic and educational advantage. Regarding socio-economic advantages, positive evaluation of family happiness, health, nutrition, and personal possessions were highly positively associated with life satisfaction. Regarding educational advantages, satisfactions with education and career guidance are highly significantly correlated with life satisfaction.

Exposure to development opportunities was not tightly associated with life satisfaction. This might be expected, as exposure does not bring immediate returns. Nevertheless, some of the development opportunity indicators feature among the life satisfiers: Youth who had visited a nature reserve, knew of the National Youth Commission, were motivated to do community service to gain life skills, and had acquired some job or life skills training. Technically, participation in a Grahamstown festival should have been excluded on grounds of its low rho value, but is shown for completeness sake. Although not statistically significant, festivalgoers do score above-average on life satisfaction.

As anticipated, Table 5.3 shows that satisfied youth are more self-confident than others, proud of their neighbourhood, and keen to learn life skills.

A separate analysis of factors that might inhibit personal and collective youth development are shown in Table 5.4. For technical reasons some survey items were easier to express in the negative, as factors which would prevent youth development and depress subjective well-being. Some indicators which feature in Table 5.3 are repeated in Table 5.4, for example self-esteem. Some indicators which did not qualify for inclusion in Table 5.3 due to their low rho values, reappear as satisfaction inhibitors in Table 5.4.

Generally, youth who score on more than 4 and up to 11 risk factors identified in the survey, expressed below-average life satisfaction although not statistically significant at the 0.05 level. Educational inhibitors which also depress life satisfaction include a poor school rating, a frustrating school life and being off-track in one's education. Youth who lack ambitions to continue their education or training report below-average satisfaction although only the former indicator qualified for inclusion in Table 5.4.

A number of attributional variables which identify youth who move in risk behaviour circles or tough neighbourhoods act as well-being depressants. Prominent in this group are the more common youth 'vices' of dagga smoking and unprotected sex (cigarette smoking was not included in the analysis), and anti-social and criminal behaviours.

Variables that did not quality for inclusion in Tables 5.3 and 5.4 also deserve a mention as they give insight into the distribution of development opportunities. Several domain items, which were virtually saturated on the satisfaction and dissatisfaction pole, did not discriminate between satisfied and dissatisfied youth. For example, most youth were satisfied with the self and their leisure activities. On the other hand, most youth were discontent with job opportunities and family income. Job opportunities featured in two regression solutions. Participation variables, such as membership in clubs and organisations, church attendance and singing in choirs, all popular spare-time pursuits among Grahamstown East youth, were excluded.

Several variables on commitment to staying or leaving Grahamstown in order to find work did not discriminate. Only one statistically non-significant item met the criterion for inclusion under the attitudes heading.

The subjective indicators of satisfaction with education and evaluation of the school and school life discriminated better than the objective indicator of school performance based on the proportion of pupils earning a matriculation pass.

Noteworthy is that some signs are counter-intuitive. Pre-school attendance, which was positively correlated with educational advantages and exposure to development opportunities throughout the survey, features as a satisfaction depressant. Sex and fun in life were domains which correlated negatively with life satisfaction. Technical factors might be involved here as the latter item drew an above-average number of non-responses which were excluded in Table 5.1 but included in this analysis in the 'non-satisfied' category. Alternatively, both items, sex and fun in life, might be regarded as 'escapism' in view of the seriousness with which youth take their leisure activities. Disillusioned youth who score lower on life satisfaction might find outlets for their frustration in these domains.

In contrast to the risk behaviours, negative lifestyle factors did not appear to have an impact on life satisfaction. One explanation is that township youth come into contact with school pregnancy, rape and anti-social and criminal behaviour at an early age. These problems are so ubiquitous in everyday life that youth learn to rise above them.

5.8. CONCLUSIONS

The study of 862 Grahamstown East youth and the special analysis of their subjective well-being has provided a number of leads for youth development under depressed economic conditions. Three dominant themes are isolated by way of pulling together the findings.

In spite of the generally depressed economic situation, a major divide is evident between youth who have a headstart in personal development owing to their family and educational background. The two appear to be intimately intertwined. Youth from better-off circumstances are more likely to score high on all indicators of access to development opportunities. Youth from better-off homes with an advantaged school background (e.g., pre-school education, being 'on-track' in education, attendance at a school affording a 'quality' education according to youth assessments, a rewarding school life, and a better chance of achieving a matriculation pass rate) were more likely than others to have acquired jobs skills training, to have visited educational destinations in Grahamstown, to know of local organisations and the National Youth Commission, and to have participated in Grahamstown festivals.

Self-esteem emerged as an important asset for youth who are more satisfied and positive about their life chances.

A major discrepancy exists between what the youth 'want' and what they 'have' to use Michalos' descriptors of reference standards for personal evaluations of quality of life. Youth identify jobs as their life's ambitions, lack of job opportunities as a major youth concern, and stated they were more dissatisfied with job opportunities than with any other of 22 domains in life. Less than 5% had gained any training in job skills such as typing, a driver's license, computer literacy, or in life skills. Domain satisfactions show up the discrepancy between education that satisfies while job opportunities do not. However, only minorities (36%) attend a high school that has a track record of 60% or more pupils earning a matriculation pass which is widely regarded as a minimal requirement for entry into the labour market at a level beyond the most menial of jobs. Some 44% attend high schools with a matriculation pass rate of less than 39% in the year of the survey.

What the youth 'want' beyond jobs is squarely within the scope of any municipality to deliver. Beyond jobs and jobs training, life skills emerged as a major motivator and engine for youth development. Life skills training, which featured prominently in the wish list of the satisfied youth, was seen as a carrot to engage in a community service programme. The fact that mobility for jobs received such short shrift in the analysis of subjective well-being is indicative of a youth population that wishes to develop 'in place' rather than seek their fortunes elsewhere. Thus, the conclusion lies close at hand that volunteer jobs, which offer life skills, might operate as stopgap solutions. In response to ideas for youth initiatives, life skills training featured along with youth clubs and centres which are among the few agencies that provide practical life skills training. Youth made specific mention of 'church' youth clubs with reference to the important role of the churches in youth work and guidance. Ironically, it may have required the AIDS pandemic to draw policy makers' attention to the need for life skills training in South African schools. A larger amount has been set aside for this purpose in the 2002/03 national budget (Hartley, 2001).

In sum, even an economically depressed South African city such as Grahamstown, has a lot to offer young people who wish to develop 'in place'. The youth themselves have identified what might be the most effective means to develop their potential. The advantaged youth who have a headstart in accessing the unique development opportunities afforded by Grahamstown show that outcomes are promising. Headstart youth are more self-confident, satisfied with life and proud to be citizens of their city and South Africa. A positive youth development initiative for Grahamstown might seek to engage youth in life skills training, youth clubs, and community service with a view to unlocking potential among young people before they become disillusioned with their life chances.

5.9. REFERENCES

Community Agency for Social Enquiry (CASE). (2000). *Youth 2000: A Study of Youth in South Africa.* Johannesburg.

Cummins, R. A. (2000). Personal income and subjective well-being: a review. *Journal of Happiness Studies*, **1**(2), 133–158.

Everatt, D. (ed.) (1994). *Creating a Future: Youth Policy for South Africa.* Johannesburg: Ravan Press.

Everatt, D. (ed.) (2000). Youth in post-apartheid South Africa: The dead decade? *Development Update*, special issue, July.

Everatt, D. and Jennings, R. (undated). Educated for servitude? A national survey of 'out-of-school' youth in South Africa. Johannesburg: *Community Agency for Social Enquiry* (CASE).

Furstenberg, F. E. (2000). The sociology of adolescence and youth in the 1990s: A critical commentary. *Journal of Marriage and Family*, **62**(4), 896–910.

Leggett, T., Møller, V., and Richards, R. (1997). *'My Life in the New South Africa': A Youth Perspective.* Pretoria: HSRC Publishers.

Leggett, T., Møller, V., and Sotshongaye, A. (1997). Youth brigades of Natal? On the possibility of a national youth service programme. *Indicator South Africa*, **14**(3), 68–72.

Haines, R. and Wood, G. (1994). Region of hope and despair: Perceptions and attitudes of black matriculants in Grahamstown and Port Elizabeth towards employment and unemployment and future policy options. In F. van Zyl Slabbert, C. Malan, H. Marais, J. Olivier, and R. Riordan (eds.), *Youth in the New South Africa: Towards Policy Formulation* (pp. 295–299). Pretoria: HSRC Publishers.

Hartley, W. (2001). State boosts AIDS spending. *Business Day*, October 31, p. 3.

Kelly, J. R. (1983). *Leisure Identities and Interactions.* London: George Allen and Unwin.

Manona, C. (1987). Land tenure in an urban area. *Development Southern Africa*, **4**(3), 569–581.

Manona, C. (1994). The impact of political conflict and violence on the youth in Grahamstown. In: F. van Zyl Slabbert, C. Malan, H. Marais, J. Olivier, and R. Riordan (eds.), *Youth in the New South Africa: Towards Policy Formulation* (pp. 357–362). Pretoria: HSRC Publishers.

Michalos, A. C. (1985). Multiple discrepancy theory (MDT). *Social Indicators Research*, **8**, 385–442.

Møller, V. (ed.). (1991). Lost generation found: black youth at leisure. *Indicator South Africa Press*, University of Natal, Durban.

Møller, V. (1992). Spare time use and perceived well-being among black South African youth. *Social Indicators Research*, **26**(4), 309–351.

Møller, V. (1993). *Quality of life in Unemployment: A Survey Evaluation of Black Township Dwellers.* Pretoria: HSRC Publishers.

Møller, V. (1994a). *Township Youth and Their Homework.* Pretoria: HSRC Publishers.

Møller, V. (1994b). Intergenerational relations in a society in transition: a South African case study. *Ageing and Society*, 14, 155–189.

Møller, V. (1995). Home environment and educational achievement among high-school pupils living in three-generation urban black households. *South African Journal of Sociology*, **26**(3), 87–97.

Møller, V. (1996). Intergenerational relations and time use in urban black South African households. *Social Indicators Research*, 37, 303–332.

Møller, V. (ed.) (2001). Living in Grahamstown East/Rini: A social indicators report. Research Report Series No. 6, *Institute of Social and Economic Research*, Rhodes University, Grahamstown.

Møller, V. and Dickow, H. (2002). South Africa's 'rainbow people', national pride and optimism: A trend study. *Social Indicators Research*, 59, 175–202.

Møller, V., Dickow, H., and Harris, M. (1999). South Africa's "rainbow people", national pride and happiness. *Social Indicators Research*, **47**, 245–280.

Møller, V., Mthembu, T., and Richards, R. (1994). The role of youth clubs in youth development: A South African case study. *Journal of Social Development in Africa*, 9(2), 5–29.

Møller, V. and Richards, R. (1990). The feasibility of a youth centre for Pinetown: A survey evaluation of young people's aspirations and expectations. CSDS Research Report No. 2, *Centre for Social and Development Studies*, University of Natal, Durban.

National Youth Commission (NYC). (1997). *National Youth Policy*. Pretoria: NYC.

National Youth Commission (NYC). (1998). *Green paper on the National Youth Service*. Pretoria: NYC.

Neugarten, B. L., Havighurst, R. J., and Tobin, S. S. (1961). The measurement of life satisfaction. *Journal of Gerontology*, 16, 134–143.

Slabbert, F. van Zyl, Malan, C., Marais, H., Olivier, J., and Riordan, R. (eds.) (1994). *Youth in the New South Africa: Towards Policy Formulation*. Pretoria: HSRC Publishers.

South African Institute of Race Relations (SAIRR). (2000). *Fast Facts No. 2*, Johannesburg.

Van Hees, C. (2000a). Youth development in Grahamstown: A social map. Research Report Series No. 3, *Institute of Social and Economic Research*, Rhodes University, Grahamstown, South Africa.

Van Hees, C. (2000b). "It takes a whole village to raise a child": Youth development in Grahamstown. Research Report Series No. 4, *Institute of Social and Economic Research*, Rhodes University, Grahamstown, South Africa.

Zeldin, S. (2000). Integrating research and practice to understand and strengthen communities for adolescent development. *Applied Developmental Science, Supplement 1*, **4**(3), 2–9.

5.10. ACKNOWLEDGEMENT

A generous grant from the South Africa-Netherlands Research Programme on Alternatives in Development (SANPAD) to conduct the survey is gratefully acknowledged. Thanks go to colleagues who were part of the Grahamstown East research team in the Institute of Social and Economic Research, Dr. Cecil Wele Manona and Andile Tobi, and Charlotte van Hees, University of Utrecht. Richard Devey, University of Natal, kindly assisted with data processing. Views are those expressed by the author and should not be attributed to the sponsor or colleagues.

Giampaolo Nuvolati

6. SOCIOECONOMIC DEVELOPMENT AND QUALITY OF LIFE IN ITALY

ABSTRACT: The paper concerns the analysis of the evolution of Quality of Life (QOL) in Italy considering the size of the cities and the geo-economic division of the country. In particular, starting from the model of the *Three Italies* elaborated by Bagnasco in the seventies, it shows the linkages existing between different types of socioeconomic development and living conditions in the Italian regions. Ranks based on social indicators and survey data are presented in order to quantify and compare QOL during the last 12 years in the ex-industrial and metropolitan regions of the North-West, in the *multi-cephalic* urban system of the North-East-Center as well as in the poor Meridione. New possible trends in the evolution of QOL are also presented.

6.1. The Size of the City

The relationship between city size and QOL is an important point to start with in order to make hypothesis about QOL in the cities. A large part of the literature points out the negative relationship between urban size and QOL and many authors, speaking about the American cities, have emphasized the negative aspects related to the larger urban context in terms of social exclusion, limits of democracy, criminality and pollution.

"(1) The size of an urban place is an important factor that can contribute to and detract from quality of life conditions; it therefore deserves a primary place in the formulation of national growth policy. (2) In general, the quality of urban life, as measured across non-economic dimensions, seems to decline as urban scales increase. (3) The extent to which this quality of life difference is acceptable seems to depend largely upon economic trade-offs; the economic rewards must compensate sufficiently for apparent net social, environmental, political preferential and systematic disamenities which accrue as urban scale increases; otherwise, one could expect a spontaneous reversal in migration patterns away from larger cities to occur" Elgin et al. (1974: 16).

Although the European metropolis historically presents different morphological, cultural and social characteristics from the USA case, it is possible to say that also in Europe the process of migration and concentration of population in the larger cities determined serious disamenities.[1]

Of course, this statement does not imply that small urban units necessarily present only positive situations. In fact, several towns, also because of their small size, are still nowadays not well prepared to deal with issues like immigration, territorial redistribution of industrial settlements, rapid diffusion of urban living styles, reorganization of transport system, while local metropolitan governments often present a quite consolidated tradition and know-how in managing these problems.

In general, the relationship between QOL and city size is not very clear as far as large cities and small-medium ones go. Both present specific positive and negative

M. Joseph Sirgy et al. (eds.), Advances in Quality-of-Life Theory and Research, 81–98, 2003.

aspects which can also be interpreted and measured using not always converging methodological approach (Burnell and Galster, 1992). It is also difficult to define a standard urban threshold, in terms of *acceptable* number of residents, because of the complex and often contradictory phenomena characterizing the modern urban societies in terms of differentiated individual needs and expectations and in terms of alternative policies for gaining collective well-being. Nevertheless, the idea that QOL is higher in the small-medium cities seems to be still predominant.

6.2. Quality of Life, Urban Size, and Urban System

The statement that QOL is higher in the small-medium cities can be reinforced by specific characteristic of the urban system. As a matter of fact, in a properly distributed urban system, the QOL of the inhabitants of the small-medium sized centres is guaranteed not only by the sufficient availability of basic resources and services in their own town, but also by the rapid accessibility of the more sophisticated services located in the nearest metropolis. The dimension and the density of the urban network, in terms of distances between centers, is therefore crucial in generating positive effects linked to the preservation of the local community and context, on one side, and the increment of the capabilities and opportunities for the individuals in the core of the metropolitan area, on the other side. Modern cities, however, not really any more able to satisfy the needs of the residents and of the transient populations (commuters and city users), are now constantly spreading. This includes, from a morphological and cultural point of view, new urban units in a more wide metropolitan area.

This QOL is, therefore, the result of controversial processes in which medium sized towns try to remain self-protected and hold self-reliant *niches*, *while*, at the same time, seek to gravitate on the largest cities for specific activities, exploiting them as pivots of resources. Of course, a metropolis reacts to these tendencies through the decentralization, not only of the services, but also of the *disamenities*. Historical centres become more safeguarded, factories as sources of pollution are located in the countryside, traffic flows are limited in some part of the city and more bounded in the external rings. Moreover, local authorities of the large cities develop experiences and competence in dealing with urban problems, while small town seems to be less prepared in fighting new issues generated by the diffusion of the urbanization.

For these reasons, QOL is nowadays a concept not simply valuable in regards to the size of the city, but also for looking at the urban system, at the mobility patterns of the populations and goods, and at their conflicts in *using* the city.

The Italian urban system is one of the more *multi-cephalic* in Europe. The origins of such a system can be found in the economic and political autonomy of the Italian Cities State of the Middle Age in the Central and Northern parts of the country. Other similar examples are historically observable in the so-called Old European Cities Belt including – besides Italy – Switzerland, Germany, Belgium and the Netherlands. As a matter of fact, the later State formation in these countries contributed to determining a low level of *welfare stateness* and to develop a fruitful web of urban units and of *decentralized* structures.

In Italy there are 103 cities *capoluoghi* of provinces: 3 with more than 1 million of inhabitants, 8 with more than 300,000 and 39 with more than 100,000. Also two cities *non-capoluogo* count more than 100,000 inhabitants. Cities are equally distributed between Northwest, Northeast, Center, and South, also the level of urbanization is higher in the Northern part of the country (see Table 6.1).

The first hypothesis tested in this paper is that QOL in Italy is related to the size of the cities and also to the scattering of the urban system. Is the ongoing process of *megalopolization* and the consequent homogenization of the more developed area of the country making differences between large and medium-small city more and more narrow?

6.3. ECONOMIC AND PRODUCTIVE FEATURES OF THE CITIES AND QUALITY OF LIFE

Another important point related to the QOL of local communities concerns their dominant economic-productive sector. For Europe, several findings indicate a quite clear relationship between light and flexible productive systems and living conditions. In particular, the crisis of the heavy and centralized industry model and the consequent process of productive decentralization and tertiarization constitute fundamental trends to observe in order to analyze not only the economic development but also the QOL in terms of:

- decreasing pollution in the cities;
- increasing and diffused level of education and civic participation;
- reduced social conflict and active participation in the decision process by the workers occupied in the medium size firms, in services cooperatives, in familial enterprises.

Cheshire et al. (1988), analyzing empirically the urban decline[2] of the cities and of their FUR (Functional Urban Regions) in the European Communities, stress the negative relationship between the QOL, the large size of the firms and the over-representation of the heavy industry. In fact, the older European industrial regions, dominated by wide plants and economies of scale, tend to present a more evident slope.

> "Healthy growing cities have little heavy industry in their cores, lower crime rates, less crowding (than problem growing cities), more cars per head and more favorable changes in hospital bed provision, than problem cities" (Cheshire et al., 1988: 178).

Final findings for the Italian case show that declining regions in the North of the country are Liguria and Piemonte (the first region mainly relies on the port economy and the steel industries concentrated in Genoa, the second on the historical absolute predominance of the FIAT's car industry in Turin), while non-declining regions are Lombardia, Veneto, Emilia Romagna and Toscana. Unemployment rates in Italy in 1999 clearly reveal the economic disparities between regions

Table 6.1. Italian Cities by Size and Geographical Area.

North-West	North-East	Centre	South	Islands
Cities-capoluogo with more than 1 million inhabitants (3)				
Milano		Roma	Napoli	
Cities-capoluogo with more than 300,000 inhabitants (8)				
Torino	Venezia	Firenze	Bari	Palermo
Genova	Bologna			Catania
Cities-capoluogo with more than 100,000 inhabitants (39)				
Novara	Bolzano	Ancona	Salerno	Messina
Alessandria	Trento	Livorno	Pescara	Siracusa
La Spezia	Verona	Pisa	Foggia	Sassari
Bergamo	Vicenza	Prato	Taranto	Cagliari
Brescia	Padova	Perugia	Lecce	
	Udine	Terni	Cosenza	
	Trieste	Latina	Catanzaro	
	Piacenza		Reggio C.	
	Parma			
	Reggio E.			
	Modena			
	Ferrara			
	Ravenna			
	Forli'			
	Rimini			
Cities-capoluogo with less than 100,000 inhabitants (53)				
Vercelli	Belluno	Pesaro	Caserta	Trapani
Cuneo	Treviso	Macerata	Benevento	Agrigento
Asti	Rovigo	Ascoli P.	Avellino	Caltanissetta
Verbania	Gorizia	Massa C.	L'Aquila	Enna
Biella	Pordenone	Lucca	Teramo	Ragusa
Aosta		Pistoia	Chieti	Nuoro
Imperia		Arezzo	Campobasso	Oristano
Savona		Siena	Isernia	
Varese		Grosseto	Brindisi	
Como		Viterbo	Potenza	
Sondrio		Rieti	Matera	
Pavia		Frosinone	Vibo Valentia	
Cremona			Crotone	
Mantova				
Lecco				
Lodi				
Total cities-capoluogo				
24	22	21	23	13 (total: 103)
Cities-non-capoluogo with more than 100,000 inhabitants (2)				
Monza (Milano)			Torre Del Greco (Napoli)	
Total cities				
25	22	21	24	13 (Total 105)

Source: Istat, Census, 1981, 1991.

confirming the declining trends inside the Northern regions described for the 80s by the European research and also the classical gap between North and South. Toscana seems to constitute an exception being characterized by a more negative pattern in the 90s (see Table 6.2).

The second hypothesis of the paper is that, in Italy, there is a strong relationship between QOL and socioeconomic growth of the regions, even if differences inside the more developed parts of the countries are emerging. We also assume that areas or regions explain QOL better than city size, being the geographical disparities deeply grounded in the history of Italy, while the city network is traditionally *multi-cephalic* and therefore internally quite balanced (See Table 6.3).

6.4. THE REGIONAL SOCIO-ECONOMIC DEVELOPMENT IN ITALY AFTER THE SECOND WORLD WAR

In Italy, where the differences between regions are extremely meaningful, the interpretation of the socioeconomic development has been characterized for a long time by the simple distinction between the more developed areas in the Centre North of the country and the distressed regions in the Meridione. Although this gap is

Table 6.2. European Regions Classified as Being Associated with Urban Decline or Non Decline.

	Decline	Non decline
Belgium	Hainaut Liège	Antwerpen Ost Vlaanderen
Germany	Saarbrücken Düsseldorf Münster Arnsberg	Köln Rheinhessen Pfalz Schwaben Mittelfranken Oberbayern Stuttgart
UK	North West Scotland W. Midlands	East Anglia South East South West E. Midlands
France	Nord Pas de Calais Lorraine	Alsace Bourgogne Procence-Aples-Côte d'Azur Centre
Italy	Piemonte Liguria	Emilia Romagna Lombardia Toscana Veneto
Denmark	Hovedstadsregionen	Vest for Storebaelt

Source: Cheshire et al. (1988).

Table 5.3. Unemployment Rate in Italy, 1999.

Regions	Rate	Regions	Rate
Piemonte	7.2	Campania	23.7
Valle d'Aosta	5.3	Abruzzo	10.1
Liguria	9.9	Molise	16.2
Lombardia	4.8	Puglia	19.0
North-West	6.0	Basilicata	17.1
		Calabria	28.0
Trentino Alto Adige	3.4	South	21.2
Veneto	4.5		
Friuli Venezia Giulia	5.6	Sicilia	24.5
Emilia Romagna	4.6	Sardegna	21.0
North-East	4.6	Islands	23.5
Marche	6.1	Italy	11.4
Toscana	7.2		
Umbria	7.6		
Lazio	11.7		
Centre	9.2		

Source: Istat, Labour Forces, 1999.

still evident and prominent, other theories became popular in the 70s in order to explain in a more articulated and appropriated ways the social and economic disparities in Italy. In particular, in 1977 Arnaldo Bagnasco modified the classical distinction between the rich North and the poor South, introducing a new model: the so called *Three Italies* (see Figure 6.1). This approach singled out three different socioeconomic homogeneous geographic areas. These are:

- the Northwestern *Industrial Triangle* characterized by a sort of *monocephalic* urban system based on the concentrations of the heavy industry in three large metropolitan areas: Turin, Genoa and Milan;
- the Central and Northeastern part of Italy with a much more fragmented urban and economic system based on networks of many small and medium sized cities (*Third Italy*);
- the South and the Islands (Meridione) characterized by a deep and persistent economic delay and on the dominance of some large problematic cities (Naples and Palermo in particular) surrounded by even more deprived rural areas.

In the 50s and 60s *Third Italy* was demarcated by the presence of industrial firms with specific features:

- small or medium size;
- traditional sectors of activity (food, clothing, shoes, textile, furniture, etc.);
- entrepreneurs with both skills and managerial capacities;
- high level of territorial specialization and co-ordination between firms (for example: the clothes area in Carpi-Correggio, the textile area in Prato, etc.);

Figure 6.1. The Three Italies Subdivision.

- reduced fix capital and low investment in technology;
- products with relatively low cost and good quality;
- low cost and flexibility of the labor forces in terms of decentralization, seasonal activities, part-time, home-made work.

All these characteristics favored the development of the so-called *peripheral economy* in the Northeast and Center of Italy, and a consequent competitive position of these regions, not only on the national market, but also on the international one, according to the international labor division.[3]

Especially at the beginning, this economic model was based on cheap labor costs, low wages, low consumption and high occupational instability of the workers. Therefore, the cultural, political and social system tried to solve the economic and social needs of the families involved in such a process in two different ways. On the one hand, thank to the relatively high political stability, the public administration (see, for example, the local governments with the enduring presence of Communist Party in Emilia Romagna) made many efforts in order to organize an efficient and effective system of social services in the welfare sector, also favoring the constitution of intermediate economic institutions like *cooperative* as strong instruments for the integration process. On the other hand, a sort of continuity between the agricultural and the family-based model and the modern industrial development was maintained with the purpose of reducing economic marginality and social protest. To such a purpose, the Catholic tradition in Veneto and, more generally, the role of the Church in developing solidarity networks, were crucial.

During the 70s the position gained on the international market by the enterprises was largely confirmed,[4] causing a general increase in the wealth of the *Third Italy*, followed by a growth of the labor cost and, consequently, by:

- a process of a larger decentralization of the production in the more marginal areas of the South of Italy;
- a tendency toward technological improvements for some manufacturing industries.

Nevertheless, these conditions did not imply a radical change of the nature of the firms that continued to be medium-size enterprises; instead, a trend towards a more advanced production and organization of the labor could be observed.

Living conditions in the Northwestern regions of the country were quite similar to the Northeast ones. But these regions,[5] after the economic boom of the post war and the industrialization phase of the 60s and the 70s, in the 80s started to show serious problems linked to the crisis of the heavy industry sector and to the difficulties in the regeneration processes. Of course, the situation in Meridione was and is, even worse, being characterized by a more historical and structural underdevelopment (King, 1992).

6.5. Quality of Life in the Italian Provinces

According to several empirical research studies on QOL conducted in Italy during the last decades, the *Third Italy* is the area where living conditions always appear to be better.

The following figures (see Figures 6.2 and 6.3) are based on the annual collection and analysis of social indicators on QOL performed by the most important Italian economic newspaper *il Sole 24 Ore* during the last 12 years (from 1990 till 2001). They regard the position of the 103 Italian provinces on the rank of the final index of QOL (range from 1 = best position to 103 = worst position) constructed collecting official statistical data.[6]

Provinces grouped in the three geographical areas according to the Bagnasco's theory: Northwest (Industrial Triangle: 4 regions), Northeast and Center (Third Italy: 7 regions) and South and Islands (Meridione: 9 regions) show clear differences in terms of QOL.

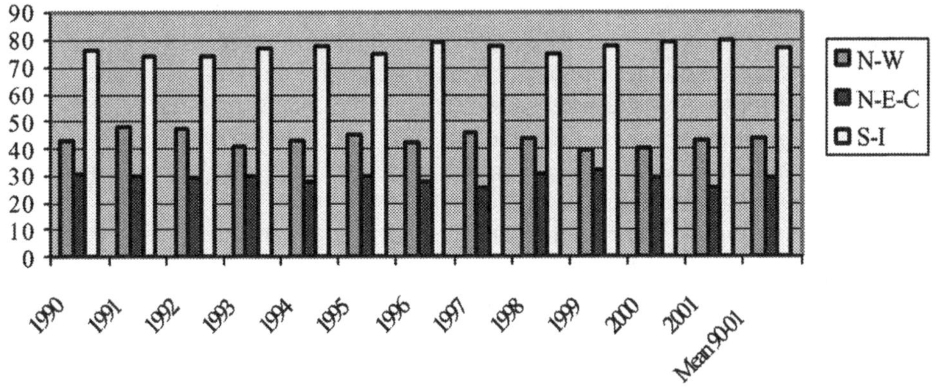

Source: il Sole 24 Ore (QOL range from 1 = best position to 103 = worst position).

Figure 6.2. Average Position of the Provinces in the Final Rank of the QOL Index by Geographical Areas and Years.

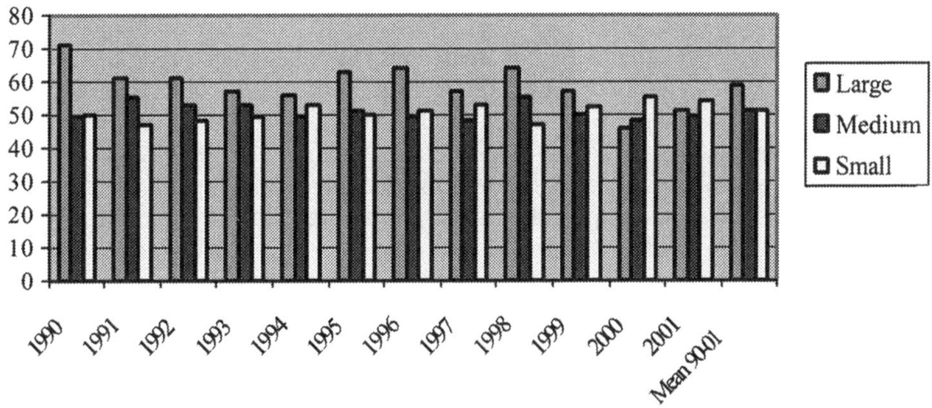

Source: il Sole 24 Ore (QOL range from 1 = best position to 103 = worst position).

Figure 6.3. Average Position of the Provinces in the Final Rank of the QOL Index by Capoluogo Size and Years.

In particular, rank scores are higher (and therefore more negative) for provinces located in the South than in the Center and in the North, but quite evident differences can be observed also between the Northwestern and the Northeastern and Central part of Italy. These data were confirmed by other studies made by the Italian economic magazine *il Mondo* in 1986, 1989, 1991 an 1994 and, more recently in 1999, 2000 and 2001, by a research published by another economic newspaper *Italia Oggi*. Both using different or more sophisticated methods, but presenting results that are very similar to the findings of the *il Sole 24 Ore*: the division of Italy in three parts, and the primacy of the provinces located in the Third Italy. As it is pointed out in the next table, many provinces are also recurrent in their very good or very bad positions demonstrating a quite high stability of the ranks.

Geographic location of the provinces explains QOL better than the size of their *capoluogo*; however data show quite clearly that living conditions in the provinces with large *capoluogo* are generally worse than in the small and the medium sized, despite the unusual results for 2000 and 2001.[7]

In particular, in 2001 the group of the three large cities located in the Northeast and Center (Bologna, Venezia, and Firenze) show the best average score on the QOL index, while the group of the 13 medium cities of the South and Islands (Latina, Salerno, Pescara, Foggia, Taranto, Lecce, Cosenza, Catanzaro, Reggio Calabria, Messina, Siracusa, Sassari, and Cagliari) display the more negative average (see Table 6.4).

In order to test the relationship between QOL and the geo-economic division of Italy, it is also very interesting to consider survey data on the perceived importance of different problems. Data here presented are from a survey on 43 Italian cities conducted by the Censis-Rur Research Institute in 1992 (see Table 6.5).

These data show that in the Northeast (*Third Italy*) services, criminality, social integration, employment, and also housing costs are not very problematic, in comparison with the situations of other areas. This is probably due to the economic, institutional and the cultural system, capable to provide, on the one hand, a good quality of the services and, on the other hand, networks of relations and practices of informal economy and reciprocal support between individuals. Medium and small sized cities, more diffused in these areas, also guarantee a higher social control. Looking at the other geographical contexts it is interesting to see that in the Northwest, the more industrialized one, the high living and housing costs and the low quality of environment constitute the more problematic aspects. In the South and in the Islands, QOL is perceived as very negative because of the unemployment, criminality, inefficient services, and restricted cultural opportunities. The situation in the Center of Italy, regarding various aspects, is not so good as it is in the North and it is, instead, more similar to the situation of the Meridione, contrasting in such a result the model of the *Three Italies*. But this result is also due to the object and instrument of investigation (a survey finalized to collect subjective indicators) and to the territorial data aggregation, which are different from the ones adopted by Bagnasco. In particular, Lazio in the model of the *Three Italies* is considered as a Southern region while in the Istat system is included in the Central regions.

Survey data also show that all the problems are, or are perceived as, more serious in the large cities than in the small or medium sized ones. Except for the lack of job opportunities, the high cost of living – compensated in a trade-off perspective by the higher level of income in the large cities – and the fewer cultural opportunities (see Tables 6.6 and 6.7).

Findings from another survey, show that differences tend to disappear when satisfaction for the life as a whole is considered, also if people living in the North and in the Centre as well in the small cities are more satisfied about their life than

Table 6.4. First and Last Ten Provinces in 1989 and 2001 by QOL.

	il Sole 24 Ore, 1990		*il Sole 24 Ore, 2001*		*Italia Oggi, 2001*	
First ten (1 = first)						
1.	**Belluno**	NEC, S	**Bolzano**	NEC, M	**Bolzano**	NEC, M
2.	**Gorizia**	NEC, S	Sondrio	NW, S	**Reggio E.**	NEC, M
3.	Ravenna	NEC, M	**Trieste**	NEC, M	**Trento**	NEC, M
4.	**Trento**	NEC, M	Bologna	NEC, L	**Modena**	NEC, M
5.	**Modena**	NEC, M	**Belluno**	NEC, S	Mantova	NW, S
6.	Aosta	NW, S	**Gorizia**	NEC, S	**Belluno**	NEC, S
7.	Forlì	NEC, M	Rimini	NEC, M	Parma	NEC, M
8.	Bergamo	NW, M	**Trento**	NEC, M	Siena	NEC, S
9.	**Trieste**	NEC, M	Firenze	NEC, L	Cuneo	NW, S
10.	**Reggio E.**	NEC, M	**Ancona**	NEC, M	**Ancona**	NEC, M
Last 5en (10 = last)						
1.	Avellino	SI, S	Caltanissetta	SI, S	**Brindisi**	SI, S
2.	**Reggio C.**	SI, M	**Trapani**	SI, S	Crotone	SI, S
3.	**Taranto**	SI, M	**Catania**	SI, L	**Taranto**	SI, M
4.	Agrigento	SI, S	**Catanzaro**	SI, M	**Catanzaro**	SI, M
5.	**Brindisi**	SI, S	**Taranto**	SI, M	**Palermo**	SI, L
6.	Napoli	SI, L	Salerno	SI, M	Isernia	SI, S
7.	**Trapani**	SI, S	Lecce	SI, M	Oristano	SI, S
8.	**Palermo**	SI, L	**Caserta**	SI, S	Vibo Valentia	SI, S
9.	**Caserta**	SI, S	Benevento	SI, S	**Caserta**	SI, S
10.	**Catania**	SI, L	**Palermo**	SI, L	**Reggio C.**	SI, M

Bagnasco's geographic division of the provinces and regions:
NW = North West: 24 provinces. Regions: Valle d'Aosta, Piemonte, Liguria, Lombardia.
NEC = North East and Centre: 38 provinces. Regions: Veneto, Trentino Alto Adige, Friuli Venezia Giulia, Emilia Romagna, Marche, Toscana, Umbria.
SI = South Islands: 41 provinces. Regions: Lazio, Abruzzi, Molise, Campania, Puglia, Basilicata, Calabria, Sicilia, Sardegna.

Division of the provinces by size of capoluogo:
L = Province with large capoluogo: more than 300,000 inhabitants – 11 provinces
M = Province with medium capoluogo: 100,000–300,000 inhabitants – 39 provinces
S = Province with small capoluogo: less than 100,000 inhabitants – 53 provinces

Note: In bold characters recurrent provinces at least in two of the three ranks.
Source: il Sole 24 Ore, Italia Oggi.

people living in the Meridione and in the large cities (Nuvolati, 1998) (see Tables 6.8 and 6.9).

6.6. LINKAGES BETWEEN THE SOCIOECONOMIC DEVELOPMENT AND QUALITY OF LIFE IN ITALY

According to the objective and subjective data presented, the main collective problems appear to be less serious in the *Third Italy* than in the other areas of the

Table 6.5. Average Position and Standard Deviation of the Provinces in the Final Rank of the QOL Index by Geographical Areas and City Size in 2001.

	Cases	Average*
North-West	24	43
Large	3	35
Medium	5	55
Small	16	41
North-East-Center	38	26
Large	3	19
Medium	21	23
Small	14	33
South-Islands	41	80
Large	5	80
Medium	13	89
Small	23	76

* Range from 1= best position to 103 = worst position.
Source: il Sole 24 Ore.

Table 6.6. Urban Problems in Different Geographical Areas.

	North West	North East	Centre	South Islands	Total
Few job opportunities	54.4	53.0	64.9	79.9	64.6
Cost of living	48.6	43.4	38.1	33.5	40.6
Housing cost	29.6	20.4	25.4	20.1	23.9
Criminality	27.5	19.0	30.9	42.0	31.4
Low quality of environment	37.3	35.1	28.9	22.7	30.4
Inefficient services	28.9	22.2	35.1	40.4	32.5
Spatial mobility time	11.3	11.8	10.7	4.1	8.9
No cultural opportunities	6.3	9.0	10.3	16.4	10.9
Low social integration	9.3	8.6	14.1	9.9	10.3
Others	3.2	3.2	0.3	0.6	1.8

Sample: 1.500 cases (43 cities).
Source: Censis-Rur (1992).

country. Such a situation can be quite easily explained by the type of economic development, the old administrative tradition in providing good services, as well as by the established processes of cultural and social integration. In other words, the social, cultural and economic background, as well as the urban systems of these regions, can be considered as a remote, but still valid, cause of the more recent patterns of QOL.

In general, the QOL, as measured across non-economic dimensions, declines as urban scales increase. Italian provinces with small and medium sized *capoluoghi* are normally characterized by a faster socioeconomic development, by less acerb internal

Table 6.7. Urban Problems by City Size.

	Small	Medium	Large	Total
Few job opportunities	67.0	62.5	61.8	64.4
Cost of living	42.9	39.8	35.7	40.5
Housing cost	19.7	23.2	35.4	23.9
Criminality	29.1	30.3	38.6	31.3
Low quality of environment	25.2	32.6	38.9	30.4
Inefficient services	31.4	33.5	32.9	32.4
Spatial mobility time	5.9	10.1	13.9	8.9
No cultural opportunities	11.5	12.8	5.7	10.9
Low social integration	8.8	11.2	12.1	10.3
Others	1.9	2.1	1.1	1.8

Sample: 1,500 cases (43 cities).
Source: Censis-Rur (1992).

Table 6.8. Annual Net Family Income (in Italian lira) by City Size.

	Small	Medium	Large	Total
Till 10 millions	14.2	9.8	10.1	11.9
10–20 millions	42.7	37.1	30.6	
20–30 millions	27.9	33.1	35.3	31.1
40–50 millions	12.8	16.2	19.0	15.2
50–100 millions	1.9	3.4	3.1	2.6
Over 100 millions	0.5	0.4	1.9	0.7

Sample: 1,500 cases (43 cities).
Source: Censis-Rur (1992).

Table 6.9. Life Satisfaction by Geographical Area and City Size.

	% enough or very satisfied
North-West	86.1
North-East	85.5
Centre	84.3
South and Islands	77.1
Rural communities	84.6
Small city	82.2
Medium city	81.4
Large city	79.9

Sample: 4,000 cases.
Source: Abacus, Barometro sociale (1998).

conflict, by a larger and more articulated set of public services and by more opportunities in terms of participation in the economic, as well in the social and political arenas. Even if these trends are changing toward more homogeneous standards of living, for a long time the *Third Italy* has been marked and identified as a thick network of medium sized cities, contrasting the *mono-cephalic* model of the largest city in the Northwest and Meridione, and getting a lot of advantages from this structure. The Italian industrial districts of the *Third Italy* based on the inter-firm cooperation and on a favorable socio-economic and political context for a long time has been considered as a positive example of equilibrate growth also for other European countries.[8]

Of course, in the *Third Italy* several problems can also be observed. In particular, the rapid growth of the wealthy of the local communities are causing phenomena of varying crises (school drop-outs, strong conflicts more inside the private sphere than in the public one) of the more traditional values based on the family cohesion. The increased socioeconomic development and the QOL of these regions are also generating new flows of population (mainly non EU immigrants) looking for working opportunities or better living conditions. These flows determine new kind of problems related to the availability of finite resources, but are also are fundamental in maintaining a demographic and productive equilibrium (Salvatori, 1997). In any case, the picture seems to be still better in the multi-centered urban systems than in the metropolitan ones. In particular, the antique presence in the cities of the *Third Italy* of *intermediary structures* – like religious and political local institutions – and of private networks generating practices of informal economy can be considered as crucial issues in producing a more *participatory* framework. In this framework, the heritage of a solidarity system based on spatial identity, social control and mutual help constitute the starting point in the direction of a more integrated society.

6.7. CONCLUSIONS

Traditionally, QOL is higher in the cities of the *Third Italy*, in the Northeast and Center of Italy, even if the *Three Italies* model of socioeconomic growth presents, nowadays, some digressions. The possibility of a new *Italian dualism*, based on the division of the *Third Italy* into more dynamic economic sectors and regions in the North of the country (Veneto, Trentino Alto Adige, Friuli Venezia Giulia, Emilia Romagna) and more peripheral-traditional-static productions and regions in the Centre (Marche, Toscana, Umbria) (*Inchiesta*, 1990)[9] can be suspected as one. Another one regards the individuation of two main leading development axes in North Italy. The first relates to the urban continuum between Milan and Bologna (along the Via Emilia, through the so called Food Valley), the second to a more horizontal, ex-industrial dorsal, crossing Turin, Milan and Venice, expanding especially in the eastern direction.[10] According to these alternative spatial interpretations of the economic expansions, Milan plays one of the most important roles, although traditionally not included in the *Third Italy*.

In general, small and medium sized cities score better than the large ones, but some Italian metropolises show also new positive trends, while minor units start to deal with serious problems. Moreover, the homogenization of the living conditions, linked to the on going process of urbanization and to the daily mobility in the North of Italy, makes it more and more difficult to distinguish between metropolitan and semi-urban areas in term of QOL.

Next, the map (see Figure 6.4) shows quite clearly that the distribution of QOL by provinces – position in the rank: from 1 to 103 – in 2001 is very similar to a leopard skin outline of the *Third Italy* model that can be recognized behind. This means that the *Third Italy* model is still valid, but we are going toward more articulated regional profiles in which historical components and more contingent

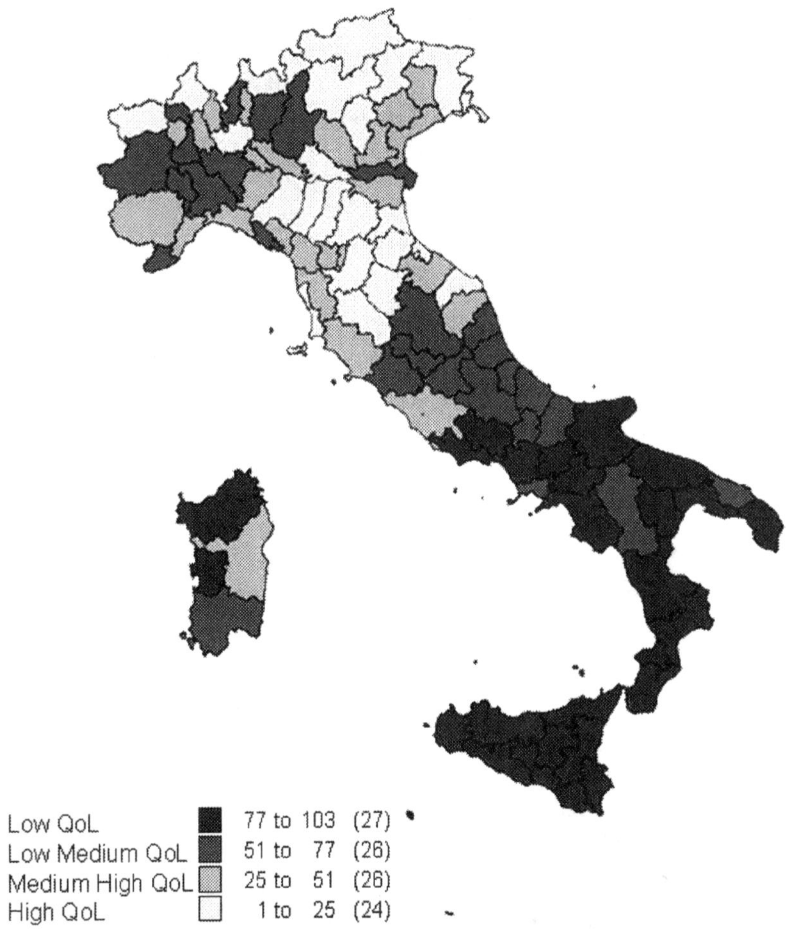

Figure 6.4. Position of the Provinces in the Rank of the QOL Index in 2001.

patterns of development can concur in determining new paths of concentration and diffusion of the QOL.

Also the concept of QOL is changing and new variables linked to the capabilities of the people in moving, using technological devices and communicating are becoming more and more important. The interaction between the individuals and the territory is starting to mutate as well, even in a traditional society like the Italian one, which has been characterized for a long time by forms of strong local identity. The geography of the QOL in the future will be deeply conditioned by the process of *disembedding* (Giddens, 1990), which is already typical of the more advanced society and is transforming the framework of the private and public relationships between the citizens and the cities.

The question of "quality of life, for whom?" is pertinent here. The formation of communities without propinquity (Webber, 1963) and, more in general, the increase of people traveling and presenting intensive long distance communication needs are *imposing* new life styles. Major societal changes are appearing on the wake of the diffusion of Information and Communication Technologies (ICT). The diffusion of time saving and time consuming technologies is now so widespread that they affect every aspect of our every-day life. Working, shopping, traveling, banking, receiving services from the public administration, going to the hospital or to the cinema are all activities that come in contact with ICT to a greater or lesser extent generating emancipation processes but also distinct types of marginality for the weakest segments of the population (Craglia et al., 1999).

In such a panorama, new positive trends like the improvement of the level of education and participation, as well as negative ones like the reduction of identity, the impoverishment of personal contacts, the exclusion from the more sophisticated technological services, are possible. The consolidated analyses simply based on the territorial distribution of the socioeconomic resources appear to be to some extent obsolete for the study of QOL. Nevertheless, these analyses are still very important in order to establish the context in which innovative patterns are taking place.The model of the *Three Italies* can be considered as one of the most fruitful for interpreting the Italian case. Of course, past and new perspectives of development at urban, regional, and global levels are overlapping, making it difficult to delineate precise scenarios on economic growth, as well as on QOL in Italy, at least in the long run.

6.8. NOTES

[1] Even, the most efficient urban size, in terms of low per capita costs for *running* the cities, has been indicated by many studies in the small-medium ones (Vanhove and Klaassen, 1987).

[2] According to the OECD (1983), urban decline regards problems experienced by larger metropolitan areas, which are losing population and employment from the central or even the entire metropolitan area. Urban decline is considered as the spatial concentration in large cities of social, economic and environmental problems such as high levels of unemployment and poverty, housing deterioration and decay of the urban infrastructure.

[3] Agricultural production and tourist activities were other two important aspects of the economic

development of the *Third Italy*. In fact, these two sectors continued to be a source of social integration, labor and income. As Bianchini points out (1991: 338): "many agricultural workers in the *Third Italy* worked on rented land, or were small farm-owners. These systems were very different from those used in the Meridione, where large landed estates prevailed and agricultural workers were mainly salaried day laborers".

[4] Although in the 80s the growth of the *Third Italy* was slowed down by a crisis in global demand for the products which the area was specialized in and by an increase in the competition from Brazil, Singapore, South Korea (Bianchini, 1991: 340).

[5] The metropolitan areas of Turin and Genoa, in particular.

[6] Despite some variations year by year regarding the number and type of indicators utilized, the QOL index is normally based on a non-weighted sum of 36 standardized social indicators related to 6 main areas: wealth and consumes, business and labor, services and environment, criminality, population, leisure. Final QOL ranks from 1990 to 1995 regard 95 provinces and from 1996 till 2001 regard 103 provinces, but for this paper they have been made comparable. Il Sole 24 Ore also performed two data collections on QOL in 1988 and 1989, but the methods adopted were completely different. Although many criticisms have been moved, from a methodological point of view, to the research of *il Sole 24 Ore* (Vitali and Merlini, 1999), such a research constitutes the most regular collection and analysis of data on QOL in Italy. Results must be interpreted with caution, especially in relation to the positions gained by the single province year by year on the final QOL ranks; nevertheless it is possible to assume that the general scene produced by the research is very useful in order to outline the evolution of QOL in Italy. For an overview of the research performed in Italy on QOL see also Nuvolati (1998).

[7] In particular, in the North West and in the North East, provinces with small and medium *capoluogo* are nowadays suffering more than the largest ones and this is mainly due to: a) a less experimented tradition in dealing with problems (immigration, criminality, pollution) now interesting also the small and medium size towns, c) the permanence of some functions in the large cities with positive effects in terms of occupation opportunities not yet available in the small ones, d) a transportation system not always able to support the decentralization process and still privileging a hierarchical model. Very recently several newspapers (in particular *Corriere della Sera* of Milan, for example see article of 11 April 2001 and 19 April 2001) point out the possibility of a redevelopment of the so called GE-MI-TO (Genoa-Milan-Turin) triangle based on the improvement of the transport infrastructures connecting the three cities but also the Italian triangle with France (Lyon in particular), Switzerland and Germany.

[8] Specific European areas with flexible production that could be compared with the *Third Italy* were: Jutland, the German Land of Baden-Württemberg, the industrial districts of Oyonnax near Lyon, and the Eastern Valles near Barcelona (Sabel, 1989; Bianchini, 1991).

[9] See also the unemployment rate outlined in Table 6.3.

[10] These two axes form the cores of a larger urban continuum defined by Turri (2000) with the term of *Megalopoli Padana*, according to the Gottmann's model (1961).

6.9. REFERENCES

Bagnasco, A. (1977). *Tre Italie: la problematica territoriale dello sviluppo italiano*. Bologna: Il Mulino.

Bianchini, F. (1991). The Third Italy: Model or Myth? *Ekistics*, n. 350–351, 336–345.

Burnell, J. D. and Galster, G. (1992). Quality of Life Measurements and Urban Size: An Empirical Note. *Urban Studies*, **29**, 727–735.

Cheshire, P., Hay, D., Carbonaro, G., and Bavan, N. (1988). *Urban Problems and Regional Policy in the European Community*. Brussels: Commission of the European Community.

Craglia, M., Leontidou, L., Nuvolati, G., and Schweikart, J. (1999). *Evaluating Quality of Life in European Regions and Cities*. Brussels: Committee of the Regions – European Union.

Elgin, D., Thomas, T., Logothetti, T., and Cox, S. (1974). *City Size and the Quality of Life. An Analysis of Policy Implications and Continued Population Concentration*. National Science

Foundation – Research Applied to National Needs Program. Stanford: The Stanford Research Institute.

Giddens, A. (1990). *The Consequences of Modernity.* Stanford: Stanford University Press.

Gottmann, J. (1961). *Megalopolis.* Cambridge (MA): MIT Press.

King, R. (1992). Italy: From sick man to rich man of Europe. *Geography*, **77**, 153–169.

Inchiesta (1990). *Tre Italie o nuovo dualismo*, vol. 20, n. 88–89.

Nuvolati, G. (1998). *La qualità della vita delle città. Metodi e risultati delle ricerche comparative.* Milano: Franco Angeli.

Nuvolati, G. (1998). La qualità della vita, valutazione e trade off. In P. Natale (ed.), *Abacus. Italia al macroscopio* (pp. 85–108). Milano: Feltrinelli.

OECD (1983), *Managing Urban Change: Policies and Finance*. Paris: OECD.

RuR-Censis (1992). Sviluppare reti di città e migliorare la qualità urbana. *Strumenti per valorizzare la rete delle Piccole Capitali.* Roma: Censis.

Sabel, C. (1989). Flexible specialisation and the reemergence of regional economies. In P. Hirst and J. Zeitlin (eds.), *Reversing Industrial Decline? Industrial Structures and Policy in Britain and Her Competitors* (pp. 17–70). Oxford: Berg.

Salvatori, F. (1997). Population mobility and new industrial districts: The case of the third Italy. In H. H. Blotevogel, and A. J. Fielding (eds.), *People, Jobs and Mobility in the New Europe* (pp. 217–225). Chichester: John Wiley and Sons.

Turri, E. (2000). *La megalopoli padana.* Venezia: Marsilio.

Vanhove, N. and Klaassen, L. H. (1987). *Regional Policy: A European Approach.* Aldershot: Ashgate.

Vitali, O. and Merlini, A. (1999). La qualità della vita: metodi e verifiche. *Rivista italiana di economia, demografia e statistica*, **53**, 5–93.

Webber, M. M. (1963). Order in diversity: Community without propinquity. In L. Wingo (ed.), *Cities and Spaces* (pp. 23–56). Baltimore: Johns Hopkins Press.

6.10. AFFILIATION

Giampaolo Nuvolati, University of Milan Bicocca, Italy.

Joseph Deutsch, Xavier Ramos, and Jacques Silber

7. POVERTY AND INEQUALITY OF STANDARD OF LIVING AND QUALITY OF LIFE IN GREAT BRITAIN

ABSTRACT: Most empirical analyses on inequality and poverty use either income or consumption to approximate the standard of living and/or quality of life of individuals (or households). Notwithstanding this, it is well known that these measures are seriously deficient. Moreover, it is a handicap to be concerned with goods, as such, to the exclusion of what goods "do to human beings" (Sen, 1998, 1999). We take on Sen's concepts of 'resources' and "functionings" and measure poverty and inequality of standard of living and quality of life in Great Britain using the British Household Panel Study (BHPS) data. Sen defines "resources" as the material goods and services, which confer capability on individuals. That is, provide them with the capacity to do things. His concept of "functionings," however, captures the notion of how well individuals are functioning as human beings. Following Lovell et al. (1994) we use distance functions to estimate standard of living, quality of life and the efficiency in transforming resources into functionings. Standard of living is measured as a mixture of resources by means of an index, which is analogous to the input quantity index of production economics, whereas quality of life gets measured by an index of individual functionings, which is analogous to the output quantity index of production economics. We then analyse the distributions of standard of living and quality of life and their relationship with the efficiency in transforming resources into functionings. We find little correlation between the first two distributions and very low inequality and poverty.

7.1. Introduction

Few people would doubt about the multidimensional nature of the two notions central to this paper: the standard of living and the quality of life. To show the complexity of the latter, Sen (1999) argues:

> One could be *well off*, without being *well* (due to health problems). One could be *well*, without being able to lead the life he or she *wanted* (due to cultural restrictions and bounds). One could have got the life he or she *wanted*, without being *happy* (due to psychological problems). One could be *happy*, without having much *freedom* (due to society's norms). One could have a good deal of *freedom*, without *achieving* much (due to lack of self-confidence or self-esteem). We can go on. [Sen, 1999: 3; parentheses are ours]

Clearly, there are many dimensions of these two notions that are not easy to capture by any economic measure of income or wealth. Yet, economists have traditionally identified well-being with market command over goods, thus, confounding the "state" of a person – well-being – with the extent of his or her possessions – being well-off. To some extent, such an "opulence-focused approach" (Sen, 1999) could be empirically justified by the scarcity of (individual) data. From a theoretical point of view, however, "economics has not been very interested in the plurality of focus in judging a person's states. In fact, often enough the very richness of the subject matter has been seen as an embarrassment. There is a powerful tradition in economic analysis that tries to eschew the distinctions and make do with one simple measure of a person's interest and its fulfillment" (Sen, 1999).

M. Joseph Sirgy et al. (eds.), Advances in Quality-of-Life Theory and Research, 99–128, 2003.

Not to overlook the plurality embedded in the standard of living and the quality of life notions we adopt Sen's "capability approach," which views individual well-being as a combination of various functionings. A functioning is an achievement of a person: what she manages to do or to be, and reflects a part of the "state" of that person. These functionings are then the constituents of an individual's quality of life, and the evaluation of the latter must take the form of valuing the functioning vectors.[1] In other words, according to Sen, the mere command over commodities cannot determine the valuation of the goodness of the life that one can lead for "the need of commodities for any specified achievement of living conditions may vary greatly with various physiological, social, cultural and other contingent features." (Sen, 1999: 25) Commodity command is a means to the end of well-being.

In accordance to Sen's "capability approach" we see the standard of living primarily as a basket of multiple resources – commodities – and the quality of life as a basket of functionings. To evaluate these two vectors we give them a numerical representation in the form of an index. The aggregation of individual resources into an index of standard of living, and of individual functionings into a measure of quality of life are based on the application, originally suggested by Lovell et al. (1994), of the concept of distance function, widely used in production theory, to individual data for Great Britain.

Lovell et al.'s methodology and estimation procedures are explained in section 7.2 and Appendix A. Section 7.3 and Appendix B describe the data used for the empirical investigation: the British Household Panel Survey (BHPS). This data set collects information on several aspects of people's life such as their state of health, housing conditions, self-esteem, mobility problems, community life and so on. Section 7.4 focuses on the resources and functionings used to measure the standard of living and quality of life, whereas Sections 7.5 and 7.6 present the main results on inequality and poverty. Finally, Section 7.7 concludes.

7.2. ESTIMATION PROCEDURES

The evaluation of standard of living and quality of life raises several complex empirical issues. In our understanding, two are of special importance and have not yet been resolved: the specification of a complete list of resources and functionings – see Section 7.4 –, and the relative valuation of each functioning or resource.

To tackle the latter we have several options. One possibility is to treat all attributes equally. This strategy, which has been associated to an "agnostic" attitude or to a wish to minimize interference, is as arbitrary as any other one. A second possibility is to use frequency-based weights. This weighting strategy has been mainly used in the construction of multidimensional deprivation indicators,[2] the basic idea being to give a larger weight to those vector constituents for whom there is a lower proportion of people in deprivation. Finally, those using multivariate techniques let the method and the data determine the weights. This is, indeed, our case. A drawback of this strategy is that it does not provide any indication about the relative valuation of functionings.

Following Lovell et al. (1994), we use distance functions to estimate standard of living, quality of life and the efficiency with which individuals are able to transform resources into functionings. The latter is an empirical approximation of Sen's converting function,[3] which, as pointed out in the introduction, will depend on contextual factors as well as personal characteristics.

Of course, this is not the only way to empirically implement Sen's "capability approach." With individual data, one could use standard multivariate statistical techniques to manage the problems posed by the multidimensionality. In one of the few applications of this sort of techniques to the "capability approach," Schokkaert and Van Ootegem (1990) employ factor analysis to identify the functionings of a group of Belgian unemployed. As they point out, the problem with this technique is that it is a "mere data reduction technique" which does not guarantee that the list of functionings is complete. As mentioned above, it does not provide either any indication about the relative valuation of functionings.[4] As it will be clear below, this is also a drawback of the methodology we employ. Alternatively, one could also use multidimensional inequality and poverty indices – see Maasoumi (1986, 1989), Tsui (1995), and Bourguignon and Chakravarty (1998).

Other techniques have been used with aggregate or macroeconomic data. In particular, the use of stochastic dominance to vectors of average functionings – see, for instance, Gaertner (1993) – and the use of composite indices such as the Human Development Index – see UNDP (1995).

7.2.1. *Estimating the Standard of Living Index*

Let $x = (x_1, \ldots, x_N) \in \mathbb{R}^N_{++}$ denote the resources vector and $u = (u_1, \ldots, u_M) \in \mathbb{R}^M_{++}$ denote the functionings vector. Then an individual's resources and functionings are denoted by the pair (x^i, u^i), $i = 1, \ldots, I$.

A theoretical standard of living index SL can be estimated using a Malmquist input quantity index:

$$\mathrm{SL}(u, x^s, x^t) = \frac{D_{in}(u, x^s)}{D_{in}(u, x^t)}$$

where x^s and x^t are two different resource vectors and D_{in} is an input distance function. The idea behind the Malmquist index is to provide a reference set against which to judge the relative magnitudes of the two resource vectors. That reference set is the isoquant $L(u)$ and the radially farther x^i is from $L(u)$ the higher its standard of living, for x^i must be shrunk more to move back onto the reference set $L(u)$.

There is, however, a difficulty because the Malmquist index depends generally on u. One could use an approximation of this index such as the Tornquist index, but such an index requires price vectors as well as behavioral assumptions.[5] Since we do not have prices for resources we have to adopt an alternative strategy. The idea is to get rid of u by treating all individuals equally and assume that each individual has the same level of functionings: one unit for each functioning. Let e represent such a vector of functionings – a M-dimensional vector of ones. Thus, the reference set becomes $L(e)$ and bounds the sample resource vectors form below. Individuals with resource vectors onto $L(e)$ share the lowest standard of living, with an index value of unity, whereas individuals with large resources vectors will then have higher standards of living, with index values above unity.

To estimate the distance function, let $\lambda = (1/x_N)$ and define a $(N-1)$ dimensional vector z as $z = \{z_j\}=\{x_j/x_N\}$ with $j = 1, \ldots, N-1$. Then $D_{in}(z, e) = (1/x_N) \geq D_{in}(z, e)$ and, since $D_{in}(z, e) \geq 1$,[6] we have

$$\frac{1}{x_N} \leq D_{in}(z, e).$$

This implies that we may also write

$$\frac{1}{x_N} \leq D_{in}(z, e) \cdot \exp(\varepsilon), \qquad \varepsilon \leq 0.$$

By assuming that $D_{in}(z, e)$ has a translog functional form, we have

$$\ln(u_N^{-1}) = \alpha_0 + \sum_{j=1}^{N-1} \alpha_j \ln z_j + \frac{1}{2} \sum_{j=1}^{N-1} \sum_{k=1}^{N-1} \alpha_{jk} \ln z_j \ln z_k + \varepsilon$$

Estimates of the coefficients α_j and α_{jk} may be obtained using COLS (corrected ordinary least squares) or Maximum Likelihood methods – see the Appendix for details – while the input distance function $D_{in}(z^i, e)$ for each individual i is provided by the transformation

$$D_{in}(z^i, e) = \exp\{\max(\varepsilon_i) - \varepsilon_i\}.$$

This distance will, by definition, be greater than or equal to one (since its logarithm will be positive) and will hence indicate by how much an individual's resources must be scaled back in order to reach the resource frontier. This procedure guarantees that all resources vectors lie on or above the resource frontier $L(e)$. The standard of living for individual i will then be obtained by dividing $D_{in}(z^i, e)$ by the minimum observed distance value – which by definition equals 1.

7.2.2. *Estimating the Quality of Life Index*

The quality of life index, QL, can be derived and estimated in a similar manner. Now, though, instead of an input distance function we use an output distance function $D_{out}(x, u)$ defined as

$$D_{out}(x, u) = \mathrm{Min} \left\{ \theta\colon \left(\frac{u}{\theta}\right) \in P(x) \right\}$$

where $P(x)$ is the set of all functioning vectors which can be realized with the resource vector x. A theoretical Standard of Living index, QL, can be estimated using a Bergson-Moorsteen output quantity index

$$\mathrm{QL}(x, u^s, u^t) = \frac{D_{out}(x, u^s)}{D_{out}(x, u^t)}$$

where u^s and u^t are two functionings vectors and x is a resource vector. Clearly, the further inside the isoquant $P(x)$ a functioning vector is, the more it must be radially expanded in order to meet the standard and the lower the corresponding quality of life.

Here also the problem is to choose a reference vector, in this case a resource vector x. We will, this time, define a N-dimensional vector e of ones. That is, we will assume that each individual is endowed with one unit of each resource. This implies that we define a reference set $P(e)$ which bounds from above the observed functionings of the various individuals. If an individual has a vector of functionings which places him on the frontier $P(e)$, this implies that she has the maximum level of quality of life and, hence, an output index of unity. Individuals with smaller functionings will have a lower quality of life and, hence, index values below unity. As before, note that this index is independent of units of measurement of functionings.

To estimate the output distance functions we proceed as in the input distance case. We assume a translog functional form

$$\ln(u_M^{-1}) = \beta_0 + \sum_{f=1}^{M-1} \beta_f \ln v_f + \frac{1}{2} \sum_{f=1}^{M-1} \sum_{h=1}^{M-1} \beta_{fh} \ln v_f \ln v_h + \varepsilon$$

where $v_f = (v_f/u_M)$, $f = 1, \ldots, M-1$. Here, again, we may use either COLS or maximum likelihood methods to obtain estimates of the β coefficients. The (modified) residuals which are then derived will provide output distance functions for each individual by means of the transformation

$$D_{out}(e, u^i) = \exp\{\min(\varepsilon_i) - \varepsilon_i\}$$

This distance will by definition be smaller than one (since its logarithm will be negative or at most equal to zero) so that all individual functionings vectors will lie on or beneath the functioning frontier corresponding to $P(e)$. Hence, the output distance function $D_{out}(e, u^i)$ gives the maximum amount by which individual functionings vectors must be radially scaled up in order to reach the functioning frontier. Finally, a quality of life index $\mathrm{QL}(x, u^s, u^t)$ is obtained by dividing all the output distance functions by the maximum observed distance – by definition equal to 1.

7.2.3. *Estimating the Transformation Efficiency Index*

We estimate the Transformation Efficiency index, TE, using a Malmquist productivity index

$$\mathrm{TE}(x^s, x^t, u^s, u^t) = \frac{D_{out}(x^s, u^s)}{D_{out}(x^t, u^t)}$$

Note that now the reference set $P(x^i)$ is defined as

$$P(x^i) = \left\{ \left(\frac{u^i}{\theta}\right) : D_{out}\left(x^i, \left(\frac{u^i}{\theta}\right)\right) = 1 \right\}, \quad i = 1, \ldots, I$$

where i is the number of individuals. All individuals will therefore be compared to the relevant reference set and for those who are able to convert relatively small resources into relatively large functionings the distance function will be unity while less efficient individuals will have a smaller score. The same technique used previously in estimating distance functions for the standard of living and the quality of life is applied here. Note, however, that this time both resource and functioning data are used. The translog output distance function can then be expressed as

$$\ln(u_M^{-1}) = \delta_0 + \sum_{j=1}^{N-1} \alpha_j \ln x_j + \frac{1}{2}\sum_{j=1}^{N-1}\sum_{k=1}^{N-1} \alpha_{jk} \ln x_j \ln x_k + \sum_{f=1}^{M-1} \beta_f \ln v_f + \frac{1}{2}\sum_{f=1}^{M-1}\sum_{h=1}^{M-1} \beta_{fh} \ln v_f \ln v_h + \sum_{f=1}^{M-1}\sum_{j=1}^{N-1} \gamma_{fj} \ln v_f \ln x_i + \varepsilon$$

Again, coefficient estimates may be obtained using either COLS or maximum likelihood methods. The (modified) residuals, which are then derived, provide output distance functions for each individual by means of the transformation used to obtain the quality of life index

$$D_{out}(x^i, u^i) = \exp\{\max(\varepsilon_i) - \varepsilon_i\}$$

This distance will by definition be smaller than one (since its logarithm will be negative or at most equal to zero) so that all individual resource and functionings vectors will lie on or beneath the frontier $P(x)$.

These output distance functions measure the efficiency with which individuals convert their resources into functionings. Since, by construction, the maximum observed output distance function is unity, the distance $D_{out}(x^s, u^s)$ will also be equal to the Malmquist Productivity Index $\mathrm{TE}(x^s, x^t, u^s, u^5)$ – when divided by the maximum output distance.

7.3. THE DATA

Data used in this study come from the 7th wave of the British Household Panel Study (BHPS), conducted in 1997. The BHPS is a longitudinal data set consisting of some 5,500 households (approximately 10,000 individuals) first interviewed in the autumn of 1991 (wave 1) and followed and re-interviewed every year subsequently. This initial sample represents a response rate of about 69% (proxies included) of the effective sample size. Wave-on-wave attrition rates for the subsequent waves are very small.[7] The sample used in this study consists of 7,545 individuals who provide valid answers to the questions relevant to our investigation.

The BHPS questionnaire provides information on the possession and quality of several durable goods – which we use as resources – as well as objective and subjective information on several aspects of the respondent's life such as health, physical mobility, ability to undertake mental tasks, self-worth, etc. – which we use to estimate functioning scores. A complete list of the variables used is given in Appendix B.

7.4. RESOURCES AND FUNCTIONINGS

Arguably, there is no such a thing as the complete list of functionings. Actually, the identification of certain resources and functionings as objects of value is itself a valuation exercise (Sen, 1998). As such, our efforts should shift to specifying a reasonably parsimonious but comprehensive enough resource and functioning vectors by making sure that two minimum requirements are satisfied. First, that the different constituents are not very correlated, that is, each constituent of the, say, functionings vector reflects and measures different "doings or beings"; and second, that the vectors do not neglect any important aspect (Brandolini and D'Alessio, 1998). Of course, most times, data restrictions will hamper the completeness of the vectors.

Given the richness of the BHPS, this has, however, not been our major problem and hence we believe we have reasonable resource and functioning vectors. Our resources vector contains 5 elements: durable goods for leisure, durable goods for home work, other type of property, quality of the dwelling and income; and the constituents of the functionings vector are: living in the right environment, mobility and able to undertake usual physical tasks, ability to undertake usual mental tasks, self-respect and self-worth, ability to socialize and network, and health state.

A second empirical issue is to choose the variables to appropriately approximate those resources and functionings. We have chosen to use more than one variable for each resource and functioning and to estimate them by means of the methodology outlined above – Table 7.1 shows summary statistics. That is, we use a two stage procedure to estimate the SL, QL, and TE indices. In the first step we estimate 4 resource vectors[8] and 6 functionings vectors using the information contained in Appendix B. In this first stage we use a Malmquist input quantity index.[9] These resource and functionings vectors are then used in the second stage to finally estimate the SL, QL and TE indices.

All these resources and functionings vectors have their own (unequal) distribution. However such inequalities will be most worrying when they are highly correlated. That is, when one's standing in one distribution determines one's standing in other distributions (Walzer, 1983). Arguably, then, a certain degree of independence is to be favored.

Our analysis for Great Britain suggests a high level of equality in the different

Table 7.1. Summary Statistics of Resources, Functionings, Equivalent Income, Standard of Living, Quality of Life and Transformation Efficiency Vectors.

	Mean	St. Dev.	Min.	Max.
Equivalent income	10,292.99	10,990.67	3.01	250,440.1
Standard of living	2.34	0.24	1	2.74
Quality of life	0.62	0.07	0.22	1
Transformation efficiency	0.45	0.00	0.16	1
Resources				
Durables leisure	2.52	0.10	1	2.56
Durables home work	2.42	0.28	1	2.54
Other property	3.21	0.65	1	5.92
Quality of dwelling	2.29	0.24	1	2.43
Functionings				
Right environment	5.18	1.30	1	19.88
Able to undertake physical tasks	4.41	0.53	1	5.52
Able to undertake mental tasks	3.08	0.41	1	6.60
Self-worth	3.31	0.49	1	8.17
Socialise	4.57	0.59	1	7.55
Health related	6.11	1.43	1	20.40

Table 7.2. Inequality indices of Functionings, Equivalent Income, Standard of Living, Quality of Life and Transformation Efficiency Vectors.

	GE(0)	GE(1)	Gini	A(0.5)	A(1)
Equivalent income	52.977	40.406	47.654	19.894	41.126
Standard of living	0.789	0.641	3.866	0.354	0.786
Quality of life	0.707	0.67	6.018	0.343	0.704
Transformation efficiency	0.708	0.698	6.347	0.35	0.705
Resources					
Durables leisure	0.123	0.096	0.746	0.054	0.123
Durables home work	0.998	0.789	3.807	0.441	0.993
Other property	2.466	2.198	11.01	1.155	2.436
Quality of dwelling	0.796	0.641	3.355	0.355	0.793
Functionings					
Right environment	3.877	3.303	13.014	1.756	3.803
Able to undertake physical tasks	1.213	0.895	3.692	0.514	1.205
Able to undertake mental tasks	1.007	0.915	6.516	0.477	1.002
Self-worth	1.316	1.171	7.347	0.616	1.307
Socialise	0.94	0.87	6.409	0.449	0.936
Health related	3.264	2.908	12.869	1.522	3.211

All Indices are multiplied by 100.

GE(a) are the Generalised Entropy indices, where a = income difference sensitivity parameter. The more positive a is, the more sensitive GE(a) is to income differences at the top of the distribution. GE(0) is the Mean Log Deviation and GE(1) is the Theil Index.

$A(e)$ are the Atkinson indices, where $e > 0$ is the inequality aversion parameter. The more positive $e > 0$ (the 'inequality aversion parameter') is, the more sensitive $A(e)$ is to income differences at the bottom of the distribution.

resources and functionings – see Table 7.2 – and very low correlations – see Table 7.3. One can have low levels of resource yet be functioning well, and vice-versa.

Such low correlations raise several points. First, the low correlations among resources and among functionings suggest that each resource or functioning index is capturing a different aspect relevant for the standard of living and the quality of life. Thus, we avoid the risk of redundancy mentioned above. Second, the low correlations between resources and functionings imply that the possession of any single resource – more precisely, of any set of "commodities" embedded into each resource score – does not determine doing well with respect to a certain functioning. Moreover, as we will show below, this is also true in a more "aggregate" level for the correlation between the standard of living and the quality of life is also very low. Third, it is also interesting to notice the very low correlation between equivalent income and the different resources and functionings. On the one hand, this lack of correlation shows that our resource vectors measure something different from income. On the other hand, the lack of correlation between income and the different functionings suggest that, as it happened with the resources, income does not guarantee doing well in any functioning. This might be obvious for some cases: why should a higher level of income imply more (physical) mobility, a higher self-respect or a better socializing?[10] However, at least for the health related functioning, this lack of correlation is, to some extent, surprising. As it is well known among health economists, there seems to be a non-negligible effect of individual income on her health state.[11]

7.5. (IN)EQUALITY OF STANDARD OF LIVING AND QUALITY OF LIFE

One of the most striking results of our empirical analysis is the high concentration around the median/(mean) of the Standard of Living and the Quality of Life indices – see Figure 7.1. As much as 87% of standard of living individual scores lie within one standard deviation of the mean value, and the Gini coefficient is 0.038 – see Table 7.2. As far as quality of life is concerned, the figures are very similar: 80% of individuals lie within one standard deviation of the mean value and the Gini coefficient is 0.060.

Although this result is not new[12] it is still surprising for inequality of equivalent income is much higher – the Gini is 0.48. Notwithstanding this, there is no doubt that these findings are encouraging. On the one hand, when standard of living is estimated by an index that includes resources other than income, inequality decreases drastically. On the other hand, quality of life, as measured by basic functionings, also displays a very low level of inequality.

As Table 7.4 shows, resources are more equally distributed than functionings for the first nine deciles. In other words, the quality of life Lorenz curve crosses the standard of living one from below in the ninth decile – see Table 7.6. This, in turn, means that the highest standard-of-living-decile is less "efficient" in transforming resources into functionings than the rest of the population – actually, the

Table 7.3. Correlations between Resources, Functionings, Equivalent Income, Standard of Living, Quality of Life and Transformation Efficiency.

	DL	DHW	OP	QDW	REN	AUPT	AUMT	SR	SAL	HTH	EI	SL	QL	TE
Durables Leisure (DL)	1													
Durables Home Work (DHW)	0.253 (0.00)	1												
Other Property (OP)	0.1066 (0.00)	0.2604 (0.00)	1											
Quality of Dwelling (QDW)	0.0166 (0.15)	0.0532 (0.00)	0.0606 (0.00)	1										
Right Environment (REN)	0.0407 (0.00)	0.0371 (0.00)	0.1513 (0.00	0.1099 (0.00)	1									
Able Undertake Physical Tasks (AUPT)	0.013 (0.26)	0.0244 (0.03)	0.0564 (0.00)	0.0186 (0.11)	0.0347 (0.00)	1								
Able Undertake Mental Tasks (AUMT)	0.01 (0.39)	–0.008 (0.49)	0.0048 (0.68)	0.0152 (0.19)	0.0875 (0.00)	0.1351 (0.00	1							
Self-worth (SR)	0.033 (0.00)	0.0119 (0.30)	0.0299 (0.01)	0.0393 (0.00)	0.1125 (0.00)	0.1307 (0.00)	0.5276 (0.00)	1						
Socialise (SAL)	0.0226 (0.05)	0.0353 (0.00)	–0.0057 (0.62)	0.0251 (0.03)	0.0912 (0.00)	0.0313 (0.01)	0.1079 (0.00)	0.1286 (0.00)	1					
Health Related (HTH)	0.0019 (0.87)	0.0082 (0.48)	0.0308 (0.01)	0.0382 (0.00)	0.194 (0.00)	0.1487 (0.00)	0.1702 (0.00)	0.1819 (0.00)	0.071 (0.00)	1				
Equivalent Income (EI)	0.0183 (0.11)	–0.0364 (0.00)	0.0091 (0.43)	0.0342 (0.00)	0.0306 (0.01)	0.0372 (0.00)	0.0002 (0.99)	0.0322 (0.01)	–0.0007 (0.95)	0.0301 (0.01)	1			
Standard of Living (SL)	0.0189 (0.10)	0.0469 (0.00)	0.0604 (0.00)	0.9859 (0.00)	0.1133 (0.00)	0.0257 (0.03)	0.017 (0.14)	0.0461 (0.00)	0.0263 (0.02)	0.0428 (0.00)	0.1815 (0.00)	1		
Quality of Life (QL)	0.033 (0.00)	0.0437 (0.00)	0.0473 (0.00)	0.0706 (0.00)	0.3948 (0.00)	0.0769 (0.00)	0.1658 (0.00)	0.1935 (0.00)	0.8433 (0.00)	0.4978 (0.00)	0.0173 (0.13)	0.0737 (0.00)	1	
Transformation Efficiency (TE)	–0.0031 (0.79)	0.0055 (0.63)	–0.0005 (0.97)	0.0018 (0.88)	0.353 (0.00)	0.0548 (0.00)	0.1451 (0.00)	0.1709 (0.00)	0.7689 (0.00)	0.4825 (0.00)	0.0006 (0.96)	0.0056 (0.63)	0.9043 (0.00)	1

Significance levels in parentheses.

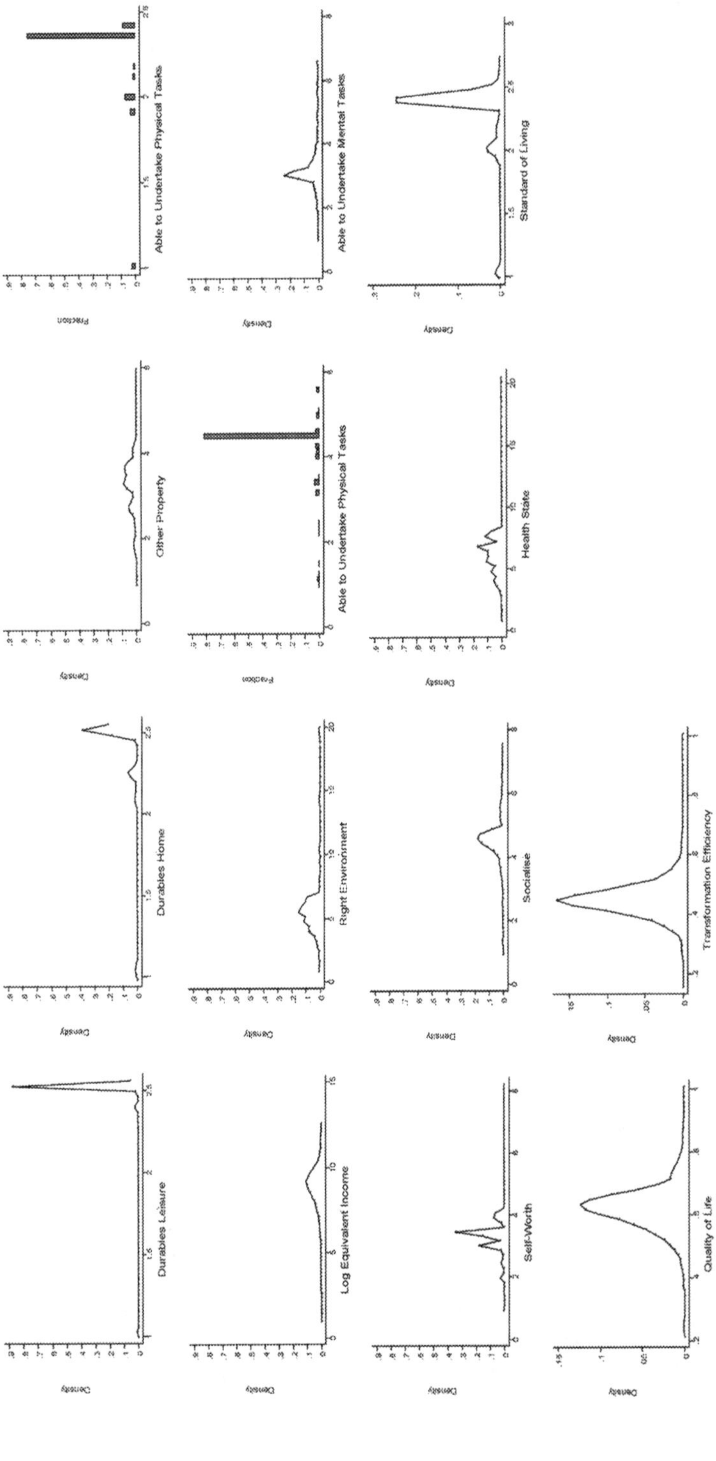

Figure 7.1. Kernel Density Estimates.

Table 7.4. Ventile Lorenz Ordinates and Shares (in percentage).

Percentiles	Lorenz Ordinates				Shares			
	EI	SL	QL	TE	EI	SL	QL	TE
5	0.006	0.046	0.039	0.038	0.58	4.63	3.92	3.84
10	0.016	0.093	0.082	0.081	1.06	4.71	4.31	4.24
15	0.030	0.141	0.127	0.125	1.37	4.73	4.49	4.40
20	0.047	0.188	0.173	0.170	1.64	4.76	4.57	4.53
25	0.065	0.236	0.219	0.216	1.88	4.78	4.65	4.60
30	0.087	0.284	0.267	0.263	2.12	4.80	4.71	4.69
35	0.110	0.332	0.314	0.311	2.37	4.81	4.76	4.76
40	0.136	0.380	0.362	0.359	2.61	4.82	4.81	4.81
45	0.165	0.429	0.411	0.408	2.90	4.84	4.85	4.88
50	0.197	0.477	0.460	0.457	3.17	4.85	4.90	4.93
55	0.232	0.526	0.509	0.507	3.47	4.86	4.96	5.00
60	0.270	0.575	0.559	0.557	3.82	4.88	5.01	5.05
65	0.312	0.624	0.610	0.608	4.20	4.89	5.05	5.10
70	0.359	0.673	0.661	0.660	4.67	4.92	5.13	5.18
75	0.411	0.722	0.713	0.713	5.20	4.92	5.20	5.24
80	0.469	0.771	0.766	0.766	5.84	4.94	5.29	5.34
85	0.537	0.821	0.820	0.821	6.80	4.96	5.41	5.46
90	0.619	0.873	0.876	0.876	8.22	5.17	5.55	5.59
95	0.727	0.930	0.934	0.935	10.78	5.71	5.79	5.82

EI: Equivalent Income.
SL: Standard of Living.
QL: Quality of Life.
TE: Transformation Efficiency.

Table 7.5. Standard of Living and Quality of Life Sorted by Standard of Living Deciles (%).

SL-Deciles	Shares		Accumulated Shares	
	QL	SL	QL[a]	SL
1	9.8	9.3	9.8	9.3
2	9.9	9.5	19.7	18.8
3	10.0	9.6	29.7	28.4
4	10.0	9.6	39.7	38.0
5	10.0	9.7	49.7	47.7
6	10.1	9.7	59.8	57.5
7	10.0	9.8	69.8	67.3
8	10.1	9.9	80.0	77.1
9	10.1	10.1	90.1	87.3
10	9.9	12.7	100.0	100.0

These are actually the concentration curve ordinates.
SL: Standard of Living.
QL: Quality of Life.

average transformation efficiency of the highest SL-decile is slightly lower than that for the other nine deciles. Therefore, the mean quality of life share of the highest SL-decile is slightly lower than the standard of living share of the same SL-decile – see Table 7.5.

Notwithstanding this, the relationship between standard of living and quality of life is very weak. That is, these two dimensions (distributions) are independent. The correlation coefficient is very small – see Table 7.3 – and the joint distribution – see Table 7.9 – is almost flat, denoting a very even joint distribution. This means that, as happened with every pair of individual functionings or resources,

Table 7.6. Lorenz Dominance Results.

	EI	SL	QL
SL	LD		
QL	LD	Cb (18)	
TE	LD	Cb (18)	Cb (18)

EI: Equivalent Income.
SL: Standard of Living.
QL: Quality of Life.
TE: Transformation Efficiency.
Let rows denote distribution A and columns distribution B.
LD: A Lorenz Dominates B.
Cb (#): A Crosses B from Below at the #-th ventile.

Table 7.7. Quintiles of Equivalent Income and Standard of Living.

Quintiles	1	2	3	4	5	Total
1	8.0	8.9	0.9	1.2	1.0	20.0
2	3.7	11.1	3.4	1.4	0.4	20.0
3	2.9	0.0	13.5	1.7	1.8	20.0
4	2.9	0.0	2.3	12.1	2.7	20.0
5	2.5	0.0	0.0	3.5	14.0	20.0
Total	20.0	20.0	20.0	20.0	20.0	100.0

Table 7.8. Quintiles of Equivalent Income and Quality of Life.

Quintiles	1	2	3	4	5	Total
1	3.6	4.2	4.1	4.4	3.6	20.0
2	4.2	4.3	4.3	3.6	3.6	20.0
3	4.1	4.1	3.9	4.0	3.9	20.0
4	4.2	3.6	3.9	4.0	4.4	20.0
5	3.9	3.8	3.8	4.0	4.6	20.0
Total	20.0	20.0	20.0	20.0	20.0	100.0

when these are aggregated the possession of resources does not guarantee the enjoyment of functionings, and that the enjoyment of the latter does not necessarily comes through the possession of the former. In other words, it shows that the ranking in terms of resources does not determine the ranking in terms of more general well-being, and vice-versa. As Lovell et al. (1994) point out, this does not mean that the possession of material resources is of no value. An individual can enjoy having a large house equipped with lots of good quality durables, several cars, etc. and yet not rank highly in terms of health, mobility, self-worth, social interaction or any other functioning. In fact the importance of the material resources could stem from the fact that these provide utility – seen either as satisfaction or as happiness, or as desire-fulfillment (Sen, 1982). However, utility – defined this way – need not have anything to do with quality of life, and, indeed, this is the

Table 7.9. Quintiles Standard of Living and Quality of Life.

Quintiles	1	2	3	4	5	Total
1	4.9	4.0	3.8	3.8	3.4	20.0
2	3.6	4.3	4.2	4.3	3.6	20.0
3	3.8	4.2	3.9	3.9	4.1	20.0
4	3.6	3.6	4.0	4.2	4.6	20.0
5	4.0	3.9	4.1	3.7	4.3	20.0
Total	20.0	20.0	20.0	20.0	20.0	100.0

Table 7.10. Quintiles of Standard of Living and Transformation Efficiency.

Quintiles	1	2	3	4	5	Total
1	4.8	3.8	3.5	3.7	4.2	20.0
2	4.3	4.2	3.2	4.3	4.0	20.0
3	3.5	4.4	3.9	4.5	3.7	20.0
4	3.6	3.7	4.4	4.2	4.1	20.0
5	3.9	3.8	5.0	3.3	3.9	20.0
Total	20.0	20.0	20.0	20.0	20.0	100.0

Table 7.11. Quintiles of Quality of Life and Transformation Efficiency.

Quintiles	1	2	3	4	5	Total
1	16.5	2.9	0.4	0.1	0.1	20.0
2	3.0	13.7	2.6	0.5	0.2	20.0
3	0.4	3.3	13.1	2.7	0.5	20.0
4	0.1	0.1	3.9	13.0	3.0	20.0
5	0.1	0.0	0.1	3.6	16.2	20.0
Total	20.0	20.0	20.0	20.0	20.0	100.0

lesson Sen tried to teach us in several of his writings (*inter alia*, 1980, 1982, 1998a, b, 1999).

As mentioned above for the resources and functionings, the equality in, and the lack of correlation between, the distributions of the standard of living and the quality of life is a positive result for a low score in the resources dimension does not necessarily imply a low level of quality of life. In addition to that, the correlation between the standard of living and the different functionings as well as that between the quality of life and the different resources is extremely low – see Table 7.3. That is to say, a person can still enjoy a high quality of life without having certain durable goods or certain properties, and a high standard of living does not necessarily imply doing well in any of the functionings considered.

6. POVERTY (OR INDIVIDUAL BELOW THE MEDIAN)

Since the standard of living and quality of life distributions are very concentrated, it does not make much sense setting the poverty line at the level usually set when using income, i.e. around 50% of the median of the distribution. As Table 7.12 shows, when the poverty line is set at those levels there is hardly any poverty in the distributions. Only when the poverty line reaches the level of 90% of the median the proportion of poor exceeds 5% of the population.

Poverty, either on the basis of standard of living or quality of life is low, and certainly much lower than it is on the basis of equivalent income. According to the standard of living, only 2.4% of the population is poor when the poverty line is set at 80% of the median. However, when the latter is set at 90% of the median,

Table 7.12. Foster-Greer-Thorbecke Poverty Indices, FGT(a) for Different Poverty Lines.

Poverty Line (% Median)	0.5	0.6	0.7	0.8	0.9
FGT(0): headcount ratio (proportion poor)					
Equivalent Income	0.2626	0.3132	0.3629	0.4105	0.4577
Standard of Living	0.0237	0.0237	0.0237	0.0237	0.1381
Quality of Life	0.0035	0.0052	0.0127	0.0424	0.1596
FGT(1): average normalized poverty gap					
Equivalent Income	0.1380	0.1632	0.1882	0.2130	0.2377
Standard of Living	0.0032	0.0066	0.0091	0.0109	0.0194
Quality of Life	0.0006	0.0012	0.0022	0.0049	0.0143
FGT(2): average squared normalized poverty gap					
Equivalent Income	0.0953	0.1123	0.1292	0.1460	0.1627
Standard of Living	0.0005	0.0019	0.0035	0.0050	0.0069
Quality of Life	0.0001	0.0004	0.0007	0.0013	0.0029
Gini amongst the poor					
Equivalent Income	0.0358	0.0356	0.0.354	0.0353	0.0352
Standard of Living	0.0130	0.0130	0.0130	0.0130	0.0874
Quality of Life	0.0524	0.0994	0.1045	0.0729	0.0513

the proportion of poor is 6 times higher and the average normalized poverty gap is 1.7 times larger – from 0.0109 to 0.0194. When poverty is measured on the quality of life space, the proportion of poor increases slightly but becomes less severe – the average normalized poverty gap is smaller. Notwithstanding this, when poverty is measured on the quality of life space and with a poverty line of 90% of the median, the proportion of poor is only 16%. This means that the ten percentage points of the median before the median concentrates 34% of the population.

One may also note the very low inequality among the poor, whether it concerns the standard of living or the quality of life.

Poverty is clearly very low according to these two indices. What proportion of this small part of the population is poor when the two criteria are used together? Using the 90% threshold for both distributions, as few as 3% of the population gets classified as poor according to their standard of living and quality of life. That is, 22% of those who are poor according to the standard of living are also poor according to the quality of life. Using this same (90%) threshold, Table 7.13 shows conditional poverty (proportion of poor) figures. It is interesting to note that only around 16% of those who are poor according to the conventional equivalent income measure are also poor according to our measures of standard of living and quality of life.

7.7. Concluding Comments

Standard of living and quality of life are two ideas of extremely wide relevance to economics and, especially, to social policy. Such relevance lies on the extent to which they are able to capture, or encompass, a set of important aspects to evaluate individuals' living. In spite of this, economists have traditionally used an "opulence-focused approach" (Sen, 1998), whereby these two notions are reduced to an individual's command over goods or some income or wealth indicator, thence neglecting many relevant aspects of an individual's life. To do justice to the richness of the standard of living and quality of life notions, we adopt the "capability

Table 7.13. Conditional Proportion of Poor (%) for Different Poverty Lines.

Poverty Line (% Median)	0.6	0.7	0.8	0.9
Poor according to Equivalent Income				
Standard of Living	2.3	2.7	2.7	16.5
Quality of Life	0.5	1.2	4.0	16.0
Poor according to Standard of Living				
Equivalent Income	30.7	40.8	46.4	54.6
Quality of Life	1.1	1.7	8.9	22.0
Poor according to Quality of Life				
Equivalent Income	30.8	35.4	38.4	46.0
Standard of Living	5.1	3.1	5.0	19.0

approach" proposed by Sen (1980). This approach shifts the attention from material attributes to "doings and beings," which reflect the different "states" of a person.

Given, on the one hand, the complexity – multidimensionality – of the notions we try to measure and, on the other hand, the informational requirements of the "capability approach" few studies have empirically implemented it. We have approximated the concepts of standard of living and quality of life by means of resources and functionings, respectively, which in turn, were estimated using BHPS information for Great Britain. The measurement of individual scores is based on an application of distance functions, originally put forth by Lovell et al. (1994) and estimated by corrected ordinary least squares (COLS).

According to our results, in Great Britain, there is hardly any inequality – and thus relative poverty – neither in the distribution of the standard of living nor in that of the quality of life. Though surprising, our conclusions are in line with those of studies for other countries that use the same methodology.

Certainly, these results call for further research. Emerging empirical research to implement Sen's "capability approach" has recently employed alternative methodologies to that suggested by Lovell et al. and used in this paper. Our intention is to contrast our results for Great Britain using those techniques, which range from other multivariate techniques to multidimensional indices of inequality and poverty. The next step in the research agenda should be to explain the levels of standard of living and quality of life in terms of observable characteristics. Here much can be learned from the incipient analyses on multidimensional deprivation (Layte et al., 2000). Another important avenue for future research is the study of the dynamics of quality of life and standards of living. Panel data econometric techniques are one method that could be used to empirically analyze the evolution and determinants of the dynamics of these two notions.

7.8. APPENDIX A: DUALITY THEORY AND THE CONCEPT OF DISTANCE FUNCTION

A1. *The Distance Function in Consumption Theory*

Let q be a vector of quantities and p the corresponding price vector. One way of defining the consumer's problem is to assume that she wants to maximize utility u for a given outlay $o = p \cdot q$. It is well known that the solution to this maximization problem yields the Marshallian demand functions $q = g(p, o)$. By substituting these solutions into the original problem we then derive the indirect utility function $\psi(p, o)$, the maximum utility which may be reached at prices p with an outlay o.

An alternative approach is to assume that the consumer wants to minimize the expenditure required to reach utility u. This cost minimization problem yields the Hicksian or compensated demand functions $q = h(p, u)$, which, when substituted into the original problem, gives the cost function $o = c(p, u)$ which is defined as the minimum cost of attaining u at prices p.

By deriving the cost function with respect to prices we obtain the Hicksian demand function while by using Roy's identity one may derive the Marshallian demand function from the indirect utility function. Hence, there is a duality between a direct and indirect representation of preferences. The *distance function* is an inverse representation of the direct utility function – see Deaton (1979), and Deaton and Muellbauer (1980), for more details.

Let q represent an arbitrary quantity vector and u an arbitrary utility indifference curve. It is not assumed that $u = v(q)$. The distance function $D(u, q)$, defined on u and q, represents the amount by which q must be divided in order to bring it on to the indifference curve, so that $v[q/D(u, q)] = u$. Geometrically, in Figure 7.2 (A1), $D(u, q)$ is the ratio OB/OA. Note that if q happens to be on u, B and A coincide so that $u = v(q)$ if and only if $D(u, q) = 1$. There is thus an analogy with the indirect representation of preferences since $u = \psi(p, o)$ if and only if $c(p, u) = o$.

This link between the distance and the cost functions may be expressed also in

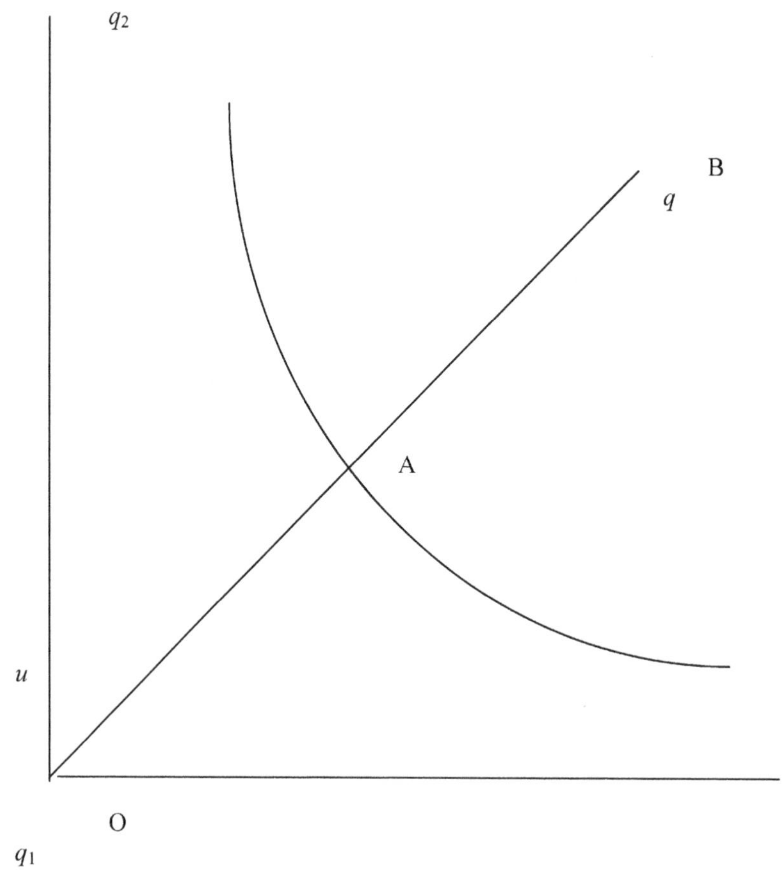

Figure 7.2 (A1).

the following way. Let q' be equal to OA in Figure 7.2 (A1) and let λ be equal to the ratio OB/OA. We can then write that $q' = q/\lambda$ so that

$$D(u, q) \cdot c(p, u) = \lambda \cdot c(p, u) \leq (\lambda q') \cdot p = q \cdot p$$

In other words q', which is obtained by a proportional change λ in the quantities defined by q, does not necessarily yield the cheapest cost $c(p, u)$ of reaching utility u at prices p. But there exists at least one vector price p for which $D(u, q) = \mathrm{q} \cdot p/c(p, u)$.

We may therefore write that

$$D(u, q) = \mathrm{Min}_p \; p \cdot q \text{ such that } c(u, p) = 1$$

as well as

$$c(p, u) = \mathrm{Min}_q \; p \cdot q \text{ such that } D(u, q) = 1.$$

The distance and cost functions are clearly dual to one another: just as the cost function seeks out the optimal quantities given u and p, the distance function finds the prices that will lead the consumer to reach utility u by acquiring a vector of quantities proportional to q.

When deriving the distance function $D(u, q)$ with respect to prices we obtain functions $a_i(q, u)$ which are dual to the Hicksian demand functions $h_i(p, u)$ and are compensated inverse demand functions, that is we may write:

$$\frac{\delta D(u, q)}{\delta q_i} = a_i(q, u) = \frac{p_i}{o}$$

For any quantity vector q and any utility level u, these compensated inverse demand functions give the prices as a function of o that will cause u to be reached at a point proportional to q – see Figure 7.3 (A2). These inverse demands may be given a simple intuitive interpretation: they represent the amounts of money an individual on u, consuming quantities proportional to those defined by the vector q, will be willing to pay for one more unit of each of the goods. It should be stressed that such inverse demand functions are convenient to use when prices do not exist because they then define shadow prices associated with u and the quantity proportions defined by the vector q. It is therefore not surprising that the concept of distance function is often used when prices are not available and such an application has turned out to be very useful in production theory – see Coelli, Prasada Rao and Battese (1997), for a detailed introduction to the topic.

A2. *The Distance Function in Production Theory*

A2.1. *Input Distance Function*

Let $L(y)$ represent the input set of all input vectors x which can produce the output vector y. That is,

$$L(y) = \{x\text{: } x \text{ can produce } y\}.$$

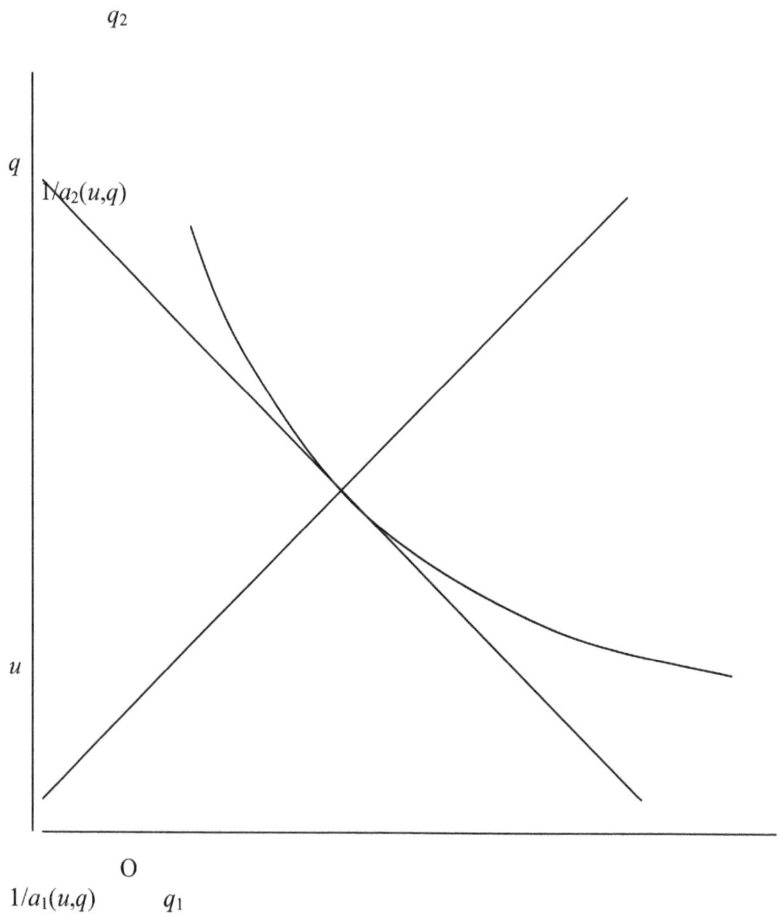

Figure 7.3 (A2).

The input distance function $D_{in}(x, y)$ involves then (in a way similar to that in which this concept is used in consumption theory) the scaling of the input vector and will be defined as

$$D_{in}(x, y) = \text{Max} \left\{ \rho = \left(\frac{x^i}{\rho} \right) \in L(y) \right\}$$

It may be proven that:

- the input distance function is increasing in x and decreasing in y;
- it is linearly homogeneous in x;
- if x belongs to the input set of y (i.e. $x \in L(y)$) then $D_{in}(x, y) \geq 1$;
- the input distance function is equal to unity if x belongs to the "frontier" of the input set (the isoquant of y).

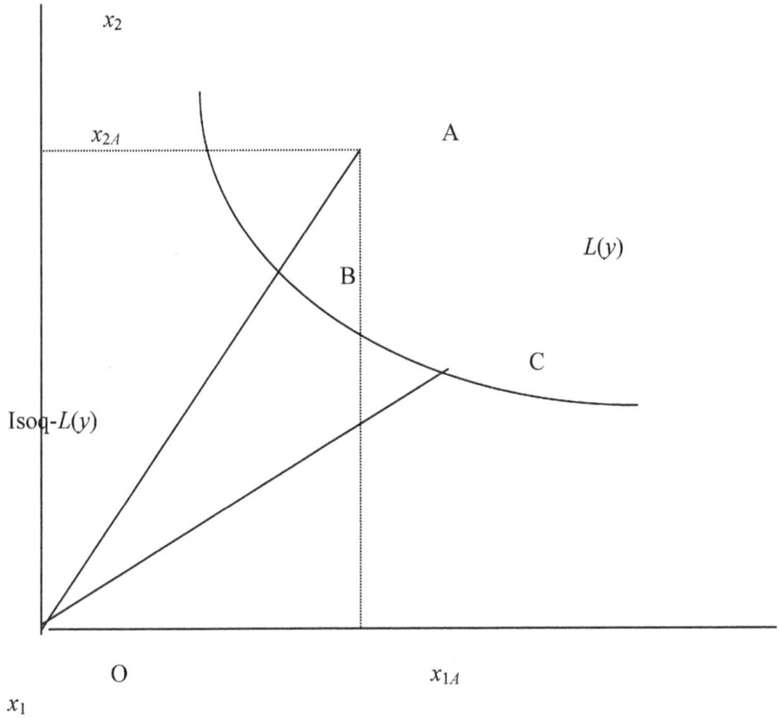

Figure 7.4 (A3).

A representation of the input distance function is given in Figure 7.4 (A3).

A2.2. *Input Distance Function*

Distance functions may also be used in the context of a multi-input, multi-output production technology. Let $P(x)$ represent the set of all output vectors y which can be produced using the input vector x. That is

$$P(x) = \{y: x \text{ can produce } y\}$$

The output distance function $D_{out}(x, y)$ is then defined as

$$D_{out}(x, y) = \text{Min}\left\{ \delta: \left(\frac{y^i}{\delta}\right) \in P(x) \right\}$$

The following properties of the output distance function may be proven:

- $D_{out}(x, y)$ is increasing in y and decreasing in x;
- $D_{out}(x, y)$ is linearly homogeneous in y;
- if y belongs to the production possibility set of x (i.e. $y \in P(x)$), then $D_{out}(x, y) \leq 1$;

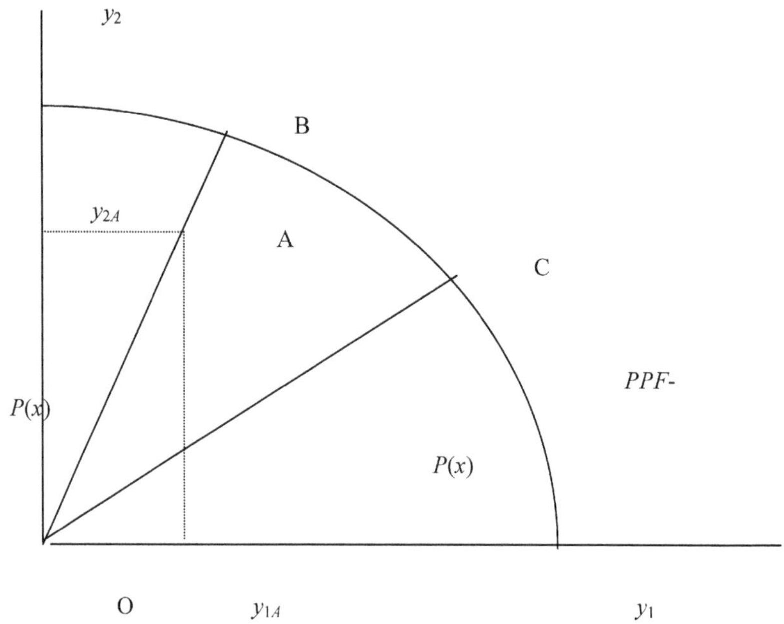

Figure 7.5 (A4).

– the output distance function is equal to unity if y belongs to the "frontier" of the production possibility set (to the production possibility curve of x).

An illustration of this concept is given in Figure 7.5 (A4).

A2.3. *Productivity Indices and the Distance Function*

Another interesting application of the concept of distance function concerns productivity indices.

A2.3.1. *The Malmquist Output Index*

Let y_t, y_s, x_t and x_s represent respectively the quantities of output y produced by a firm and the input x it uses at times t and s.

Using the concept of output distance function defined previously, the Malmquist output index, based on technology at time t, is defined, for an arbitrarily selected input vector x, as:

$$Q^t_{out}(y_s, y_t, x) = \frac{D^t_{out}(x, y_t)}{D^t_{out}(x, y_s)}$$

A similar Malmquist output index may be defined using the technology available at time s. Naturally we can define alternative indices using different levels of x. It should be stressed that the Malmquist output index will be independent of the technology involved if and only if the technology exhibits Hicks output neutrality. Similarly it will be independent of the input level x if and only if the technology is output homothetic.

If we consider output quantity indices based on technology in periods s and t, together with the inputs used in these periods, we have then two possible measures of output change, $Q^s_{out}(y_t, y_s, x_s)$ and $Q^t_{out}(y_t, y_s, x_t)$.

It can be proven that if the distance functions for periods s and t are both represented by translog functions with identical second-order parameters, then a geometric average of the Malmquist output indices $Q^s_{out}(y_t, y_s, x_s)$ and $Q^t_{out}(y_t, y_s, x_t)$ is equivalent to the Tornquist output quantity index (this index is a weighted geometric average of the ratios of the quantity at periods t and s, the weights being the simple arithmetic averages of the value shares in periods s and t). Note also that the Malmquist index is the only one which satisfies the homogeneity property according to which if $y_t = \lambda \cdot y_s$, then $Q^t_{out}(y_s, y_t, x) = Q^t_{out}(y_s, \lambda \cdot y_s, x_t) = \lambda$.

A2.3.2. *The Malmquist Input Index*

Using the concept of input distance function, the Malmquist input quantity index $Q^t_{in}(x_s, x_t, y)$ will be defined as

$$Q^t_{in}(x_s, x_t, y) = \frac{D^t_{in}(x_t, y)}{D^s_{in}(x_s, y)}$$

Naturally we can define in a similar way an input quantity index $Q^s_{in}(x_s, x_t, y)$ based on period-s technology. It can also be proven that when the distance functions are of the translog form and have in both periods identical second-order parameters and if the assumptions of allocated and technical efficiency[13] hold, then the geometric average of these two indices is equal to the Tornquist input quantity index (this index is a weighted geometric average of the ratios of the inputs at periods t and s, the weights being the simple arithmetic averages of the input cost-shares in periods s and t).

A2.3.3. *The Malmquist Productivity Index*

Output-oriented indices: They focus on the maximal level of outputs that could be produced using a given input vector and a given production technology relative to the observed level of outputs. Their computation is based on the use of output distance functions and the period-s Malmquist productivity index $M^s_{out}(y_s, y_t, x_s, x_t)$ is then defined as

$$M^s_{out}(y_s, y_t, x_s, x_t) = \frac{D^s_{out}(y_t, x_t)}{D^s_{out}(y_s, x_s)}$$

If we assume that the firm is technically efficient in both periods, $D^s_{out}(y_s, x_s) = 1$ so that

$$M^s_{out}(y_s, y_t, x_s, x_t) = D^s_{out}(y_t, x_t)$$

One can define in a similar way an output-oriented Malmquist productivity index based on period-t technology.

Input-oriented indices: It can be shown similarly that the input-oriented Malmquist productivity index $M^s_{in}(y_s, y_t, x_s, x_t)$ is equal to $D^s_{in}(y_t, x_t)$ if the firm is technically efficient in both periods.

A3. *Estimation Procedures*

Let us take as a simple illustration the case of a Cobb-Douglas production function. Let ln yi be the logarithm of the output of firm $i = 1$ to I and x_i a $(N + 1)$ row vector, whose first element is equal to one and the others are the logarithms of the N inputs used by the firm. We may then write that

$$\ln (y_i) = x_i \cdot \beta - u_i, \quad i = 1, \ldots, I$$

where β is a $(N + 1)$ column vector of parameters to be estimated and u a non-negative random variable, representing the technical inefficiency in production of firm i.

The ratio of the observed output of firm i to its potential output will then give a measure of its technical efficiency T_i so that

$$T_i = \frac{y_i}{\exp(x_i \cdot \beta)} = \frac{\exp(x_i \cdot \beta - u_i)}{\exp(x_i \cdot \beta)} = \exp(-u_i).$$

One of the methods allowing the estimation of this output-oriented Farrell measure of technical efficiency T_i (see Farrell, 1957) is to use an algorithm proposed by Richmond (1974) which has become known as corrected ordinary least squares (COLS). This method starts by using ordinary least squares to derive the (unbiased) estimators of the slope parameters. Then in a second stage the (negatively biased) OLS estimator of the intercept parameter β_0 is adjusted up by the value of the greatest negative residual so that the new residuals have all become non-negative. Naturally the mean of the observations does not lie any more on the estimated function: the latter has become in fact an upward bound to the observations.

One of the main criticisms of the COLS method is that it ignores the possible influence of measurement errors and other sources of noise. All the deviations from the frontier have been assumed to be a consequence of technical inefficiency. Aigner, Lovell and Schmidt (1977) and Meeusen and van den Broeck (1977) independently suggested an alternative approach called the stochastic production frontier method in which an additional random error v is added to the non-negative random variable u.

$$\ln (y_i) = x_i \cdot \beta + v_i - u_i$$

The random error v is supposed to take into account factors such as the weather, the luck, etc. v is assumed to be i.i.d. normal random variables with mean zero and constant variance σ_v^2, independent of u, the latter being taken generally to be i.i.d. exponential or half-normal random variables. In the latter case where u is assumed to be i.i.d truncations (at zero) of a normal variable $N(0, \sigma)$, Battese and Corra (1977) suggested to proceed as follows. Calling σ_s^2 the sum $(\sigma^2 + \sigma_v^2)$, they defined the parameter $\gamma = (\sigma^2/\sigma_s^2)$ – so that γ has a value between zero and one – and showed that the log-likelihood function could be expressed as

$$\ln(L) = -\frac{N}{2}\ln\frac{\pi}{2} - \frac{N}{2}\ln\sigma_s^2 + \sum_{i=1}^{I}[1 - \Phi(z_i)] - \left(\frac{1}{\sigma_s^2}\right)\sum_{i=1}^{I}\ln y_i - x_i\beta)^2$$

where $z_i = [(\ln y_i - z_i \cdot \beta)/\sigma_s] \cdot \sqrt{[\gamma/(1-\gamma)]}$ and $\Phi(\cdot)$ is the distribution function of the standard normal random variable.

The Maximum Likelihood estimates of β, σ_s^2 and γ are obtained by finding the maximum of the log-likelihood function defined previously where this function is estimated for various values of γ between zero and one. More details on this estimation procedure is available in programs such as FRONTIER (Coelli, 1992) or LIMDEP (Green, 1992). The same methods (COLS and Maximum Likelihood) may naturally be also applied when estimating distance functions.

7.9. APPENDIX B: VARIABLES USED TO ESTIMATE THE RESOURCES AND FUNCTIONINGS VECTORS

RESOURCES

BHPS Variable Name	Description
Durables Leisure	
wCD1USE	Colour TV in accommodation
wCD2USE	VCR in accommodation
wCD8USE	Home computer in accommodation
wCD9USE	CD player in accommodation
wCD10USE	Satellite dish at accommodation
wCD11USE	Cable TV in accommodation
wCD12USE	Telephone in accommodation
Durables Home Work	
wCD3USE	Freezer in accommodation
wCD4USE	Washing machine in accommodation
wCD5USE	Tumble dryer in accommodation
wCD6USE	Dish washer in accommodation
wCD7USE	Microwave oven in accommodation
Other Property	
wNCARS	Household member owns vehicle
wHSOWND	House owned or rented
wHSROOM	Number of rooms in accommodation
wHSTYPE4	Type of accommodation (wHSTYPE)

RESOURCES *(Continued)*

BHPS Variable Name	Description
Quality of Dwelling	
wHEATCH	Household has central heating
wHSPRBG	Accom: shortage of space
wHSPRBH	Accom: noise from neighbours
wHSPRBI	Accom: street noise
wHSPRBJ	Accom: not enough light
wHSPRBK	Accom: lack of adequate heating
wHSPRBL	Accom: condensation
wHSPRBM	Accom: leaky roof
wHSPRBN	Accom: damp walls, floors etc.
wHSPRBO	Accom: rot in windows, floors
Income	
wFIYR	Annual income (1.9.96–1.9.97)

FUNCTIONINGS

BHPS Variable Name	Description
Right Environment	
wCRDARK	Feel safe walking alone at night
wHSPRBP	Accom: pollution/environmental problems
wHSPRBQ	Accom: vandalism or crime
wLKMOVE	Prefers to move house
wLKNBRD	Likes present neighbourhood
wLFSAT3	Satisfaction with: house/flat
Mobility and Able to Undertake Usual Physical Tasks	
wHLLTB	Health hinders climbing the stairs
wHLLTC	Health hinders getting dressed
wHLLTD	Health hinders walking more than 10 mins
wHLENDW	Health prohibits some types of work
wHLLT	Health limits daily activities
wHLLTA	Health hinders doing the housework
wHLLTWA	How far health limits amount of work
Able to Undertake Usual Mental Tasks	
wGHQA	GHQ: concentration
wGHQB	GHQ: loss of sleep
wGHQD	GHQ: capable of making decisions
wGHQE	GHQ: constantly under strain
wGHQF	GHQ: problem overcoming difficulties
wGHQG	GHQ: enjoy day-to-day activities
wGHQH	GHQ: ability to face problems
wGHQI	GHQ: unhappy or depressed
wGHQL	GHQ: general happiness

FUNCTIONINGS *(Continued)*

BHPS Variable Name	Description
Self-Respect, Self-worth	
wGHQC	GHQ: playing a useful role
wGHQJ	GHQ: losing confidence
wGHQK	GHQ: believe in self-worth
Able to Socialize and Network	
wFRNA	Frequency of talking to neighbours
wFRNB	Frequency of meeting people
wSSUPA	Is there someone who will listen
wSSUPB	Is there someone to help in a crisis
wSSUPC	Is there someone you can relax with
wSSUPD	Anyone who really appreciates you
wSSUPE	Anyone you can count on to offer comfort
wXSUPA	Someone outside HH can help if depressed
wXSUPC	Someone outside HH can borrow money from
wNORGA	Number of organisations active in
wNORGM	Number of organisations member of
wORGMB	Member of trade union
wTUIN1	Member of workplace union (**wTUIN2**)
wLFSAT6	Satisfaction with: social life
Health Related	
wHLPRBA	Health problems: Arms, legs, hands, etc.
wHLPRBC	Health problems: Hearing
wHLPRBD	Health problems: Skin conditions/allergy
wHLPRBE	Health problems: Chest/breathing
wHLPRBF	Health problems: Heart/blood pressure
wHLPRBG	Health problems: Stomach or digestion
wHLPRBI	Health problems: Anxiety, depression, etc.
wHLPRBL	Health problems: Migraine
wHLPRBM	Health problems: Other
wHLSTAT	Health over last 12 months
wHOSP	Hospital in-patient since 1.9.96
wHL2GP	Number of visits to GP since 1.9.96
wHLSVI	Health service: used physiotherapist
wLFSAT1	Satisfaction with: health

7.10. NOTES

[1] More precisely, in his 'capability approach', Sen proposes to evaluate quality of life in terms of capabilities, defined as "the alternative combinations of functionings individuals can achieve, and from which they can choose one collection". (Sen, 1993: 31) The notion of capability is thus conceptually superior to that of functioning in that it reflects the freedom individuals have in terms of the choice of functionings. Due to the difficulty in measuring such freedom to pursue different functionings, we will not use capabilities but will focus on achieved functionings. According to Sen (1999: 38–40), our exercise constitutes then an "elementary evaluation" of the capability set.

[2] See Cerioli and Zani (1990) and Desai and Shah (1988).

[3] In his only attempt at formalising the 'capabilities approach' (Sen, 1999, Section 7.2) Sen defines a (not necessarily lineal) 'converting' or 'utilization' function $f(\cdot)$ which reflects one of the many ways in which individual can transform commodities into functionings. The 'converting' function $f(\cdot)$ belongs to a set F of functions from which individuals can in fact choose.
[4] See also Nolan and Whelan (1996a, b) for two additional applications of factor analysis to the study of deprivation in Ireland.
[5] This is also the case of other indices that are usually used to approximate the Malmquist index such as the Paasche index, the Laspeyres index or the Fisher index.
[6] See the Appendix for the properties of the distance functions.
[7] For a detailed discussion of the BHPS methodology and representative ness see Taylor (1994) and Taylor (1995).
[8] We only estimate 4 resource vectors (and not the 5 we use to estimate the standard of living) because the vector of incomes comes directly from the BHPS data.
[9] In this first stage it does not matter whether we use input or output distance functions to estimate the resource and functioning indices.
[10] Of course, the lack of correlation between every single functioning and income requires a deeper analysis – often carried on by sociologists rather than economists. For instance, as Lovell et al. (1994) point out, poverty is often thought of causing people to be excluded from participation in the society in which they live. Notwithstanding this, the lack of correlation between the 'socialising' functioning and income suggests that such link does not exist in the British society. In their study for Australia Lovell et al. find exactly the same result.
[11] The magnitude of this effect, though, is the object of discussion between the health economist supporting the absolute income hypothesis and those in favour of the relative income hypothesis – which introduces income inequality as an important determinant of health and argues for a lower effect of individual income levels. See Kawachi et al. (1999) for more on this.
[12] The other studies we know of obtain similar results. In particular, Deutsch, Silber and Yacouel (2000) find that the Gini of Standard of Living and Quality of Life in Israel are 0.1 and 0.082, respectively; Lovell et al. (1994), in their study for Australia, find Gini coefficients of 0.009 and 0.048 for Standard of Living and Quality of Life; and Delhause (1996) gets Ginis of 0.029 and 0.021 for Standard of Living and Quality of Life in France.
[13] Technical efficiency refers to the fact that the firm operates on the production frontier while allocated efficiency refers to the selection of a mix of inputs that produces a given quantity of output at minimum cost.

7.11. REFERENCES

Aigner, D., Lovell, C. A. K., and Schmidt, P. (1977). Formulation and Estimation of Stochastic Frontier Production Function Models. *Journal of Econometrics*, **6**, 21–37.

Battese, G. E. and Corra, G. S. (1977). Estimation of a Production Frontier Model: With Application to the Pastoral Zones of Eastern Australia. *Australian Journal of Agricultural Economics*, **21**, 169–179.

Bourguignon, F. and Chakravarty, S. R. (1998). The Measurement of Multidimensional Poverty, DELTA Working Paper, 98-12, Paris.

Brandolini, A. and D'Alessio, G. (1998). *Measuring Well-being in the Functionings Space*. Banca d'Italia, unpublished paper.

Cerioli, A. and Zani, S. A (1990). Fuzzy Approach to the Measurement of Poverty. In C. Dagum and M. Zagna (eds.), *Income and Wealth Distribution, Inequality and Poverty*, Springer-Verlag, Berlin.

Coelli, T. A (1992). Computer Program for Frontier Production Function Estimation: Version Frontier 2.0. *Economic Letters*, **39**, 29–32.

Coelli, T., Prasada Rao, D. S. and Battese, G. E. (1997). *An Introduction to Efficiency and Productivity Analysis*. Boston: Kluwer Academic Publishers.

Deaton, A. (1979). The Distance Function in Consumer Behaviour with Application to Index Numbers and Optimal Taxation. *Review of Economic Studies*, **46**, 391–405.

Deaton, A. and Muellbauer, J. (1980). *Economics of Consumer Behaviour.* Cambridge: Cambridge University Press.

Desai, M. and Shah, A. (1988). An Econometric Approach to the Measurement of Poverty. *Oxford Economic Papers*, **40**, 505–522.

Deutsch, J., Silber, J., and Yacouel, N. (2000). *On the Measurement of Inequality in the Quality of Life in Israel.* Bar-Ilan University, unpublished paper.

Farrell, M. J. (1957). The Measurement of Productive Efficiency. *Journal of the Royal Statisctical Society, Series A*, **CXX**, 253–290.

Gaertner, W. (1993). Commentary to: 'Amartya Sen: Capability and Well-being'. In M. C. Nussbaum, and A. Sen (eds.), *The Quality of Life* (pp. 62–66). Oxford: Clarendon Press.

Green, W. H. (1992). *LIMDEP Version 6.0: User's Manual and Reference Guide.* Econometric Software Inc., New York.

Kawachi, I., Wilkinson, R. G., and Kennedy B. P. (1999). *Income Distribution and Health: a Reader.* New Press N.Y.

Layte, R., Maitre, B., Nolan, B., and Whelan, C. (2000). Explaining Levels of Deprivation in the European Union, *EPAG Working Paper 12*, Institute for Social and Economic Research, University of Essex.

Lovell, C. A. K, Richardson, S., Travers, P., and Wood, L. (1994). Resources and Functionings: A New View of Inequality in Australia. In W. Eichhorn (ed.), *Models and Measurement of Welfare and Inequality*. Heidelberg: Springer-Verlag.

Maasoumi, E. (1986). The Measurement and Decomposition of Multi-Dimensional Inequality. *Econometrica*, **54**, 991–997.

Maasoumi, E. (1989). Continuously Distributed Attributes and Measures of Multivariate Inequality. *Journal of Econometric*s, **42**, 131–144.

Meeusen, W. and Van Den Broeck, J. (1977). Efficiency Estimates From Cobb-Douglas Production Functions with Composed Error. *International Economic Review*, **18**, 435–444.

Nolan, B. and Whelan, C. T. (1996a). *Resources, Deprivation and Poverty.* Oxford: Clarendon Press.

Nolan, B. and Whelan C. T. (1996b). The Relationship Between Income and Deprivation: A Dynamic Perspective. *Revue Économique*, **3**, 709–717.

Richmond, J. (1974). Estimating the Efficiency of Production. *International Economic Review*, **15**(2), 515–521.

Schokkaert, E. and Van Ootegem, L. (1990). Sen's Concept of the Living Standard Applied to the Belgian Unemployed. *Recherches Economiques de Louvain*, **56**, 429–450.

Sen, A. (1980). Equality of What. In S. McMurrin (ed.), *Tanner Lectures on Human Values*, Reprinted in A. Sen, Cambridge University Press, Cambridge, 1980.

Sen, A. (1982). *Choice, Welfare and Measurement.* Oxford: Blackwell.

Sen, A. (1998a). The Standard of Living: Lecture I, Concepts and Critiques. In G. Hawthorn (ed.), *The Standard of Living*. Cambridge University Press.

Sen, A. (1998b). The Standard of Living: Lecture II, Lives and Capabilities. In G. Hawthorn (ed.), *The Standard of Living*. Cambridge University Press.

Sen, A. (1999). Commodities and Capabilities, Oxford University Press, Oxford India Paperbacks.

Taylor, A. (1994). Appendix: Sample Characteristics, Attrition and Weighting. In N. Buck, J. Gershuny, D. Rose, and J. Scott (eds.), *Changing Households: The British Household Panel Study 1990–1992*. Colchester: Institute for Social and Economic Research, University of Essex .

Taylor, M. F. (1995). *British Household Panel Survey User Manual Volume A: Introduction, Technical Report and Appendices.* Colchester: Institute for Social and Economic Research, University of Essex. An up-to-date version of the BHPS documentation is available at: http://www.iser.sx.ac.uk/bhps/doc/

Tsui, K. Y. (1995). Multidimensional Generalizations of the Relative and Absolute Inequality Indices: The Atkinson-Kolm-Sen Approach. *Journal of Economic Theory*, **67**, 251–265.

UNDP (1995). *Human Development Report*. New York and Oxford: United Nations Development Programme and Oxford University Press .

Walzer, M. (1983). *Spheres of Justice*. New York: Basic Books.

7.12. AFFILIATIONS

Joseph Deutsch and Jacques Silber, Department of Economics, Bar-Ilan University, Ramat-Gan, Israel.

Xavier Ramos, Departament d'Economia Aplicada, Universitat Autònoma de Barcelona, Edificio B, 08193 Bellaterra, Spain. E-mail: xavi.ramos@uab.es

Ivan Brown

8. ABUSE AND NEGLECT OF DISABLED AND NON-DISABLED CHILDREN: ESTABLISHING A PLACE IN QUALITY OF LIFE STUDY

ABSTRACT: Addressing the basic necessities of life is an important place to start when studying the quality of life of individuals who experience maltreatment. Published literature has consistently pointed to a link between disability and maltreatment, especially to the over-representation of people with disabilities. An analysis of data from the *Canadian Incidence Study on Reported Child Abuse and Neglect*, for subsets of 666 children (8.68% of the total sample) with and 7,006 children without intellectual disability (ID) revealed that 1) neglect was the single type of maltreatment most frequently reported and substantiated for both the ID and the non-ID children; 2) neglect and several subtypes of neglect were reported and substantiated significantly more frequently for the children with ID; 3) children with ID were described more frequently for 11 of 15 child functioning concerns examined; 4) consequences of maltreatment, including physical harm, emotional harm, emotional harm requiring treatment, out of home placement, and the number of child welfare court applications made, were significantly higher for the children with ID, and 5) children with ID in the sub-sample who had experienced sexual abuse were more likely than the non-ID children to continue living with the perpetrator of the abuse.

8.1. Introduction

The importance and relevance of the term quality of life has been demonstrated over the past few decades, particularly in three broad areas of study: social indicators, health-related quality of life, and whole-person quality of life. While social indicators work typically examines broader concepts associated with quality living, and health-related quality of life emphasizes the impact of health conditions and interventions on people's lives, whole-person quality of life focuses on all aspects of life for individuals in the environments in which they live. Because of this orientation, whole-person quality of life is considered highly appropriate to the study of quality of life of individuals who are particularly impacted by their environments – such as children who experience child abuse and neglect within family life.

Whole-person quality of life was influenced by social indicators study, but emerged primarily from an area of sociology concerned with comparing expected and actual life goals, and from an area of psychology concerned with life satisfaction and personal happiness. Although these and several other disciplines pursue quality of life studies the emphasize the individual, interestingly, some of the best and most thoughtful development of whole-person quality of life work has been carried out for populations that are typically marginalized in society, especially people with intellectual disabilities (mental retardation). A strong and persistent guiding principle of the quality of life work for people with intellectual disabilities has been that its concepts, measures and applications need to be relevant for all people, with or without disabilities and across cultures and time. Thus, this body of work

M. Joseph Sirgy et al. (eds.), Advances in Quality-of-Life Theory and Research, 129–141, 2003.

combines well with work from other disciplines to provide a comprehensive theoretical and practical framework for examining people's lives and how they are impacted by their environments (for a summary of the historical development and current conceptualization, measurement and application of this body of work, see IASSID-QOL-SIRG, 2000).

One question that has begun to be addressed in literature on whole-person quality of life conceptualization and measurement is the degree to which some aspects of life are more fundamental to improved quality of life than others. This question becomes crucial when considering very negative aspects of life, such as abuse and neglect. Brown (1999; in press) began to address this question by suggesting a 3-level quality of life hierarchy that assumed the lower levels need to be satisfactorily in place before the higher levels can be fully attained. The hierarchy comprises: level 1, the basic necessities of life; level 2, happiness or satisfaction with aspects of one's life experiences and environment; and level 3, personal empowerment, enrichment, and expansion of one's life experiences and environment. This simple hierarchy does not allow for developing the complexities of whole-person quality of life, but it does provide a straight-forward framework for considering the place of abuse and neglect in the study of child and family quality of life.

8.1.1. *Abuse and Neglect in Disabled and Non-Disabled Children*

The literature of the past three decades has built a strong case for the importance of child abuse and neglect for children, with and without disabilities. The overall incidence reported by Trocmé et al. (2001) was 9.71 substantiated cases per 1,000 children for Canada and 13.8 substantiated cases per 1,000 children for the United States (from the National Incidence Study 3, 1993), indicating that approximately 1% of all children are reported for child maltreatment and that these reports are substantiated as having occurred. A number of comprehensive studies have, more specifically, documented both incidence and factors associated with physical abuse, sexual abuse, emotional maltreatment, and neglect (Trocmé et al., 2001), and these have been supported by numerous smaller studies in maltreatment in general or specific aspects of maltreatment. Together, this body of work presents clear evidence that child maltreatment is a concern of considerable importance for children's well-being.

This literature of the past three decades has also documented a strong link between incidence of abuse and neglect and the presence of disabilities in children (for a review, see Westcott and Jones, 1999). Further, some convincing data has been presented to support the view that children with disabilities are actually at increased risk of maltreatment, compared to children who do not have disabilities. For example, in one study of children under the age of 19, 11.5% of those with disabilities were maltreated and only 1.5% of age-matched control children experienced similar maltreatment (Salamanca, 1995). Data of this type underscores concern for children with disabilities, and especially so since children with intellectual and other disabilities are typically under-diagnosed in infancy and early childhood (Daily,

Ardinger, and Holmes, 2000; Percy and Brown, 1999). Although there has been some debate in the literature about whether disability contributes to increases in maltreatment or if maltreatment contributes to disability, the link between the two has been primarily seen for at least 15 years as part of the complex mix of individual and social factors within which child maltreatment is likely to occur (Belsky, 1993; Westcott and Jones, 1999).

The link between child abuse and neglect and reduced quality of life for children is implicit in the large maltreatment literature, but this literature has produced no explicit framework for examining the implications of maltreatment on children's quality of life. Similarly, the quality of life literature has not yet included maltreated children among those populations on whom quality of life is particularly important to focus.

The present analysis sought to establish a place for the study of child abuse and neglect within whole-person quality of life, by analyzing reported child maltreatment data from a national study carried out across Canada and considering the findings from a quality of life perspective. Specifically, it compared two subsets of children, those with and without developmental delay (children with intellectual disability) to 1) determine whether or not children with developmental delay are over-represented in reported child maltreatment compared to non-disabled children; 2) tabulate the extent to which types and subtypes of maltreatment were reported for children with and without developmental delays; 3) examine the degree to which each of 15 child functioning concerns is present in the delayed and non-delayed groups of maltreated children; and 4) document the importance of a number of variables relating to the consequences of maltreatment, and compare these for the delayed and non-delayed children.

8.2. METHOD

8.2.1. Participants

Participants were those selected for the Canadian Incidence Study of Reported Child Abuse and Neglect (CIS), the first Canada-wide study to examine incidence of reported child maltreatment and the characteristics of children and families investigated by Canadian child welfare services. The CIS sample comprised 7,672 child maltreatment investigations in total, with 666 (8.68%) described as having developmental delays. It was this group that was selected for the analysis reported here.

In this group of children with developmental delays, 130 (19.52%) children were also described as having physical or developmental disabilities; in the non-delayed sample, by contrast, only 135 (1.76%) children were described in the same way. Boys were more highly represented than girls overall (of the 662 for whom sex was recorded, 402 were boys and 260 were girls), as well as in each of four age categories: for infants age 0–3, there were 94 boys and 63 girls; for children age 4–7, there were 138 boys and 74 girls; for children age 8–11, there were 96 boys and 56 girls; and for teens age 12–15, there were 74 boys and 67 girls.

Most of the children (91.9%) lived with their biological parents, although others lived with adoptive parents, foster parents, step-parents, and others. Of the 612 children who lived with their biological parents, ethno-racial heritage data was not collected for the province of Québec but was collected for the 392 who lived outside Québec: 70.9% were white, 18.1% aboriginal, 4.5% Asian, 3.3% black, 0.8% Arab, .5% Latin American, and 1.8% were of other heritage. Household source of income was recorded for 607 (99.2%) of the families: of these, 57.7% received benefits, 27.7% were employed full time, 8.6% were employed part time or seasonally, and 6.1% had unknown or other sources of income. Regarding total family income, 35.0% of the children were from families whose total income was less than $15,000, 33.2% were from families whose income was $15,000–$40,999, 7.0% were from families whose income was more than $41,000, and for 24.9% of the children family income information was not available. Most children's families lived in rental housing (56.9% in market-value units, and 12.0% in geared-to-income units), but 17.0% lived in purchased homes, 1.7% in shelters, and 11.7 in a variety of other accommodation.

8.2.2. *Procedures*

The CIS used a four-stage strategy to select a representative sample of child maltreatment investigations: first, 51 sites were randomly selected from 327 child welfare service areas across Canada; second, 9,909 cases were selected that were opened between October 1 and December 31, 1998; third, 5,449 suspected child maltreatment cases were selected; and, finally, 7,672 child maltreatment investigations that resulted from these cases were identified. CIS researchers collected information directly from child welfare workers and from their file reports (for a full explanation of the sampling methodology see Trocmé et al., 2001).

8.2.3. *Instrumentation and Analysis*

The main instrument used to collect data was the CIS Maltreatment Assessment Form, which was developed through extensive consultation and pre-testing for the purpose of capturing standardized information about child maltreatment, characteristics of maltreating families, and characteristics of maltreated children. The CIS Maltreatment Assessment Form comprises three sections: 1) an Intake Face Sheet, which provides a method of documenting information related to the referral and identification of children referred for investigation; 2) a Household Information sheet, which contains multiple-response questions under 12 headings concerning characteristics of the child's caregiver(s) and household; and 3) a Child sheet, which contains multiple-response questions under 13 headings concerning characteristics related to the maltreated child and consequences of the maltreatment. Data from the CIS Maltreatment Assessment Form was entered into SPSS as 455 variables. It is the data from the Child sheet that is the primary focus of this analysis. These data provided descriptive information concerning children with developmental delays and child maltreatment that goes beyond that which is available from other sources, and is the first comprehensive set of such data on Canadian children. In addition, though, it provided an opportunity to contrast children with and without developmental delays regarding types of maltreatment experienced, child functioning concerns, and consequences of the maltreatment.

8.3. RESULTS

8.3.1. *Types of Maltreatment Reported*

The percentage of children with and without developmental delays who were reported for physical abuse, sexual abuse, neglect, emotional maltreatment, and multiple types of maltreatment, are shown in Table 8.1. Of the four main maltreatment types, all children – and especially those with developmental delays – were most likely to be reported for neglect. About one-third of those reported allegedly experienced physical abuse, and nearly as many had allegedly experienced emotional maltreatment. Slightly more than one-tenth of the children were reported because of sexual abuse.

Sub-types of maltreatment were also identified for each of the four main maltreatment types (also see Table 8.1). About two-thirds of the children who were reported for physical abuse were more specifically reported for inappropriately punishment. Among the sub-types of sexual abuse, touching and fondling genitals was the most frequently reported. The most common form of neglect was failure to physically provide and protect. For emotional maltreatment sub-types, emotional abuse was most frequently identified, although emotional neglect for the delayed children and exposure to family violence among the non-delayed children were also frequently reported.

A series of cross tabulation analyses using chi-square tests were conducted to contrast the number of children with and without developmental delays reported for the four general maltreatment categories and for each sub-type. Neglect was the only single type of maltreatment that was significantly higher for the developmentally delayed children than for the non-delayed children ($\chi^2 = 29.88$, $p < 0.001$), and post hoc analyses revealed that this finding accounted for multiple-category maltreatment for delayed children being higher than for non-delayed children. Several sub-types of neglect were also more frequently reported for the delayed children than for the non-delayed children: physical neglect, medical neglect, failure to provide treatment, maladaptive behaviour, and educational neglect. Although the two groups did not differ overall for rates of reported emotional maltreatment, the delayed group was reported to experience significantly more emotional neglect than the non-delayed group, and the non-delayed group were exposed to significantly more family violence than the delayed group.

Table 8.1. Percentage Of Children With And Without Developmental Delays Reported And Suspected/ Confirmed For Four Types of Maltreatment.

Type of maltreatment	Reported No delay (n = 7006)	Delay (n = 666)	Substantiated No delay (n = 3225)	Delay (n = 344)
Any physical abuse	34.8	34.2	28.7	25.0**
Inappropriate punishment	22.6	22.1	19.5	15.7
Other physical abuse	12.7	11.9	9.8	8.7
Shaken baby syndrome	0.4	0.8	0.3	1.2
Any sexual abuse	11.4	12.3	9.5	8.1
Sexual activity attempted	2.8	2.6	1.4	1.5
Sexual activity completed	1.8	2.1	1.7	2.0
Touching/fondling genitals	6.1	7.2	6.1	4.7
Exposure of genitals	1.1	1.2	1.0	1.2
Exploitation: pornography/ prostitution	0.4	0.3	0.4	0.3
Sexual harassment	0.4	0.3	0.5	0.3
Voyeurism	0	0	0	0.3
Any neglect	49.7	60.8**	52.77	74.1**
Failure to supervise/protect (physical)	25.1	24.2	24.1	27.9*
Failure to supervise/protect (sexual)	3.1	4.4	2.4	4.7
Physical neglect	12.0	16.5**	9.3	16.3**
Medical neglect	3.4	10.1**	3.9	12.2**
Failure to provide treatment	0.9	3.0**	1.0	3.2
Maladaptive behaviour	6.3	9.9**	9.4	15.7**
Abandonment	3.8	2.6	5.3	3.8
Educational neglect	5.7	9.8**	8.6	23.8**
Any emotional maltreatment	26.8	31.4	35.8	34.9
Emotional abuse	12.3	13.7	12.4	11.9
Non-organic failure to thrive	0.1	0.2	0.1	0.3
Emotional neglect	5.0	11.4**	5.2	11.6**
Exposed to family violence	15.1	9.6**	21.3	12.8**
Multiple categories	23.1	34.8**	–[a]	–[a]

* $p < 0.05$; ** $p < 0.01$.
[a] Data not available from dataset.

8.3.2. *Types of Maltreatment Substantiated*

Of the 7,672 cases reported for maltreatment in the sample, child welfare investigators substantiated 3,569 (46.52%) in at least one category of abuse or neglect (46.03% of non-delayed children and 51.65% of children with developmental delays). The percentage of children who were substantiated as experiencing the four main types of maltreatment and each of the sub-types of maltreatment is also shown in Table 8.1. The results here generally mirror those of the reported cases. Important differences, when substantiation is taken into account, include slightly lower rates of physical abuse and higher rates of emotional maltreatment. In addition, neglect is even more commonly experienced for the children with developmental disabilities now, and this is primarily accounted for by educational neglect and maladaptive behaviour.

8.3.3. *Child Functioning Concerns*

All children who were reported for child maltreatment were rated for 15 confirmed or suspected child functioning concerns. The number and percentage of delayed and non-delayed children reported for maltreatment who were described by each of these concerns are shown in Table 8.2. Among the 15 child functioning concerns, exhibiting behaviour problems was most frequently recorded for both the delayed and the non-delayed groups. Physical health conditions and mental health difficulties are noteworthy among the delayed group, as is apparent difficulty getting along with other children (negative peer involvement; violence toward others).

A series of cross tabulations was again conducted to contrast the number of children with and without developmental delays for the 15 child functioning concerns studied. The children with developmental delays in the sample were described

Table 8.2. Number and Percentage of Children Reported for Maltreatment with and without Developmental Delays Who were Described by 15 Child Functioning Concerns.

Type of maltreatment	Developmental Delay Status	
	No Developmental Delay	Developmental Delay
Health condition	208 (3.0%)	97 (14.6%)**
Depression / anxiety	587 (8.4%)	74 (11.1%)*
Substance abuse related birth defects	85 (1.2%)	64 (9.6%)**
Psychiatric disorder	106 (1.5%)	36 (5.4%)**
Self-harming behaviour	160 (2.3%)	35 (5.3%)**
Any behaviour concerns	2,009 (28.7%)	310 (46.5%)**
Behaviour problems	1,414 (20.2%)	240 (36.0%)**
Irregular school attendance[a]	435 (8.1%)	68 (13.5%)**
Negative peer involvement	417 (6.0%)	74 (11.1%)**
Violence toward others	313 (4.5%)	67 (10.1%)**
Age inappropriate sexual behaviour	165 (2.4%)	39 (5.9%)**
Running away (multiple incidents)	148 (2.1%)	19 (2.9%)
Substance abuse	237 (3.4%)	14 (2.1%)*
Running away (1 incident)	118 (1.7%)	12 (1.8%)
Criminal involvement	109 (1.6%)	12 (1.8%)
Involvement in prostitution	9 (0.2%)	1 (0.2%)

* $p < 0.05$; ** $p < 0.01$.

[a] Only children age 4–15 included: 5364 (76.56%) non-delayed children and 505 (75.83%) delayed children.

significantly more frequently than the non-delayed children for 11 of the concerns. The non-delayed children were described more frequently only for substance abuse, a concern that was rated low for both groups.

8.3.4. *Consequences of Child Maltreatment*

Some of the consequences of reported child maltreatment were investigated by the CIS Maltreatment Assessment Form. The number and percentage of delayed and non-delayed children for the consequence types recorded on the form are presented in Table 8.3. Once again, a series of chi-square test analyses was conducted to contrast the number of children of the two types who were recorded or not recorded in each consequence type category. One-fifth of the children with developmental delays reported for maltreatment experienced physical harm, and were significantly more likely to do so than the non-delayed children. Fortunately, most of that harm appears not to be of an extremely serious nature. More than half of the delayed children reported showed signs of emotional harm and almost half of these required treatment. These rates were more than twice as high as for the non-

Table 8.3. Number and Percentage of Children Reported for Maltreatment with and without Developmental Delays Who were Described by Consequences of Maltreatment.

Consequences of maltreatment	Developmental Status	
	No Developmental Delay	Developmental Delay
Any physical harm	882 (12.6%)	135 (20.3%)**
Bruises/cuts/scrapes	618 (8.8%)	74 (11.1%)
Burns/scalds	38 (0.5%)	3 (0.5%)
Broken bones	29 (0.4%)	8 (1.2%)*
Head trauma	34 (0.5%)	7 (1.1%)
Fatal	1 (0%)	0 (0%)
Other physical harm	206 (2.9%)	58 (8.7%)**
Exhibits signs of emotional harm	1,665 (23.8%)	340 (51.1%)**
Emotional harm required treatment	742 (10.6%)	184 (27.6%)**
Out of home placement	1,191 (17.0%)	166 (24.9%)**
Child welfare court application made	231 (3.3%)	39 (5.9%)**
Police investigation made	1,247 (17.8%)	116 (17.4%)
Criminal charged were laid	544 (7.8%)	50 (7.5%)
Responses to substantiated sexual abuse		
Non-offending caregiver believes child[a]	387 (92.8%)	29 (80.6%)*
Caregiver(s) provide emotional support[b]	380 (90.9%)	31 (75.6%)**
Caregiver(s) protect child from further abuse[c]	385 (91.7%)	32 (80.0%)*
Alleged perpetrator continues living with child[d]	52 (11.9%)	15 (34.9%)**

* $p < 0.05$; ** $p < 0.01$.
[a] Applicable $n = 453$; [b] Applicable $n = 459$; [c] Applicable $n = 460$; [d] Applicable $n = 479$.

delayed children. One-quarter of the children with developmental delays reported were placed out of their family homes as a consequence of a maltreatment investigation, again significantly higher than the rate for the non-delayed children. Child welfare court applications were also higher for the delayed group, although these were made for only 5.9% of the children. Interestingly, the number of police investigations and criminal charges laid did not differ for the two groups.

Four responses to substantiated sexual abuse were recorded for those children who had experienced sexual abuse. Higher percentages of caregiver support were recorded for the non-delayed children than for the delayed children in three categories: non-offending caregiver believes child, caregiver(s) provide emotional support, and caregiver(s) protect child from further abuse. The alleged perpetrators of sexual abuse continued to live with 34.9% of the children with developmental delays, but the percentage of alleged perpetrators who continued to live with non-delayed children was significantly lower at 11.9%.

8.4. DISCUSSION

This analysis sought to achieve four things: 1) determine whether or not children with developmental delay are over-represented compared to non-disabled children; 2) tabulate the extent to which types and subtypes of maltreatment were reported for children with and without developmental delays; 3) examine the degree to which each of 15 child functioning concerns is present in the delayed and non-delayed groups of children; and 4) document the importance of a number of variables relating to the consequences of maltreatment, and compare these for the delayed and non-delayed children.

Children with developmental delays appear to be considerably over-represented at 8.68% of the children reported for possible child maltreatment. Prevalence of developmental delay in children has been reported at various rates in literature, reflecting a discrepancy between the percentage of children who are expected to have delay, and the percentage of children tabulated from various service and educational organizations (Brown, 1999). It is usually expected, however, that about 3.0% of the population might have an intellectual disability, with about 0.5–1.0% known to service systems (Nuyen, 1996; Roeleveld, Zielhuis, and Gabreels, 1997; Yu and Atkinson, 1993). Given that the information on developmental delay for this study was collected from the files of child welfare workers and that developmental delay is often under-diagnosed (Percy and Brown, 1999), we might expect that only 1% or fewer of the children reported would be identified as having a developmental delay. Thus, it appears that delayed children are over-represented in the sample of children reported for maltreatment by at least eight times what might be expected from general prevalence rates.

This over-representation makes all types of child maltreatment matters of concern for children with developmental delay. Over and above this, though, there were differences among the types of maltreatment reported. Neglect was most frequently reported for children with developmental delay (60.8% of all delayed children), followed by physical abuse (34.2%), emotional maltreatment (31.4%), and sexual abuse (12.3%). Neglect was also the one maltreatment type that was experienced by a significantly higher number of delayed children in the sample when compared with their non-delayed peers. The additional finding that five sub-types of neglect and emotional neglect were all significantly higher for the delayed children in the sample than for the non-delayed children points to neglect being a particularly serious issue for children with intellectual disabilities. This information contributes to the overall literature on intellectual disability and child maltreatment by providing detail about the extent to which specific types of maltreatment are experienced by children with intellectual disability.

The 15 child functioning concerns examined were developed by the research team in consultation with child welfare agency partners. The list is clearly not exhaustive, but rather it represents commonly-perceived concerns in the child welfare field. Increased physical and emotional health problems for people with intellectual disability are recognized in the literature (Bradley and Summers, 1999; Cheetham, 1999), and, perhaps not surprisingly, such increases are confirmed in the present sample of children with developmental delays. Still, increased physical and emotional health concerns co-existing with both maltreatment and developmental delay is reason for additional caution. The significantly higher percentage of delayed children with substance abuse related birth defects is perhaps not unexpected, since some (but not all) substance abuse related birth defects are related to delayed functioning (e.g., fetal alcohol syndrome). But when approximately one in ten of the children in the sample of maltreated children with developmental delays is described in this way, it is a concern that needs to be taken very seriously. Increased behaviour concerns for children with intellectual disability are also well documented in the literature, but, again, when these are coupled with maltreatment, there is reason for particular attention.

The consequences of maltreatment that were examined in this analysis also produced some noteworthy results. Children with developmental delays were described as having experienced both physical and emotional harm significantly more frequently than their non-disabled peers. Such increases for one of the most vulnerable sub-populations of children is worrying, although it is possible that harm may have been recorded more frequently for this sub-population because they were considered to be more vulnerable or that the harm may not have been accompanied by actual maltreatment. It is also possible that the significantly higher percentage of delayed children who were said to experience "other physical harm" could result from neglect rather than from physical abuse, and that this type of physical harm would be less specifically related to a single incident than the other physical harm categories.

It is interesting to note how the increased levels of neglect and harm for the delayed children were treated by law enforcement and child welfare workers. The percentage of reports that resulted in police investigations and criminal charges being laid were virtually the same for the delayed and non-delayed children, in spite of increased harm and neglect. On the other hand, both child welfare applications and out-of-home placements were made for a significantly higher proportion of delayed children than for non-delayed children.

The analysis of four variables related to sexual abuse involved only the smaller sub-sample of children who were suspected or confirmed as having experienced sexual abuse (data was available for 453, 459, 460 and 479 children for the four variables respectively), and the number of children with developmental delays was relatively small. Still, the findings that the delayed children, compared with their non-delayed peers, were believed less, received less emotional support, and were protected from further sexual abuse to a lower degree are worthy of strong note. What makes these all the more noteworthy is the finding that showed the alleged perpetrator of sexual abuse to continue living with the developmentally delayed children in more than one-third of the cases, nearly three times the rate for the non-delayed children.

It might seem obvious to argue that child abuse and neglect function as negative factors in quality of life for children who experience such maltreatment, but this point needs to be stressed because it has not arisen in the whole-person quality of life literature to date. The question of how to position such negative factors in quality of life study might be addressed in part by borrowing from the literature on people with intellectual disabilities. Here, disability is regarded as a negative aspect of life – one that is associated with many challenges, some of which are quite substantial in nature – but the emphasis is on ways to maintain and enhance other positive contributors to quality of life and to minimize negative influences. Study of abuse and neglect in a quality of life context might do the same, but maltreatment is different from disability in that it is both preventable and able to be redressed. Its place in whole-person quality of life study, then, might also centre around minimizing or stopping child maltreatment and its negative effects. In the 3-stage hierarchy referred to earlier, abuse and neglect might best be thought of as aspects of level 1, basic necessities of life. As such, they would be regarded as factors essential to address first before proceeding with other aspects of quality of life, such as increasing satisfaction or enriching personal life experiences.

The secondary analysis that was conducted here is limited to the purposes and methodology of the original study. Still, the purposes are sufficiently general that they are of interest to an international audience, and the study's careful sampling methods within child welfare agencies throughout Canada appear to provide assurance that known child welfare systems are well represented. A more important limitation, perhaps, was that the analysis could examine only variables that were included in the original collection of data. Developmental delay was a single variable, for example, and there was no way to analyse the data for specific sub-types. There was also no clear data on children who have only sensory or physical disabilities (e.g., hearing impairment, blindness, mobility problems); this group would have constituted another interesting comparison group in addition to the large "non-delayed" group.

The analysis does suggest a number of interesting areas for further research. Factors associated with the over-representation of children with intellectual disability in reports of child maltreatment need to be explored and clearly specified so that child welfare practitioners can develop effective prevention strategies and respond to reported maltreatment in the most appropriate ways. Although all types of maltreatment are important to address, neglect, in particular, needs to be described both quantitatively and qualitatively to develop an understanding of what it consists of and why it is the most frequently reported type of maltreatment. The relationship between child functioning concerns and maltreatment of children with intellectual disability needs to be examined closely, and we need further information about the possible differential treatment of children with intellectual disability by professionals and caregivers following reported maltreatment.

On the whole, this analysis has provided some valuable new information about the types of maltreatment experienced by children with intellectual disability, it has identified some interesting associations between maltreatment and child functioning concerns, and it has pointed out some potential problems with the response to reports of child maltreatment. Such additions to the literature are crucial in our efforts to better understand abuse and neglect – phenomena that are surprisingly much less understood than should be the case.

8.5. References

Belsky, J. (1993). Etiology of child maltreatment: A developmental-ecological analysis. *Psychological Bulletin*, **114**(3), 413–434.

Bradley, E. and Summers, J. (1999). Developmental disability and behavioural, emotional and psychiatric disturbances. In I. Brown and M. Percy (eds.), *Developmental Disabilities in Ontario* (pp. 409–428). Toronto, ON: Front Porch Publishing.

Brown, I. (1999). What do we mean by developmental disabilities in Ontario? In I. Brown and M. Percy (eds.), *Developmental Disabilities in Ontario* (pp. 17–31). Toronto, ON: Front PorchPublishing.

Brown, I. and Brown, R. I. (in press). *Quality of Life: Practice and Practitioners.* London: Jessica Kingsley Publishers.

Cheetham, T. (1999). Physical health and people with developmental disabilities. In I. Brown and M. Percy (eds.), *Developmental Disabilities in Ontario* (pp. 339–350). Toronto, ON: Front Porch Publishing.

Daily, D., Ardinger, H., and Holmes, G. (2000). Identification and evaluation of mental retardation. *American Family Physician*, **61**, 1059–1067.

Nuyen, M. (1996). *What is the prevalence of Ontarians labelled as having a "developmental disability"?* Toronto, ON: Developmental Services Branch, Ministry of Community and Social Services.

IASSID-QOL-SIRG (International Association for the Scientific Study of Intellectual Disability, Quality of Life Special Interest Research Group). (2000). *The conceptualization, measurement, and application of quality of life: An international consensus.* http://www.iassid.org: Author.

Percy, M. and Brown, I. (1999). Causes and contributing factors, and approaches to intervention. In I. Brown, and M. Percy (eds.), *Development Disabilities in Ontario* (pp. 223–252). Toronto, ON: Front Porch Publishing.

Roeleveld, N., Zielhuis, G. A., and Gabreels, F. (1997). The prevalence of mental retardation: a critical review of recent literature. *Developmental Medicine and Child Neurology*, **39**, 125–132.

Trocmé, N., MacLaurin, B., Fallon, B., Daciuk, J., Billingsley, D., Tourigny, M., Mayer, M., Wright, J., Barter, K., Burford, G., Hornick, J., Sullivan, R., and McKenzie, B. (2001). *Canadian incidence study of reported child abuse and neglect: Final report.* Ottawa, ON: Minister of public Works and Government Services Canada.

Westcott, H. L. and Jones, D. P. H. (1999). The abuse of disabled children. *Journal of Child Psychology and Psychiatry and Allied Disciplines*, **40**(4), 497–506.

Yu, D. and Atkinson, L. (1993). Developmental disability with and without psychiatric involvement: Prevalence estimates for Ontario. *Journal on Developmental Disabilities*, **2**(1), 92–99.

8.6. AFFILIATION

Ivan Brown is Director of the Disability Support Unit, Centre for Health Promotion, University of Toronto, Canada.

Mark Peterson

9. CLIMATE AS A COMPONENT OF OBJECTIVE QUALITY OF LIFE IN COUNTRIES OF THE WORLD

ABSTRACT: A unique contribution of this study is the explicit inclusion of a natural endowment for a country – climate – in a theoretical framework for objective QOL. This study investigates the relationship of climate favorableness for the world's countries with other objective QOL indicators previously researched. The group of higher-QOL countries is compared with the group of lower-QOL countries on climate favorableness, as well as on the correlations among the dimensions of objective QOL in each group of countries. Finally, confirmatory factor analysis with latent variables is employed within each group of countries to understand the underlying relationships of climate with other indicators of country QOL.

9.1. Introduction

Interest in economic geography has revived in recent years as scholars have broadened their view about influential variables in country development. Previously, scholars had presented geographical determinism to explain country development almost exclusively through geographical endowments (Mellinger, Sachs, and Gallup, 2000). From the end of World War II through the mid 1980's, such a narrow notion of country development prompted a backlash against the study of economic geography in much of the academic world because it smacked of racism and undermined the concept of equal opportunity among nations and individuals (Hausmann, 2001). At about the same time of economic geography's temporary wane, social indicators research began in earnest with the establishment of the social science journal *Social Indicators Research* (Sirgy, 2001: 14). Not surprisingly, geography has been an almost invisible element on the landscape of country QOL research since the beginning of QOL scholarship.

Both climate and topography have been cited as being important elements of geography, and as being influential in developing the markets and living standards of locales around the world (Cateora, 1996). In explaining country prosperity, some scholars have focused on the set of enabling conditions that leads to increased economic productivity. In this view, prosperity can be conceptualized as a set of stocks or capital upon which a society can draw (Fairbanks, 2000). Natural endowments, such as location, subsoil assets, forests, beaches and climate lead the list of such stocks. In keeping with a broadened view of influential variables in country development, other stocks would be used in country development. Such stocks would include 1) financial capital, 2) infrastructure assets (for example, roads, as well as grids for electrical energy and telecommunication transmissions), 3) institutional capital (for example, legal systems that actually work), and 4) social capital (such as skills, R&D capabilities, and cultural attitudes toward innovation).

This view of prosperity as a set of capital or stocks on which to draw provides scholars both with a theoretical perspective close to those of researchers of

M. Joseph Sirgy et al. (eds.), Advances in Quality-of-Life Theory and Research, 143–162, 2003.

objective QOL (Peterson and Malhotra, 1997), and also with new theoretical breadth. Not only is prosperity conceptualized as being close to other definitions of objective QOL, but now a distinctly natural endowment of countries is included with the usual man-made features of countries, such as economic life, infrastructure, and culture. According to Sirgy (2001), thirteen measures of overall country QOL are currently in widespread use. While four of these address ecological conservation, only one – the Weighted Index of Social Progress (WISP) (Estes, 1988) – addresses natural endowments of nations in some direct way. Here, the WISP includes the arable land mass of countries, and susceptibility to natural disasters among 45 elements for overall country QOL. By comparison, Fairbanks' (2000) conception that natural endowments include location, subsoil assets, forests, beaches and climate offers a more complete view of geography's potential influence on country QOL. In this way, Fairbanks makes an important theoretical contribution – natural endowments (not just the preservation of what is endowed) are now explicitly conceived as being ingredients to prosperity or objective QOL.

After a review of recent research on climate and country development, this study will investigate the relationship of climate favorableness for the world's countries with indicators of objective QOL or standards of living that mirror the dimensions of Fairbanks' framework. Such indicators will include 1) cost of living, 2) culture and recreation, 3) economy, 4) environment, 5) freedom, 6) health, 7) infrastructure, and 8) personal safety. Correlation analysis and confirmatory factor analysis with latent variables will allow conceptual insights into the current situation faced by developing countries of the world in their pursuit of improved quality of life.

9.2. CLIMATE AND COUNTRY DEVELOPMENT

Two main branches have emerged in the "new economic geography" – clusters of activity (such as Silicon Valley in California for software development), and regional growth disparities (Economist, 1999). Although geographers decry these revivals of what was studied more than thirty years ago by scholars of geography proper (Martin, 1999), the new economic geographers, like Paul Krugman, have brought more sophisticated modeling approaches than what was attempted thirty years ago (Krugman, 1995).

Climate figures most directly in the regional-growth disparity debate. According to neo-classical economic-growth theorists, incomes across regions should converge because of the greater diminishing returns to the investments made by developed countries. In this view, poor regions should catch up (Economist, 1999). But empirically, this proposed convergence has occurred much more slowly than the standard neoclassical growth model would predict. For example, 1997 estimates of the richest twenty per cent of the world's population were 74 times the income of the lowest twenty per cent. In 1960, income estimates of the top twenty per cent of developed countries were 30 times those of the lowest twenty per cent.

Critics of the new economic geography would assert that scholars of traditional geography long ago recognized the limits of formal mathematical modeling in making predictions of such complex phenomena as country development. Accordingly, geographers turned away from advances in modeling. As a result, "Geographers became more interested in real economic landscapes with all their complex histories and local contexts and particularities." (Martin, 1999: 66).

Indeed, some of the new economic geographers imply the role of weather as a causal factor in slowing the convergence of regional incomes by referring to "tropical countries", instead of "third-world" or "underdeveloped" countries (Easterly, 2001). Others, like Sachs (2000), are direct in asserting that the temperate regions of the world are vastly more developed than the tropics. "We don't really have a North-South division in the world; instead, we have a temperate-tropical division" (Sachs, 2000: 32).

Indeed, temperate regions of the world are strikingly more developed than the tropical countries. Of the 24 countries classified as "industrial", not one lies between the Tropics of Cancer and Capricorn – except a bit of Australia and the Hawaiian Islands (Hausmann, 2001). In 1995, tropical countries had an average income equivalent to roughly one-third of the income of temperate zone countries. The slow convergence of incomes across regions predicted by neo-classical economic theorists can be seen in disparities in annual rates of economic growth. Tropical nations have rates of annual economic growth that are between one-half and a full percentage point lower than temperate zone countries. Previous centuries' philosophers, and social scientists fielded simplistic explanations for such latitude differences. For example, Montesquieu believed climate might have a direct effect on human temperament, work effort and social harmony (Mellinger, Sachs, and Gallup, 2000). During times of colonial rule and widespread embracing of social Darwinism, such ideas were popular.

Some social scientists have argued that climate helps determine the means of production – small farming in the temperate regions, plantation farming in the tropics. With such profound effect on production, climate would thereby indirectly affect the organization of society and the possibilities for development.

While rejecting notions from past eras regarding climate's links with race, work effort or culture, the new economic geographers view climate as one of many important influences on development. Coastal location (with resulting lower transportation costs and with increased access to markets and to technological new approaches and ideas) would be another dimension of geography critical to development.

Three reasons for tropical countries being consistently poorer than temperate ones have been recently offered. Agricultural factors, health factors and factors related to the mobilization of scientific resources (Sachs, 2000). Eurasia's east-west geographical layout and the north-south layout in Africa and the Americas have influenced historical patterns of agricultural innovation and thus, economic growth (Diamond, 1997). Because climate changes little with longitude, but markedly with latitude, the countries of Eurasia happily had fairly common climatic conditions. Such uniformity would therefore, allow agricultural innovations developed in one region to travel long distances and be shared by many regions. On the contrary, new agricultural varieties developed in the tropics of Africa or the Americas could not travel very far before the climate changed dramatically.

Other problems unique to agriculture in the tropics have reduced productivity of perennial crops and staple foods, especially: 1) weak soils, high soil erosion and depletion of nutrients due to tropical rain forest conditions, 2) difficulties of water control and risk of drought in wet-dry tropics, 3) high incidence of pests, and 4) high rate of spoilage for food in storage (Sachs, 2000).

The incidence of infectious disease is also higher in the tropics. Flies and mosquitoes that flourish in the warm climate carry major vector-borne diseases, such as malaria, hookworm, schistasomiasis, river blindness, and yellow fever. Because the afflicted countries tend to be poor and underdeveloped with respect to the temperate countries, tropical diseases do not receive R&D investments that instead might be directed to cures for baldness in Western markets (Hausmann, 2001).

In sum, changes in latitude have had a profound inhibiting effect on the diffusion of technological innovations to the tropics in crucial sectors for development, such as agriculture, health and construction (Sachs, 2000). Despite criticisms of economic globalization, it appears that increased globalization in these economic sectors could help overcome what has been called "the tyranny of geography" in the tropics.

When considering the needed linkages between R&D advances in the temperate countries and those of the tropics, recent warnings about global warming would suggest that the temperate and tropical countries are already linked in an ecological sense (Timoshenko, 1992). With ongoing encroachments on rain forests and wetlands in the tropics, the temperate-zone countries are thus impacted by development activities in the tropics (Schultz and Holbrook, 1999). Ominously, environmental degradation today can be much worse in developing countries than developed ones (Blaikie, 1985; Sponsel et al., 1996; Thompson and Nachtwey, 1991). With such trends, researchers should note that the theoretical causal paths might be becoming bi-directional with development now influencing climate (specifically, deforestation), as well as the historically theorized relationship of climate influencing development.

9.3. CLIMATE AS A DIMENSION OF COUNTRY OBJECTIVE QOL

QOL studies can be classified by their focus on subjective well-being (SWB – perceptions of life satisfaction), or on objective well-being (OWB – material conditions of life) (Paim, 1995; Sirgy, 2001). This study addresses objective QOL, as climate is one of the material conditions of life.

One of the 22 QOL indexes recently evaluated by Hagerty et al (2001) for use in national public policy is the objective QOL index produced annually by *International Living* (IL). For the past eighteen years, IL has rated countries on multiple dimensions using a 0–100 interval scale. IL is a publication with more than 50,000 subscribers worldwide. Its annual QOL index uses a variety of statistical inputs from secondary sources, as well as primary sources (a network of several dozen writers stationed around the globe). IL's QOL ratings have demonstrated high year-to-year reliability (Peterson, Malhotra, and Kleiser, 1998). In their evaluation of QOL indices, Hagerty et al. (2001) gave IL's rating a higher evaluation for public policy use than the UN's Human Development Index (HDI).

In previous studies, IL's ratings have allowed rigorous examination of the underlying dimensions of objective QOL across the countries of the OECD (Peterson and Malhotra, 1995), and across the countries of the world (Peterson and Malhotra, 1997). In a recent study, two tiers of countries appeared to emerge when analyzing country QOL – the "haves" (with higher objective QOL) and "have nots" (with lower objective QOL).

Currently, IL rates countries on nine dimensions: 1) freedom, 2) safety, 3) infrastructure, 4) economy, 5) cost of living, 6) culture and recreation, 7) environment, 8) health, and 9) climate. One previous study (Peterson and Malhotra, 1997) showed how the seven dimensions of IL's QOL study at that time were very similar to other QOL dimension sets used to study small business and entrepreneurship (Morris and Lewis, 1991). Another previous study showed the matching of IL's dimensions to those used to by scholars to study foreign direct investment (Peterson, Malhotra, and Wagner, 1999).

In 2000, IL introduced a safety and risk dimension (Peterson, 2000), and in 2001 a climate dimension was introduced for the first time. IL operationalized its climate dimension by incorporating 1) average temperature for countries, 2) average annual rainfall, and 3) risk for natural disasters. Table 9.1 presents IL's nine dimensions of QOL in more detail.

IL's recent introduction of a separate indicator representing climate provides an opportunity for QOL researchers to obtain theoretical insights into the relation of

Table 9.1. Elements of *International Living's* Dimensions for Objective QOL.

Dimension	Elements
• Cost Of Living (favorability)	– US State Dept. Index of Overseas Living Costs, and income taxes.
• Culture	– Literacy rate, newspaper circ. per 1,000, primary and secondary school enrollment ratios, museums.
• Economy	– GDP per capita, GDP growth, inflation.
• Environment	– Population density, population growth, greenhouse gas emissions per capita, "total land/protected land".
• Freedom	– Citizen's political rights and civil liberties.
• Health	– Calorie consumption, physicians, hospital beds per 1,000, safe water access, infant mortality, life expectancy, "public health expenditures/country GDP".
• Infrastructure	– Railways, highways, airports, waterways, ISPs, phones, motor vehicles, radios.
• Safety & Risk	– US State Department's hardship differentials and danger allowances.
• Climate	– Average annual rainfall, average temperature, and risk for natural disasters.

climate and QOL. Previous to this, climate was either ignored by researchers of objective QOL (likely because climate was considered to be a natural endowment which could not be modified by human intervention), or was considered as a part of the ecological environment (Cravens and Hills, 1978; Pepptelenbosch and Tempelman, 1989; Morris, Sexton, and Lewis, 1995). However, in research of tourism and QOL, Ritchie (1987) identified climate as a factor in destination attractiveness. In Ritchie's view, climate influenced the attractiveness of a tourist region in five measurable ways: 1) amount of sunshine, 2) temperature, 3) winds, 4) precipitation, and 5) a discomfort index. In this way, Ritchie's framework suggests climate's inclusion as a distinct factor of country QOL.

Research of business relocation decisions using a behavioral approach has provided empirical support for climate's positive relationship with two dimensions of QOL. Love and Crompton (1999) submitted scaled survey items to 174 key decision-makers in businesses that had relocated, expanded or been launched in Colorado in a five-year period. In the subsequent factor analysis of these items, five factors emerged: 1) QOL, 2) labor and cost issues, 3) government involvement and taxes, 4) daily living concerns, and 5) proximity to relevant publics. The scaled item for climate/weather loaded on the first factor – QOL – along with items representing other traditional QOL dimensions, such as cultural and recreational opportunities, as well as environmental quality. Based on these results, climate would be expected to be positively related with two dimensions of IL's QOL index – culture and environment.

Fairbanks (2000) provides a conceptual framework for climate's positive relationship with other dimensions of QOL. Based on the work of Ray (1998), Fairbanks (2000) proposes a view of prosperity that is similar to one for objective QOL. Here, prosperity is regarded as both a flow (ability) and a set of stocks or capital. According to Fairbanks (2000), such flows and stocks provide the following: "the ability of an individual, group, or nation to provide shelter, nutrition, and other material goods that enable people to live a good life, according to their own definition" (Fairbanks, 2000: 270). Sen has also elaborated on the conceptualization of flows and stocks as applied to national wealth (Sen, 1996).

Table 9.2 presents a comparison between Fairbanks' (2000) physical and social capital of prosperity with the nine dimensions of IL. As can be seen, each of Fairbanks' dimensions for prosperity has a corresponding dimension in IL's scheme for QOL. The point of this is to show the theoretical basis for climate being positively related to the other eight dimensions of objective QOL.

Based on the empirical findings of Love and Crompton (1999), and on Fairbanks' analogous rendition of objective QOL, eight hypotheses are proposed for empirical evaluation using the 2001 IL QOL Index. Climate is hypothesized to be positively related to the eight other dimensions of objective QOL. For the favorability of cost of living (H_1), the proposed relationship is based on the financial reserves of a nation being one of the stocks of prosperity or objective QOL (Fairbanks, 2000). In addition, Sachs' (2000) work shows the difficulties of overcoming weak soils, and of surmounting challenges for water and food storage in

Table 9.2. Fairbanks' (2000) Prosperity Stocks (or Capital) and Corresponding Dimensions for Objective QOL.

Fairbanks (2000)	*International Living* (2001)
1. Natural endowments, such as location, subsoil assets forests, beaches, and climate.	Environment
2. Financial resources of a nation, such as savings and international reserves.	Economy, and Cost of Living (favorability)
3. Humanly made capital, such as buildings, bridges, roads, and telecommunications assets.	Infrastructure
4. Institutional capital, such as legal protections of tangible and intangible property, efficient government departments, and firms that maximize value to shareholders and compensate and train workers.	Freedom, Safety & Risk, Health, and Economy
5. Knowledge resources, such as international patents, and university and think-tank capabilities.	Economy
6. Human capital, which represents skills, insights, and capabilities.	Economy
7. Culture capital, which means not only the explicit articulations of culture like music, language, and ritualistic tradition but also attitudes and values that are linked to innovation.	Culture

harsh climates. Agricultural problems imposed or exacerbated by a harsh climate would contribute to a higher cost of living.

For culture (H_2), Fairbanks' conceptualization of culture being a stock of prosperity or objective QOL is complemented by the empirical work of Love and Crompton (1999) who found culture to be positively related to climate in their business relocation study. For the vitality of national economies (H_3), Fairbanks proposes that knowledge and human capital are also stocks of prosperity or objective QOL. Additionally, Hausmann reports that tropical countries had income levels only a third of the income levels of countries with temperate climates. For the environment (H_4), Love and Crompton's work offered empirical support for the positive linkage between climate and the environment. Additionally, environmental degradation can be much worse in the developing countries that are also non-temperate.

For freedom (H_5), Fairbanks regards freedom as one of the outcomes of institutional capital – another stock of prosperity or objective QOL. For health (H_6), the challenges for overcoming malaria and other pest-borne diseases in non-temperate climates would be greater. Therefore, health and climate would be positively related. For infrastructure (H_7), Fairbanks conceives of humanly made capital as being one of the stocks of prosperity. Additionally, increased difficulties would be encountered in establishing and maintaining elements of infrastructure (roads, bridges, sewer systems, ports, airports, as well as communication and energy grids) in non-temperate climates. For personal risk (H8), is hypothesized to be positively related to climate because of the increased institutional capital in temperate-climate countries, such as effective systems of justice, and government departments.

H_{1-8}: Climate will be positively related to each of the other dimensions of objective QOL.

This study also seeks to examine the question of whether climate actually matters in overall objective QOL for countries. Based on the work of the new economic geographers (Sachs, 2000), we propose that countries with high QOL and countries with low QOL will differ on their climate rating. Therefore, we propose a ninth hypothesis:

H9: The group of countries with higher objective QOL will post a higher rating on the climate variable than the group of countries with lower objective QOL.

Finally, we will utilize the dichotomy of "haves" and "have nots" cited previously by Peterson and Malhotra (2000) to better understand the correlations between the QOL dimensions in both underlying structure for objective QOL using covariance analysis (Norusis 1990; Bollen, 1989). No specific hypothesis will be proposed for this modeling effort that is exploratory in nature. These factor analyses include IL's new variables of safety and risk, and climate for the first time.

9.4. RESULTS

Figure 9.1 depicts the frequency distribution of the climate variable for the 199 countries evaluated. The mean value for climate across these countries is 68.1 with a standard deviation of 18.94. The distribution has a negative skew with a longer tail on the left of Figure 9.1. Countries scoring high on the climate variable include Senegal (98) and Burundi (94). Those scoring worst were Mongolia and Oman (both with 10).

Table 9.3 presents the results of computing correlations between climate and the other eight IL variables for objective QOL across the 199 countries. As can be seen, all of the Pearson product correlation coefficients are positive in sign. Six of the eight correlation coefficients are statistically significant at $p = 0.05$ and are noted with an asterisk. The binary correlations for climate and cost of living (H_1), as well as for climate and health (H_6) are not statistically significant at $p = 0.05$. Therefore, six of the eight proposed hypotheses were supported.

The final index score for QOL is a weighted average of the nine variables comprising IL's QOL Index. Each of the variables receives a ten per-cent weighting in IL's scheme for computing this composite score with the exception of Cost of Living and Economy which both receive a fifteen per-cent weighting. The mean of this final score for QOL is 50.5 with a standard deviation of 11.11. A median split was used on the frequency distribution of this final index score for QOL to divide the 199 countries into a lower-QOL group ($n = 100$) and a higher-QOL group ($n = 99$). A complete listing of the countries comprising the two groups

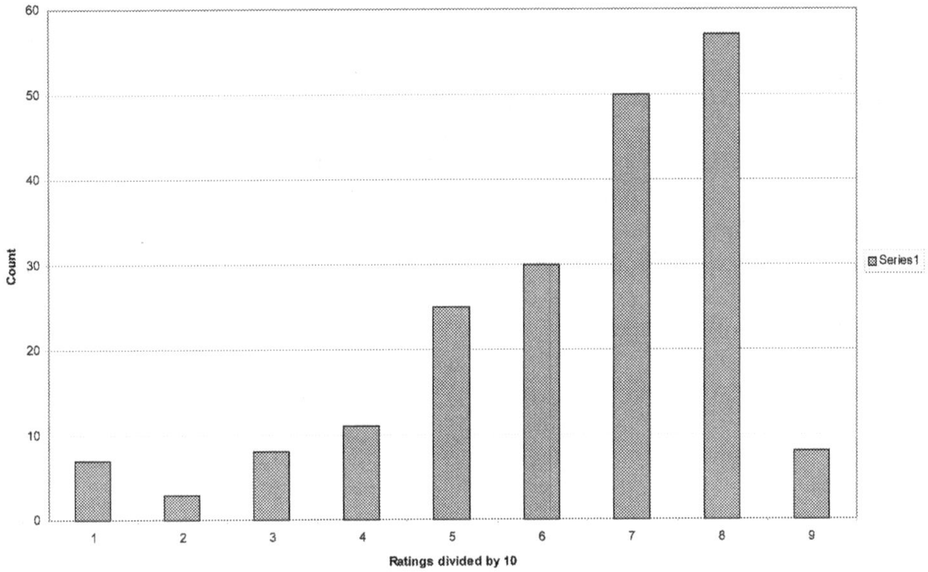

Figure 9.1. Frequency Distribution for Country Climate Ratings.

along with the countries' ratings on the climate variable and the countries' final index score for QOL are included in Tables A9.1 and A9.2.

On the climate variable, the lower-QOL group – the "have nots" – has a mean of 61.8 and a standard deviation of 22.06. The higher-QOL group – the "haves" – has a mean of 74.4 and a standard deviation of 12.37 on the climate variable. In short, the higher-QOL group has a noticeably different mean value on the same climate variable, as well as less dispersion about the mean. In evaluating H_9 to see if the higher-QOL group had a statistically higher value on the climate variable than the lower-QOL group, a *t*-test was utilized (Norusis, 1990). This test returned a *t*-value of 4.95 with 195 degrees of freedom. This result was statistically significant at $p = 0.05$, and provided support for H_9.

Table 9.3. Pearson Correlations for Eight Objective QOL Dimensions and Climate – Total Group.

	Col H_1	*p*	Cult H_2	*p*	Econ H_3	*p*	Enviro H_4	*p*
Climate	0.03	0.66	0.15*	0.03	0.24*	0.00	0.19*	0.01

	Freedom H_5	*p*	Health H_6	*p*	Infra H_7	*p*	Safety H_9	*p*
Climate	0.23*	0.00	0.12	0.09	0.2*	0.01	0.15*	0.04

* Correlation coefficient is statistically significant at $p = 0.05$.

The final analysis consisted of sub-group analysis for the lower and higher QOL groups. Pearson product correlations were computed for all binary relationships among the objective QOL dimensions. These are presented side-by-side in Table 9.6. As can be seen, some of the same binary relationships have correlations that are opposite in sign across the lower and higher QOL groups. Such opposing sets of correlation coefficients are outlined with boxes in Table 9.4. Of the 36 unique sets of correlation coefficient pairs in Table 9.4, nine of these sets have correlation coefficients that are noticeably opposed in sign. Each of the nine objective QOL dimensions of this study is involved in at least one of these sets of opposite-signed binary relationships. Such results underline the possibly different nature of the phenomena occurring in countries with higher QOL than in countries with lower QOL. Some economists have referred to a "take-off" point in economic development where rapid and sustained productivity growth occurs (Porter, 2000). In terms of objective QOL relationships, this would seem to correspond to a point where the relationships among some of these objective QOL relationships (such as those outlined with boxes in Table 9.4) would actually reverse themselves in sign.

Noteworthy for our current study, climate and economy have a –0.17 correlation for the higher-QOL group and a 0.31 correlation for the lower-QOL group. This suggests that a more temperate climate would seem to be found with those countries in the lower-QOL group that are above the average for this group in terms of the final QOL index score. Likewise, less temperate climates would be found with those countries in the lower-QOL group that are below the average for this group in terms of the final QOL index score. In short, climate and progress in QOL move together in the lower-QOL countries.

The negative correlation between climate and economy in the higher-QOL group suggests that less favorable climatic conditions are associated with the best economies. This finding implies that other factors, such as the social capital as proposed by Fairbanks (2000) are overcoming the drag that climate makes on the attainments of the highest scoring countries on the final QOL index score.

Following correlation analysis, factor analysis was conducted using both the common factor analysis technique, as well as confirmatory factor analysis using structural equation modeling (Bollen, 1989; Hair et al., 1998). Both of these techniques were executed using the data of the separate groups for lower and higher QOL. The outcome of these analyses can be seen in the different resulting factor structures in both groups.

Figure 9.2 depicts the underlying factor structure for the lower-QOL group that was modeled using confirmatory factor analysis. The model chi-square was 32.3 with 23 df ($p = 0.095$) and a comparative fit index (CFI) of 0.93 (Bentler, 1990). During the exploratory factor analysis using the maximum likelihood extraction with oblimin rotation, three factors were extracted which are labeled as 1) Temperate Climate, 2) Social Development, and 3) Environmental Disregard. All depicted factor loadings were statistically significant at $p = 0.05$. Both climate and economy loaded positively on the Temperate Climate factor with climate being the more dominant item in identifying this factor. Social Development was identified by the high

Table 9.6. Pearson Correlations for Objective QOL Dimensions for High-QOL and Low-QOL Country Groups.

	hi-qol col	**lo-qol col**	hi-qol cult	**lo-qol cult**	hi-qol econ	**lo-qol econ**	hi-qol enviro	**lo-qol enviro**	hi-qol freedom	**lo-qol freedom**	hi-qol health	**lo-qol health**	hi-qol infra	**lo-qol infra**	hi-qol safety	**lo-qol safety**
Col	1.00	**1.00**														
Cult	–0.21	**0.03**	1.00	**1.00**												
Econ	–0.36	**0.19**	0.51	**0.34**	1.00	**1.00**										
Enviro	0.08	**0.21**	0.17	**0.11**	–0.17	**0.20**	1.00	**1.00**								
Freedom	–0.33	**–0.10**	0.34	**–0.22**	0.28	**–0.04**	0.03	**–0.32**	1.00	**1.00**						
Health	–0.16	**0.13**	0.44	**0.63**	0.50	**0.27**	–0.01	**0.08**	0.31	**–0.24**	1.00	**1.00**				
Infra	–0.35	**0.20**	0.44	**0.25**	0.58	**0.06**	–0.05	**0.25**	0.45	**–0.21**	0.39	**0.26**	1.00	**1.00**		
Safety	–0.33	**–0.34**	0.17	**0.09**	0.34	**0.05**	–0.15	**–0.34**	0.30	**0.32**	0.19	**–0.01**	0.28	**–0.21**	1.00	**1.00**
Climate	–0.13	**0.00**	–0.21	**–0.03**	–0.17	**0.31**	0.04	**0.14**	–0.01	**0.03**	–0.13	**–0.12**	0.01	**0.03**	0.05	**–0.08**

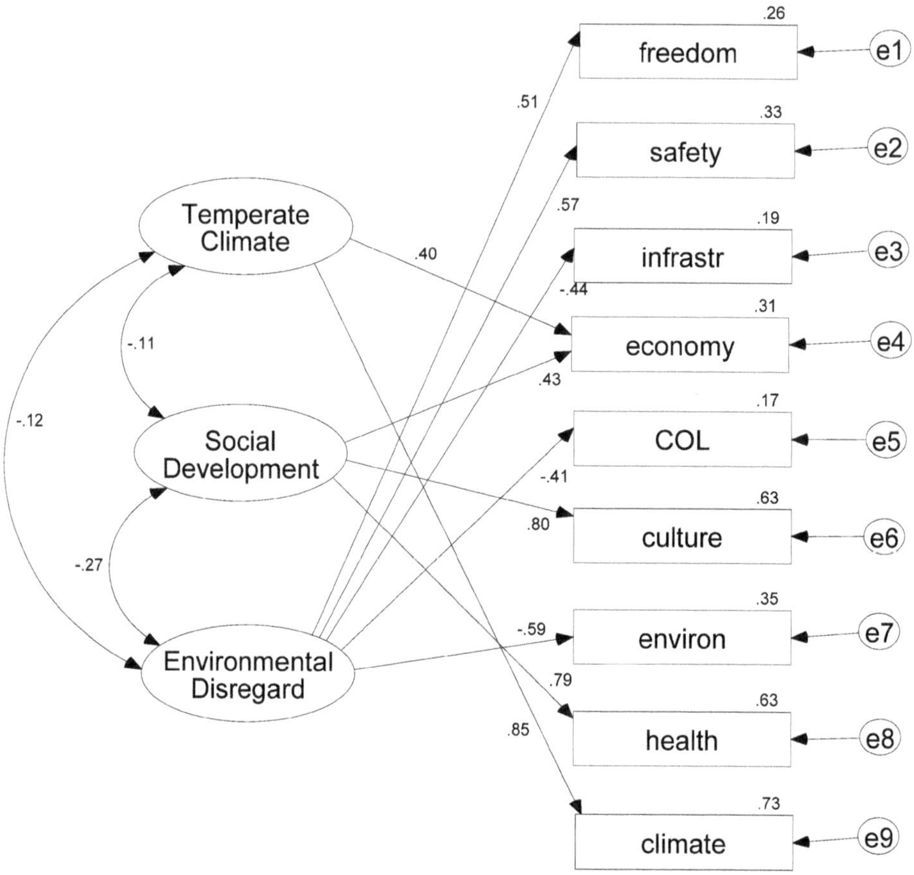

Figure 9.2. Lower-QOL-Country Confirmatory Factor Analysis: Chi-square = 32.3, df = 23, p = 0.10, CFI = 0.93.

loadings for culture and recreation, as well as health. Economy was also an item that loaded on this Social Development factor. Finally, five items loaded on the Environmental Disregard factor. Both freedom, and safety and risk posted positive loadings, while environment, cost of living, and infrastructure each posted negative loadings.

These results from this multivariate analysis receive support from previously discussed theory and research. First, as discussed earlier, the new economic geography has reinforced the proposed theoretical connection between climate and economic development. Second, social development corresponds with the social capital stocks proposed by Fairbanks (2000) – institutional capital (health), knowledge resources and human capital (economy), and culture capital (culture). Third, Environmental Disregard is manifested by its loadings on five objective QOL dimensions.

The story emerging about environmental degradation in the Third World is similar to the pattern of loadings returned in the exploratory factor analysis. As preliminary development occurs, infrastructure and cost of living favorableness improves, environmental degradation declines. The final two loadings suggest that as social institutions related to freedom, as well as safety and risk improve, so would environmental degradation. This becomes more understandable when thinking of countries moving out of subsistence farming or social collapse, such as Cambodia or Haiti. Here, initial moves by more citizens to seek individual prosperity in a new era of social history for their countries could likely result in environmental setbacks, such as deforestation (Sponsel et al., 1996).

The only correlation between the factors of the model that was statistically significant at $p = 0.05$ was that between Social Development and Environmental Disregard. This association of –0.27 also supports the idea that the less developed countries of this lower-QOL group will be prone to environmental mismanagement. The lack of association between Temperate Climate and the other two factors suggests that having a temperate climate is very weakly related to Social Development and Environmental Disregard.

Figure 9.3 depicts the underlying factor structure for the higher-QOL group that was modeled using confirmatory factor analysis. The model chi-square was 27.9 with 23 df ($p = 0.022$) and a comparative fit index (CFI) of 0.97 (Bentler, 1990). During the exploratory factor analysis using the maximum likelihood extraction with oblimin rotation, three factors were extracted which are similar, but nevertheless distinct from those of the lower-QOL group. These factors are labeled as 1) Smooth Operations, 2) Social Development, and 3) Environmental Regard. All depicted factor loadings were statistically significant at $p = 0.05$. Both freedom, safety and risk, and infrastructure all loaded positively on the Smooth Operations factor, while the cost of living favorableness item loaded negatively on this factor. Social Development was identified by the high positive loadings for economy, culture and recreation, as well as health. The climate item loaded negatively on Social Development. Finally, two items loaded on the Environmental Regard factor. Environment posted a positive loading, while economy posted a negative loading. The emergence of this factor suggests that environmental protection and economy are inversely related in the higher-QOL group. In other words, more environmental protection occurs in the less thriving economies of the higher-QOL group. This finding might occur because there is simply not as much environment to protect anymore in the most advanced economies. Ecuador would be an example of a country scoring high on the environment variable (86) in this higher-QOL group which has laws enacted to protect its wilderness areas. Conversely, the Netherlands would be an example of a country scoring low on the environment variable (58) most likely because it is the most densely populated country on earth.

The only correlation between the factors of the model that was statistically significant at $p = 0.05$ was that between Smooth Operations and Social Development. This association of 0.72 is very strong and suggests that the institutions in higher-QOL countries are highly functional, which in turn reinforces support for these

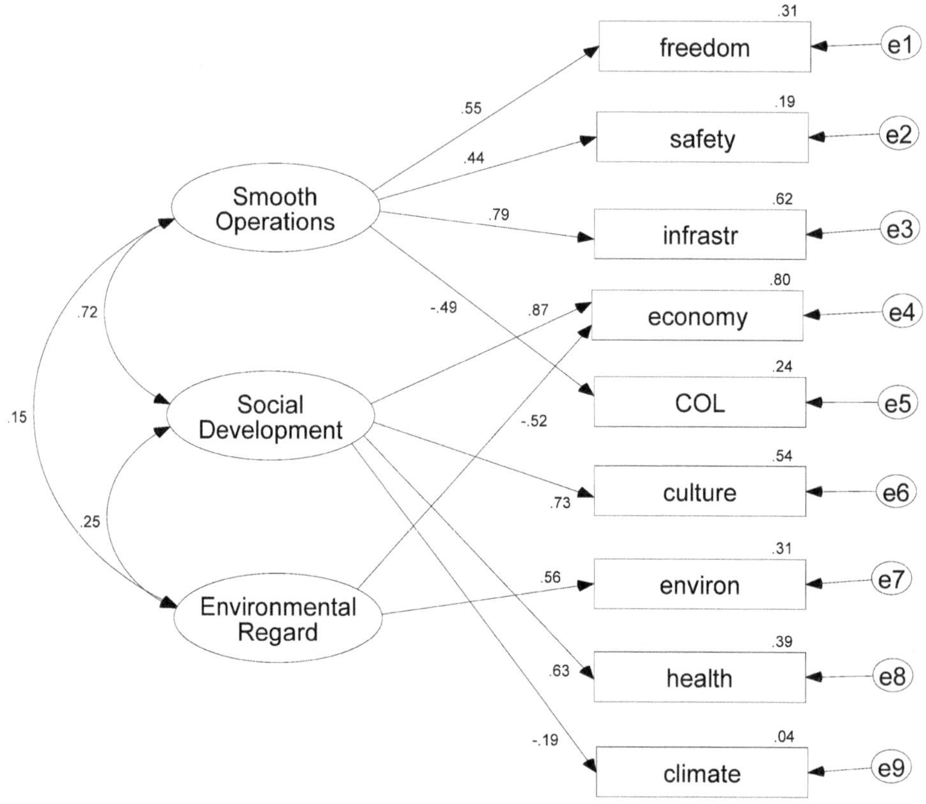

Figure 9.3. Higher-QOL-Country Confirmatory Factor Analysis: Chi-square = 27.9, df = 23, p = 0.22, CFI = 0.97.

institutions from the citizens of the higher-QOL countries. The lack of association between Environmental Regard and the other two factors suggests that regard for the environment in these higher-QOL countries is no more than weakly related to the stocks and flows of prosperity as represented by Social Development and Smooth Operations, respectively.

9.5. DISCUSSION

A unique contribution of this study is the explicit inclusion of a natural endowment – climate – in a theoretical framework for objective QOL. In short, the results of this study highlight the importance of climate in overall country QOL. Specifically, climate has the strongest binary correlation (which is positive in sign) with economic vitality than with any other dimension of objective QOL investigated in this study. But when high and low-QOL countries are examined separately using both simple and sophisticated correlation analysis, climate's relationship with economic vitality becomes more complex. In the group of high-QOL countries, climate has an inverse relationship with economic vitality. This suggests that objective QOL in countries of the world with lower levels of objective QOL is more dependent on a natural endowment, such as climate, than in countries of the world with higher QOL. Looking again at Figure 9.3, it appears that improvements in the non-climate dimensions of QOL comprising the Social Development construct (specifically, economy, culture, and health) might be the principal dimensions higher-QOL countries have emphasized in becoming less dependent on their geography. In a sense, the high-QOL countries have found ways to liberate themselves from "the tyranny of geography". As this study highlights, high-QOL societies now draw more on stocks of social capital, such as economic, cultural, or health-care systems, than on stocks of natural endowments.

The standardized loadings for the manifest variables of the three constructs in Figures 9.2 and 9.3 correspond, in general, to those found in earlier studies (Peterson and Malhotra, 1998). For example, in high-QOL countries, the favorableness of cost of living is inversely related to country development. For example, highly developed countries, such as Switzerland and Japan, typically have less favorable costs for living. This relationship can be seen in the negative relationship (standardized loading of –0.49) between cost of living and the Smooth Operations construct.

9.6. CONCLUSION

Our study used an empirical set of objective QOL indicators to understand the relationship between climate and objective quality of life (QOL). Specifically, this study investigated the relationship of climate favorableness for the world's countries with other indicators of objective QOL or standards of living. Such indicators included 1) cost of living, 2) culture and recreation, 3) economy, 4) environment, 5) freedom, 6) health, 7) infrastructure, and 8) personal safety. Using correlation analysis, support was found for six of eight proposed hypotheses proposing a positive relationship between climate and these other eight dimensions of objective QOL. In general, these statistically significant correlations in the total group of countries were small (economy and climate posted the highest correlation at 0.24). The two dimensions that were not found to have a statistically significant relationship with climate were 1) cost of living, and 2) health. More research is needed to understand the unexpected outcome of these two hypothesis tests.

By dividing the total group of 199 countries into lower and higher-QOL groups, the higher-QOL group was found to have a higher mean value on the climate variable than the lower-QOL group. This finding provided support for the ninth proposed hypothesis of this study. In all, seven of the nine hypotheses of this study were supported.

The sub-group analysis also allowed the observance of some striking differences existing between the correlations for the same binary relationships between objective QOL dimensions across the two groups of countries. This finding underlines the complex linkages between inputs and substantial improvements in objective

QOL. Subsequent to this comparative analysis, confirmatory factor analysis with latent variables allowed conceptual insights into the distinct development-related phenomena occurring across groups of lower-QOL countries and higher-QOL countries. In brief, the confirmatory factor analyses highlighted how environmental degradation looms for lower-QOL countries in their pursuit of improved objective QOL, and how environmental regard appears to be independent of social development in the higher-QOL countries. Together these insights lend support to repeated concern about the "tragedy of the commons" (Schultz and Holbrook, 1999), and the linkage between what transpires in the lower-QOL countries with what transpires in the higher-QOL countries.

Looking to future research, our study has demonstrated not only the connection between climate and prosperity, as well as climate and the other dimensions of objective QOL. Including disease ecology in the computation of a revised climate variable would be one step to refine the climate variable used in this study (Mellinger, Sachs, and Gallup, 2000). In this way, a formidable climate-related challenge to development in the tropics would be included.

Importantly, our study also demonstrated the value of examining lower and higher-QOL groups separately in sub-group analyses. Hausmann (2001) describes the dominant development paradigm these days as insisting that market-oriented economic policies and rule of law are all that matter for economic progress.

"In other words, Mozambique could become Singapore if it would only get its institutions and policies in order; in the meantime, we could alleviate poverty through targeted social spending for the poor, such as the financing of education for girls. But this mantra vastly oversimplifies the challenges of development" (Hausmann, 2001: 49).

The empirical results of our study support the complex differences between lower and higher-QOL countries. We look forward to development researchers joining us in using the lens of objective QOL to better understand the complex phenomena facing lower-QOL countries in their pursuit of improved QOL.

9.7. APPENDIX

Table A9.1. Higher-QOL-Country Climate Ratings and Final Scores.

Country	Clim.	Final	Country	Clim.	Final	Country	Clim.	Final
Andorra	73	59	Greece	69	63	New Zealand	75	71
Antigua & Barbuda	88	52	Grenada	88	57	Nicaragua	73	58
Argentina	83	60	Guatemala	83	56	Norway	67	69
Australia	82	72	Guyana	64	55	Panama	80	66
Austria	69	70	Honduras	91	58	Papua New Guinea	79	55
Bahamas	90	62	Hong Kong	78	56	Paraguay	88	60
Barbados	88	64	Hungary	69	65	Philippines	33	53
Belgium	77	68	Iceland	68	61	Poland	69	64
Belize	77	58	India	56	51	Portugal	83	69
Bermuda	90	57	Indonesia	70	51	Puerto Rico	71	56
Bolivia	75	57	Ireland	76	67	Romania	76	57
Botswana	84	54	Isle of Man	76	59	Seychelles	85	54
Brazil	82	53	Israel	86	58	Singapore	63	55
Bulgaria	73	61	Italy	78	68	Slovakia	74	55
Canada	61	73	Jamaica	78	58	Slovenia	76	65
Cayman Islands	88	59	Japan	74	64	South Africa	86	64
Channel Islands	78	59	Jordan	59	54	South Korea	74	64
Chile	41	59	Kuwait	52	50	Spain	67	64
Colombia	86	56	Latvia	67	61	Sri Lanka	65	54
Costa Rica	66	64	Liechtenstein	74	64	St. Kitts & Nevis	88	53
Croatia	84	56	Lithuania	73	58	Swaziland	85	51
Cyprus	38	56	Luxembourg	76	64	Sweden	64	67
Czech Rep	62	68	Macedonia	71	53	Switzerland	70	66
Denmark	72	69	Malawai	86	51	Thailand	57	57
Domican rep	88	59	Malaysia	56	57	Trinidad & Tobago	88	58
Dominica	88	53	Malta	75	57	Tunisia	74	52
Ecuador	85	61	Mauritius	85	60	Ukraine	72	51
El Salvador	63	55	Mexico	87	61	United Kingdom	76	67
Estonia	22	56	Moldova	70	54	United States	76	75
Fiji	71	54	Monaco	80	54	Uruguay	82	64
Finland	70	67	Morocco	81	52	Venezuela	82	59
France	82	75	Namibia	69	58	Zambia	91	51
Germany	72	66	Netherlands	77	70	Zimbabwe	87	56

Table A9.2. Lower-QOL-Country Climate Ratings and Final Scores.

Country	Clim.	Final	Country	Clim.	Final	Country	Clim.	Final
Afghanistan	54	23	French Polynesia	54	47	Niger	47	34
Albania	79	43	Gabon	82	43	Nigeria	82	44
Algeria	86	43	Gambia	93	43	North Korea	26	32
Angola	76	37	Georgia	71	46	Oman	10	42
Armenia	63	48	Ghana	89	47	Pakistan	69	41
Azerbaijan	34	44	Guinea	52	37	Palau	40	47
Bahrain	57	46	Guinea-bissau	74	44	Peru	41	45
Bangladesh	83	47	Haiti	80	43	Qatar	41	40
Belarus	71	48	Iran	55	45	Russia	66	48
Benin	73	49	Iraq	57	25	Rwanda	10	31
Bhutan	59	37	Kazakhstan	19	39	Samoa	64	42
Bosnia	74	34	Kenya	89	47	Saudi Arabia	57	46
Brunei	56	48	Kiribati	53	45	Senegal	98	48
Burkina Faso	46	40	Kyrgyzstan	24	40	Serbia	70	33
Burundi	94	32	Laos	75	40	Sierra Leone	51	32
Cambodia	64	43	Lebanon	89	48	Solomon Islands	70	42
Cameroon	85	43	Lesotho	83	48	Somalia	40	17
Cape Verde	65	48	Liberia	45	34	Sudan	13	28
Cen. African Rep.	87	47	Libya	61	43	Suriname	64	47
Chad	66	39	Macau	75	38	Syria	52	42
China	81	49	Madagascar	82	49	Taiwan	83	47
Comoros	75	42	Maldives	59	44	Tajikistan	54	37
Congo Dem. Rep.	89	36	Mali	65	41	Tanzania	77	46
Congo Rep of	89	37	Marshall Islands	45	41	Togo	83	44
Congo-Kinshassa	89	35	Martinique	75	48	Tonga	84	44
Cote d'Ivoire	86	46	Mauritania	48	37	Turkey	65	49
Cuba	90	48	Mayotte	55	36	Turkmenistan	52	36
Dijbouti	11	32	Micronesia	31	41	Tuvalu	34	44
Egypt	45	48	Mongolia	16	41	Uganda	87	45
Equitorial Guniea	80	39	Mozambique	60	35	Un. Arab Emirates	30	46
Eritrea	64	38	Myanmar	55	41	Uzbekistan	36	37
Ethiopia	80	44	Nauru	54	44	Vanuatu	36	38
French Guiana	57	41	Nepal	82	47	Viet Nam	83	48
						Yemen	12	31

9.8. REFERENCES

Bentler, P. M. (1990). Comparative fit indexes in structural models. *Psychological Bulletin*, **107**, 238–246.

Blaikie, P. M. (1985). *The Political Economy of Soil Erosion in Developing Countries*. New York: John Wiley and Sons.

Bollen, K. A. (1989). *Structural Equation Modeling with Latent Variables*. New York: John Wiley and Sons.

Cateora, P. R. (1996). *International Marketing*, ninth edition. Chicago, Irwin, 65.

Cravens, D. W. and Hills, G. E. (1978). Measurement issues in studying marketing and the quality of life. In F. D. Reynolds and H. C. Barksdale (eds.), *Marketing and the Quality of Life* (pp. 51–60). Chicago: American Marketing Association.

Diamond, J. (1997). *Guns, Germs, and Steel: The Fates of Human Societies*. New York: W.W. Norton & Company.

Easterly, W. (2001). *The Elusive Quest for Growth*. Cambridge, MA: The MIT Press.

Economist Staff (1999). Knowing your place. *The Economist* (March 13), 92.

Estes, R. J. (1988). *Trends in World Social Development*. New York: Praeger.

Fairbanks, M. (2000). Changing the Mind of a Nation: Elements in a Process for Creating Prosperity. In L. E. Harrison and S. P. Huntington (eds.), *Culture Matters: How Values Shape Human Progress* (pp. 268–281). New York: Basic Books.

Finlay, R. and Galvin, L. (2001). 2001 Quality of life index. *International Living*, **20**(9), 1–10.

Fisk, G. (1974). *Marketing and the Ecological Crisis*. New York: Harper and Row.

Hair, J. F., Jr., Anderson, R. E., Tatham, R. L. and Black, W. C. (1998). *Multivariate Data Analysis*, 4th edition. New York, NY: MacMillan.

Hausmann, R. (2001). Prisoners of geography. *Foreign Policy* (January/February), 45–53.

Hagerty, M. R., Cummins, R., Ferriss, A. L., Land, K., Michalos, A. C., Peterson, M., Sharpe, A., Sirgy, M. J., and Vogel, J. (2001). Quality of life indexes for national policy: review and agenda for research. *Social Indicators Research*, **55**(1), July 2001, 1–96.

Hardin, G. (1968). The tragedy of the commons. *Science*, **162**, 1243–1248.

Inter-American Development Bank (2000). Geography and development in *Development Beyond Economics: Economic and Social Progress in Latin America 2000 Report*.

Krugman, P. (1995). *Development, Geography and Economic Theory*. Cambridge, MA: MIT Press.

Malhotra, N. K. and Peterson, M. (2001). Marketing research in the new millennium: emerging Issues and Trends. *Marketing Intelligence and Planning*, **19**(4), 216–235.

Malhotra, N. K. and Peterson, M. (2000). *Marketing Research: An Applied Orientation*, 3rd edition. Upper Saddle River, NJ: Prentice Hall.

Malhotra, N. K., Peterson, M., and Kleiser, S. B. (1998). Assessing the reliability and validity of international secondary data used to design competitive strategies for global marketing. In A. Manrai and L. Manrai (eds.), *Research in Marketing, Vol. 14, Designing Competitive Strategies for Global Marketing* (pp. 185–228). Stamford, CT: JAI Press.

Malhotra, N. K., Agarwal, J., and Peterson, M. (1996). Methodological issues in cross-cultural marketing research: a state-of-the-art review. *International Marketing Review*, **13**(5), 7–43.

Martin, R. (1999). The new 'geographical' turn in economics. *Cambridge Journal of Economics*, **23**(1) (January), 65–92.

Mellinger, A. D., Sachs, J. D., and Gallup, J. L. (2000). Climate, coastal proximity, and development. In G. L. Clark, M. P. Feldman, and M. S. Gertler (eds.), The Oxford Handbook of Economic Geography (pp. 169–194). Oxford, UK: Oxford University Press.

Morris, M., Sexton, D. L., and Lewis, P. L. (1995). Small business, entrepreneurship, and quality of life: a growth perspective. In M. J. Sirgy and A. C. Samli (eds.), *New Dimensions in Marketing/Quality-of-Life Research* (pp. 71–94). Westport, CT: Quorum Books.

Morris, M. and Lewis, P. L. (1991). Entrepreneurship as a significant factor in societal quality of life. *Journal of Business Research*, **23** (August), 21–36.

Norusis, M. (1990). *SPSS Advanced Statistics' User's Guide*. Chicago, IL: SPSS Inc.

Paim, L. (1995). Definitions and measurements of well-being: a review of literature. *Journal of Economic and Social Measurement*, **21**, 297–309.

Pepptelenbosch, P. and Tempelman, G. (1989). The pros and cons of international tourism to the third world. In S. V. Singh (ed.), *Towards Appropriate Tourism: The Case of Developing Countries*. Bern, Switzerland: Peter Lang Publishing.

Peterson, M. and Malhotra, N. K. (2000). Country segmentation based on objective quality-of life measures. *International Marketing Review*, **17**(1), 56–73.

Peterson, M. (2000). *Personal risk as a component of objective QOL*, paper presented at the ISQOLS Conference, Gerona, Spain, July 22.

Peterson, M., Malhotra, N. K., and Wagner, J. (1999). Country quality of life and foreign direct investment decisions. *Global Outlook*, **11**(1), 51–62.

Peterson, M. and Malhotra, N. K. (1997). Comparative marketing measures of societal quality of life: substantive dimensions in 186 countries. *Journal of Macromarketing*, **17** (1) (Spring), 25–38.

Peterson, M. and Malhotra, N. K. (1994). Global marketing: quality of life in OECD countries. In S. Neelamegham (ed.), *Competing Globally: Challenges and Opportunities* (pp. 153–161). New Delhi: Allied Publishers.

Porter, M. E. (2000). Attitudes, values, beliefs and the microeconomics of prosperity. In L. E. Harrison and S. P. Huntington (eds.), *Culture Matters: How Values Shape Human Progress* (pp. 14–28). New York: Basic Books.

Ray, D. (1998). *Development Economics*. Princeton, NJ: Princeton University Press, 9.

Ritchie, J. R. B. (1987). Tourism, marketing, and the quality-of-life. In A. C. Samli (ed.), *Marketing and the Quality-of-Life Interface* (pp. 47–62). New York: Quorum Books.

Sachs, J. (2000). Notes on a new sociology of economic development. In L. E. Harrison and S. P. Huntington (eds.), *Culture Matters: How Values Shape Human Progress* (pp. 29–43). New York: Basic Books.

Schulz, C. J. II and Holbrook, M. B. (1999). Marketing and the tragedy of the commons: a synthesis, commentary and analysis for action. *Journal of Public Policy & Marketing*, **18**(2), 218–229.

Sen, A. (1996). The concept of wealth. In R. Myers (ed.), *The Wealth of Nations in the Twentieth Century: The Policies and Institutional Determinants of Economic Development*. Stanford, CA: Hoover Institution Press.

Sirgy, M. J. (2001). *Handbook of Quality-of-Life Research: An Ethical Marketing Perspective*. New York: Kluwer Academic Publishers.

Sponsel, L. E., Headland, T. N., and Bailey, R. C. (eds.) (1996). *Tropical Deforestation: The Human Dimension*. New York: Columbia University Press.

Thompson, J. and Nachtwey, J. (1991). East europe's dark dawn: the iron curtain rises to reveal a land tarnished by pollution. *National Geographic*, **179** (June), 36–69.

Timoshenko, A. S. (1992). Ecological security: response to global challenges. In E. Brown (ed.), *Environmental Change and International Law: New Challenges and Dimensions*.

Tokyo: United Nations University Press. www.unu.edu/unupress/unubooks/uu25ee/uu25ee00.htm# Contents

9.8. AFFILIATION

Mark Peterson is an associate professor of marketing at the University of Texas at Arlington, USA.

PART III:

MEASUREMENT ISSUES AND RESEARCH IN TECHNIQUES IN QOL STUDIES

Perhaps primarily because quality of life is a very broad and far-reaching discipline in the making it attracts many scholars from other disciplines with different orientation, perception, background and above all research skills. In this section, five chapters deal primarily with different research orientations and measurement attempts that are quite novel. Research techniques presented and measurement issues explored are likely to make a major contribution to research methodologies in quality of life studies. Although all of the papers in this book present important research orientation, the chapters in this section revolve more predominantly on research methodologies.

Kaufman-Scarborough presents a measure of retail quality of life for color deficiency. Clearly, such an approach can be used in many other areas where consumer deficiency is an issue. Furthermore, the methodology presented can be expanded into many other areas of business as well as service delivery situations.

Huebner, Nagle and Suldo construct a measurement concept dealing with child and adolescent health care which they coin multidimensional students' life satisfaction scale (MSLSS). Their scale is constructed on the basis of five specific domains: self, family, friends, school and living environment. However, it is possible to add or delete a number of other domains and assess the role of each in the quality of life consideration. Similarly, the same approach certainly can be used for other important areas of life and for other population segments than children.

Frisch, Clark, Rouse (others Joe Help) attempt to undertake a very difficult task of determining the predictive validity and sensitivity to change as quality of life assessment attempts are made. Although they use a mental health setting for their analyses, the same type approach can be used for other settings as well. They truly present a quality of life inventory that will be quite valuable for future researchers.

Dickson and Littpell present a unique approach of connecting qualitative and quantitative data in order to obtain a better evaluation of quality of life. The authors generated a basic minimum needs ratio by dividing average total household income by essential expenses of housing, food, transportation and utilities. Such an approach can be repeated in many parts of the third world to determine relative well being of people in different areas.

Maggino and D'andrea explore the use of different scales in different survey methods. All scales are not appropriate for all surveys in quality of life research. They posit the importance of measurement instrument being good for one survey as opposed to not being suitable for another. It is critical to realize that generalizations regarding quality of life without paying proper attention to scaling and the survey method could very well be misleading. Therefore, this chapter makes a special contribution to research undertakings.

Carol Kaufman-Scarborough

10. TOWARD THE DEVELOPMENT OF A MEASURE OF RETAIL QUALITY OF LIFE FOR COLOR-DEFICIENT CONSUMERS

ABSTRACT: An integrative model of quality of life is proposed that specifically represents perceptually disabled consumers' experiences in the marketplace. Components of the model include the relationship between the "destination retail environment" and the preconceived expectations formed about the capabilities of potential customers. Color-deficient consumers are chosen as the sample for analysis. Their responses to a semi-structured surveys and interviews are examined in determining the level of congruity among the attributes of the retail environment, the attributes of the color deficient consumers, and their expected "performance" in processing consumer information.

> *Clothing + Make-up + Accessories should have color name tags . . . I have had sales people laugh at me and walk away . . . there should be more awareness of this disability . . . we love to shop too . . . but the market does not cooperate with people who have problems with colors . . . shopping is a very frustrating experience for me in every aspect . . . I really don't think it should be this way.*
>
> *(Female, 39).*

10.1. Introduction

The Census Bureau indicates that there are over 54 million Americans limited in one or more major life activities, including physiological and psychological disorders, amassing approximately one-fifth of the US population. Despite progress through legislation such as the Americans with Disabilities Act, many disabled persons continue to encounter obstacles in retail stores and shopping areas (Stephens and Bergman, 1995). Quite often, the needs of disabled persons are addressed via architectural changes mandated by law that may overlook how barriers affect quality-of-life as experienced through the retail setting (Kaufman-Scarborough, 1999). In fact, one might say that disabled persons are treated as if they are "unexpected" visitors to the settings where nondisabled persons actually shop.

In many instances, persons with disabilities are discounted as retail stores and shopping centers, products, and advertising messages are developed with the able-bodied consumer in mind. Fortunately, substantial progress can bc documented for persons who are mobility-disabled, given the universal acceptance of and demand for amenities such as ramps and electronic doors. In contrast, the needs of perceptually disabled persons have lagged behind (Inana, 1980; Macias and Rucker, 1979). Perhaps this lag occurs since perceptual needs are not simple to comprehend nor easy to test. Perceptual disabilities may also be less concretely defined in terms of marketplace problems and solutions.

It might be said that retailers tend to consider perceptual limitations as

M. Joseph Sirgy et al. (eds.), Advances in Quality-of-Life Theory and Research, 165–178, 2003.

"unexpected" disabilities in planning their retail environments. The retail atmosphere is typically constructed assuming that the expected consumer is fully capable or at least "capable enough" in their sensory capacities. Given the unanticipated nature of perceptual disabilities, the perceptually disabled shopper is hypothesized to experience reduced quality of life related to their inability to retrieve needed information that critically affects their abilities to function successfully as a fully-participating shopper. That is, while they may be able to travel to the marketplace and enjoy physical access to the retail space, their experiences are similarly limited because they cannot access nor process needed information.

Since color is a predominant marketplace cue, the case of persons with color vision deficiencies is chosen as a case analysis. Color vision deficiencies are likely to be "unexpected" disabilities to account for in the retail setting. As a result, persons with color vision deficiencies report encountering information presented with color as the only visual cue, confounding their abilities to make wise selections or follow directions. In addition, since common knowledge of color vision deficiencies is often stereotypically limited to males wearing "mismatched socks", applications to both genders of all ages in various scenarios tend to be limited.

Recent awareness of the importance of understanding perceptual disabilities has been stimulated by the growing interest in web site development practices. Color vision professionals such as eye doctors, scientists, and web designers have created numerous web sites and publications that are devoted to accurately presenting the multiple causes of color vision deficiencies in the general population. Their work also considers the impact of color deficiencies on the accurate interpretation of color-coded information on the web. Thus the case of color-deficient shoppers is likely to have significant implications for the future.

10.2. BACKGROUND

In the decade since the enactment of the Americans with Disabilities Act, considerable progress has been made in widening doors, building ramps, and otherwise reducing barriers to access that have been experienced by persons with disabilities. Nowhere is this more evident in the retail sector as public accommodations have undergone considerable evaluation, assessment, and modifications.

While many initiatives have been put into place, much more work remains to be done (Baker, Stephens, and Hill, 2001b; Gould, 1997). Disabilities activist groups routinely profile "gaps" in accommodations, while litigation continues to be filed against retailers and service providers who have not fully integrated the sense of the ADA into their establishments. However, researchers have found that many retailers do not fully understand the actual ramifications of the ADA or may be searching for practical affordable methods of increasing their "fit" with the needs of persons with disabilities (Baker, Stephens, and Hill, 2001a; Kaufman-Scarborough, 1998).

A useful approach to ADA assessment is found in the retail environment, self-congruity, and retail patronage model proposed by Sirgy, Grewal, and Mangleburg

(2000). The basic model postulates that the attributes of retail environment enable a consumer to determine if they "match" the image of a typical store patron. Such a match with their own self-image is thought to lead to increased retail patronage. While the authors' treatment focuses on more traditional image variables such as trendy upscale shoppers and bargain shoppers, a valuable extension may be made by considering the matching process that is often reported by mobility-disabled shoppers (Kaufman-Scarborough, 1999). That is, persons who use walkers, wheelchairs, and motorized carts are known to critically assess the match of their actual mobility abilities with the physical design of a store that they are considering patronizing. Similarly, policymakers attempt to diagnose the congruity between the access desired by disabled persons, the actual accommodations that have been made, and the effectiveness of the ADA.

For instance, when policymakers and store planners consider persons who are mobility disabled, layout designs that accommodate walkers, wheelchairs, and motorized carts can be anticipated and evaluated. However, the congruity may be more difficult when perceptual disabilities are considered. Perceptual disabilities involve the ability to utilize information as intended by the retailer, which is less intuitive to conceptualize and test in a reliable manner. A basic assumption for perceptually disabled persons is that the nature of their disability may make it difficult, if not impossible, to perceive, interpret, and use marketplace information that directs their behavior as consumers, enables them to make comparisons, and provides essential information for their purchases. Unfortunately, the quality of such consumers' experiences may depend on certain assumed abilities to perceive product information as intended by the marketer (Bettman, 1970; Bettman and Kakkar, 1997; Bettman, Luce, and Payne, 1998). Such information includes stimuli such as auditory messages, visual images, and scents.

At the simplest level, perceptually disabled persons vary in their abilities to perceive and interpret parts of stimuli in their environments (Reedy, 1993). As a result, standard shopping information, such as printed texts, colors, sounds, scents, and lighting, might be partially perceptible, distorted, or totally imperceptible. Accurate information retrieval that relies on such cues may become impossible, potentially limiting the perceptually disabled consumer's "successful" shopping experiences. Several researchers have examined specific cases of perceptual stimuli in the retail context (see the following for discussions of these stimuli: Adkins and Ozanne, 1997; Milliman, 1986; Mitchell, Kahn, and Knasko, 1995).

10.3. PROBLEM STATEMENT – COLOR VISION DEFICIENCIES

Color vision deficiencies are thought to affect a minimum of 19 million persons in the United States, with approximately 10 percent of white males and a substantially smaller proportion of women (1 out of 225) being color-deficient from birth (Rosenthal and Phillips, 1997). Based on these statistics, color vision deficiency appears to be a problem faced predominantly by men. However, when persons are included who experience changes in color vision due to illness, aging, head trauma, and the side effects of medications, the estimate increases to approximately 41 million men and women in the United States alone. Color vision capabilities are also known to vary with environmental conditions, such as lighting, specific combinations of colors, and the level of contrast in the stimuli. Thus, unlike other disabilities, color vision deficiencies are generally invisible to the observer and may cause subtle and situational changes in the consumer's abilities to perceive.

Color vision deficiency is a disability that is frequently overlooked in research since it is an "invisible" disability that can both be congenital or acquired. About 19 million persons in the United States are color-blind or color deficient (Rosenthal and Phillips, 1997). Approximately 10 percent of white males in the US have some aspect of color deficiency, with much less prevalence among females. However, the statistics can be deceiving, since color vision deficiencies can be acquired, can be temporary, and can vary with conditions in the environment. For instance, color vision deficiencies can be caused by diseases such as diabetes and macular degeneration, head or eye injury, side effects of medications such as contraceptives and antidepressants, plus the natural process of aging. While the inability to distinguish between reds and greens is the most common form, color deficiencies of other types can cause people to confuse blues and yellows, confuse yellows and greens, see all objects as yellow, see all objects as blue, or see objects tinged with red. Thus, it is not a uniformly described disability inherited solely by men. Its implications for correct information transmission are significant.

Figure 10.1 diagrammatically organizes and suggests a framework representing the anticipated experiences of color deficient persons in the retail environment. Following the concepts introduced in the discussion above, the figure is made up of four key components: the attributes of the destination retail environment, the attributes of color deficient persons, the psychological negotiation of consumer identity, and the resultant experience of the color deficient person in the retail setting. Han et al.'s measures of quality of life in relation to social functioning (1998) were adapted for application in the model and extended to the notion of consumer functioning in the retail setting. The specific variables expected to emerge are: 1) perceptual barriers and abilities to function in information retrieval, in consumer tasks, and following in-store directions; 2) psychological reactions expressed in feelings of well-being and frustrations; and 3) interpersonal barriers found in misunderstanding by retail personnel and lack of training. This organizing framework is an adaptation of Kaufman-Scarborough's (2001) model of the factors affecting mobility disabled consumers in shopping environments.

10.4. METHOD

The data are drawn from the author's larger study of color-deficient consumers that has been ongoing since 1997 (Kaufman-Scarborough, 2000). Currently, 70 color-deficient persons have provided their input, together with the insights of 18 professionals, including optometrists, color design professionals, and educators. Responses have been gathered through several methods: unstructured interviews,

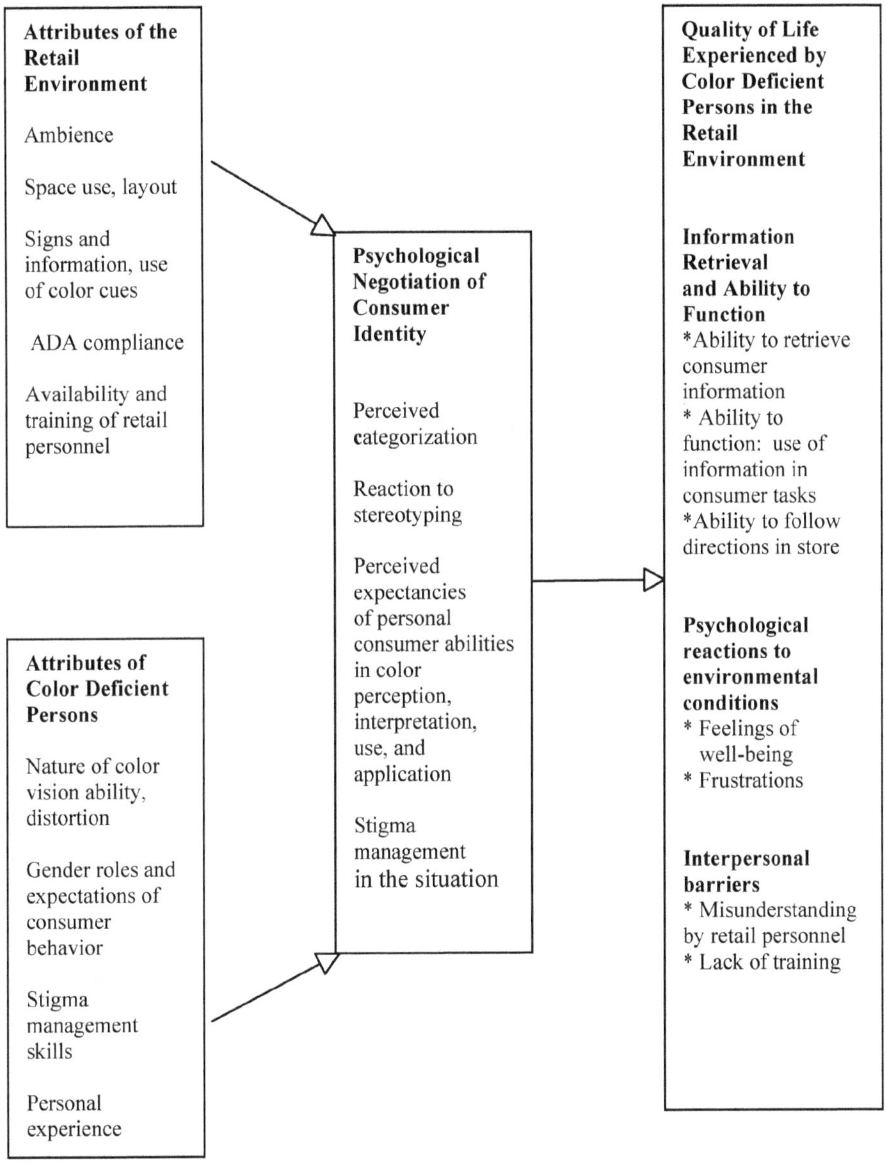

Figure 10.1. Factors Affecting the Quality of Life Experienced by Color Deficient Persons in the Retail Environment.

semi-structured interviews, written surveys and free response comments, web page postings and email communications from informants, personal communications from eye care professionals, and personal communications from color designers.

In attempting to understand what color-deficient shoppers actually experience, the respondents were asked to think about problems they encountered as consumers. After first describing their vision in their own words, they were asked to think about problems that they had in their own lives with product use, reading or watching ads, and shopping in retail stores. Product, advertising, and shopping issues were then discussed separately, asking them to describe problems in free format, how often they occurred, and what companies could do to help them.

10.4.1. *Attributes of the Color-deficient Persons*

At the time of the current analysis, the total number of respondents is 70 color-deficient individuals plus 18 other informants, including eye doctors, educators, color design professionals, and professors of vision studies. The current sample is composed of 16 females and 54 males with diagnosed color vision deficiencies. The color deficient men and women who responded to the survey did so in several ways: some by filling in the survey independently, others by emailing comments that summarized their reactions. Others instead preferred to speak by telephone. Questions throughout the survey requested the respondent to report on problems related to color in using the products that are bought, in advertising, and while shopping.

10.4.2. *Analysis*

The responses were arrayed in spreadsheet format in order to systematize their analysis. The interview data, depth interviews, and survey responses were read and re-read in order to identify a set of codes that could be used in examining the information (Strauss and Corbin, 1998). In doing so, a set of themes emerged that represented the characteristics of the retail environment, displays, and products as perceived by the respondents. In addition, themes also emerged that revealed the feelings of the respondents as they were confused, unable to retrieve information, or were uncertain about the accuracy of their perceptions. Finally, respondents also recounted the reactions of salespersons who treated them as curiosities rather than customers, greatly diminishing their quality of life in the retail environment.

10.5. RESULTS

The responses of both men and women are examined in determining how their quality of life as shoppers is experienced in terms of their own color vision abilities. In addition, particular attention will be paid to the effects of those experiences on their self-confidence and their anticipated successful performance as consumers.

10.5.1. *Attributes of the Retail Environment*

Marketplaces ideally provide clear access to product information so that consumers can make the choices that are in their best interests or meet their specific decision criteria. Such environments, in turn, are ideally supported by well-trained salespersons and informative displays. However, color-deficient respondents reported great difficulty with color-related product choices and unhelpful personnel. Many reported that color information was often missing in useable formats, such as standard color systems with numbered colors or color names that are were indecipherable. In addition, safety-related perceptual problems included difficulties with reading instructions or warnings printed in red, as well as interpreting product information in which background and textual information are printed in similar colors with low contrast.

The respondents were asked to provide details on types of marketplace characteristics where color vision presented a problem. The respondents argued that lighting in stores made a considerable difference in their abilities to perceive, interpret, and process product-information, whether textual or color-coded.

10.5.2. *Attributes of the Color-Deficient Respondents*

The respondents provided a variety of descriptions of their color-vision deficiencies, indicating a wide range of colors, contrast levels, and color combinations that were perceptually challenging to them. Only 17 out of the 70 respondents indicated specifically that their color blindness involved confusions with red and green. Three of the respondents were achromatic; that is, they see only in black, gray, and white. Two indicated that they were proantopes causing them to be blind specifically to red, yet others reported confusing yellow and green. Others simply reported that they were color blind without providing specific details.

Many spoke in illustrative anecdotes, such as not being able to visually spot fruit on a tree or a golf ball on a golf course if it were a certain color. Interestingly, the respondents varied widely in their ages at which their color deficiencies were formally identified. That is, some reported considerable problems as youngsters in school, causing their parents to seek professional eye care to identify their visual problems. Others apparently did not have problems in school, but instead were diagnosed through formal career-based vision screenings whose purposes was to diagnose color deficiencies. In several cases, the diagnosis resulted in rejection from a career field or educational training program. Finally, some in the sample reported that the onset of color deficiencies accompanied conditions such as macular degeneration, causing their formerly-accurate color vision to be changed due to their physiological changes.

Each type of manifestation of color deficiency is likely to affect an individual's quality of life in substantially different ways. When color deficiencies result in poor performance in school, embarrassment in front of one's peers, and inability to complete color-coded work, the individual is likely to experience feelings of incompetence at an early age until a diagnosis is made and coping skills are learned. In contrast, some individuals are successful in school up until their "failure to pass" a conventional color vision test. That failure instead is reported to be a sometimes traumatic and unexpected barrier that disrupts the individual's lifetime plans.

Finally, persons who acquire color deficiencies later in life have a very different impact on their quality of life. In contrast to those who are color deficient from birth, this latter group has been able to perceive color accurately throughout their lives until the onset of their illness or until the prescription of their medication. For them, color deficiency is a new condition that distorts and reduces their capabilities to function as they had in the past. Such color distortions are often subtle and slow to develop over time, causing deterioration in performance in careers or in activities that were formerly carried out successfully.

10.5.3. *Psychological Negotiation of Consumer Identity*

People learn to be consumers through socialization to the customs and practices of the marketplace. They typically develop strategies that allow them to maximize their benefits and use their resources well. Color deficient persons are no exception.

The female respondents had an interesting perspective in that they felt that society has stereotyped color-deficient persons to be men. That is, they felt pressure as females to be able to match products and they felt failure if they could not do so successfully. In addition, they indicated that individuals tended not to believe them when they attempted to describe their color vision limitations:

> I realize that the type of colorblindness I have (yellow-green) is fairly rare, and VERY RARE for a female. (Female2, 42).

> Being a color blind woman leads to a world of misunderstanding (Female, 50)

As mentioned earlier, some persons who were color-blind from birth indicated that their color deficiencies were unknown to them until they were administered career-specific color vision testing, such as that given for admission to the armed forces. Interestingly, they had been learning consumer cues for almost 20 years without the realization that their color processing did not match that of the general public. They reported having to re-learn consumer cues such as what the color that they actually saw "translated into" in terms of color-accurate perception.

Many reported developing strategies throughout their lives that enabled them to function in a color-coded environment. From past experience, they appeared to expect that they would be met with curiosity if they self-identified their disabilities to store personnel. Such experiences led them to manage their stigma via coping mechanisms that did not assume the risk of asking an unfamiliar salesperson for assistance: *I have had sales people laugh at me and walk away. There should be more awareness of this disability (Female, 39).*

10.6. Emergent Themes Illustrating Retail Quality of Life Experiences

The responses of the study participants can be organized according to the three major variables indicated by "Quality of Life Experienced by Color Deficient Persons in the Retail Environment," using the framework proposed in Figure 10.1. These variables are: Information Retrieval and Ability to Function, Psychological Reactions to Environmental Conditions, and Interpersonal Barriers. Each is considered in turn.

10.6.1. *Experience in the Retail Environment: Information Retrieval and Ability to Function*

In examining the color-deficient persons' experiences, a key concept focuses on their abilities to fully function as consumers with access to all needed cues. I was interested in determining whether respondents would discuss whether they felt that they could retrieve needed information, use that information in capably functioning in consumer tasks, and use it to follow directions. In order to stimulate their responses, I asked them to respond to the open-ended question: "Have you ever had a color-related problem while shopping?" If, yes, describe the type of store. Interestingly, many respondents indicated that they had problems in all types of stores, while others specifically indicated retail settings in which they were expected to perform some type of "matching" function independently. Examples included matching clothing, items of home dÈcor, items for home repair such as paint, and cosmetics. The following quotation illustrates frequent responses indicating when the need to interpret color information posed a real problem for the respondent:

> When trying to buy coordinating items such as towels, sheets, two-piece clothing items, threads, zippers, trim for fabrics. In crafting, items that need to match such as paper, paints, ribbons, and embellishments (Female, 64).

Some indicated that the information provided in retail environments actually maximized their disabilities since color was used as the only visual cue to correct shopping behavior. Such problems occurred when specific merchandise was color-coded in some way that was not obvious from any other type of information. Thus, the retail environment can be designed to make the shopping work easy or difficult. For instance, sometimes color is simply used as a cue *"when stores distinguish between different areas using color" (Female, 38).* That is, certain sales displays or sections may be color-coded to assist the typical consumer finding their location. The familiar "Blue lights" at Kmart, yellow "smiling face" specials at Wal-Mart, and markdowns in red ink at Barnes and Noble are illustrations of information that retail planners assume to be retrievable by all customers. In fact, color can become a useless point of information when customers are told to *"ask a store clerk wearing a certain color vest (Male, 12)*:

> Orange label items half price! . . . Are there any yellow label items which are not half price, but which I would mistake for orange? (Male, 26).

Write the name of the color of the product on the label or package (if the product line is differentiated by color). Also, DON'T identify a product by a pseudo-color name like "Misty" or "Army" or "Steel" without another qualifier, like "misty blue", "army green", "steel grey". (Male, 49).

Product designers often use color as a cue to product line extensions such as low salt, diet, and different flavor varieties of products. However, when color is used as an informative cue, product information cannot be perceived in ways that meets the real informational needs of color deficient consumers, as in *"supermarkets . . . wrong product but right brand . . . special information in circles or logos that blends in with the background . . . special discounts are missed . . . dietary warnings are missed" (Male, 42)*. Such color-coding proves to be quite frustrating for persons with color deficiencies, especially when packaging is similar or when lighting is poor:

> But different lighting in different stores makes it hard to tell if one product coordinates or matches another. Trying to find a product someone has described to me (blue "Dawn" dish detergent vs. green) . . . I have found this mainly happens in fabric stores, department stores (Sears, Dillards), and general merchandise stores (Kmart, Wal-Mart, etc.), and seldom in grocery stores. This may be because I have less need to know colors in grocery stores, so I simply don't notice it (Female 2, 42).

10.6.2. *Experience in the Retail Environment: Psychological Reactions, Well-Being, and Frustration*

Persons who have color vision deficiencies tend to report problems with everyday information as illustrated by the following statement:

> Simple directions to a friend's house can present problems: Turn left at the big blue house and we're in the green house on the right. The tan van is in the driveway. I sometimes feel like an adult illiterate finding ways to cope without drawing attention to my disability, especially if the situation involves a contact with a prospective or new employer (Male, no age given).

Feelings of well-being seemed to revolve around feelings of competence and the satisfaction or frustration that comes with being able to shop capably through one's own adaptive behaviors. Many reported shopping with someone else, being careful to note that the person was someone who was "trusted." In many cases, the trusted companion was a spouse, significant other, or close friend. On other occasions, the respondent indicated that they had identified certain retail personnel whom they felt that they could trust to assist them in a respectful manner:

> Where colour selection is important, as in home furnishing, I take advice, usually from my wife or shop assistant. Trained staff in a good furnishing store can be very helpful, as are the suggestions for co-ordinates put out by some manufacturers (Male1, 60)

> When clothes shopping, I have to have someone come along with me if I am going to buy separate pieces to put together an outfit. When sewing my own clothes, I often choose the wrong color thread and buttons . . . I am a "reading" shopper because of the problems with colors . . . I can't shop for clothes by myself . . . I can't see the difference in the color coding (Female, 53)

Others were able to articulate clear feelings about the retail characteristics that caused them problems and inability to function:

> Make it easier for me to buy your product. I would like to buy it, and as I consider this to be a fairly serious problem, I am willing to pay more, go further, or invest more time with a product

that makes it easier. I get frustrated that it is so difficult to buy a product in a color I would like to have, but am not comfortable choosing, simply because I don't know what color it is, or whether I can coordinate something else with it later (Female2, 42).

. . .We have trouble reading advertisements, with directions and matching our clothes. It is extremely frustrating to me to try to shop. I am tired of asking for assistance when making purchases and I wish they would stop color coding things (Female, 38).

Store personnel often say look for the green box of it by the red tubs (Male, 40).

10.6.3. *Experience in the Retail Environment: Interpersonal Barriers*

My expectations of interpersonal barriers in the retail setting were of store personnel who were uncomfortable with persons who are disabled or who simply have not received training in meeting their needs in a respectful manner. Surprisingly, many respondents indicated that store clerks reacted to their requests for help with intrusive questions about color blindness:

. . . Irritating shop assistants who think my colour blindness is an invitation to start an amateur biology discussion rather than tell me what colour the bloody item I want to buy is. I don't have time to discuss my eyesight with every shop assistant in the world. (Male, 26)

Put a label on the clothes that states the color; and teach their sales people, or cashiers about color blindness. These people sometimes look at you like you're stupid, or they think its neat and want to test you. (Male, 38).

10.7. IMPLICATIONS

The study reported in the present paper only begins to touch the surface of the experiences of persons who are perceptually-disabled through color vision deficiencies. Their quality of life in the retail environment is substantially affected by assumptions of full or partial color abilities being possessed by all consumers. Their self-reports instead indicate that the Americans with Disabilities Act has not fully provided accessibility for persons with invisible disabilities such as those related to perception. Several managerial and research implications can be considered.

10.7.1. *Managerial Implications*

Clearly, persons with color vision deficiencies do not uniformly feel welcomed in the retail environment. Their problems occur in the use of color in display, advertising, and signage, as well as in the preparation training of personnel. They appear to feel disenfranchised and ignored as consumers particularly when color is used as an essential cue to some type of information. For instance, goods may require matching to some other color cue for a successful purchase and reliable assistance may be needed. The importance of addressing this problem is likely to increase significantly given the increased aging of the population. Larger numbers of consumers are likely to acquire color vision confusions due to typical effect of age, increased illness, and increased use of prescription medications.

First, color is often used as a cue to product, pricing, and location information. While color is accessible and attractive to the majority of consumers, it is not identifiable nor uniformly perceptible to between 8 and 10 percent of consumers who see it. When described in these terms, the failure of color to communicate in all cases becomes a more relevant problem than considered in retail settings in the past.

Secondly, color deficient persons indicate unpleasant encounters with salespersons who do not treat their disability with respect or understanding. While perceptual disabilities may be less understood, they are being identified in the general population with increased frequency. It is the retailer's responsibility to ensure that personnel receive adequate training that enables them to respond appropriately to a customer who asks for assistance with color selection and interpretation. These issues provide areas for future concern and discussion.

10.7.2. *Research Implications*

The themes that emerged in the present study suggest that the quality of shoppers' experiences are linked with their abilities to function as capable, respected, and independent persons. They experience well-being through the ability to perform successfully in the marketplace with full utilization of needed consumer information.

However, studies that examine perceptions of and reactions to color often fail to prescreen respondents on their individual color perception abilities. Thus, the experiences and reactions of color-deficient persons remain under-researched. Despite conventional use in marketing, color does not affect all persons uniformly. It does not and cannot attract everyone in the same way. It does not and cannot provide the same information to all consumers. It does not and cannot provide the same cues to quality, branding, and product differentiation when color is the only cue that is used.

The research presented in this study provides the foundation for the development of a scientific survey-based instrument capturing retail quality of life for color deficient consumers. Basically, it would attempt to capture the relative strength of the feelings that color-deficient persons experience. The survey items could potentially represent their feelings of competence, ability to complete a desired task, level of difficulty with carrying out tasks, concern for making an incorrect consumer decision, and satisfaction with employee assistance. The statements would be adjusted for the three key areas of product use, reading or watching ads, and shopping in retail stores. Examples of possible survey items are given in Table 10.1, using 5-point Likert scales to assess agreement or disagreement with each item. The items in boldface would be reverse-scaled on this additive index. Scores on this suggested index would range from a low of 12 to a high of 60, with a low score representing lower levels of perceived quality of life in the retail and consumer settings.

In conclusion, it is important to recognize that color deficiencies occur in every

Table 10.1. Suggested Survey Items.

1. It is difficult to make purchases that require me to match colors.
2. I feel that retailers include my needs in the design of their stores.
3. I am concerned that I will buy something that is a different color from what I need.
4. Store displays that use many colors are confusing to me.
5. Salespersons are willing to help me with color-related problems.
6. I feel that advertisers expect me to rely on color to understand their ads.
7. I feel competent to evaluate products based on their colors.
8. Color does not interfere with my ability to use products.
9. I worry that I will make incorrect consumer decisions based on color.
10. I feel that marketers consider my needs in the design of their products.
11. It is challenging for me to purchase clothing by myself.
12. Color blindness makes it difficult for me to make certain purchases.

Note: Scores represent the following scale items:
1 = strongly agree, 2 = agree, 3 = neutral, 4 = disagree, 5 = strongly disagree.

day life among men and women of all ages. Some are born with it, while others acquire it through aging, illness, drug effects, and other causes. While color vision deficiencies are not well understood, they are beginning to gain increased attention through the growth of web technologies.

10.8. REFERENCES

Adkins, N. R. and Ozanne, J. L. (1997). Johnny's Mom Can't Read: The Stigma of Low Literacy in the Marketplace. In E. Iyer and G. R. Milne (eds.), *Proceedings of the 1997 Marketing and Public Policy Conference*, Vol. 7, pp. 9–10. Chicago, Illinois: American Marketing Association.

Baker, S. M. and Kaufman-Scarborough, C. (2001). Marketing and Public Accommodation: A Retrospective On Title III Of The Americans With Disabilities Act. *Journal of Public Policy and Marketing*, **20** (Fall), 297–304.

Baker, S. M., Stephens, D. L., and Hill, R. P. (2001a). How Can Retailers Enhance Accessibility? Giving Consumers with Visual Impairments a Voice in the Marketplace. *Journal of Retailing and Consumer Services*, **9**(4), 227–239.

Baker, S. M., Stephens, D. L., and Hill, R. P. (2001b). Marketplace Experiences of Individuals with Visual Impairments: Beyond the Americans with Disabilities Act. *Journal of Public Policy and Marketing*, **20** (Fall), 215–224.

Bettman, James R. (1970). Information Processing Models of Consumer Behavior. *Journal of Marketing Research*, **7** (August), 370–378.

Bettman, J. R. and Kakkar, P. (1977). Effects of Information Presentation Format on Consumer Information Acquisition Strategies. *Journal of Consumer Research*, **3** (March), 233–240.

Bettman, J. R., Luce, M. F., and Payne, J. W. (1998). Constructive Consumer Choice Processes. *Journal of Consumer Research*, **25**(3) (December), 187–217.

Gould, Steven (1997). Leveling the Playing Field for Visually Impaired Consumers: A Public Policy and Research Agenda. In Debbie Thorne LeClair and Michael Hartline, *1997 AMA Winter Educators' Conference: Marketing Theory and Applications*, 8, eds. Chicago: American Marketing Association, 142-148.

Han, T. S., Tijhuis, M. A. R., Lean, M. E. J., and Seidell, J. C. (1998). Quality of Life in Relation to Overweight and Body Fat Distribution. *American Journal of Public Health*, **88**(12) (December), 1814–1820.

Inana, Marjorie (1980). Grocery Shopping: Principles and Techniques for the Blind Consumer. *Journal of Visual Impairment and Blindness*, **74** (November), 329–332.

Kaufman-Scarborough, Carol (1998). Retailers' Perceptions of the ADA: Suggestions for Low-Cost, High-Impact Accommodations for Disabled Shoppers. *Journal of Consumer Marketing*, **15**(2/3), 94–110.

Kaufman-Scarborough, Carol (2001). Sharing the Experience of Disabled Consumers: Building Understanding Through Ethnography. Special Issue of the *Journal of Contemporary Ethnography focusing on Marketing, Consumer Behavior, and Ethnography*, edited by Eric J. Arnould, Volume 30, Number 4 (August), 430–464.

Kaufman-Scarborough, Carol (2000). Seeing Through the Eyes of the Color -Deficient Shopper: Consumer Issues for Public Policy. *Journal of Consumer Policy*, **23**(4), 461–492.

Kaufman-Scarborough, Carol (1999). Reasonable Access for Mobility-Disabled Persons is More Than Widening the Door. *Journal of Retailing*, **75**(4), 479–508.

Macias, P. and Rucker, M. (1979). Clothing Selection and the Visually Impaired Consumer. *Journal of Visual Impairment and Blindness*, **73** (December), 400–404.

Milliman, Ronald E. (1986). The Influence of Background Music on the Behavior of Restaurant Patrons. *Journal of Consumer Research*, **13** (September), 286–289.

Mitchell, D. J., Kahn, B. E., and Knasko, S. (1995). There's Something in the Air: Effects of Congruent or Incongruent Ambient Odor on Consumer Decision Making. *Journal of Consumer Research*, **22** (September), 229–238

Reedy, Joel (1993). *Marketing to Consumers with Disabilities: How to Identify and Meet the Growing Market Needs of 43 Million Americans*. Chicago, Illinois: Probus Publishing Co.

Rosenthal, O. and Phillips, R. H. (1997). *Coping with Color-Blindness*. Garden City Park, New York: Avery Publishing Group.

Sirgy, M. J., Grewal, D., and Mangelburg, T. (2000). Retail Environment, Self-Congruity, and Retail Patronage: An Integrative Model and a Research Agenda. *Journal of Business Research*, **49**, 127–138.

Strauss, A. and Corbin, J. (1998). *Basics of Qualitative Research: Techniques and Procedures for Developing Grounded Theory*. Thousand Oaks, California: SAGE Inc.

Stephens, D. L. and Bergman, K. (1995). The Americans with Disabilities Act: A Mandate for Marketers. *Journal of Public Policy and Marketing*, **14**(1) (Spring), 164–168.

10.9. AFFILIATION

Carol Kaufman-Scarborough XXX

E. SCOTT HUEBNER, RICHARD J. NAGLE AND SHANNON SULDO

11. QUALITY OF LIFE ASSESSMENT IN CHILD AND ADOLESCENT HEALTH CARE: THE MULTIDIMENSIONAL STUDENTS' LIFE SATISFACTION SCALE (MSLSS)

ABSTRACT: The major trends and measurement issues for quality of life assessment in children and adolescents for the purposes of health care and problem prevention are reviewed. Next, the Multidimensional Students' Life Satisfaction Scale, a self-report quality of life scale appropriate for children and youth, is discussed. This multidimensional scale was designed to measure general life satisfaction and satisfaction within five specific domains (Self, Family, Friends, School, and Living Environment) among students of ages 8–18. Its rationale, development, psychometric properties, and applications to health care assessment of children and youth are outlined with an emphasis on the incremental validity of quality of life assessments. Future research directions are also discussed.

11.1. INTRODUCTION

Health care professionals from a variety of theoretical orientations have shown an increasing interest in expanding the criteria for mental and physical health to include perceived quality of life (QOL) in addition to the absence of physical or psychiatric illness (Cowen, 1991; Kazdin, 1993; Raphael et al., 1996; Seligman and Csikszentmihalyi, 2000). Comprehensive evaluations of individual's well-being thus are expected to incorporate positive indicators of well-being along with the traditional negative indicators (e.g., symptoms, risk behaviors). This perspective suggests that those health care professionals who are interested in health promotion must evaluate changes in positive indicators, such as QOL, as well as negative indicators (Frisch, 2000).

Perceived QOL, or life satisfaction, has been defined "as a global evaluation by the person of the quality of his or her life" (Pavot et al., 1991: 150). Life satisfaction reports have been studied with respect to evaluations of overall life and/or specific life domains (e.g., family, school). Perceived QOL reports encompass the complete spectrum of subjective well-being, ranging from very negative (e.g., "terrible") to neutral to very positive (e.g., "delighted"); thus they offer the possibility of reflecting high levels of wellness as well as disturbances in adaptive functioning. Although QOL reports relate to a variety of psychological and health disorders (see Frisch, 2000), they are also discriminable from disorders. For example, QOL reports have been differentiated from depression (Lewinsohn, Redner, and Seeley, 1991; Headey, Kelly, and Wearing, 1993), anxiety (Huebner, 1991b; Huebner, Funk, and Gilman, 2000), and self-esteem (Huebner, Gilman, and Laughlin, 1999; Lucas et al., 1996). Furthermore, Greenspoon and Saklofske (2001) have provided preliminary empirical support for a dual-factor model of child mental health, which theorizes that psychopathology and subjective well-being (including perceived QOL) are not opposite poles of a single continuum but rather comprise two separate

M. Joseph Sirgy et al. (eds.), Advances in Quality-of-Life Theory and Research, 179–189, 2003.

dimensions of functioning worthy of examination. Thus, researchers have demonstrated the incremental contribution of QOL judgments to multidimensional models of well-being.

Raphael et al. (1996) have identified four benefits of a QOL perspective for health care efforts. First, they suggest that QOL approaches integrate psychological and sociological perspectives with medical and rehabilitation perspectives. Second, they argue that QOL approaches highlight multiple determinants of health, including personal, community, and structural determinants. Third, QOL perspectives relate to health promotion and rehabilitation perspectives, suggesting health promoting conditions and behaviors. Fourth, QOL measures offer a sensitive method to assess the effects of illness, disability, and associated interventions and treatments.

Despite the increased attention to QOL of adults, little research attention has been devoted to QOL in children and youth. Systematic research related to the determinants, correlates, and sequelae of individual differences in perceived QOL reports of children and adolescents have been hampered by the lack of developmentally appropriate, well-validated measures. To date, few life satisfaction measures suitable for children and/or adolescents exist. Notable exceptions include The Quality of Life Profile-Adolescent Version (Raphael et al., 1996), the Comprehensive Quality of Life Scale (Gullone and Cummins, 1999), Multidimensional Students' Life Satisfaction Scale (Huebner, 1994; Huebner et al., 1998), Students' Life Satisfaction Scale (Huebner, 1991a), and Perceived Life Satisfaction Scale (Adelman, Taylor, and Nelson, 1989). It should be noted that of the five measures, four of the measures appear to be designed to provide only a summary score of general or global life satisfaction. In contrast, the Multidimensional Students' Life Satisfaction Scale was constructed to provide a general life satisfaction score along with scores on five domains (Family, Friends, School, Self, Living Environment). Although the preliminary findings with all of these measures are promising for research purposes, additional validation work needs to be done with each of them to enhance confidence in their validity (see Gilman and Huebner, 2000, for a review).

Although measures of global (i.e., domain-free) life satisfaction offer useful information (see Pavot and Diener, 1993), multidimensional measures potentially offer more differentiated assessments for use in applied and research contexts. Multidimensional measures can provide useful information related to developing goals and assessing health care interventions. For example, Frisch (2000) has discussed how domain-specific life satisfaction measures can inform client goal setting through the determination of the specific life contexts that are most dissatisfying for a given individual. For example, the quality of life of a child undergoing medical treatment for cancer whose satisfaction decreases in a single life domain is quite different from one whose satisfaction decreases in several important life domains. The use of multidimensional life satisfaction measures offers the promise of considerable incremental validity over the use of global measures in health care research and practice.

The major purpose of this paper is to summarize the development, psychometric properties, health applications, and directions for future research related to a multidimensional life satisfaction measure suitable for children and youth (grades 3–12), the Multidimensional Students' Life Satisfaction Scale (MSLSS: Huebner, 1994). The MSLSS was designed to provide a profile of children's satisfaction with important specific domains (e.g., family, friends, school) in their lives as well as assess their total life satisfaction. Furthermore, the MSLSS was designed for use with children across a wide array of ages, ability levels (e.g., gifted students, students with learning problems), and physical and mental health concerns. In contrast to the many existing disorder-specific quality of life measures, the MSLSS was thus designed to be useful across a wide variety of children with and without health care concerns.

11.2. Overview of the MSLSS

11.2.1. *Item Selection, Administration, and Clinical Follow-Up*

In the initial test development, 14 items were developed to represent each of the five specific domains of family, friends, school, living environment, and self. The particular life satisfaction domains were selected on the basis of a literature review, pilot interviews with school age students, student essays, and previous research (e.g., Huebner, 1991b). The items were written to be easy to read and comprehend, thus being potentially useful across a wide range of age and ability levels. The results of subsequent item and factor analyses yielded a 40-item final version of the scale. The items and scoring procedures can be found in Huebner (1994).

The 40-item final version of the MSLSS may be administered to children and adolescents in groups as well as individually. Written directions are provided prior to the items. With younger children (grades 3–5) and children with learning difficulties (e.g., learning disabilities, mental disabilities), it is recommended that researchers read aloud the directions and encourage students to ask questions as necessary. The readability of the scale is estimated at the 1.5 grade level; therefore most students require little assistance in responding to the questions.

The usefulness of the MSLSS for clinical applications with individuals may be enhanced by conducting a more detailed inquiry following the administration of the scale. The MSLSS does not directly enable the examiner to derive inferences about the processes used by individual children to make life satisfaction judgments. The nature of the comparative processes may differ across individual children or groups of children (Huebner et al., 2002). For example, some students may evaluate their life satisfaction on the basis of comparisons with their ideal lives, others' lives, previous experiences, predominant affective states in particular contexts, cultural norms, and so forth (Diener et al., 1999; Dube, Jodoin, and Kairouz, 1998; Michalos, 1985). Open-ended interview questions may thus be useful as part of a clinical follow-up to provide more comprehensive interpretations of the meaning of MSLSS "scores." Adapting procedures recommended by Harter (1985) for self-concept measurement, follow-up inquiry questions such as the following have been found to be useful: "What makes you agree/not agree that your school experiences are interesting?" "What makes you agree/disagree that your life is good?" "What are the main things you think about when you say your family gets along well together?" Such procedures may also yield information that helps clarify discrepancies between self-reports and the reports of significant others (Huebner et al., 2002).

11.2.2. *Normative Data*

To date, the MSLSS has been administered to four samples of students in South Carolina, USA. These samples have included 312 students in grades 3–8 (Huebner, 1994), 413 students in grades 3–5 (Huebner, 1994), 291 students in grades 6-8 (Huebner et al., 1998), and 321 students in grades 9–12 (Gilman, Huebner, and Laughlin, 2000). Validation studies have also been completed in Spain (Casas et al., 2000), Korea (Park, 2000), and Canada (Greenspoon and Saklofske, 1997). An abbreviated version of the MSLSS, which contains five items, has been developed for use in large-scale surveys and screening (Huebner et al., 2002; Seligson, Huebner, and Valois, in press).

Mean scores for all domains and the total score were above the midpoint of the scale in all samples, indicating positive levels of life satisfaction. Such findings are consistent with studies of adults (Diener, 1984, 1994) and children and youth (e.g., Huebner, 1994; Huebner, Drane, and Valois, 2000).

11.2.3. *Reliability*

The MSLSS has consistently yielded acceptable internal consistency coefficients. Alpha coefficients from the normative samples have compared favorably to those reported for adult life satisfaction scales (Bender, 1997). Further, the internal consistency estimates for the five domains are acceptable for research purposes. Obtained alphas coefficients have ranged from 0.79 to 0.85 for the Family domain, 0.81 to 0.85 for the Friends domain, 0.83 to 0.85 for the School domain, 0.72 to 0.84 for the Self domain, and 0.79 to 0.83 for the Living Environment domain.

Test-retest coefficients have also been reported (Gilligan and Huebner, 2002; Huebner et al., 1998) for two- and four-week time intervals, falling mostly in the 0.70–0.90 range. One-year reliability coefficients range from 0.47 (School) to 0.64 (Total) (Funk, 2001). These data provide preliminary support for the temporal stability of the scale.

11.2.4. *Validity*

The results of exploratory factor analyses have supported the dimensionality of the MSLSS (Greenspoon and Saklofske, 1997; Huebner, 1994). Confirmatory factor analyses, conducted on samples of children in grades 6–8 (Huebner et al., 1998) and grades 9–12 (Gilman, Huebner, and Laughlin, 1998) have provided further support for the multidimensional hierarchical model, which consists of a general life satisfaction higher-order factor at the apex of the hierarchy along with five lower-order specific domains.

Convergent and discriminant validity have also been demonstrated through predicted correlations with other self-report well-being indexes (Greenspoon and Saklofske, 1997; Huebner, 1994; Gilman et al., 1998; Huebner et al., 1998), parent reports (Gilligan and Huebner, 2002; Huebner et al., 2002), teacher reports (Greenspoon and Saklofske, 1997), and social desirability scales (Huebner et al., 1998). For example, the MSLSS School domain correlated 0.68 with the Quality of School Life Scale (Epstein and McPartland, 1977), the MSLSS friends domain correlated 0.56 with the Loneliness and Social Dissatisfaction Scale (Asher, Hymel, and Renshaw, 1984), the Family domain correlated 0.61 with the Parent scale from the Behavioral Assessment Scale for Children (Reynolds and Kamphaus, 1992), and the MSLSS Self domain correlated 0.62 with the General Self-Esteem scale of the Self-description Questionnaire-I (Marsh, 1988). It should be noted that a suitable criterion measure for the Living Environment domain has yet to be identified.

The predictive validity of the MSLSS has received minimal attention. Correlations between MSLSS Total scores and measures of depression ($r = 0.52$), anxiety ($r = -0.39$), and social stress ($r = -0.64$) taken one year later provide preliminary support for its predictive utility (Huebner, Funk, and Gilman, 2000). Clearly, additional research is needed to demonstrate the predictive power of this measure across a broad range of child and contextual factors.

The sensitivity of the MSLSS to health care interventions has yet to be investigated thoroughly. One study (Gilman and Handwerk, 2001) has demonstrated changes in a modified version of the MSLSS as a result of a psychosocial intervention (i.e., placement in a residential treatment program for adolescents). Another study (Farrell et al., in press) demonstrated changes in a short form of the MSLSS following a conflict management program for middle school students.

11.2.5. *Applications to Health Care*

Limited research has been undertaken on the use of the MSLSS with children with health care concerns. One notable exception concerns a study by Griffin and Huebner (2000) in which MSLSS reports of adolescents with serious emotional disturbance (SED) were compared to a sample of non-SED controls. Although there were no differences on overall life satisfaction between the two groups, the students with SED reported significantly lower satisfaction on the domain of friends. Similarly, in a study of adolescent students with mild mental disabilities (MMD), Brantley, Huebner, and Nagle (2002) found that students with MMD reported lower satisfaction with friends, higher satisfaction with school experiences, and comparable levels of overall life satisfaction relative to a normally achieving control sample. Similar studies are underway with children with chronic hearing conditions and attention deficit disorders (Gilman, Easterbrooks, and Frey, 2001).

According to Wallander, Schmitt, and Koot (2001), much research on children's QOL has been aimed at distinguishing generic measures of QOL from "health-related" QOL measures (HRQOL). They argue that since QOL is a "holistic" concept, it is difficult to differentiate the influences of a health condition from the collective influence of present and past experiences of the child. In view of this, they recommend the use of generic instruments of QOL to study the health outcomes of children. It has also been suggested that generic measures, such as the MSLSS, can allow for comparisons between specific health conditions as well as comparisons with children with no health conditions (Levi and Drotor, 1998; Wallander, Schmitt, and Koot, 2001). Given the multidimensional nature of the MSLSS, it has the potential to assess domain differences across groups of healthy and chronically ill children. Health-related QOL measures may serve the useful purpose of assessing symptoms or outcomes that are known to be associated with a specific condition (Levi and Drotor, 1998; Wallander, Schmitt, and Koot, 2001) but all definitions of QOL should be considered relative to the general population (Eiser and Morse, 2001).

11.3. CONCLUSIONS

The initial research findings provide support for the use of the MSLSS for research purposes with students in grades 3–12. Given that the item content and response options incorporate both positive and negative indicators of subjective well-being, the MSLSS should be sensitive to changes across the spectrum of well-being (e.g., from "mild" to "moderate" life satisfaction). The MSLSS may thus serve as a useful research tool, whenever the perspective of the child is to be considered.

Various researchers have speculated on possible clinical applications of life satisfaction measures, such as the MSLSS. For instance, Frisch (2000) has articulated numerous specific potential uses of life satisfaction measures in health care contexts. He has argued for considerations of life satisfaction in the general medicine, psychiatry, clinical psychology, behavioral medicine, and gerontology arenas. These considerations involve possible functions in assessment, program planning, program evaluation, and mental health screening. First, life satisfaction measures can be incorporated in comprehensive assessments of the effects of health care programs. Through the inclusion of life satisfaction data, health care professionals can extend beyond the measurement of "symptom" changes to investigate broader effects of prevention and intervention programs, including child and adolescent perceptions of quality of life in various domains (e.g., school, family, self). For example, health care professionals could explore how the experiences of medical, psychosocial, and education interventions might differ in terms of the effects on different life domains for children with a potentially chronic health condition (e.g., asthma, cancer, ADHD). Second, life satisfaction measures could provide useful planning instruments in the development and implementation of health care programs. Multidimensional life satisfaction measures offer useful information with respect to both diagnostic and treatment decisions. Child and adolescent perceptions of the specific environmental risks and protective factors that may be operating in their lives may be suggested by particular life satisfaction profiles. For example, the determination of etiology will likely differ for a child with emotional problems who reports high satisfaction with family, self, and living environment, but low satisfaction with peers and school experiences in comparison to a child who reports high satisfaction with self, peers, and school, along with low satisfaction with family and living environment. Furthermore, based upon such information, the subsequent treatment plans are likely to differ as well. Finally, life satisfaction scales may eventually be useful for screening purposes, that is, identifying persons who are most at risk for the development of health problems and/or relapses before such problems occur. Longitudinal investigations have shown that life satisfaction reports predict a variety of subsequent pathological outcomes, such as depression, suicide, and physical illness (see Frisch (2000) for a review). Therefore, life satisfaction measures may eventually be applied in the context of screening programs for children and youth.

In addition to health care contexts, Huebner et al. (1998) and Gilman and Huebner (in press) have discussed applications in education. Considering that the maintenance and enhancement of quality of life, including perceived quality of life, is a major goal of all human service interventions, and given the wide nomological network of important related variables (cf. Huebner, in press), it is not surprising that researchers such as Kazdin (1993) have stated" there are few constructs this broad, global, and yet as clinically important" (p. 296). Thus, periodic multidimensional "checkups" of life satisfaction (see Frisch, 2000) of individuals, groups, and nations should provide crucial information for the design of intervention programs to enhance the quality of life of children and youth in various human services contexts. Indeed, Wallander, Schmitt, and Koot (2001) suggest that QOL reports have "the potential to represent the ultimate standard against which to judge the impact on children from whatever conditions they encounter (e.g., physical, social, environmental) and the efforts of society to enhance their development (e.g., policy, resource allocation, interventions)" (p. 583).

To achieve these goals, additional research is clearly needed. First, more representative samples must be employed to assess the generalizability of the current findings with the MSLSS. Eiser and Morse (2001) state that even a QOL measure with well-established psychometric properties in one population may not generalize to another population. There is also increasing recognition that cultural, racial, and ethnic differences can play a role in influencing perceptions of HRQOL among children, adolescents, and parents (Drotor et al., 1998). Therefore, nationally representative samples that include children and adolescents from other parts of the US and different ethnic backgrounds (e.g., Hispanic, Asian Americans, etc.) are crucial to promote our understanding of the impact of cultural and family influences on children's appraisal of QOL. The availability of norms from other nations is also necessary as a prerequisite for the use of the MSLSS for potential clinical purposes. Normative data for particular child health care populations should be gathered as well for comparison purposes.

Second, further studies are needed that establish the stability and changes related to MSLSS scores. Studies of the sensitivity of the scale to naturally occurring and induced life changes (e.g., school or neighborhood changes, medical or psychosocial interventions) are imperative for demonstrating the usefulness of the MSLSS as an outcome measure in clinical and non-clinical health care contexts. Studies that make comparisons of the sensitivity of the MSLSS relative to traditional symptom-based measures of mental health are also needed to establish the utility of the MSLSS.

Third, additional validation studies of the MSLSS should be undertaken, particularly with respect to possible clinical applications. For example, additional concurrent and predictive validity studies (e.g., determining the ability of the MSLSS to predict important mental and physical health outcomes) must be conducted to establish its utility for diagnostic and screening purposes. Predictive validity studies of the relationship between MSLSS scores and subjective and objective health indices should be especially illuminating for subsequent health care applications. Furthermore, the interplay of MSLSS scores with proxy ratings of QOL from significant others in the child's environment (i.e., parents and teachers) will allow health providers the opportunity to examine the impact of the health issues in a more systemic context.

Much additional research remains to be done to clarify the utility of the MSLSS in the child health care arena. Improved rates of survival among children with chronic health conditions have increased the importance of examining the construct of quality of life in these populations (Rodrigue, 2000). According to Rodrigue, there is a need for psychometrically sound instruments that are well grounded in conceptual foundation. Preliminary empirical scrutiny of the MSLSS has revealed promising validity findings across divergent age, cultural, and disability groups. Future research by the authors will be extended to populations of children and youth with chronic health conditions.

Our findings offer considerable support for health care researchers interested in measuring the perceived QOL of children and adolescents (ages 8–18). The MSLSS studies reported herein are consistent with the recommendations of Andelman et al. (2000) following their review of the child QOL literature. Their recommendations for improved trends in child QOL research included greater diversity in study populations, sophistication in psychometric and measurement methodology, and attention to theoretical underpinnings. It is hoped that this research with the MSLSS, as well as other child QOL measures, will stimulate additional research in this area of inquiry, based upon such guidelines.

11.4. REFERENCES

Adelman, H., Taylor, L., and Nelson, P. (1989). Minors' dissatisfaction with their life circumstances. *Child Psychiatry and Human Development*, **20**, 135–147.

Andelman, R. B., Attkinsson, C. C., Zima, B. T., and Rosenblatt, A. B. (1999). Quality of life of children: Towards conceptual clarity. In M. Maruish (ed.), *The Use of Psychological Testing in Treatment Planning and Outcomes Assessment*, 2nd edition (pp. 1383–1413). Mahwah, NJ: Lawrence Erlbaum Associates.

Asher, S. R., Hymel, S., and Renshaw, S. D. (1984). Loneliness in children. *Child Development*, **55**, 1456–1464.

Brantley, A., Huebner, E. S., and Nagle, R. J. (2002). Multidimensional life satisfaction reports of adolescents with mild mental disabilities. *Mental Retardation*, **40**, 321–329.

Casas, F., Alsinet, F., Rossich, M., Huebner, E. S., and Laughlin, J. (2000, July). *Cross-cultural investigation of the Multidimensional Students' Life Satisfaction Scale with Spanish adolescents*. Paper presented at the Third Conference of International Quality of Life studies. Girona, Spain.

Cowen, E. L. (1991). In pursuit of wellness. *American Psychologist*, **46**, 404–408.

Dew, T. (1996). *The preliminary development and validation of a multidimensional life satisfaction scale for adolescents*. Unpublished doctoral dissertation, University of South Carolina, Columbia.

Diener, E. (1994). Assessing subjective well-being: Progress and opportunities. *Social Indicators Research*, **31**, 103–157.

Drotor, D., Levi, R., Palmero, T. M., Riekert, K. A., Robinson, J. R., and Walders, N. (1998). Recommendations for research concerning the measurement of pediatric health-related quality of life. In D. Drotor (ed.), *Measuring Health-Related Quality of Life in Children and Adolescents: Implications for Research and Practice* (pp. 341–350). Mahwah, NJ: Lawrence Erlbaum Associates.

Dube, L., Jodoin, M., and Kairouz, S. (1998). On the cognitive basis of subjective well-being analysis: What do individuals have to say about it? *Canadian Journal of Behavioural Science*, **30**, 1–13.

Epstein, J. L. and McPartland, J. M. (1977). The concept and measurement of the quality of school life. *American Educational Research Journal*, **13**, 15–30.

Eiser, C. and Morse, R. (2001). The measurement of quality of life in children: Past and future perspectives. *Journal of Developmental and Behavioral Pediatrics*, **22**, 248–256.

Farrell, A. D., Valois, R. Fl, and Meyer, A. A. (in press). Impact of the RIPP Violence Prevention Program on rural middle school students. *Journal of Primary Prevention*.

Frisch, M. (2000). Improving mental and physical health care through Quality of Life Therapy and assessment. In E. Diener and D. R. Rahtz (eds.), *Advances in Quality of Life Theory and Research* (pp. 207–241). Dordrecht, Netherlands: Klewer Academic Press.

Funk, B. A. (2001). *The Reliability and Predictive Utility of the Multidimensional Students' Life Satisfaction Scale*. Unpublished masters thesis, University of South Carolina.

Gilligan, T. D. and Huebner, E. S. (2002). Multidimensional life satisfaction reports of adolescents: A multitrait-multimethod study. *Personality and Individual Differences*, **32**, 1149–1155.

Gilman, R., Easterbrooks, S., and Frey, M. (2001, November). *Assessment of the Quality of Life among Children Diagnosed with Hearing Loss or Attention Deficit Disorders*. Paper presented at the International Society for Quality of Life Studies, Washington, DC.

Gilman, R. and Handwerk, M. L. (In press). Changes in life satisfaction as a function of stay in a residential setting. *Residential Treatment for Children and Youth*.

Gilman, R. and Huebner, E. S. (2000). Review of life satisfaction measures for adolescents. *Behaviour Change*, **17**, 178–195.

Gilman, R. and Huebner, E.S. (in press). A review of life satisfaction research with children and adolescents. *School Psychology Quarterly*.

Gilman, R. C., Huebner, E. S., and Laughlin, J. E. (2000). A first study of the Multidimensional Students' Life Satisfaction Scale with adolescents. *Social Indicators Research*, **52**, 135–160.

Greenspoon, P. J., and Saklofske, D. H. (1997). Validity and reliability of the Multidimensional Students' Life Satisfaction Scale with Canadian children. *Journal of Psychoeducational Assessment*, **15**, 138–155

Greenspoon, P. J. and Saklofske, D. H. (2001). Toward an integration of subjective well-being and psychopathology. *Social Indicators Research*, **54**, 81–108.

Griffin, M. and Huebner, E. S. (2000). Multidimensional life satisfaction reports of students with serious emotional disturbance. *Journal of Psychoeducational Assessment*, **18**, 111–124.

Gullone, E., and Cummins, R. A. (1999). The Comprehensive Quality of Life Scale: A psychometric evaluation with an adolescent sample. *Behaviour Change*, **16**, 127–139.

Harter, S. (1985). *Manual for the Self-Perception Profile for Children*. Unpublished manuscript, University of Denver.

Headey, B., Kelley, J., and Wearing, A. (1993). Dimensions of mental health: Life satisfaction, positive affect, anxiety, and depression. *Social Indicators Research*, **29**, 63–82.

Huebner, E. S. (1991a). Initial development of the Student's Life Satisfaction Scale. *School Psychology International*, **12**, 231–240.

Huebner, E. S. (1991b). Correlates of life satisfaction in children. *School Psychology Quarterly*, **6**, 103–111.

Huebner, E. S. (1994). Preliminary development and validation of a multidimensional life scale for children. *Psychological Assessment*, **6**(2), 149–158.

Huebner, E. S. (in press). Research on assessment of life satisfaction research of children and adolescents. *Social Indicators Research*.

Huebner, E. S., Brantley, A., Nagle, R. J., and Valois, R. F. (2002). Correspondence between parent and adolescent ratings of life satisfaction for adolescents with and without mental disabilities. *Journal of Psychoeducational Assessment*, **20**, 20–29.

Huebner, E. S., Drane, W., and Valois, R. (2000). Adolescents' perceptions of their quality of life. *School Psychology International*, **21**(3), 187–198.

Huebner, E. S., Funk, B. A., and Gilman, R. (2000). Cross-sectional and longitudinal psychosocial correlates of adolescent life satisfaction reports. *Canadian Journal of School Psychology*, **16**, 53–64.

Huebner, E. S., Gilman, R., and Laughlin, J. E. (1999). A multimethod investigation of the multidimensionality of children's well-being reports: Discriminant validity of life satisfaction and self-esteem. *Social Indicators Research*, **46**, 1–22.

Huebner, E. S., Laughlin, J. E., Ash, C., and Gilman, R. (1998). Further validation of the Multidimensional Students' Life Satisfaction Scale. *Journal of Psychoeducational Assessment*, **15**, 118–134.

Huebner, E. S., Suldo, S., Valois, R. F., Drane, J. W., and Zullig, K. (2002). *Brief Multidimensional Students' Life Satisfaction Scale (BMSLSS): Gender, Race, and Grade Effects*. Manuscript submitted for publication.

Kazdin, A. E. (1993). Treatment of conduct disorder: Progress and directions on psychotherapy research. *Development and Psychopathology*, **5**, 277–310.

Levi, R. and Drotor, D. (1998). Critical issues and needs in health-related quality of life assessment of children and adolescents with chronic health conditions. In D. Drotor (ed.), *Measuring Health-Related Quality of Life in Children and Adolescents: Implications for Research and Practice* (pp.3–24). Mahwah, NJ: Lawrence Erlbaum Associates.

Lewinsohn, P., Redner, J., and Seeley, J. (1991). The relationship between life satisfaction psychosocial variables: New perspectives. In F. Strack, M. Argyle, and N. Schwartz (eds.), *Subjective Well-Being* (pp. 193–212). New York, NY: Plenum.

Lucas, R. E., Diener, E., and Suh, E. (1996). Discriminant validity of well-being measures. *Journal of Personality and Social Psychology*, **71**(3), 616–628.

Michalos, A. (1985). Multiple discrepancies theory (MDT). *Social Indicators Research*, **16**, 347–413.

Marsh, H. W. (1988). *Self-Description Questionnaire I*. San Antonio, Texas: The Psychological Corporation.

Pavot, W. and Diener, E. (1993). Review of the Satisfaction With Life Scale. *Psychological Assessment*, **5**, 164–172.

Pavot, W., Diener, E., Colvin, C. R., and Sandvik, E. (1991). Further validation of the Satisfaction With Life Scale: Evidence for the cross-method convergence of well-being measures. *Journal of Personality Assessment*, **57**, 149–161.

Raphael, D., Rukholm, E., Brown, I., Hill-Bailey, P., and Donato, E. (1996). The Quality of Life Profile-Adolescent Version: Background, description, and initial validation. *Journal of Adolescent Health*, **19**, 366–375.

Reynolds, C. R. and Kamphaus, R. W. (1992). Manual for the Behavior Assessment System for Children. *Circle Pines*. MN: American Guidance Service.

Rodrigue, J. R. (2000). Quality of life. In J. R. Rodrigue, G. R. Geffken, and R. M. Streisand (eds.), *Child Health Assessment: A Handbook of Measurement Techniques* (pp. 170–195). Needham Heights, MA: Allyn and Bacon.

Seligman, M. E. P. and Csikszentmihalyi, M. (2000). Positive psychology: An introduction. *American Psychologist*, **55**, 5–14.

Seligson, J., Huebner, E. S., and Valois, R. F. (in press). Preliminary validation of the Brief Multidimensional Students' Life Satisfaction Scale. *Social Indicators Research.*

Valois, R. F., Zullig, K. J., Huebner, E. S., and Drane, J. W. (2001). Relationship between life satisfaction and violent behaviors among adolescents. *American Journal of Health Behavior*, **25**(4), 353–366.

Wallander, J. L., Schmitt, M., and Koot, H.M. (2001). Quality of life measurement in children and adolescents: Issues, instruments, and applications. *Journal of Clinical Psychology*, **57**, 571–585,

11.5. Acknowledgements and Affiliation

Appreciation is extended to Jerlean Noble for word-processing the paper. Paper presented at the Fourth Annual Conference of the International Society for Quality of Life Studies, Washington, DC: November, 2001. Address correspondence to: Scott Huebner, Ph.D., Department of Psychology, University of South Carolina, Columbia, SC, 29208. Phone: (803) 777-4137. Email: huebner@sc.edu

Michael B. Frisch, Michelle P. Clark, Steven V. Rouse, M. David Rudd, Jennifer Paweleck, Andrew Greenstone, and David A. Kopplin

12. PREDICTIVE VALIDITY AND SENSITIVITY TO CHANGE IN QUALITY OF LIFE ASSESSMENT AND LIFE SATISFACTION: FURTHER STUDIES OF THE QUALITY OF LIFE INVENTORY OR QOLI IN MENTAL HEALTH SETTINGS

ABSTRACT: The clinical usefulness of quality of life assessments depends upon their ability to predict clinically important outcomes and to detect treatment-related change. In addition, norms for clinical – and not just nonclinical – samples are needed to demonstrate clinically significant change. These issues were explored in the context of a program of instrument validation for the QOLI or Quality of Life Inventory involving 3,927 clients from various clinical settings. Clinical norms for community mental health centers and university counseling centers were also generated that supplement existing nationwide, nonclinical norms. The predictive validity of the QOLI in a university counseling center was supported in terms of its ability to predict academic retention both by itself and in conjunction with cumulative G.P.A. one to three years in advance. The QOLI was also found to be sensitive to treatment-related change in two, naturalistic clinical settings and samples, that is, a managed care/substance abuse and a university counseling center setting. The interpretation and clinical utility of measures of quality of life and life satisfaction are discussed along with an agenda for further research.

12.1. Introduction

To be accountable to patients and to payers, health care professionals in mental health and physical medicine, must demonstrate clinically significant change as a result of treatment. According to Kazdin (2003, 1993a, b, 1994 – also see Frisch, 1998a, 2000, in press); Heimberg and his colleagues (Eng, Coles, Heimberg, and Safren, 2001; Safren et al., 1997; Jenkins, 1992; Matarazzo, 1992; Rush, 2000; Seligman and Csikszentmihalyi, 2000; Seligman, 2002; Spilker, 1996; Strupp, 1996; Chambliss, 2000; Mendlowicz and Stein, 2000; Ogles, Lunnen, and Bonesteel, 2001; Burlingame et al., 1995; Sirgy, 2002), no variable is more clinically important or significant than quality of life, a very noticeable and central part of patients' everyday functioning and experience. To the extent that treatment leads to improved quality of life as well as to symptomatic improvement, it can be said that clinically significant change has occurred. Besides outcome evaluation, quality of life measures can assist in assessing 'problems of living', treatment planning, and screening those at high risk for future health, relapse, and work problems (Kazdin, 1993a, 1994; Frisch, 1998a, 2000; Jenkins, 1992; Matarazzo, 1992; Safren et al., 1996/1997; Seligman, 1995; Spilker, 1996; Strupp, 1996; Diener et al., 1999).

Quality of life is usually equated with life satisfaction in psychology and psychiatry, and, to a lesser extent, in general medicine and cancer treatment (Rabkin et al., 2000; Mogotsi, Kaminer, and Stein, 2000; Endicott et al., 1993; Diamond and Becker, 1999; Ferrans, 2000; Ferrans and Powers, 1992; Heimberg and his

M. Joseph Sirgy et al. (eds.), Advances in Quality-of-Life Theory and Research, 191–210, 2003.

colleagues [Eng, Coles, Heimberg, and Safren, 2001; Safren et al., 1997]; Huebner, 1994; Crowley and Kazdin, 1998; Kazdin, 2003, 1993a; Frisch, 1998a, 2000; Snyder et al., 2000; Huebner, Drane, and Valois, 2000; Lambert and Ogles and their colleagues [Burlingame et al., 1995; Ogles, Lambert, and Masters, 1996; Ogles, Lunnen, and Bonesteel, 2001]; Woody and Adessky, 2002; Carlbring et al., 2001; Rapaport, Endicott, and Clary, 2002; Rush, 2000). In addition, studies of life satisfaction judgments support the use of *domain-based* measures of life satisfaction that take into account the *importance of particular domains* to particular respondents (Schimmack, Diener, and Oishi, 2002; Pavot and Diener, 1993). For example, in psychiatry, life satisfaction is usually measured by Endicott et al.'s (1993) domain-based "Short Form Q-LES-Q". While the QOLI or Quality of Life Inventory has been evaluated as "the most promising quality of life instrument available" for adults (Ogles, Lambert, and Masters, 1996: 92; see also Mogotsi, Kaminer, and Stein, 2000; Crits-Christoph and Connolly, 1997; Cornell et al., 1997; Crowley and Kazdin, 1998; Eng et al., 2001; Constance Hammen, personal communication, January 4, 1991; Horowitz et al., 1997; Kazdin, 1993a, b, 1994; Theodore Millon, personal communication, February 11, 1995; Moras, 1997; Rabkin et al., 2000; Ben-Porath, 1997; Safren et al., 1997), additional research is needed to see if its promise is fulfilled, especially in light of a revision aimed at securing nationwide norms and a 6th-grade reading level (Frisch, 1994). Quality of life measures, in general, and the QOLI in particular, need further evaluation with respect to predictive validity, sensitivity to treatment-related change, and diverse norms for determining the amount of change needed to denote clinical significance.

12.1.1. *Predictive Validity*

Life satisfaction measures of quality of life have the potential to predict and to identify those at high risk for health problems, relapse, and impaired functioning in school, work, and social relationships. In one of the few prospective studies of its kind, Lewinsohn and his colleagues (Lewinsohn et al., 1991) found that low life satisfaction preceded or predicted episodes of clinical depression in an undepressed subsample of community volunteers. Participants evidenced low life satisfaction just prior to the onset of clinical depression. Life satisfaction ratings tended to worsen during the depressive episode, only to move up into the average or normal range once the depression abated. Low life satisfaction was the only variable found to be "prodromal, or an early manifestation, of depression's onset" (p. 163) both in this study and in a prospective study of depressive relapse which followed patients after being successfully treated for depression (Gonzales, Lewinsohn, and Clarke, 1985). The results of these studies were corroborated and extended in a prospective study of 184 randomly selected community volunteers in which levels of life satisfaction assessed two years earlier significantly predicted the onset of DSM depressive, anxiety, and somatoform disorders (Baruffol et al., 1995). The authors concluded that low life satisfaction is a major risk factor for psychological disturbance.

Moum (1996) found that low life satisfaction predicted suicide over the following five years. Life satisfaction predicts the response of depressed patients to pharmacotherapy and may identify those in need of both medication *and* psychotherapy for depression (Miller et al., 1998). Low life satisfaction has also been identified as a predictor for cardiovascular diseases such as myocardial infarction (see Vitaliano, Dougherty, and Siegler, 1994, for a review), "chronic pain syndrome" (Dworkin et al., 1992), and physical illness such as respiratory tract infections and colds in both healthy individuals and those afflicted with cancer (Anderson et al., 1994). Life satisfaction predicts job performance and satisfaction as much as five years in advance (Judge and Hulin, 1993; Judge and Watanabe, 1993) and may predict a willingness to participate in prevention programs aimed at eliminating unhealthy behaviors like smoking (Wagner et al., 1990). With respect to the former, quality of life is thought to affect our ability to function in major life tasks such as 'love and work' (and not just our vulnerability to disorder and disease). In the context of college, 'work' includes the ability to stay in school and complete a degree, that is, 'academic retention' as defined here.

The present study aimed to extend quality-of-life predictive validity studies to an entirely new domain by assessing the ability of life satisfaction to predict academic retention in university counseling center clients. By using the QOLI in this analysis, its predictive validity could be assessed for the first time in the literature.

12.1.2. *Sensitivity To Treatment-Related Change*

In the interest of parsimony and clarity, the cumbersome phrase, sensitivity to treatment-related change may also be referred to as *treatment validity*. While it is a requirement for psychometric adequacy, treatment validity is not always documented for quality of life measures (Frisch, in press, 1999, 1998a; Ogles, Lambert, and Masters, 1996). Only a few clinical trials and case studies (Kazdin, 1993a; Frisch in press, 1999, 1992) have examined the QOLI's treatment validity. In a study carried out at the Center for Stress and Anxiety Disorders of cognitive-behavioral treatment for chronic and treatment-resistant Social Anxiety Disorder – also known as Social Phobia, QOLI scores were low at pretreatment (9th percentile of non-clinical standardization sample) and improved significantly after therapy along with benchmark measures of anxiety and social functioning (Safren et al., 1997); these findings have been replicated with other samples suffering from Social Anxiety Disorder and extended to patients with Generalized Anxiety Disorder at the Adult Anxiety Clinic of Temple University (Eng, Coles, Heimberg, and Safren, 2001; Eng, Coles, Turk et al., 2001; Turk et al., 2000). As in these studies, evidence for sensitivity is bolstered when measures change in ways that mirror more established benchmark measures of change in addition to demonstrating treatment-related change by themselves. In a related finding from this clinic, a cluster analysis of socially anxious patients revealed a lower quality of life/life satisfaction in patients with disordered adult attachment styles versus those with mature attachment styles

(Eng, Heimberg, Hart, Schneier, and Liebowitz, 2001). After administration of Heimberg's treatment in a different laboratory, socially anxious patients' QOLI scores moved to within one standard deviation of a nationwide nonclinical normative sample, suggesting clinically significant change in response to treatment although the statistical significance of this finding was marginal, that is, $p = 0.07$ (Woody and Adessky, 2002). Evidence for the QOLI's sensitivity to treatment-related change was also found in a study of an Internet-delivered treatment for Panic Disorder (Carlbring et al., 2001).

In a study of Quality of Life Therapy (Frisch, in press), a cognitive therapy for depression, related disorders, and quality of life problems per se, QOLI scores improved significantly along with benchmark measures of depression with gains maintained at a follow-up assessment (Grant et al., 1995). These findings have been replicated with a larger sample of depressed women with alcoholic partners at the University at Buffalo's Research Institute on Addictions (Robert G. Rychtarik, personal communication, September 9, 2002). In a treatment study of 119 alcoholics conducted at the Rutgers' Center of Alcohol Studies, QOLI, psychiatric symptom, and benchmark substance abuse scales improved significantly after treatment with gains maintained at 6- and 12-month follow up assessments (Jon Morgenstern, personal communication, September 12, 2002). Initial results from a study of naltrexone treatment of alcoholism conducted at the Yale School of Medicine also support the QOLI's sensitivity to treatment-related change in so far as the QOLI scores of treatment responders, that is, abstainers, increased significantly after treatment (Stephanie S. O'Malley, personal communication, September 6, 2002). The QOLI also seems to be sensitive to treatment related change in the National Institute on Aging's PEARL (Project to Enhance Aged Rural Living) study in so far as the quality of life of older rural home health care patients and their caregivers improved following a psychosocial intervention aimed at improving their emotional well being and the quality of life, while the quality of life of delayed treatment patients and caregivers did not, according to initial findings (Forrest Scogin, personal communication, August 7, 2002).

The present study aimed to extend these findings to larger samples in more naturalistic settings, that is, a managed care, HMO program for substance abuse and the ongoing treatment program of a university counseling center.

12.1.3. *Clinical Norms*

Clinical significance is defined both in terms of a: 1) a *construct*, such as quality of life or life satisfaction, that is clinically and practically important, a basic or central aspect of a patient's experience or functioning that is easily noticeable to the patient (Kazdin, 1993a) and; 2) the *amount of change* on a measure deemed to be of clinical or ractical importance (Kazdin, 2003; Kendall and Grove, 1988; Ogles, Lambert, and Masters, 1996; Jacobson and Truax, 1991). In terms of the latter, change to *within* one standard deviation of a functional, nonclinical norm group or change that is two standard deviations or more *away from* a clinical, dysfunctional norm group is considered to be a clinically significant amount of change, using the most stringent standards (Ogles, Lambert, and Masters, 1996). While comparisons of patients to nonclinical functional peers is the preferred 'gold standard' for establishing clinical significance in the amount of change on a measure (Kazdin, 2003; Kendall and Grove, 1988; Miller et al., 1998; Ogles, Lambert, and Masters, 1996; Jacobson and Truax, 1991), clinical, dysfunctional norm groups can be necessary as in cases of highly impaired or chronic samples in which change approaching a nonclinical sample is unrealistic even when treatment has been rather successful as in the case of patients with schizophrenic disorders or very few resources (Frisch and MacKenzie, 1991). Dysfunctional norms can also be helpful in cases of overlapping nonclinical and clinical distributions (Jacobson and Truax, 1991).

Despite nationwide nonclinical norms in a sample that approximates the US Census in ethnic make-up, clinical or dysfunctional norms for the QOLI are lacking. The present study tried to address this deficiency by collecting data from naturalistic samples of community mental health center (CMHC) patients and university counseling center clients.

12.2. METHOD

12.2.1. *Validation Samples, Measures, and Procedures*

Managed care substance abuse sample

In order to assess the QOLI's sensitivity to change, a Midwestern managed care substance abuse sample was administered the QOLI and Brief Symptom Inventory (BSI; Derogatis and Lynn, 1999) at intake, discharge, and at 3- and 6-month follow up assessments. A demographic questionnaire was also administered at intake. Follow-up assessments were administered by mail. The BSI was selected to represent the state of the art in well-validated measures of psychiatric symptoms; the BSI would thereby serve as the benchmark against which QOLI results could be compared for its sensitivity to treatment-related change.

As clients first entered the treatment program at intake, they were asked for their informed consent to participate in the study. Data collection stopped after 90 participants successfully completed the program. In addition to the 90 clients who successfully completed treatment and agreed to participate, 5 clients did not wish to participate, and 2 dropped out of treatment prematurely – data from these 7 clients are not included in these analyses. Of the 90 participants, 82 (91.11%) were treated for alcohol dependence and 8 (8.88%) were treated for either methamphetamine, cocaine, benzodiazepine, cannabis or opioid dependence. Of participants, 67% were admitted for outpatient treatment (Mean duration = 71 days) and 33% were admitted for inpatient treatment (Mean duration = 19 days). The predominantly male (73.33% versus 26.66% female) sample averaged 38.50 years of age (SD = 9.20). The sample was overwhelmingly white (94.4%) with a few (5.6%)

African-, Hispanic-, Asian- and Native-American participants. The percent of participants married, divorced, widowed, or single was 28.9, 17.8, 13.3, and 38.9, respectively.

University Counseling Center Sample

The 3,638 participants in this study were comprised of college students seeking services at a mid-sized land-grant university counseling center located in the Midwestern United States. The study aimed to: 1) generate normative statistics on the QOLI for a university counseling center; 2) test the QOLI's sensitivity to treatment-related change for a subsample of participants and; 3) test the QOLI's validity in predicting the academic retention of clients both by itself and in conjunction with cumulative G.P.A. for a subsample of participants. Prior to being seen at the center, participants gave their informed consent for the center to gather psychological test data and academic performance information as part of an ongoing effort at program evaluation. The predominantly female (57.2% versus 42.8% male) sample averaged 23.01 years of age (SD = 5.42). The sample was predominantly white (86.0%) with some international students (5.5) as well as African- (4.7), Hispanic- (2.2), Asian- (1.3) and Native- (0.3) American participants. The percent of participants classified as freshmen, sophomores, juniors, seniors, graduate and special (e.g., non-degree seeking) students was 18.4, 20.1, 22.0, 25.1, 13.2, and 1.2, respectively.

Over a four year period, all clients referred for individual psychotherapy were administered the QOLI and a demographic questionnaire prior to their first session. As part of this process, clients who had a planned termination from therapy were asked by their counselor to complete a second, posttreatment QOLI. Of the clients who had a planned termination from counseling (n = 1,505) during this period, 56.9% (n = 857) were administered a posttreatment QOLI.

In an effort to predict academic retention and assess outcome, retention status was checked in 1998 for students who had either completed counseling or dropped out of counseling in 1995–1997 and in 2000 for students who had either completed counseling or dropped out of counseling in 1997–1999.

The time between QOLI testing and the check on students' retention status ranged from 12 to 36 months with a mean of 24.8 months. Students who were still enrolled or had graduated at the time that their enrollment status was checked were considered 'retained', while students who were no longer enrolled and had not graduated were considered 'not-retained'. Of the students who completed counseling between 1995–1999, registration data was available for 2,245 subjects. Of these, 2,179 had complete QOLI data. Of the subjects with complete data, 1,796 (82.4%) were counted as retained, and 383 (17.6) were counted as not retained. In the discriminant analysis, the most recent QOLI score the client had obtained prior to terminating services was utilized. For those students who failed to follow-through on counseling, the pretest was their most recent QOLI (n = 1,568). For those students who completed a planned termination from counseling, the posttest was utilized (n = 611). Because one year had not elapsed since the completion of their counseling, data from 246 counselees that were used in the sensitivity to change analyses, were excluded from the prediction of retention analyses.

Community Mental Health Center Sample (CMHC)
This sample was tested in order to obtain normative statistics on the QOLI for a CMHC. Until such time that about 200 participants gave their informed consent to participate, all clients presenting for services at a Community Mental Health Center in the greater Waco area of about 200,000 inhabitants were administered the QOLI. Twenty clients were unable or unwilling to participate because of illiteracy or acute agitation; 2 patients submitted data with missing values that were unusable. A demographic questionnaire was completed archivally at a later date based on clients' medical records. The predominantly female (63.6% versus 36.4% male) sample averaged 34.52 years of age (SD = 9.85). The sample was predominantly white (71.6%) with significant African-American (17.6%) and Hispanic-American (10.8%) representation. All of the Hispanic-American participants were Mexican-American. The percent of participants married, separated, divorced, widowed, or single was 19.8, 6.4, 30.7, 3.0, and 40.1 respectively.

12.3. RESULTS

12.3.1. *Sensitivity To Treatment-Related Change*

Counseling Center Sample
Evidence in support of the QOLI's treatment validity was found in both the Managed Care Substance Abuse and Counseling Center samples and is displayed in Table 12.1. According to the results of a correlated *t*-test, QOLI raw scores increased significantly from pre- to posttreatment in the Counseling Center sample, $t(857) = -20.23$, $p < 0.001$, effect size = 0.57. When evaluating the between-group differences, caution was taken not to emphasize differences that were statistically but not clinically significant; for this reason, Cohen's (1988) cut-offs – 0.20 standard deviation units for a small or 'weak', but important effect size; 0.50 for a 'moderate' effect size and; 0.80 for a 'large' effect size – were used in analyzing results. Thus, the effect size of 0.57 was evaluated as 'moderate'.

Managed Care Substance Abuse Sample
The overall repeated measures MANOVA was significant, $F(12, 833) = 5.86$, $p < 0.001$, for the QOLI raw score and general indices of the BSI – GSI, PSDI, and PST – administered at pretreatment, posttreatment, and 3- and 6-month follow-up assessments to the Managed Care Substance Abuse sample. The significant MANOVA result was followed by univariate analyses, that is, four repeated measure ANOVAS to determine which measure(s) evinced significant change over time. All four measures displayed significant change over time: QOLI $F(3, 38) = 8.97$, $p < 0.001$, effect size = 0.42; GSI $F(3, 38) = 22.13$, $p < 0.001$, effect size = 0.64; PSDI $F(3, 38) = 19.53$, $p < 0.001$, effect size = 0.61; PST $F(3, 38) = 19.12$, $p <$

Table 12.1. Treatment Validity for Substance Abuse and Counseling Center Samples.*

Scale		Time of Assessment			
		Pretreatment	Posttreatment	3-month Follow-up	6 month Follow-up
Substance Abuse Sample					
QOLI	M	1.07 a	2.16 b	2.30 b	2.47 b
	SD	1.79	1.41	1.50	1.43
GSI	M	64.45 a	56.41 b	53.74 b	52.18 b
	SD	12.90	11.28	11.71	10.70
PSDI	M	59.28 a	52.93 b	50.94 b	49.68 b
	SD	9.56	7.97	7.82	6.73
PST	M	63.31 a	56.62 b	53.79 b	52.75 b
	SD	12.34	11.54	11.69	11.48
Counselling Center Sample					
QOLI	M	1.09 a	2.22 b		
	SD	1.69	1.58		

* The Ns for the Substance Abuse sample at pretreatment, posttreatment, 3-, and 6-month follow-up were 90, 90, 58, and 48, respectively. The N for the counselling center sample at pretreatment and posttreatment was 858. All pretreatment Means differ significantly, from the posttreatment, 3-month follow-up, and 6-month follow-up Means using the Bonferroni correction. Row means with different subscripts differ significantly using the Bonferroni correction.

0.001, effect size = 0.60 (see Table 12.1 for means and standard deviations). Bonferroni-adjusted pairwise comparisons revealed a significant increase in QOLI raw scores from pretreatment to posttreatment that was maintained at 3- and 6-month follow up assessments. Furthermore, these results were exactly mirrored in the analysis of benchmark BSI measures. That is, psychiatric symptom scores on the GSI, PSDI, and PST significantly dropped from pretreatment to posttreatment with the drop maintained at 3- and 6-month follow up assessments. While QOLI results mirrored those of the BSI, correlational analyses revealed that these were not isomorphic measures of the same construct. While significant, correlations between the QOLI and the BSI – its three overall scales and the depression scale – at intake and discharge, with all 90 patients providing data, ranged from –0.41 to –0.53 (also see Frisch et al., 1992). The R^2 values corresponding to these correlations indicate that the QOLI only accounts for between 17% and 28% of the variance of the BSI indices. Thus, while the pattern of change is similar for the BSI and QOLI, they should not be misconstrued as measures of the same construct.

12.3.2 *Predictive Validity of the QOLI*

Validation Sample Results

Using the cross-validation approach of Butcher and his colleagues at the University of Minnesota (Rouse, Butcher, and Miller, 1999), a discriminant analysis was conducted to determine the predictive utility of clients' QOLI scores and cumulative GPA in assessing academic retention one to three years in advance (see 'Method' for procedural details). The sample of 2,179 was randomly divided into two halves, with 1,089 subjects in the validation sample and 1,090 subjects in the cross-validation sample. The mean GPA and QOLI scores of the two samples did not differ significantly.

Three discriminant function equations were generated from the validation sample with GPA and QOLI scores considered separately as predictors of retention, followed-by a step-wise discriminant analysis in which *both* variables were included. These equations, each of which was statistically significant, and their associated group centroids are presented in Table 12.2. Efficiency statistics are presented in Table 12.3. Of the three discriminant equations, all reached statistical significance. The classification ratio and all efficiency statistics were highest for the stepwise analysis containing both GPA and QOLI scores.

Table 12.2. Discriminant Functions for Classifying Students' Academic Retention Based on GPA and QOLI Scores.*

Discriminant Scales	Unstandardized Functions	Group Centroids	
		Retained	Not Retained
GPA	GPA (1.153) – 3.06	0.122	–0.573
QOLI	QOLI (0.571) – 0.914	0.083	–0.391
Stepwise: GPA & QOLI	GPA (0.948) + QOLI (0.313) – 3.012	0.146	–0.685

* Each function was found to be statistically significant, $p < 0.050$.

Table 12.3. Efficiency of GPA and QOLI in the Discrimination of Students Who were Retained as Students Versus Those Who were not Retained.†

Discriminant Scales	Sens.	Spec.	PPP	NPP	Class.	Chi^2
GPA	0.58	0.678	0.27	0.884	0.661	73.59
QOLI	0.57	0.611	0.238	0.87	0.604	34.81
GPA & QOLI	0.61	0.714	0.311	0.895	0.695	103.58

† GPA = cumulative grade point average; Sens. = sensitivity, or the percentage of non-retained students who were correctly classified; Spec. = specificity, or the percentage of retained students correctly classified; PPP = percent of subjects in the group predicted to "not retained" who actually were not retained; NPP = percent of subjects in the group predicted "retained" who actually were retained. All Chi^2 values listed were significant at $p = 0.001$.

Table 12.4. Classification Rates Using GPA and QOLI to Predict Academic Retention.*

Actual Group Membership	Predicted Group Membership	
	Not Retained	Retained
Not Retained		
Number	116	75
%	60.7%	39.3%
Retained		
Number	257	641
%	28.6%	71.4%

* Values on the diagonal that are correctly classified cases and are underlined and in bold type. There were a total of 757 correctly classified cases, or 69.5%.

Table 12.4 contains the classification rates from the stepwise discriminant function. 69.5% of the cases were correctly classified when both GPA and QOLI score was considered. In a two-sample case with equal membership in each group, the percentage of correct predictions based on chance would be 50%. When the group sizes are unequal, however, as they were in this study with 898 or 82.4% of students retained and 191 or 17.6% students not retained, the percentage of correct predictions based on chance is higher than 50%. In cases with unequal distributions, Betz (1987) recommends two methods for determining the chance rate of correct prediction. If the risk of misclassification is equal for both groups, the formula n/N (n = the size of the largest group and N = total sample size) is appropriate. In this case that would result in a chance rate of prediction of (898/1,089) 82.4%. However, that would classify all students as likely to be retained. In this situation, where the cost of misclassifying a student as retained when they are likely to drop out is higher than the reverse, Betz (1987) suggests using a formula that assumes a comparable rate of error across all groups: $p_1a_1 + p_2a_2 + p_3a_3 + \ldots p_ka_k$ (p = proportion of cases in each group, a = proportion actually classified in that group, and k = the number of groups). In this case, the formula would calculate a chance rate of correct prediction of (0.175)(0.342) + (0.825)(0.657) = 59.3%. The 69.5% rate of correct prediction, using the discriminant function is significantly higher than the 59.3% chance rate of correct prediction, according to the z test for the difference in proportions (Glass and Stanley, 1970), $z = 6.84$, $p < 0.05$). Thus, the discriminant function was significantly more accurate than chance in predicting which students would not be retained. This finding is corroborated by the significant Wilks lambda for the step-wise discriminant function, Wilks lambda = 0.909, with a chi-square distribution of (2) = 103.585, $p < 0.001$, $R = 0.302$. Thus, significant differences in the group centroids were found, with the predictor variables (GPA and QOLI) accounting for 9% of the variance in retention.

Cross-validation Sample Results
Discriminant analysis is a maximization procedure that capitalizes on random, sample-specific error (Betz, 1987; Klecka, 1980). For this reason, a prediction equation developed on one sample may not be as effective when utilized with a subsequent sample. To address this problem, the second half of the sample was used to cross-validate the discriminant equation generated with the first sample. Using the discriminant function generated by the initial stepwise procedure [GPA (0.948) + QOLI (0.313) – 3.012], we classified each subject in the cross-validation sample as retained or not retained. The correct classification rate for the cross-validation sample was 69% compared with 69.5% for the validation sample. The efficiency statistics generated for the cross-validation sample – sensitivity = 0.698, specificity = 0.689, PPP = 0.324, NPP = 0.914 – actually *increased* in accuracy from those of the validation sample, suggesting no shrinkage when the predication equation from the first sample was applied to the second sample.

12.3.3. *Normative Statistics for Clinical Samples*

CMHC Norms
The QOLI normative statistics for the CMHC sample are presented in Table 12.5. A one-way ANOVA of QOLI raw scores revealed a significant difference in terms of *ethnicity*, $F(2, 192) = 5.46$, $p < 0.01$, effect size (eta2) = 0.05 such that Mexican-Americans scored higher than either whites or African-Americans, according to Bonferroni-adjusted contrasts. Whites and African-Americans did not differ significantly. Since the magnitude of effect calculated for the observed ethnic difference in QOLI scores did not even meet Cohen's (1988) threshold for a 'weak' effect, separate norms for Mexican-Americans do not seen necessary in interpreting the scores of CMHC patients. Women and men did not differ significantly in QOLI scores, $t(195) = 1.68$, $p > 0.05$.

Table 12.5. Normative Statistics for Determining Clinically Significant Change in CMHC and University Counseling Center Sample.*

Statistic	CMHC	University Counselling Center
N	199	3,638
Cutoff for Clinically Significant Change	1.90	3.13
Mean	–0.17	1.32
SD	2.07	1.81
75th Percentile	1.06	2.70
Median	–0.14	1.40
25th Percentile	–0.160	0.10
Minimum	–5.75	–6.00
Maximum	5.50	6.00

* Clinically significant change is denoted by a score that is either 2 SDs higher than a dysfunctional, clinical mean or within 1 SD of a functional, nonclinical mean.

Counseling Center Norms
The QOLI normative statistics for the Counseling Center sample are presented in Table 12.5. Ethnic differences in pretreatment QOLI scores were not statistically significant in the Counseling Center sample, $F(6, 3015) = 0.86$, $p > 0.05$, supporting the practice of using aggregate norms-in terms of ethnicity – for college counseling center clients. While men from the Counseling Center scored significantly higher on the QOLI than female counselees, $F(1, 3634) = 14.89$, $p < 0.001$, effect size(eta2) = 0.004, the effect size was so small that separate norms for male and female counselees do not seem to be necessary. In terms of *class standing*, freshman counselees scored higher on the QOLI than junior, senior, graduate, and special students and sophomores scored higher than senior and graduate students, $F(5, 3028) = 14.99$, $p < 0.001$, effect size(eta2) = 0.024 – followed by Bonferroni-adjusted pairwise tests. Once again, the effect size for *class standing* was so small that separate norms for freshman or sophomore counselees do not seem to be necessary.

12.4. DISCUSSION

In terms of overall results: 1) the predictive validity of the QOLI was supported in terms of its ability to predict academic retention both by itself and in conjunction with cumulative G.P.A. one to three years in advance; 2) the QOLI was found to be sensitive to treatment-related change in two, naturalistic clinical settings and samples, that is, a managed care/substance abuse and a counseling center setting; 3) the construct validity of the QOLI was supported through its relationship to related measures and; 4) clinical norms for CMHCs and university counseling centers were generated that supplement existing nationwide, nonclinical norms.

The results of the present study extend the predictive validity of life satisfaction, in general, and the QOLI, in particular, to an entirely new domain: that is, the QOLI was able to predict academic retention both by itself and in conjunction with cumulative G.P.A. one to three years in advance. This finding lends further credence to the view that life satisfaction may be a 'trans-theoretical' and interdisciplinary construct of great heuristic and practical value. Based on the findings here and studies reviewed above, it may be time to see if quality of life measures could be used in schools, businesses, employee assistance programs (Frisch, 1998b), and clinics/hospitals – both general medical and mental health – to screen those at high risk for job or school failure, particular mental disorders – that is, depressive, anxiety, substance use, and somatoform disorders –, suicide, respiratory infections, heart disease, cancer, and excessive health-care utilization and expenditures. Toward this end, and that of preventative medicine, a brief quality of life assessment could be part of periodic physical exams or 'check ups'.

In the context of college counseling centers, the QOLI may be used as a harbinger of academic failure that can alert both psychologists and clients to the need for aggressive intervention such as that suggested by Frisch and his colleagues (Frisch, in press; Frisch and Froberg, 1987; Frisch et al., 1982; Frisch and Gerrard, 1981).

Specifically, a counseling center clinician may enter the QOLI score and the cumulative GPA of a counselee into the 'Stepwise' 'Function' or equation in Table 12.2 and predict that a student will drop out of school if the solution to the equation is closest to the 'not retained' centroid of –0.685 or predict retention if the solution to the equation is closest to the 'retained' centroid of 0.146. In an era of shrinking budgets and increased demands for service, measures like the QOLI may provide the 'proof' and accountability that funding agencies are demanding if health care services are to be maintained or expanded; QOLI results have already been used successfully to secure additional resources and staff in university counseling centers (Clark and Mason, 2001).

While quality of life in psychiatry is increasingly defined in terms of the rather psychological construct of life satisfaction, which assumes some cognitive mediation of quality of life judgments, general medicine and the pharmaceutical industry almost always ignore the psychological aspects of quality of life by defining it exclusively in terms of functional abilities or impairments as measured by either the SF-12 or SF-36 (Niemcryk, 2001; Spilker, 1996). Thus, in addition to a cure or management of symptoms/disease/disability, there is a desire to see a patient's ability to function in everyday life enhanced or at least maintained after treatment. Unfortunately, such measures of functioning can be misleading and can miss deep dissatisfaction and a very low quality of life as in patients with anxiety disorders who are extremely dissatisfied and unhappy with their life even though their functioning is only mildly or moderately impaired (Eng et al., 2001; Turk et al., 2000). In addition, patient concerns about functional impairments often dissipate with time as patients adapt to even such severe disabilities such as quadraplegia and blindness (Diener et al., 1999; Frisch, 2000). Thirdly, life satisfaction can improve without any changes in life circumstances or functional abilities whatsoever (Frisch, 1992, 1998a, 1999, in press); it is a function of attitude and expectations and not just 'objective' factors. In this regard, perhaps impairments in functioning that do *not* affect life satisfaction should not be considered in quality of life assessment to begin with (Frisch, in press). Thus, from a *psychological* perspective, particular functional impairments may or may not discourage, demoralize, or ruin patients' basic contentment or quality of life, suggesting the need to assess life satisfaction, or 'subjective well-being' (Diener et al., 1999; Diener, 2000; Frisch 1998, 1999) in order to assess quality of life – whether life satisfaction *replaces* measures of 'functional ability' or *supplements* them as part of a 'quality of life assessment battery' (Frisch, 1998a).

Alternatively, life satisfaction may be viewed as a cognitive/experiential 'function' in its own right. That is, life satisfaction may reflect a consciousness 'function' or functional ability in which a general sense of satisfaction or contentment: 1) makes a person's conscious inner experience pleasant; 2) motivates him or her to pursue goals and; 3) makes him or her attractive to friends and loved ones who then may share resources and social support (Diener, 2001; Folkman and Moskowitz, 2000; Lazarus, 1991). If, as Hans Strupp (1996) maintains, basic contentment or life satisfaction is the most important sign of mental health and positive outcome in psychology and psychiatry, it could be recast as vital human function along with the abilities to love, work, and toilet oneself. Thus, one's basic contentment, satisfaction with life, or subjective well-being may be impaired by illness, injury, or psychiatric disorder *in the same way* that one's ability to drive or work may be impaired.

The QOLI was found to be sensitive to treatment-related change in two clinical samples. In both the managed care/substance abuse and counseling center samples QOLI scores increased significantly with treatment and moved to within one standard deviation of the functional, nonclinical normative sample mean after treatment – from a mean T score of 38 to a score of 47 for both samples at posttest with scores of 48 and 50 at the 3- and 6-month follow-ups for the managed care/substance abuse sample. This change signifies a clinically, and not just a statistically, significant amount of change as discussed above (see Introduction). Improvement in QOLI scores was mirrored in the BSI, a benchmark measure of psychiatric symptoms; this finding is positive only to the extent that the QOLI measures a construct that is distinct from psychiatric symptoms. Both here and elsewhere, life satisfaction, in general, and the QOLI, in particular, have been found to be discriminable from the constructs of psychiatric symptoms, negative and positive affect, and depression (Schimmack, Diener, and Oishi, 2002; Crowley and Kazdin, 1998; Diener, 2000; Frisch et al., 1992; Headey et al., 1993; Lewinsohn et al., 1991; Gonzales, Lewinsohn, and Clarke, 1985; Lucas et al., 1996; Snyder et al., 2000; McNamara and Booker, 2000).

Since "the ultimate purpose of *all* health interventions (that is, medical and psychological – Kazdin, 1993a) is to enhance patients' quality of life" (Jenkins, 1992: 367), it may be useful to conduct quality of life assessments using the QOLI or similar measures (see Rabkin et al., 2000 for review) on a routine basis in medicine, psychology, and mental health. With respect to outcome evaluation in mental health – whether in psychiatry, psychology, social work, or counseling, the QOLI may meet the need for a measure of individual contentment cited by Strupp (Strupp, 1996; Strupp and Hadley, 1977) as the *primary* criterion of positive outcome and mental health from the perspective of a patient. Furthermore, Richard Heimberg and his colleagues at Temple University's Adult Anxiety Clinic (Eng, Coles, Heimberg, and Safren, 2001) along with Frisch (1998) suggest that quality of life *interventions* such as Frisch's Quality of Life Therapy (Frisch, in press) should be implemented to *augment* the effects of disorder- or disease-specific interventions on quality of life assessments, to minimize the negative quality-of-life side effects of some treatments such as chemotherapy, to actually treat symptoms of disorder or disease *per se* (Grant et al., 1995), and to enhance patients' quality of life in areas that have little or nothing to do with their malady, but that nevertheless compensate for the quality of life decrements caused by the malady or its treatment (Frisch, in press).

The present findings are limited to one measure and to one type of quality of life assessment, that is, life satisfaction. Life satisfaction seems to predict future problems in health and functioning whether in prospective or in discriminant analysis studies such as that reported here. Despite its predictive value and discriminability from depression and other psychiatric symptoms, life satisfaction may reflect the influence of 'third variables' on adjustment, thereby challenging current theories of its causal significance and supportive findings (e.g., Diener, 2001; Frisch, in press, 1998a; Gonzales, Lewinsohn, and Clark, 1985; Lewinsohn, 1991). It is important that research into third variables be prospective or longitudinal since high correlations are to be expected and are not usually meaningful during the acute phase of many disorders or disease as when acutely depressed patients generate a 'cry for help' profile of multiple elevations on an MMPI-2 or SCL-90-R.

The factor structure and treatment utility of the QOLI have yet to be evaluated. The treatment utility or 'treatment planning utility' (Frisch, 1992) of a measure refers to its contribution to a positive treatment outcome, usually by facilitating the ease, efficiency, or accuracy of assessment, treatment planning, and/or treatment (Hayes, Nelson, and Jarrett, 1987). In this vein, the QOLI was designed to comprehensively screen for "problems-in-living" (as well as for *strengths* in everyday functioning) just as symptom checklists screen for disorders and diseases. Problems-in-living assessment is particularly important in managed care settings where about 75% of patients present with problems in living and related adjustment, depression, and anxiety concerns (Ludden and Mandell, 1993). While anecdotal reports from the current samples and from hundreds of patients treated elsewhere are positive (e.g., Kazdin, 1993a; Frisch, 1992, 1998a, in press), the QOLI's treatment utility should be formally assessed as with the "manipulated assessment strategy" in which the outcome of clients treated with and without information from the QOLI could be compared (Hayes, Nelson, and Jarrett, 1987). Treatment utility may also be more broadly defined and assessed by simply surveying clinicians about the extent to which the QOLI facilitates assessment, treatment planning, and treatment per se. Future research should also aim at extending the predictive validity findings reported here to areas explored with other life satisfaction measures such as job or school failure, particular mental disorders – that is, depressive, anxiety, substance use, and somatoform disorders, suicide, respiratory infections, heart disease, cancer, and excessive health-care utilization and expenditures. Finally, since the QOLI and QOLT seem well-suited to adolescent treatment in psychiatry, psychology, and general medicine, adolescent norms should be developed (E. S. Huebner, personal communication, September 27, 2002).

12.5. REFERENCES

American Psychiatric Association (2000). *Handbook of Psychiatric Measures*. Washington, DC: American Psychiatric Association.

Andersen, B. L., Kiecolt-Glaser, J. K., and Glaser, R. (1994). A biobehavioral model of cancer stress and disease course. *American Psychologist*, **49**, 389–404.

Baruffol, E., Gisle, L., and Corten, P. (1995). Life satisfaction as a mediator between distressing events and neurotic impairment in a general population. *Acta Psychiatrica Scandinavica*, **92**, 56–62.

Betz, N. E. (1987). Use of discriminant analysis in counseling psychology research. *Journal of Counseling Psychology*, **34**, 393-403.

Ben-Porath, Y. S. (1997). Use of personality assessment instruments in empirically guided treatment planning. *Psychological Assessment*, **9**, 361–367.

Burlingame, G. M., Lambert, M. J., Reisinger, C. W., Neff, W. M., and Mosier, J. (1995). Pragmatics of tracking mental health outcomes in a managed care setting. *Journal of Mental Health Administration*, **22**, 226–236.

Carlbring, P., Setling, B. E., Ljungstrand, P., Ekselius, L. and Andersson, G. (2001). Treatment of Panic Disorder via the Internet: A randomized trial of a self-help program. *Behavior Therapy*, **32**, 751–764.

Chambliss, C. H. (2000). *Psychotherapy an Managed Care: Reconciling Research and Reality*. Boston: Allyn and Bacon.

Clark, M. P. and Mason, T. W. (2001). Implementation of a comprehensive system of program evaluation: The Iowa State University experience. *Journal of College Student Development*, **42**, 28–35.

Cohen, J. (1988). *Statistical Power Analysis for the Behavioral Sciences*, 2nd edition. Hillsdale, NJ: Erlbaum.

Cornell, J. E., Saunders, M. J., Paunovich, E. D., and Frisch, M. B. (1997). Oral Health Quality of Life Inventory (OH-QoL). In G. Slade (ed.), *Assessing Oral Health outcomes: Measuring Health Status and Quality of Life* (pp. 135–149). Chapel Hill, NC: University of North Carolina Press.

Crits-Christoph, P. and Connolly, M. B (1997). Measuring change in patients following psychological and pharmacological interventions: Anxiety disorders. In H. H. Strupp, L. M. Horowitz, and M. J. Lambert (eds.), *Measuring Patient Changes in Mood, Anxiety, and Personality Disorders: Toward a Core Battery* (pp. 155–190). Washington, D.C.: American Psychological Association.

Crowley, M. J. and Kazdin, A. E.(1998). Evaluation in clinical practice: Clinically sensitive and systematic methods of treatment delivery. *Journal of Child and Family Studies*, **7**, 233–251.

Diamond, R.. and Becker, M. (1999). The Wisconsin Quality of Life Index: A multidimensional model for measuring quality of life. *Journal of Clinical Psychiatry*, **60**, 29–31.

Denney, D. R. and Frisch, M. B. (1981). The role of neuroticism in relation to life stress and illness. *Journal of Psychosomatic Research*, **25**, 303–307.

Derogatis, L. R. and Lynn, L. L. (1999). Psychological tests in screening for psychiatric disorder. In M. E. Maruish (ed.), *The Use of Psychological Testing for Treatment Planning and Outcome Assessment*, 2nd edition (pp. 41–80). Mahwah, NJ: Laurence Erlbaum.

Diener, E. (2001, December). *The Benefits of Positive Affect.* Paper presented at the annual meeting of the International Society for Quality of Life Studies, Washington, D.C.

Diener, E. (2000). Subjective well-being: The science of happiness and a proposal for a national index. *American Psychologist*, **55**, 34–43.

Diener, E. and Suh, E. M. (2000). Measuring subjective well-being to compare the quality of life of cultures. In E. Diener and E. M. Suh (eds.), *Culture and Subjective Well-Being*. Boston, MA: MIT Press.

Diener, E., Suh, E. M., Lucas, R. E., and Smith, H. L. (1999). Subjective well-being: Three decades of progress. *Psychological Bulletin*, **125**, 276–302.

Endicott, J., Nee, J., Harrison, W., and Blumenthal, R. (1993). Quality of life enjoyment and satisfaction questionnaire: A new measure. *Psychopharmacology Bulletin*, **29**, 321–326.

Eng, W., Heimberg, R. G., Hart, T. A., Schneier, F. R., and Liebowitz, M. R. (2001). Quality of life following cognitive behavioral treatment for social anxiety disorder. *Emotion*, **1**, 365–380.

Eng, W., Coles, M. C., Heimberg, R. G., and Safren, S. A. (2001). Quality of life following cognitive behavioral treatment for social anxiety disorder. *Depression and Anxiety*, **13**, 192–193.

Eng, W., Coles, M. C., Turk, C. L., Heimberg, R. G., and Safren, S. A. (December, 2001). *Quality of Life in Individuals with Social Anxiety and Generalized Anxiety Disorder.* Paper presented to the International Society for Quality of Life Studies, Washington, D.C.

Ferrans, C. E. (2000). Quality of life as an outcome of cancer care. In C. Yarbro, M. Frogge, M. Goodman (eds.), *Cancer Nursing: Principles and Practice*, 5th edition (pp. 243–258). Boston, MA: Jones and Bartlett.

Ferrans, C. E. and Powers, M. J. (1992). Psychometric assessment of the Quality of Life Index. *Research in Nursing and Health*, **15**, 29–38.

Folkman, S. and Moskowitz, J. T. (2000). Positive affect and the other side of coping. *American Psychologist*, **55**, 647–654.

Frisch, Michael B. (in press). *Quality of Life Therapy: Cognitive therapy for the whole person*. New York: Wiley and Sons.

Frisch, Michael B. (2000). Improving mental and physical health care through quality of life therapy and assessment. In E. Diener and D. R. Rahtz (eds.), *Advances in Quality of Life Theory and Research* (pps. 207–241). New York: Kluwer Academic.

Frisch, M. B. (1999). Quality of life assessment/intervention and the Quality of Life Inventory (QOLI). In M. R. Maruish (ed.), T*he Use of Psychological Testing for Treatment Planning and Outcome Assessment*, 2nd edition (pp. 1227–1331). Hillsdale, NJ: Lawrence Erlbaum.

Frisch, M. B. (1998a). Quality of life therapy and assessment in health care. *Clinical Psychology: Science and Practice*, **5**, 19–40.

Frisch, M. B. (1998b). Documenting the effectiveness of Employee Assistance Programs. *Employee Assistance Research*, **2**, 2–5.

Frisch, M. B. (1994a). *Quality of Life Inventory(QOLI)*. Minneapolis, MN: National Computer Systems.

Frisch, M. B. (1994b). *Test Manual and Treatment Guide for the QOLI (Quality of Life Inventory)*. Minneapolis, MN: National Computer Systems (NCS).

Frisch, M. B. (1992). Use of the Quality of Life Inventory in problem assessment and treatment planning for cognitive therapy of depression. In A. Freeman and F. M. Dattilio (eds.), *Comprehensive Casebook of Cognitive Therapy* (pp. 27–52). New York: Plenum.

Frisch, M. B., Cornell, J., Villanueva, M., and Retzlaff, P. J. (1992). Clinical validation of the Quality of Life Inventory: A measure of life satisfaction for use in treatment planning and outcome assessment. *Psychological Assessment*, **4**, 92–101.

Frisch, M. B. and MacKenzie, C. J. (1991). A comparison of formerly and chronically battered women on cognitive and situational dimensions. *Psychotherapy*, **28**, 339–344.

Frisch, M. B. and Froberg, W. (1987). Social validation of assertion strategies for handling aggressive criticism: Evidence for consistency across situations. *Behavior Therapy*, **2**, 181–191.

Frisch, M. B. and Higgins, R. L. (1986). Instructional demand effects and the correspondence among self-report, naturalistic, and role-play measures of social skill as influenced by instructional demand. *Behavioral Assessment*, **8**, 221–236.

Frisch, M. B., Elliot, C. H., Atsaides, J. P., Salva, D. M., and Denney, D. R. (1982). Social skills and stress management training to enhance patients' interpersonal competencies. *Psychotherapy: Theory, Research, and Practice*, **19**, 349–358.

Frisch, M. B. and Gerrard, M. (1981). Natural helping systems: A national survey of Red Cross volunteers. *American Journal of Community Psychology*, **9**, 567–579.

Glass, G. V. and Stanley, J. C. (1970). *Statistical Methods in Education and Psychology*. Englewood Cliffs, JF: Prentice-Hall.

Gonzales, L. R., Lewinsohn, P. M., and Clarke, G. N. (1985). Longitudinal follow-up of unipolar depressives: An investigation of predictors of relapse. *Journal of Consulting and Clinical Psychology*, **53**, 461–469.

Grant, G., Salcedo, V., Hynan, L. S., and Frisch, M. B. (1995). Effectiveness of Quality of Life Therapy. *Psychological Reports*, **76**, 1203–1208.

Hayes, S. C., Nelson, R. O., and Jarrett, R. B. (1987). The treatment utility of assessment: A functional approach to evaluating assessment quality. *American Psychologist*, **42**, 963–974.

Headey, B., Kelley, J., and Wearing , A. (1993). Dimensions of mental health: life satisfaction, positive affect, anxiety, and depression. *Social Indicators Research*, **29**, 63–82.

Horowitz, L. M., Strupp, H. H., Lambert, M. J., and Elkin, I. (1997). Overview and summary of the Core Battery Conference. In H. H. Strupp, L. M. Horowitz, and M. J. Lambert (eds.), *Measuring Patient Changes in Mood, Anxiety, and Personality Disorders: Toward a Core Battery* (pp. 11–56). Washington, D.C.: American Psychological Association.

Huebner, E. S. (1994). Preliminary development and validation of a multidimensional life satisfaction scale for children. *Psychological Assessment*, **6**, 149–158.

Huebner, E. S, Drane, W., and Valois, R. F. (2000). Levels an demographic correlates of adolescent life satisfaction reports. *School Psychology International*, **21**, 281–292.

Jacobson, N. S. and Truax, P. (1991). Clinical significance: A statistical approach to defining meaningful change in psychotherapy research. *Journal of Consulting and Clinical Psychology*, **59**, 12–19.

Jenkins, C. D. (1992). Assessment of outcomes of health intervention. *Social Science and Medicine*, **35**, 367–375.

Judge, T. A. and Hulin, C. L. (1993). Job satisfaction as a reflection of disposition: A multiple source causal analysis. *Organizational Behavior and Human Decision Processes*, **56**, 388–421.

Judge, T. A. and Watanabe, S. (1993). Another look at the job satisfaction-life satisfaction relationship. *Journal of Applied Psychology*, **78**, 939–948.

Kazdin, A. E. (2003). *Research Design in Clinical Psychology*, 4th edition. New York: Macmillan.

Kazdin, A. E. (1993a). Evaluation in clinical practice: Clinically sensitive and systematic methods of treatment delivery. *Behavior Therapy*, **24**, 11–45.

Kazdin, A. E. (1993b). Treatment of conduct disorder: Progress and directions in psychotherapy research. *Development and Psychopathology*, **5**, 277–310.

Kazdin, A. E. (1994). Methodology, design, and evaluation in psychotherapy research. In A. E. Bergin and S. L. Garfield (eds.), *Handbook of Psychotherapy and Behavior Change*, 4th edition. NY: Wiley.

Kendall, P.C. and Trove, W. M. (1988). Normative comparisons in therapy outcome. *Behavioral Assessment*, **10**, 147–158.

Klecka, W. R. (1980). *Discriminant Analysis*. Beverly Hills, CA: Sage.

Kocis, J. H. Zisook, S., Davidson, J., Shelton, R., Yonkers, K., Hellerstein, D. J., Rosenbaum, J. and Halbreich, U. (1997). Double-blind comparison of sertraline, imipramine, and placebo in the treatment of dysthymia: Psychosocial outcomes. *American Journal of Psychiatry*, **154**, 390–395.

Lazarus, R. S. (1991). *Emotion and Adaptation*. New York: Oxford University Press.

Lewinsohn, P., Redner, J., and Seeley, J. (1991). The relationship between life satisfaction and psychosocial variables: New perspectives. In F. Strack, M. Argyle, and N. Schwartz (eds.), *Subjective Well-Being* (pp. 141–169). New York: Plenum.

Ludden, J. and Mandell, L. (1993). Quality planning for mental health. *Journal of Mental Health Administration*, **20**, 72–78.

Lucas, R. E., Diener, E., and Suh, E. (1996). Discriminant validity of well-being measures. *Journal of Personality and Social Psychology*, **71**, 616–628.

Matarazzo, J. D. (1992). Psychological testing and assessment in the 21st century. *American Psychologist*, **47**, 1007–1018.

McNamara, J. R. and Booker, D. J. (2000). The Abuse Disability Questionnaire: A new scale of assessing the consequence3s of partner abuse. *Journal of Interpersonal Violence*, **15**, 170–183.

Mendlowicz, M. V. and Stein, M. B. (2000). Quality of life in individuals with anxiety disorders. *American Journal of Psychiatry*, **157**, 669–682.

Mogotsi, M., Kaminer, D., and Stein, D. J. (2000). Quality of life in the anxiety disorders. *Harvard Review of Psychiatry*, **8**, 273–282.

Miller, I. W., Keitner, G. I., Schatzberg, A. F., Klein, D. N., Thase, M. E., Rush, A. J., Markowitz, J. C., Schlager, D. S., Kornstein, S. G., Davis, S. M., Harrison, W. M., and Keller, M. B. (1998). The treatment of chronic depression, Part 3: Psychosocial functioning before and after treatment with sertraline or imipramine. *Journal of Clinical Psychiatry*, **59**, 608–619.

Moras, K. (1997). Toward a core battery for treatment efficacy research on mood disorders. In H. H. Strupp, L. M. Horowitz, and M. J. Lambert (eds.), *Measuring Patient Changes in Mood, Anxiety, and Personality Disorders: Toward a Core Battery* (pp. 301–338). Washington, D.C.: American Psychological Association.

Moum, T. (1996, August). *Subjective Well-Being as a Short- and Long-Term Predictor of Suicide in the General Population.* Paper presented at the World Conference on Quality of Life, Prince George, British Columbia, Canada.

Newman, F. L., Ciarlo, J. A., and Carpenter, D. (1999). Guidelines for selecting psychological instruments for treatment planning and outcome assessment. In M. E. Maruish (Ed.), *The Use of Psychological Testing for Treatment Planning and Outcome Assessment*, 2nd edition (pp. 153–170. Mahwah, NJ: Lawrence Erlbaum.

Niemcryk, S. J. (2001, December). *Quality of Life Assessment: A Perspective from the Pharmaceutical Industry.* Paper presented at the annual meeting of the International Society for Quality of Life Studies, Washington, D.C.

Ogles B. M., Lunnen, K. M., and Bonesteel, K. (2001). Clinical significance: History, application, and current prratice. *Clinical Psychology Review*, **21**, 421–446.

Ogles, B. M., Lambert, M., and Masters, K. (1996). *Assessing Outcome in Clinical Practice.* Boston: Allyn and Bacon.

Ogles, B. M., Lambert, M. J., and Sawyer, J. D. (1995). Clinical significance of the NIMH treatment of depression collaborative research program data. *Journal of Consulting and Clinical Psychology*, **63**, 321–326.

Pavot, W. and Diener, E. (1993). Review of the Satisfaction with Life Scale. *Psychological Assessment*, **5**, 164–172.

Pohl, R. B., Wolkow, R. M., and Clary, C. M. (1998). Sertraline in the treatment of Panic Disorder: A double-blind multicenter trial. *American Journal of Psychiatry*, **155**, 1189–1195.

Rabkin, J., Wagner, G., and Griffin, K. W. (2000). Quality-of-Life Measures. In American Psychiatric Association, *Handbook of Psychiatric Measures.* Washington, D.C.: American Psychiatric Association.

Rapaport, M. H., Endicott, J., and Clary, D. M. (2002). PTSD and quality of life: Results across 64 weeks of sertraline treatment. *Journal of Clinical Psychiatry*, **63**, 59–65.

Rush, A. J. (Principal Investigator). (August, 2000). *Sequenced Treatment Alternatives for Resistant Depression: STAR*D Research Protocol.* Dallas, TX: Unpublished manuscript. Web address: http://www.edc.gsph.pitt.edu/stard/Private/Protocol/Post-DSMB%20Submittal.pdf.

Safren, S. A., Heimberg, R. G., Brown, E. J., and Holle, C. (1997). Quality of life in social phobia. *Depression and Anxiety*, **4**, 126–133.

Salek, S. (ed.) (1998). *Compendium of Quality of Life Instruments.* NY: Wiley.

Schimmack, U., Diener, E., and Oishi, S. (2002). Life-satisfaction is a momentary judgment and a stable personality characteristic: The use of chronically accessible and stable sources. *Journal of Personality*, **70**, 345–385.

Seligman, M. E. P. (2002). *Authentic Happiness.* New York: Free Press.

Seligman, M. E. P. (1995) The effectiveness of psychotherapy: The Consumer Reports study. *American Psychologist*, **50**, 965–974.

Seligman, M. E. P. and Csikszentmihalyi, M. (2000). Positive psychology: An introduction. *American Psychologist*, **55**, 5–14.

Sirgy, M. Joseph (2002). *The Psychology of Quality of Life.* Dordrecht, Netherlands: Kluwer Academic.

Snyder, A. G., Stanley, M. A., Novey, D. M., Averill, P. M., and Beck, J. G. (2000). Measures of depression in older adults with Generalized Anxiety Disorder: A psychometric evaluation. *Depression and Anxiety*, **11**, 114–120.

Spilker, B. (1996). *Quality of Life and Pharmacoecomonics in Clinical Trials.* New York: Lippincott-Raven Press.

Strupp, H. H. (1996). The tripartite model and the Consumer Reports study. *American Psychologist*, **51**, 1017–1024.

Strupp, H. H. and Hadley, S. W. (1977). A tripartite model of mental health and therapeutic outcomes. *American Psychologist*, **32**, 187–196.

Turk, D. L., Mennin, D. S., Fresco, D. M., and Heimberg (2000). *Impairment and Quality of Life among Individuals with Generalized Anxiety Disorder.* Paper presented at the Annual Meeting of the Association for Advancement of Behavior Therapy, New Orleans.

Vitaliano, P. P., Dougherty, C. M., and Siegler, I. C. (1994). Biopsychosocial risks for cardiovascular disease. In R. P. Abeles, H. C. Gift, and M. G. Ory (eds), *Aging and Quality of Life.* NY: Springer.

Wagner, E. H., Schoenbach, V. J., Orleans, C. T., Grothaus, L. C., Saunders, K. W., Curry, S., and Pearson, D. C. (1990). Participation in a smoking cessation program: A population-based perspective. *American Journal of Preventive Medicine*, **6**, 258–266.

Ware, J. E. (1986). The assessment of health status. In C. H. Aiken and D. Mechanic (eds.), *Application of Social Science to Clinical Medicine and Health Policy*, 9th Edition. New Brunswick, NJ: Rutgers University Press.

Ware, J. E. (1996). The MOS 36-Item Short-Form Health Survey (SF-36). In B. Dickey and L. I. Sederer (eds.), *Outcomes Assessment in Clinical Practice.* Baltimore: Williams & Wilkins.

12.6. ACKNOWLEDGEMENTS AND AFFILIATIONS

Frisch, Michael B. – Baylor University; Clark, Michelle P. – Iowa State University Student Counseling Center; Rouse, Steven V.-Pepperdine University; Rudd, M. David – Baylor University; Paweleck, Jennifer – Baylor University; Greenstone, Andrew – Baylor University; and Kopplin, David A. – Baylor University.

This chapter was supported, in part, by a 2002 summer sabbatical grant to the first author. This chapter is based, in part, upon a paper presented at the annual meeting of the International Society for Quality of Life Studies, Washington, D.C. in December of 2001. The order of authorship of the first two authors was determined by a flip of a coin. Steven Rouse is an Assistant Professor of Psychology at Pepperdine University. The authors gratefully acknowledge the invaluable assistance of Professors Olga Paradis, Billie Peterson-Lugo and Jeffrey A. Steely of the Baylor University Libraries. The authors gratefully acknowledge the following research assistants: Scott Dugan and Aimee Segura. The authors gratefully acknowledge the invaluable assistance of Professors Olga Paradis, Billie Peterson-Lugo and Jeffery Steely of the Baylor University Libraries. The authors gratefully acknowledge the invaluable assistance of the Waco branch of TDMHMR, especially that of Dr. Manuel Edquist, Grace Walton, Cindy Forcher, and Patricia Kelm. The authors gratefully acknowledge the invaluable assistance of the Behavioral Health Services Division of the Allina Health System of Minneapolis, MN, especially that of Joyce Arendt, Julie Godfrey, and Doug Nemecek. The authors gratefully acknowledge the invaluable assistance of Virginia (Ginny) Steele of NCS Assessments. Correspondence regarding this manuscript may be directed to Michael B. Frisch, Ph.D., Professor, Department of Psychology and Neuroscience, Baylor University, P.O. Box 97334 , Waco, TX 76798-7334; Telephone (254) 710-2811; Fax (254) 710-3033; Email: michael_frisch@baylor.edu.

Marsha A. Dickson and Mary A. Littrell

13. MEASURING QUALITY OF LIFE OF APPAREL WORKERS IN MUMBAI, INDIA: INTEGRATING QUANTITATIVE AND QUALITATIVE DATA ON BASIC MINIMUM NEEDS, LIVING WAGES, AND WELL-BEING

ABSTRACT: We interviewed 92 tailors and embroiderers about their wages, household income, household expenses, and quality of life. A Basic Minimum Needs Ratio was calculated by dividing average total household income by average expenses for housing, food, transportation, and utilities. The necessary living wage was calculated using a variation of a formula created at the 1998 Living Wage Summit. Open-ended questions provided qualitative data on multiple dimensions of well-being. We assess the contribution of each measure for triangulation of data in reaching valid conclusions about quality of life, business, and labor.

13.1. Introduction

Quality of life of people working in apparel production is currently a topic of interest to many people around the world. Since the mid-1990s, government officials, consumer activists, labor representatives, industry leaders, and the media have focused their attention on conditions surrounding the production of clothing (Varley, 1998). Early in the period, covert investigation by the National Labor Committee, an organization partially funded by the Union of Needletrades, Industrial and Textile Employees (UNITE), connected popular television personality Kathie Lee Gifford's clothing line sold by Wal-Mart to sweatshops in the United States and Central America. Over the ensuing years, prominent apparel manufactures and retailers, such as Nike and the Gap, were publicly linked with sweatshop production of apparel (Ramey, 1996). Throughout this period, outraged activists have targeted US firms for protests and boycotts (Varley 1998; Wazir, 2001).

One of the most contentious issues under discussion is worker wages. Groups such as the Worker's Rights Consortium demand that a 'living wage' be paid to apparel workers in developing countries (Greenhouse, 1999). In contrast, industry executives prefer paying a legal minimum wage or the prevailing wage offered by other apparel factories in the locality. A living wage directly takes into consideration the costs of basic living expenditures; whereas, the minimum wage may or may not do so, depending on the government setting the wage. It is thought that living wages are generally higher than the minimum wage (Hetter, 2001; Losciale, 2000; Sullivan, 2001; Wazir, 2001).

Alternative trading organizations are proposed as an option to consumers who wish to purchase products made under a different set of conditions than provided by multinational corporations (Ericson, n.d.; Rosenthal, 1997; Smullin, 1997). Alternative trading organizations (ATOs) are businesses that export and retail artisan products, such as ethnic apparel, from developing countries with the goal of enhancing artisan participation in the global market and ultimately improving the

M. Joseph Sirgy et al. (eds.), Advances in Quality-of-Life Theory and Research, 211–232, 2003.

quality of life of the poorest people in developing countries (Littrell and Dickson, 1997, 1999). ATOs practice "fair trade" by providing equitable wages in a safe and healthy work environment, developing sustainable business practices, fostering artisan well-being, protecting the environment, and promoting political and social justice. However, to date there has been little systematic research on the social and economic impacts of working for ATOs (Littrell and Dickson, 1999). Because of society's increased scrutiny of business claims to be fair to their workers, and the ongoing argument about appropriate remuneration, it is essential that ATOs understand and document the impact they have on artisans' lives.

The purpose of this paper is to compare and contrast a variety of quantitative and qualitative measures of quality of life of workers producing apparel for ATOs. The apparel production business for analysis involves women living in the Golibar slum of Mumbai, India who sew and embroider products for the US-based ATO, MarketPlace: Handwork of India.

We first present an overarching theoretical framework for our research and review past studies of quality of life in India. Literature discussing how to measure quality of life is also reviewed. We then examine the concept of living wages and the small body of literature discussing its measurement. Next, using the quantitative measures and narrative interviews, a portrait of the workers quality of life is revealed and discussed in relation to issues of wages, quality of life, and ATO philosophy. Within the discussion, we critically assess the quality of life measures used in the study. Unique contributions of each method are identified for triangulation of data in reaching valid conclusions about quality of life, business, and labor.

Established in 1979, MarketPlace: Handwork of India (hereafter referred to as MarketPlace), markets clothing through a mail-order catalog sent to customers throughout the United States (Littrell and Dickson, 1997, 1999). MarketPlace sells hand printed and hand embroidered clothing made in Mumbai, India under the direction of a sister organization called MarketPlace Bombay. MarketPlace and its organizational partner, Support the Handicapped Rehabilitation Effort (SHARE), commenced operations in 1980 for purposes of "providing employment opportunity to low-income women and people with handicaps" (SHARE, n.d.). By 1994, MarketPlace Bombay was providing employment for 350 workers who were organized into seven small workshops. MarketPlace Bombay and SHARE serve dual roles as a manufacturer of apparel and interiors products and a social support organization. In its role as manufacturer, MarketPlace Bombay distributes apparel orders to the seven groups of workers located in and near Mumbai. In its development role, SHARE oversees a range of activities focusing on educational, health, and social issues among MarketPlace artisans. Overarching economic and social objectives of MarketPlace Bombay and SHARE are integrated in a holistic development perspective as they strive to ensure that workers:

- are paid their fair and sustainable wages,
- enhance their self-worth and self-respect and
- feel empowered to identify and address the social issues affecting their lives and the community around them (SHARE, nd.).

In 2000, MarketPlace and SHARE asked us to conduct a social audit to determine how well they had achieved their social objectives. Beyond providing valuable information to MarketPlace and SHARE, the research directly addresses society's pressing question of how sewing and embroidering apparel for export to the United States has impacted the quality of life of workers and how best to measure this impact.

13.2. THEORETICAL FRAMEWORK

This research on ATO worker quality of life is theoretically framed by Chambers' (1992) model of well-being. A noted scholar in international development, Chambers' holds that well-being (i.e., quality of life) is measured by a range of material, social, psychological, and spiritual indicators. Economic livelihood underlies well-being and flows from a dependable source of cash and food to meet basic needs. Capabilities contribute to livelihood and well-being and are enlarged through training, learning, and practice. For this paper we focus on material well-being but bring in other aspects of well-being that were clearly important to the workers.

13.3. QUALITY OF LIFE IN INDIA

Quality of life has been measured in a variety of ways to understand social and economic development. We focused our literature review on studies examining quality of life in India. Brinkerhoff, Fredell, and Frideres (1997), like other scholars, distinguish between objective and subjective aspects of quality of life. Objective aspects are easily quantifiable at the aggregate level and include such things as mortality rate and level of education. On the other hand, subjective aspects of quality of life include psychological and attitudinal dimensions and are perceived to be difficult to measure (Brinkerhoff et al., 1997).

The Human Development Index (HDI) used by the United Nations' Development Programme is an objective measure of quality of life. Included in the index are life expectancy, educational attainment, and per capita gross domestic product, which proxy longevity, ability to have knowledge, and ability to attain a certain standard of living (Indrayan et al., 1999). The HDI was designed primarily to compare aggregate data at the nation level. Indrayan et al. (1999) used the HDI on state level quality of life in India, but the data needed for the HDI were available for only a portion of the states in India. Working with data that are disaggregated only to the state level has the potential to mask great differences in quality of life among a state's citizens. Basu (1992) contends that "macro-indices of economic growth and development often fail to capture the micro-level essence of the well-being of a population" (p. 252). For example, in Maharashta state in India, where Mumbai is located, a quick glance at the high rise apartments of the middle class, large detached houses of the wealthy, and tiny, one-room homes of the women we interviewed in the Golibar slum reveals great variability in quality of life and development within the city. Mukherjee's (1981) research with rural and urban citizens of West Bengal, including the city of Calcutta, reveals that there are multiple levels of quality of life within a region and supports the idea that groups of individuals vary greatly on which dimensions of quality of life are salient. Brinkerhoff et al. (1997) argue that social indicators, rather than objective macro-economic indices, are appropriate for measuring both the objective and subjective aspects of quality of life at individual or group levels.

13.3.1. *Social Indicators*

The social indicators approach recognizes that quality of life is multi-dimensional and includes a broad range of components beyond economic (Brinkerhoff et al., 1997); thus, this approach is compatible with Chambers' (1992) view of well-being. Social indicators can be measured at either macro or micro levels, and objectively or subjectively. At the national level, social indicators of quality of life have been correlated with macro economic, health, and education measures (i.e., objective quality of life measures). Data covering the subjective measures of quality of life are typically not available at the national level and are often collected using a combination of qualitative and quantitative research approaches (e.g., Basu, 1992; Brinkerhoff et al., 1997). Brinkerhoff et al. believe that both subjective and objective social indicators are necessary to determine a valid picture of quality of life for individuals or groups at any level. Other researchers, however, claim that subjective social indicators, such as happiness and satisfaction, are too difficult to measure (Indrayan et al., 1999).

13.3.2. *Basic Minimum Needs*

A second approach for studying quality of life in relation to development is to measure basic minimum needs – that which is required for a minimum level of living for the poorest people (Grant, 1977 as cited by Brinkerhoff et al., 1997). Basic minimum needs are considered when determining a country's poverty line (US Department of Labor [USDOL], 2000). The most fundamental of basic minimum needs are food, water, housing, and safety (Okafor, 1985). Additional basic minimum needs could include transportation and education (Brinkerhoff et al., 1997). These basic minimum needs can be measured objectively or subjectively. Yet other basic minimum needs are more subjective including appropriately paid work, participation in decision-making, freedom, access to social services, access to family planning, opportunity for spiritual growth, and satisfaction (Brinkerhoff et al., 1997).

13.3.3. *Measuring Social Indicators and Basic Minimum Needs*

Chambers (1997) contends that accurately measuring quality of life for development purposes requires that participants in a research study define what this concept means for them. Likewise, Mukherjee (1981) stresses the importance of identifying what aspects of life need to be improved for the people prior to developing strategies to improve their quality of life. Participatory action research emphasizes inclusion of the population to be measured in all phases of the research, including research design (Chambers, 1997). Brinkerhoff et al. (1997) combined qualitative and quantitative research approaches to study basic minimum needs and social indicators of quality of life among women in a rural, mountainous area of India. The researchers referred to the participatory action research approach they used as "listening to women's voices." One strategy used in early stages of their research relied on stories that revealed important aspects of quality of life to the women. From the stories and various other qualitative data gathered in early stages of the research, the researchers developed an interview instrument measuring basic minimum needs and social indicators of quality of life (Brinkerhoff et al., 1997). To measure basic minimum needs, Brinkerhoff et al. had participants consider pairs of basic needs and select what their families needed most. The Needs Index was the mean number of times a need was selected (Brinkerhoff et al., 1997).

To operationalize the various subjective social indicators of quality of life, Brinkerhoff et al. (1997) used Likert-type scales expressing degree of satisfaction with a variety of specific and general aspects of quality of life. Interviewees were presented a miniature, runged ladder and asked to relate their satisfaction to a rung on the ladder. Happiness was measured with a series of face caricatures ranging from one with a large frown to one with a large smile (Brinkerhoff et al., 1997).

In a different approach to subjectively measuring quality of life, Mukherjee (1981) asked what was missing from the individual's life and what, if removed, would make life better. Respondents from rural areas and a city (Calcutta) in the state of West Bengal described quality of life primarily in terms of what they wished they had (Mukherjee, 1981). Themes salient in discussing quality of life related to personal career, life at work, family life, personal well-being, and peace and happiness (Mukherjee, 1981).

13.3.4. *Relationship Between Basic Minimum Needs and Social Indicators*

Brinkerhoff et al. (1997) hypothesized that the extent to which basic minimum needs are met correlates positively with quality of life; however, their research did not support this hypothesis. The researchers questioned whether an objective measure of income rather than the subjective measure of satisfaction with income might have been correlated with basic minimum needs. Additionally, the researchers concluded that basic minimum needs are specific to a particular place and time. Various subjectively-measured social indicators, such as satisfaction with spiritual life were intercorrelated with specific and general measures of quality of life (Brinkerhoff et al., 1997). Based on the work of Brinkerhoff et al., we hypothesized that for this research,

H1: The ability to meet basic needs (Basic Minimum Needs Ratio) will be positively correlated with general quality of life (satisfaction).

H2: The ability to meet basic needs (Basic Minimum Needs Ratio) will be positively correlated with subjective ratings of ability to provide basic needs.

H3: Subjective ratings of ability to provide basic needs will be positively correlated with general quality of life (satisfaction).

13.3.5. *Quality of Life and Work*

Because the focus of this research was on the contribution that working with MarketPlace had made to quality of life of women artisans, we were interested in literature relating these two variables. Basu (1992) proposed that increases in income do not always positively correlate with increased quality of life because income represents a *means* to a better life, but is not always used in a way needed to achieve increased quality of life. However, most respondents in Mukherjee's (1981) study viewed their work (and concomitantly their income) as a means of improving their families' lives rather than a means of personal gratification. The urban poor in particular regarded their work as a contributing factor in their children's well-being (Mukherjee, 1981). Based on the literature, we hypothesized that,

H4: Income is not correlated with general quality of life (satisfaction).

H5: Perceived ability to provide for their families has increased since coming to work for MarketPlace.

Beyond contributing to family well-being, work also increases other aspects of quality of life. Basu (1992) studied geographically and culturally diverse groups of women that had migrated to a Delhi slum from areas throughout India. Women from North India were more likely to conform to traditions of *purdah*, which isolates women from the outside world with cloaks and veiling that cover much of their bodies. Purdah not only prevents women from being seen when they are out of their home, the tradition often keeps them indoors and out of the workplace. Basu observed that women following purdah had restricted physical movement within the slum, were less likely to work, and were more dependent on others to make decisions requiring knowledge or interaction with the outside world. The seclusion prevented women from attaining knowledge needed for improving quality of life for their families. Additionally, women from regions more likely to observe purdah were less likely to visit health care professionals (Basu, 1992). It seems that opportunity to interact with others outside the home, such as that provided by work, positively influences quality of life for both women and their families. Thus, we hypothesized that,

H6: Satisfaction with life has increased since coming to work for MarketPlace.

13.4. LIVING WAGES

We reviewed an additional body of literature more narrowly associated with material well-being that relates to the minimum compensation needed by workers to obtain an acceptable level of living. The US Department of Labor (2000) provides a brief history of the concept of living wages, from its emergence in the Middle Ages and its subsequent relevance to the writings of various economists and religious leaders in the eighteenth and nineteenth centuries. During the twentieth century, numerous studies were conducted to determine the income needed for a family to have a healthy and decent living (USDOL, 2000). Over the last decade, some metropolitan areas of the United States have passed ordinances requiring businesses to pay wages covering basic needs (Bremer, 2002; Ciscel, 2000).

Various authors define living wages differently, however, all definitions have in common the coverage of basic needs (Business for Social Responsibility [BSR], 2002). The Fair Trade Federation suggests that a living wage "covers basic needs, including food, shelter, education and healthcare for their families" (BSR, 2002, n.p.). As such, the concept of living wages links income with the previously discussed concept of basic minimum needs (i.e., USDOL, 2000). However, living wage remains an untested concept when it comes to developing countries and there is no standard method for calculating the wage. Additionally, there is disagreement about what should be included as basic needs (Bremer, 2002; BSR, 2002).

13.4.1. *Determining Living Wages*

A 1998 Living Wage Summit aimed to more precisely define the concept and its measurement. The basic needs identified at the summit included nutrition, clothing, healthcare, education, water, childcare, transportation, housing, and energy. To determine living wages, summit attendees proposed that the amount of money needed to cover the minimum amount of these basic needs for an average household be divided by the number of adult wage earners living in the average household and then 10% of income be added for savings (BSR, 2002). Bremer (2002) proposed a similar formula but suggested that one-third of available adult labor be reserved for household work.

A variety of potential issues have been raised about applying the formula established at the Living Wage Summit and other measures of living wages and basic needs. Advantages and disadvantages have been noted about using aggregate data collected at the national level versus collecting data on the actual needs of a specific workforce or community (Bremer, 2002; Steele, 2000).

Establishing a minimally acceptable level of living is also a concern (Bremer, 2002; Sweatshop Watch, 1998). Basic minimum needs can be determined by the expenditures made by families at the poverty line, or by calculating the costs of a "market basket" of goods needed for survival (USDOL, 2000). Another problem regards the under- or overestimating that occurs from use of average household size and composition in settings with diverse households (Bremer, 2002).

Additionally, some people oppose applying this or other formulas internationally because they believe that establishing the living wage should be based on a grass-roots effort that takes into consideration the views of workers about what comprises a living wage (Steele, 2000). In many ways, the problems measuring living wages parallel those found in the literature on measuring basic minimum needs and social indicators.

Srinivasin and Park (2001) pose a different sort of argument, questioning the value and relevance of requiring living wages in developing countries. The authors summarize the impact of a 1954 effort by India's government to require fair living wages and conclude that establishing living wage laws would not reach those most in need, especially since the majority of workers are employed in the informal sector where enforcement of such laws is virtually impossible. However, this perspective is less relevant among those who consider accountability for wages a voluntary action that ATOs or multinational apparel businesses might take to assure the well-being of their workforce.

13.5. METHODS

In developing this research, the US-based owner and president of MarketPlace and the Mumbai-based executive director of MarketPlace Bombay worked closely with the women artisans in Mumbai to develop a list of social indicators by which they believed that their development and quality of life should be measured. Broad social indicators included decision-making related to family matters, status in the community, self-confidence, self-improvement, economic independence, social awareness, and a variety of items related to the home and family. Like Brinkerhoff et al. (1997), MarketPlace used stories women told about their lives before and after working for MarketPlace to identify the artisans' salient dimensions of well-being. The social indicators contributed by the women reflected the material, social, and psychological dimensions of well-being, but not the spiritual dimension discussed by Chambers (1997). These social indicators were provided to us for inclusion into the interview schedule. Although aspects of economic livelihood were not included in the list of social indicators we received from the artisans, some features of material well-being were mentioned. Measuring economic livelihood was prioritized by the researchers because of society's increasing scrutiny of wages and material well-being and because of the desire to measure the complete array of factors that Chambers' proposes as influencing well-being. However, from the outset the artisans alerted us to the importance of using multiple indicators in assessing impacts of MarketPlace work on their lives. In total the interview schedule included new items to address Marketplace's social indicators and Chambers' criteria, items used in previous studies of artisans in developing countries (Dickson and Littrell, 1998), and items adapted from the instruments used by family economists and demographers who conduct research in international settings (Winter et al., 1999).

Measures of economic livelihood included open- and close-ended items about artisan monthly wages, household income provided by spouse and other household members, whether artisans had saved money, and average monthly expenditures for a variety of essential household products and services. When inquiring about income for all householders, we asked artisans to indicate both the maximum and the minimum income each person contributed per month. This measure of income recognizes that many jobs do not provide a steady income, rather the income varies with production cycles or other seasonal fluctuations.

Material well-being was measured in multiple ways. Artisans reported monthly expenses for housing, food, transportation, utilities (cooking fuel, water, and electricity), and entertainment. Additionally, annual expenses were reported for medical, education, clothing, and travel home. An objective Basic Minimum Needs Ratio was generated by dividing total household income by average monthly expenditures on food, housing, transportation, and utilities. The Basic Minimum Needs Ratio identified the extent that basic needs were met. Additionally, 7-point Likert-type scales with pictorial endpoints (sad face vs. happy face) similar to a scale used by Brinkerhoff et al. (1997), were used for artisans to subjectively rate their ability to provide for their families' basic needs, both currently and before starting work with MarketPlace. A more general, subjective measure of quality of life asked participants to rate their satisfaction with life both before working with MarketPlace and since working with MarketPlace. Participants responded on the 7-point Likert-type endpoints described earlier.

Living wages were determined by dividing the average Basic Minimum Needs by the average household size in the sample. In addition to quantitative measures, qualitative data were also collected. Participants were asked to respond to the question, "Since you have been working with MarketPlace, what are the most important changes in your life?" Additionally, throughout the interviews, interviewers recorded qualitative comments made by the artisans that provided greater context to the study.

Field research was conducted in Mumbai, India during May and June of 2001. A total of 113 in-depth interviews were conducted representing 71% of the women and men working with four different MarketPlace workshops in Mumbai. All of the women interviewed resided in the Golibar slum area of Mumbai in the northern suburb of Santa Cruz. Data were gathered from 92 women who sew or embroider apparel. The remaining 21 interviews were with male artisans (n = 5), or male and female supervisors and business owners (n = 16) whose responses are not included in this paper. Generally, the women were pleased to be included in the study and workers who were not interviewed included those who were out of town visiting relatives or those who were ill or injured.

As a criterion for Earthwatch Institute funding for the project, volunteers from around the world served as interviewers. Interviews were conducted in English and translated to Hindi by local students hired for the research project. Prior to beginning their interviews, volunteers received two and one-half days of training with the researchers to familiarize them with MarketPlace and SHARE, the artisan workshops, the Golibar slum including home visits with some of the artisans they would interview, the research instrument, and interviewing techniques. Interviews ranged from 50 to 137 minutes with the average interview lasting 80 minutes. Teams of two interviewers and one translator carried out one or two interviews each day and prepared detailed notes for each interview on the day it was conducted. During the interview one volunteer asked the questions and probed for examples while the second volunteer took detailed notes.

Quantitative data were analyzed with descriptive statistics that would provide understanding of artisan quality of life and relationships between measures. We substituted mean values for cases with some missing household expense data. Univariate analysis of variance and chi-square analyses were used for testing differences between artisans meeting basic minimum needs with their household incomes and earning living wages compared with those that did not achieve these income and wage goals. Paired sample *t*-tests were used to test differences in perceived ability to meet basic needs and satisfaction with life prior to and since coming to work for MarketPlace. Qualitative data were analyzed thematically using the constant comparative method (Glaser and Straus, 1967).

13.6. RESULTS

13.6.1. *MarketPlace Artisans*

Artisans ranged in age from 18 to 55 years with a mean age of 33.3 years. Of the women interviewed, 55.4% were Hindu, 41.3% were Muslim, and the others were Christian. The greatest number of artisans (44.6%) completed education between 6th and 9th standards (see Table 13.1). Another 17.4% had attended school at least through the 10th standard and one had attended university; however, 21.7% had no formal education. Over two-thirds of the artisans were married and had been married since age 17, on average. The range of marrying ages was from 10 to 30 years. Almost all the women (82.6%) had children and the median number of children was three. The median number of persons residing in households was five with two of those household members most often contributing money to running the household.

The median number of years working with MarketPlace was five, though the range was from less than one year to 22 years (see Table 13.2). Almost 24% of the artisans worked as tailors while 73.9% worked as embroiderers. The women most frequently came to the workshop six or seven days a week and stayed a little less than 3 hours. Additionally, over 40% of the women worked on their MarketPlace sewing or embroidery seven days a week in the home; the average workday at home was nearly six hours.[1] These figures varied with whether the artisan is involved as a tailor or embroiderer, with tailors likely to spend more time at the workshops than embroiderers.

Table 13.1. Demographic and Household Characteristics.

Characteristic	Frequency (N = 92)	%	Mean	S.D.
Education Level Completed			5.90	3.72
No formal education	20	21.7		
1st through 5th standard	15	16.3		
6th through 9th standard	41	44.6		
10th through 14th standard	16	17.4		
Marital Status				
Married	63	68.5		
Single	12	13.0		
Widowed	17	18.5		
Marrying Age			16.97	3.65
10 through 12	7	7.6		
13 through 15	14	15.2		
16 through 19	33	35.9		
20 or older	14	15.2		
Number of Children			3.39	1.72
None	16	17.4		
1 to 2	28	30.4		
3 to 5	40	43.5		
6 or more	8	8.7		
Total Household Size			5.38	2.07
1 to 3	13	14.1		
4 to 6	60	65.2		
7 or more	19	20.7		
Householders Contributing Income				
1	8	8.7		
2	50	54.3		
3	26	28.3		
4 or more	8	8.7		

13.6.2. *Economic Livelihood*

Economic livelihood was primarily based on wages. Wages were paid for the number of pieces sewn or embroidered, so the income fluctuated from month to month. In months when work was slow, artisans' salaries averaged Rs. 1,018; however, during months with heavy production, salaries averaged Rs. 1,691.[2] Overall, the artisans' average monthly income was Rs. 1,355. This income contributed from 10% to 77% of total household income that averaged Rs. 4,194 (see Table 13.3). Some artisans (38%) reported that they had been able to save money to cushion catastrophic events or periods when work was limited.

Table 13.1. Work Characteristics.

Characteristic	Frequency (*N* = 92)	%	Mean	S.D.
Number of Years with MarketPlace			5.51	4.58
1 year or less	20	21.7		
2 to 5 years	23	25.0		
6 to 9 years	25	27.2		
10 or more years	13	14.1		
Number of Days per Week Worked at Workshop			5.18	1.59
1 to 2 days	4	4.3		
3 to 6 days	60	65.2		
7 days	24	26.1		
Number of Hours per Day Worked at Workshop			2.68	2.44
3 or less hours	63	68.5		
4 to 8 hours	18	19.6		
9 or more hours	6	6.5		
Number of Days Worked per Week at Home			5.62	1.91
0 to 2 days	6	6.5		
3 to 6 days	40	43.5		
7 days	40	43.5		
Number of Hours Worked per Day at Home			5.79	2.58
3 or less hours	11	12.0		
4 to 8 hours	67	72.8		
9 or more hours	12	13.0		

Table 13.3. Economic Livelihood (in Rupes).

Source of Economic Livelihood	Mean	S.D.
Artisan Wages – Minimum Earned per Month	1,018	547
Artisan Wages – Maximum Earned per Month	1,691	633
Artisan Wages – Average of Minimum and Maximum Earned per Month	1,355	517
Average Total Household Income	4,194	2,676
Average Proportion of Artisan Wages to Total Household Income	0.41	0.23

13.6.3. *Material Well-Being*

Basic Minimum Needs Ratio

The Basic Minimum Needs Ratio was calculated by dividing monthly total household income by average monthly basic expenditures. The ratio represents the extent that household income was sufficient to meet basic minimum needs. First we summed monthly expenditures for housing, food, transportation, and utilities (water, cooking fuel, and electricity see Table 12.4). For most artisan families, these were

Table 13.4. Household Expenditures and Basic Minimum Needs (in Rupes).

	Mean	S.D.
Basic Monthly Expenditures		
Housing	262	491
Food	2,504	1,164
Transportation	147	242
Water	78	65
Cooking Fuel	224	91
Electricity	269	256
Annual Expenditures		
Education	3,856	4,337
Medical	1,667	1,903
Clothing	1,750	1,738
Travel Home or Other Destination	1,022	1,408
Entertainment	48	113
Basic Minimum Needs (housing, food, transportation, and utilities	3,484	1,398

recurring monthly expenditures. The exception was the housing expenditures. A large proportion of artisan families (65.0%) had no monthly expense for housing because they owned their homes and had no mortgage. Basic expenditures for housing, food, transportation, and utilities averaged 3,484 rupees per month. As is typical in developing countries, the greatest expenditures were for food (71.9% of total basic expenditures).

Costs for educating children were not included in our calculation of basic expenditures. Public education in India is free and transportation to and from school is likely the only additional expense required for educating children. However, expenditures for educating children were highly variable; 20.7% of artisan families had no education expenses; yet, 8.7% spent 12,000 rupees or more per year (see Table 13.4). The relatively large amount spent by some families is explained by the high priority placed on educating children in English medium schools; these schools are far more expensive and yet more desirable than public schools using the local Indian language. Other highly variable expenditures included those made for medical care, clothing, travel to visit family in other parts of the country, and entertainment. The type of entertainment enjoyed on Rs. 48 per month might be an occasional ice cream cone or transportation for a family outing to a nearby park or the beach.

The mean for the Basic Minimum Needs Ratio was 1.25 (SD = 0.59). This shows that on average families were able to cover their basic expenditures with the available income. However, the range for this measure was from 0.17 to 3.20 and 40.25 of artisan households (n = 37) had scores of less than 1.0, indicating that they were unable to cover the basic needs with their monthly incomes.

To understand more about the households that were unable to meet their basic needs, we conducted tests of difference on a veriety of household and work-related variables. We used a dummy variable that grouped together households with a 1 or greater on the Basic Minimum Needs Ratio and those that scored less than 1. The ability to meet basic minimum needs did not significantly differ by the number of years worked with MarketPlace ($F(1, 77) = 0.00$, $p = 0.961$), number of days worked in the workshop ($F(1, 84) = 0.17$, $p = 0.685$) or at home ($F(1, 82) = 0.01$, $p = 0.920$), the number of hours worked in the workshop ($F(1, 83) = 0.10$, $p = 0.754$) or at home ($F(1, 86) = 0.08$, $p = 0.774$), or the workshop employing the artisans ($\chi^2(3, 91) = 3.61$, $p = 0.548$). Additionally, ability to meet basic minimum needs did not differ for embroiderers as compared with tailors ($\chi^2(1, 90) = 0.36$, $p = 0.548$). The number of persons residing in the household did not significantly differ ($F(1, 88) = 0.39$, $p = 0.533$). However, the number of persons in the household contributing income did significantly differ between those who could and could not meet their minimum basic needs. On average, those households able to meet their basic needs had 2.73 contributing members whereas households unable to meet basic needs had only 2.00 contributing members ($F(1, 88) = 11.87$, $p = 0.001$).

13.6.4. *Relationships Between Measures*

Based on the literature, we made several hypotheses about the relationships between various measures of quality of life. Hypothesis 1 proposed that the Basic Minimum Needs Ratio would be positively correlated with general satisfaction with life. The hypothesis was rejected as no significant relationship was found between these two variables (see Table 13.5). The actual ability to cover basic needs may or may not correspond with a positive outlook on life.

Hypothesis 2 anticipated that scores on the Basic Minimum Needs Ratio, an objective measure of ability to provide, would be positively correlated with subjective measures of the ability to provide for family needs. The two measures were not significantly correlated (see Table 13.5); thus, hypothesis 2 was rejected. The actual ability to cover basic expenses did not correspond with feelings that enough had been done to provide for the family.

Hypothesis 3 stated that subjective ratings of ability to provide basic needs would

Table 13.5. Relationships between Social Indicators.

Social Indicator	1	2	3	4	5	6
1. Artisan Income	1.0					
2. Total Household Income	0.377*	1.0				
3. Basic Expenditures	0.165	0.617*	1.0			
4. Basic Minimum Needs Ratio	0.325*	0.569*	–0.195	1.0		
5. Ability to Provide Basic Needs	–0.085	0.002	–0.104	0.118	1.0	
6. Satisfaction with Life	0.111	0.090	0.006	0.163	0.551*	1.0

* $p < 0.01$.

be positively correlated with general quality of life (satisfaction) and this hypothesis was supported (see Table 13.4). The more that an artisan felt she had provided for her family, the more likely she was to be satisfied with her life.

A lack of correlation between actual income and quality of life (satisfaction) was expected with Hypothesis 4. The hypothesis was supported. Higher incomes did not lead to increased satisfaction with life.

The combination of findings for Hypotheses 1 through 4, coupled with the higher ratings given to current life satisfaction (M = 5.5, SD = 1.36) than ability to provide for basic needs (M = 5.2, SD = 1.40), all suggest that material well being is not the only dimension these women include when judging their overall well-being or satisfaction with life. Additionally, what is perceived as a basic need may be much broader than the fundamental expenditures on food, housing, transportation, and utilities that allow a family to 'get by.'

Impact of Work on Perceived Ability to Provide for Basic Minimum Needs and Satisfaction with Life

Hypothesis 5 proposed that perceived ability to provide for basic minimum needs would be increased as a result of working with MarketPlace and the hypothesis was supported. Ratings of ability to provide for family needs ranged from 2 to 7 (1 = least able – depicted by a 'sad' face, 7 = most able – depicted by a 'happy' face); the average was 5.2 (SD = 1.39), which was a significant increase over the average rating of 2.3 (SD = 1.41) prior to working with MarketPlace (t = 14.78, p = 0.000).

Hypothesis 6 suggested that satisfaction with life was increased as a result of working with MarketPlace. Artisans reported that their satisfaction with life prior to working with MarketPlace was an average of 2.7 (SD = 1.57). In contrast, current satisfaction with life averaged 5.5 (SD = 1.39), which was a significantly higher rating (t = 12.99, p = 0.000). Hypothesis 6 was supported. These findings clearly reveal the contribution that work made to quality of life.

13.6.5. *Determining Living Wages*

We used the average expenditures needed to cover basic minimum needs for food, housing, transportation, and utilities (M = 3,484) and divided it by average number of adult wage earners (M = 2.43) to determine what remuneration might be considered a living wage. To adequately cover the basic needs of the household requires wages of at least 1,434 rupees per month. When pay was at its peak (Rs. 1,691), the average artisan was generally able to cover her share of basic household expenses. However, 29.3% of artisans (n = 27) fell below the living wage level even when earning their maximum salaries. The proportion of artisans falling short of the living wage during months when earnings were low rose to 72.8% (n = 67).

To understand what factors might impact workers' ability to earn a living wage, we conducted tests of difference on several work-related variables. A dummy variable differentiated those earning the living wage (maximum salary earned by artisan was 1,434 rupees or more) from those who did not earn the living wage (maximum salary less than 1,434 rupees). Those earning and not earning a living wage did not have significantly different tenure with MarketPlace ($F(1, 77) = 0.04$, $p = 0.843$). No difference was found in number of days worked in the workshop ($F(1, 84) = 0.78$, $p = 0.380$) or at home ($F(1, 82) = 0.95$, $p = 0.332$), or the number of hours worked at home ($F(1, 86) = 1.62$, $p = 0.206$). Hours worked in the workshop came close to being significantly different for the two groups ($F(1, 83) = 3.92$, $p = 0.051$). These findings warrant further exploration as our colleagues at MarketPlace assess that women are not equally motivated to increase their workloads. Moreover, heavy household responsibilities or extended family or health emergencies can preclude some women from working longer hours or more days. Additionally, ability to meet basic minimum needs did not differ for embroiderers as compared with tailors ($\chi^2(1, 90) = 0.79$, $p = 0.374$). However, a significant difference was found regarding the workshop employing the artisans ($\chi^2(3, 91) = 26.71$, $p = 0.000$). A disproportionate number of women failing to earn a living wage worked for a particular artisan group while, in contrast, a greater than expected number of women working for another group earned a living wage. Furthermore, women earning a living wage had higher levels of educational attainment than those not earning a living wage ($F(1, 88) = 5.03$, $p = 0.027$).

13.6.6. *Multiple Dimensions of Well-Being*

To understand quality of life more fully, we next examined the qualitative data. Particular attention was paid to themes in responses to the item asking artisans about the most important changes in their lives since working with MarketPlace. Some comments did focus on material well-being resulting from the paid work; however, the responses reflected a broader range of items than had been included in quantitative measures of basic minimum needs. For example, three artisans described important material changes in their lives:

> I provide food and security for my family.
>
> My lifestyle has been improved greatly . . . food, clothing, shelter . . . all the basic things, I now have.
>
> Now I can pay for my children's education and I don't have to fear for their future.

However, far more responses centered on psychological and social aspects of well-being. Psychological well-being related to artisans' increased courage and self-confidence to stand up for themselves and for their families or to take charge of a situation. Additionally, sometimes psychological well-being resulted from actions as simple as speaking in front of others. Other times, psychological well-being was manifest by general feelings of happiness. For example, artisans commented that,

> I am very courageous. I don't think I'm weak anymore. I can face anything.

> I used to be scared to go out of the house, now I feel OK. Now I can speak confidently, even to you!
>
> I am much happier now. I never imagined that my house would be so good. Other family members are also very happy.

Social well-being was often explained regarding meaningful friendships the women developed with their co-workers. Two women explained that,

> I have the capacity to talk to people about their sorrows, which I didn't have before. At __ (name of group) __, the women all share their problems at home, and I can speak to them about how to solve them. I have an identity of my own now.
>
> I had few friends before, and now I have gained a lot of knowledge from making these new friends.

Increased respect garnered from family members also revealed the social well-being associated with MarketPlace work. Some artisans commented that,

> My husband treats me better. He has given me more independence than before.
>
> [He] never used to let me go out of house before I started working with MarketPlace.
>
> I like the respect I get from my in-laws for working.

Clearly, to these women the benefits of their work went far beyond economic livelihood gained through the wages they earned.

13.7. DISCUSSION AND CONCLUSIONS

13.7.1. *Measurement Issues Associated with Multi-Dimensionality*

By triangulating data from qualitative and quantitative measures, we obtained a rich understanding of the quality of life of women sewing and embroidering apparel for MarketPlace. The data revealed that for these women in the Golibar slum of Mumbai, India, quality of life included material, social, and psychological dimensions and each had been enhanced as a result of their employment. The multi-dimensional nature of quality of life brings several measurement issues to the forefront. Had we measured only the easily quantifiable, objective aspects of quality of life, such as income, we might have been disappointed with the level of living the women had achieved. Instead, our interpretation is balanced because we have qualitative data describing the personal growth and strength the women have gained through their work.

Brinkerhoff et al. (1997) have suggested that both subjective and objective measures of quality of life must be used to obtain a full picture of well-being. We support this view and wish to counter the idea that subjective aspects of quality of life are "difficult to measure" (Indrayan et al., 1999). A variety of subjective aspects of quality have been identified, such as personal well-being and happiness reported by Mukherjee (1981), and self-confidence, courage, decision-making, friendship, and family relationships reported in the present study. Each of these might be measured using Brinkerhoff et al.'s happy face, Likert-type scale. We found the women easily responded with this scale and the results were valid in that they followed expected patterns. We encourage researchers to incorporate this type of subjective measure in their future studies. We also encourage continued use of broad measures of quality of life, such as satisfaction with life, because the measures take into consideration the psychological and social dimensions of quality of life that might be overlooked when focusing solely on wages.

Seeking grassroots input has been championed by Chambers (1997) with regard to economic development. Likewise, Steele (2000) raises a concern about seeking grassroots input regarding living wages. We must consider the extent that wages should be the focus of discussion when it comes to evaluating employment opportunities for women in developing countries. Prior to the research, the women we were to study provided social indicators that emphasized the importance placed by both the artisans and MarketPlace on empowerment and personal self-worth. Well-being for apparel workers in Mumbai, India was clearly improved by the inner strengths the women developed from their work, the meaningful friendships that they built with co-workers, and the increased power they felt in their family relationships. We did not seek input when deciding which expenses were basic needs. In retrospect, it would have been beneficial to do this. Some women pay large amounts to educate their children at English medium schools and they may well consider this outlay of cash a basic minimum need.

Another point about measuring quality of life relates to how variables are correlated. In previous research, Brinkerhoff et al. (1997) had suggested that an objective measure of ability to cover basic minimum needs (our Basic Minimum Needs Ratio) might correlate with a subjective measure of quality of life (satisfaction). The present study did not support this hypothesis. Additionally, we found no relationship between actual income and satisfaction with life. These findings suggest that satisfaction with life might be far more dependent on social and psychological aspects than material aspects. Measuring income and basic minimum needs relates only to material well-being. On the other hand, we found a significant relationship between perceived ability to provide for family needs (a subjective income measure) and life satisfaction. This finding provides support for Basu's (1992) proposition that income is not always effectively used to enhance quality of life. Some women may be much more efficient in stretching their incomes to meet their desired family goals.

13.7.2. *Measurement Issues Associated with Basic Minimum Needs and Living Wages*

Despite the many dimensions of quality of life and the lack of relationship between income and expenses related data and satisfaction with life, we do not wish to downplay the importance of income to well-being. Chambers (1992) discusses how the economic livelihood underlying material well-being requires a dependable source of cash. We found that 40% of the artisan households in this study were unable to cover the fundamental food, housing, and utilities needed to sustain life. Households with a larger number of earners were more likely to cover basic needs. In some cases women not covering basic needs may be among those who exhibit low motivation to expand their livelihood as compared to other women who shoulder heavy responsibility and earn greater income during peak production. Additionally, heavy household and family responsibilities leave little flexibility for some women to devote more hours to sewing or embroidery as a way of increasing their incomes.

These findings related to basic needs may stem from the undependable nature of work in developing countries. We know from our colleagues in Mumbai that both unemployment and underemployment plague the Golibar slum. Many jobs are temporary, providing less consistently reliable wages. Additionally, apparel production is well-known for being cyclical – work occurs for long hours when order deadlines draw near and can come to a virtual standstill at other points in time. If a worker in a household is underemployed, it is logical that another individual would need to go to work to cover the lost income. Rates of un- and underemployment would also affect what wage level provides a living wage, since the formula for determining living wages includes the average number of working adults in a household. In situations where many are employed in part-time and temporary jobs, it might be necessary to pool the work of a number of individuals in order to approximate a full-time and dependable source of income. A more valid Living Wage formula might include the equivalent number of full-time, permanent jobs that the average household engages in, rather than the number of working adults.

As suggested by Bremer (2002), the Living Wage formula is influenced by the composition and size of households. The average household in our study included 5.38 persons and on average 2.43 of these contributed income to running the household. Yet, overall our study included a heterogeneous array of households. Some included young parents with young children, while in others the parents were older and older children were living at home. In other cases not as well represented by averages, extended families included parents, children, and in-laws. Other locales, outside India, could show very different household patterns and much less diversity. For example, much more homogeneous households would be found in and around export processing zones, such as those in Latin America, where young, single adults have migrated for work and are provided dormitory housing. In a case like this, virtually all householders would be working; an average household might include five persons with five working adults. Assuming the basic minimum needs would be roughly comparable for each household, the living wage in the homogeneous area would be lower than in the area where there is more household diversity. This has important implications. Under the pressure of activist groups to pay living wages, multinational corporations might choose to locate in export processing zones rather than in a more diverse area, such as the Golibar slum, since it would be less costly to meet activist demands for living wages. This would further contribute to the problems of un- and underemployment and widespread poverty in locations where young families with children reside.

We agree with Bremer (2002) that diverse household composition presents a special problem when defining living wages and a formula should not have the potential to discriminate against family residences. Living Wage is one valuable tool for assessing wage rates but must not be considered in isolation. We propose continued use of the Basic Minimum Needs Ratio for future studies of quality of life in developing countries because it provides an understanding of the local situation for poverty alleviation through employment. An understanding of the context helps assess the impact that any one individual company can be expected to make. Furthermore, the Basic Minimum Needs Ratio and Living Wages should be coupled with subjective measures that tap the social and psychological dimensions of quality of life.

13.7.3. *Quality of Life Resulting from Work and Alternative Trade*

The philosophy of the alternative trade movement is to provide workers in developing countries fair wages in a safe and healthy work environment. Alternative trading organizations aim to provide sustainable jobs in long-lasting businesses. Additionally, MarketPlace: Handwork of India places special importance on enhancing self-worth and empowering women to address social issues in their lives and communities. As such, social and economic goals are closely intertwined in MarketPlace's approach to their work Our findings suggest that they are meeting their dual goals. Like Basu (1992), we found that by interacting with other women at MarketPlace, the work contributed to social and psychological gains in quality of life.

Overall, MarketPlace is also meeting their alternative trade goal of providing fair wages. When work was readily available, most artisans received a living wage and the majority of households were able to cover their basic minimum needs with the average household income. However, some households were unable to meet basic minimum needs even when work was plentiful and the majority could not do so when work slowed. We do not believe that any business, whether an alternative trade organization or a multinational corporation, can be held responsible for the un- and underemployment present in an area of high poverty and in situations where women shoulder immense household responsibility, leaving them limited flexibility for devoting more hours to their artisan work. In a developing country such as India, a household requires multiple earners to meet basic needs; families piece together the income needed for survival. Smoothing out fluctuations in production will not be an easy task as the entire system of apparel contracting and sub-contracting has been designed to flexibly accommodate production fluctuations. However, any improvements are sure to help.

The fact that living wages were less likely to be earned by members of one group as compared to the others is cause for concern. Additionally, workers with lower levels of educational attainment were less likely to make a living wage. Chambers (1997) suggests that economic livelihood and well-being can be enhanced by increasing the capabilities of the individual. The United Nations' Human Development Index includes education as a proxy for ability to have knowledge

(Indrayan et al., 1999). Looking for training opportunities that will enhance the capabilities of MarketPlace artisans with lower levels of education may be one approach for expanding capabilities, and in turn earning potential. Additionally, the organization might investigate whether the work group earning lower wages has particular training needs. Enhancing the capabilities of artisans such that they are able to earn a living wage is high priority within the philosophy of alternative trade.

13.8. NOTES

[1] In charting daily activities for 30 of the MarketPlace women, we found their typical days averaged 18-20 waking hours. Approximately 9–10 of those hours were essential to the women for completing the critical tasks that provided for their family's needs. Women's activities were not linear in nature but rather jumped back and forth from one activity to another across a day, leaving a limited number of sequential, uninterrupted house for MarketPlace textile production (Littrell and Dickson, 2002).

[2] The exchange rate at time of data collection was US$1 = 46.5 rupees.

13.9. REFERENCES

Basu, A. M. (1992). The status of women and the quality of life among the poor. *Cambridge Journal of Economics*, **16**, 249–267.

Bremer, M. (2002). *Defining and Measuring a Global Living Wage: Theoretical and Conceptual Issues.* Retrieved on September 23, 2002 from www.umass.edu/peri

Brinkerhoff, M. B., Fredell, K. A., and Frideres, J. S. (1997). Basic minimum needs, quality of life, and selected correlates: Explorations in villages in northern India. *Social Indicators Research*, **42**, 245–281.

Business for Social Responsibility (2002). *Wages – Living Wage.* Retrieved on September 23, 2002 from www.bsr.org

Chambers, R. C. (1997). *Whose Reality Counts? Putting the First Last.* London: Intermediate Technology Publications.

Ciscel, D. H. (2000). The living wage movement: Building a political link from market wages to social institutions. *Journal of Economic Issues*, **34**(2), 527–535.

Dickson, M. A. and Littrell, M. A. (1998). Organizational culture for small textile and apparel businesses in Guatemala. *Clothing and Textiles Research Journal*, **16**(2), 68–78.

Ericson, R. B. (n.d.). *The Conscious Consumer: Promoting Economic Justice through Fair Trade.* Barre, MA: Fair Trade Federation.

Glaser, B. G. and Strauss, A. (1967). *The Discovery of Grounded Theory: Strategies for Qualitative Research.* Chicago: Aldine.

Greenhouse, S. (1999, October 20). Students urge colleges to join a new anti-sweatshop group. *The New York Times*, p. 23.

Hetter, K. (2001, August 7). Global labor alliance turns heat on retailers. *Newsday*, p. A31.

Indrayan, A., Wysocki, M. J., Chawla, A., Kumar, A. R., and Singh, N. (1999). 3-decade trend in Human Development Index in India and its major states. *Social Indicators Research*, **46**, 91–120

Labour Behind the Label (2000–2001). *Wearing Thin: The State of Pay in the Fashion Industry.* Norwich, UK: Author.

Littrell, M. A. and Dickson, M. A. (1999). *Social Responsibility in the Global Market: Fair Trade of Cultural Products.* Thousand Oaks, CA: Sage.

Littrell, M. A. and Dickson, M. A. (2002). *MarketPlace Handwork of India: Impacts on Artisan Capabilities.* Paper presented at the Biennial Symposium of the Textile Society of America, Northampton, MA, September 26.

Littrell, M. A. and Dickson, M. A. (1997). Alternative trading organizations: Shifting paradigm in a culture of social responsibility. *Human Organization*, **56**(3), 344–352

Losciale, A. (2000, May 7). Young and restless: Sweatshops new rally cry across US campuses. *Newsday*, p. F06.

Mukherjee, R. (1981). On the quality of life in India: An exploratory survey. *Social Indicators Research*, **9**, 455–476.

Okafor, F. C. (1985). Basic needs in rural Nigeria. *Social Indicators Research*, **17**, 115–125.

Ramey, J. (1996, March 18), Apparel's ethics dilemma. *Women's Wear Daily*, 10–12.

Rosenthal, J. (1997, August 11). Doing well while doing good. *Journal of Commerce*, p. 9A.

SHARE (n.d.). *Support the Handicappeds Rehabilitation Effort: Social Indicators* [Internal document].

Smullin, R. (1997, June 5). It takes a village to eliminate harsh labor conditions – Trade groups offer an alternative solution. *The Seattle Times*, p. D1.

Srinivasin, T. N. and Park, S. C. Jr. (2001). *Living Wage in Poor Countries.* Retrieved on September 23, 2002 from www.unc.edu/depts/livwage/clwa/srinivasin.pdf

Steele, D. (2000). *The "Living Wage" Clause in the ETI Base Code – How to Implement It?* Retrieved on September 19, 2002 from www.eti.org.uk

Sullivan, B. (2001, August 17). Whose sweat made those clothes? *The Hartford Courant*, p. D1.

Sweatshop Watch (1998). *A Working Living Wage Methodology.* Retrieved on September 19, 2002 from www.sweatshopwatch.org/swatch/wags/formula.html

US Department of Labor (2000). *Wages, Benefits, Poverty Line, and Meeting Workers' Needs in the apparel and Footwear Industries of Selected Countries.* Washington, DC: Author.

Varley, P. (ed.). (1998). *The Sweatshop Quandary: Corporate Responsibility on the Global Frontier.* Washington, DC: Investor Responsibility Research Center.

Wazir, B. (2001, May 20). Nike accused of tolerating sweatshops: New report saids workers are still on low wages despite chairman's pledge. *The Observer*, p. 12:

Winter, M., Morris, E. W., Gutkowska, K., Jezewska-Zychowicz, M., Palaszewska-Reindl, T., Zelazna, K., and Grzeszczak-Swietlikowska, U. (1999). Constraints, domain conditions, and well-being: Evidence from Poland during the transformation. *The Journal of Consumer Affairs*, **33**(1), 27–47.

13.9. ACKNOWLEDGEMENTS AND AFFILIATIONS

Marsha A. Dickson is Associate Professor in the Department of Apparel, Textiles, and Interior Design; Kansas State University; Manhattan, KS, USA.

Mary A. Littrell is Professor in the Textiles and Clothing program, Iowa State University, Ames, IA, USA

Funding for this research was provided by the Center for Field Research at the Earthwatch Institute. We appreciate the assistance of the volunteers who assisted in data collection.

F. MAGGINO AND S. SCHIFINI D'ANDREA

14. DIFFERENT SCALES FOR DIFFERENT SURVEY METHODS: VALIDATION IN MEASURING THE QUALITY OF UNIVERSITY LIFE

ABSTRACT: This chapter explores the assessment of subjective measurement instruments in terms of definition and selection of items and also in the identification of more suitable scales. The work presented here addresses the comparison of several scales in separate types of questionnaires (paper and/or CATI). It provides a conceptual framework and empirical analysis. Finally, it draws conclusions based on these analyses.

14.1. INTRODUCTION

The measurement of individual well-being and quality of life has appeared in many different forms, assessing well-being from different perspectives, and using different measures and different extensive scales to do so. The assessment of subjective measurement instruments needs special attention not only in the definition and selection of items but also in the identification of more suitable scales. This is particularly true in the measurement and assessment of the subjective perception of quality of life (in rating agreement levels, satisfaction levels, and so on), due to the disparities between areas, considered in studies found in the literature.

Synthetically, aspects involved in scale definition are:

1. Reference type (evaluation, preference, perception, image, judgment);
2. Scale type (expression of scale: verbal, rating, quantitative and graphical scale);
3. Range (number of levels for scale) in the sense of scale discriminate capacity.

The choice among all aspect combinations can mainly influence the construction and validation of indicators.

Since other elements could play important roles in this definition, such as investigated areas, semantic and cultural meanings, and survey methods, not all scales can be used in different situations. In reality, the problem of semantic definition and selection of items becomes complicated because of differences between questionnaire forms and leading survey types, such as paper questionnaire, presence of interviewers or not, Computer Assisted Telephonic Interviews (CATI), Web interviewing, and so on, particularly in the adaptation of items to more than one survey method.

The work presented here concerns the comparison of several scales in separate questionnaires (paper and/or CATI); this experience has allowed us to compare scales with:

1. Different reference (judgment vs. agreement, judgment vs. evaluation, image vs. agreement);
2. Different scale types (verbal vs. rating and/or graphical vs. numerical);
3. Rating scale with different ranges (0–10 vs. 1–7 and/or 1–7 vs. 1–4).

M. Joseph Sirgy et al. (eds.), Advances in Quality-of-Life Theory and Research, 233–256, 2003.

The goals of this study are to:

- Cross-validate different questionnaires (paper and CATI);
- Test the reliability of different scales;
- Evaluate impacts of different scores and scale meanings in selection of Quality of Life indicators (in University context);
- Compare individual levels of satisfaction and evaluation.

14.2. DIFFERENT SURVEY METHODS IN THE MEASUREMENT OF THE QUALITY OF UNIVERSITY LIFE

In order to reach our goals, we carried out surveys concerning the quality of university life, applying two different survey techniques (paper and telephonic) and three different questionnaires (paper and two telephonic, a and b), on three different samples of students (Table 14.1) of the Faculty of Economics at the University of Florence (Italy).

Table 14.1. Dimensions of the Sample.

Questionnaire		Sample dimension
Paper		**300**
CATI	a (498)	**1015**
	b (517)	

14.2.1. *The Conceptual Model*

The three questionnaires present the same conceptual model, consisting of two areas:

1. Quality of life, for which we identified three components:
   - self-esteem
   - general subjective well-being
   - subjective well-being in living contexts
2. Quality of university life, for which we identified three components:
   - personal motivation
   - university career
   - university environment

We identified a set of variables for each component, measured by means of scales with differentiated structures. The questionnaire structure also includes objective information like age, gender, birthplace, family background, etc. Table 14.2 shows the whole questionnaire structure.

Table 14.2. Questionnaire Structure.

EXTERNAL VARIABLES		o **Gender**
		o **Age**
		o **University curriculum**
		o **Employment**
		o **Distance from University**
INDIVIDUAL TRAITS AND DISPOSITION		o **Self-esteem**
		o **Personal motivation towards study**
ENVIRONMENT		o **Family support**
		o **Friends support**
VALUES		o **Importance of particular ambits in one's life**
SATISFACTION AND WELL-BEING PERCEPTION		o **General Subjective Well-being** (General Life Satisfaction)
		o **Subjective Well-being in particular life ambits** (Friendship, Family, Money, Free time, Health, Faculty, University career, University friendship)
		o **Student Life Satisfaction**
		o **Happiness** (at the present, one year ago)
UNIVERSITY LIFE	Career Performances	o **Actual Performances** (Successful Examination Number, Taking Examination Number, Marks Average, Proportion of successful exams towards requested standard, Course attendances at the present)
		o **Perceived Performances** (compared to other students, past expectations, future intentions)
		o **Attitude towards Performances**
	University evaluation	o **Faculty Evaluations**
		o **Exam Perception**

Scales for Quality of Life

To investigate Quality of Life area we considered three well-being levels:

- *Self-esteem:* We used the Rosenberg *ten-items scale*, which measures self-esteem as a personality trait and as having confidence in one's own worth and abilities. Students had to indicate their agreement on each statement regarding self-worth.
- *General subjective well-being:* The subjective well-being measurement has three identifiable components: emotional component, in the sense of *happiness*, cognitive component, in the sense of *general life satisfaction*, cognitive component for study satisfaction: in order to measure student judgment on his/her student life satisfaction.
- *Subjective well-being in living contexts:* We investigated subjective well-being in living contexts for different social domains such as friendships, family relationships, health, university career, economic status, etc. One of the goals was to synthesize these items in synthetic indexes, such as family and social relations, financial resources, and university involvement.

Scales Quality of University Life

For the Quality of University Life area, we identified three related components:

- *Motivation toward study:* Personal motivation is one of the components on which, in our opinion, both individual career and environmental perception, depend. Personal motivation towards study in the University context was assessed by student agreement towards ten statements about e.g. future expectations, learning motivations vs. dropping-out inclination, self-evaluation capacities in relation to study achievements and curricula self-evaluation.

- *Career performances:* We measured this dimension through two approaches: (1) *real performances*, which used the following indicators: grade average, mean of taken exams, and proportion of successful exams towards requested standard; and (2) *perceived performances*, the measurement of which followed the Multiple Discrepancies Theory; we defined and identified comparisons with other students, past experiences, students' own potentials, and future expectations with respect to the number of exams taken and average grades.
- *University environment:* In order to identify aspects characterizing the relationship between students and the university environment, we defined a model that highlighted the cognitive-emotional judgment on the environment, measured through two approaches: (1) satisfaction in particular domains: we identified 16 living contexts; each student had to express his/her satisfaction level for each context on an eleven-point scale (only in paper-questionnaire), and (2) subjective evaluation: students have expressed their evaluations through semantic differential scales.

14.2.2. *Different Item Approaches for Different Questionnaires*

Because of different survey techniques, our questionnaires required different item approaches and definitions with regard to:

- scale reference
- scale type
- scale range

Let us examine these different approaches.

Scale Reference

The difficulty in adapting some particular items (such as graphical scales) in forms appropriate to telephonic interviews has been overcome by asking students about their agreement regarding some defined assertions (Table 14.3). In telephonic questionnaires, in place of semantic differential scales presented in the paper-questionnaire, we defined two different adjective groups concerning university: positive and negative. This procedure allowed us to verify the real polarity of adjectives.

Table 14.3. Different Scale References Chosen for Our Three Questionnaire.

Areas	Variables	Scale reference		
		Paper-Q.	Cati-Q.	
			a	b
University Evaluation	Faculty Evaluations	Image	Agreement (Positive adjectives)	Agreement (Negative adjectives)
Satisfaction and Well-Being Perception	Student Life Satisfaction	Judgment	Agreement	Agreement
	Happiness at the Present	Judgment	Evaluation	Evaluation

Scale type
We changed graphical (Face Scale, Self Anchoring Ladder Scale, Semantic Differential Scales) and labeled scales of paper-questionnaire into equivalent rating scales in telephonic interviews. For instance, in the paper-questionnaire, students evaluated their student life by the Ladder Scale (Cantril), in graphical form, while in the CATI-questionnaires we adopted a different approach: students had to refer their agreement regarding an assertion about their student condition (Table 14.4).

Notice that the only variable measured by a verbal scale in all questionnaires is Personal Motivation towards Study scale.

Table 14.4. Different Scale Types Chosen for Our Three Questionnaires.

Areas	Variables	Scale type		
		Paper-Q.	Cati-Q.	
			a	b
University Evaluation	Faculty Evaluations	Graphical	Numerical	Numerical
Satisfaction and Well-Being Perception	Student Life Satisfaction	Graphical (Self Anchoring Ladder Scale)	Numerical	Numerical
	Happiness at the Present	Graphical (Face Scale)	Numerical	Numerical
Individual Traits and Dispositions	Self-esteem	Verbal	Numerical	Numerical

Scale Range
One of the hypotheses raised regarding rating scale concerns the discriminate capacities for scales with different rating amplitude. In order to test this hypothesis, we defined different scale ranges for our three questionnaires by assigning different scale amplitude alternatively to questionnaires (Table 14.5).

Table 14.5. Different Scale Ranges Chosen for Our Three Questionnaires.

Areas	Variables	Scale range		
		Paper-Q.	Cati-Q.	
			a	b
Satisfaction and Well-Being Perception	General Life Satisfaction	0-10	0-10	1-7
	Subjective Well-Being in Particular Ambits	0-10	0-10	1-7
	Student Life Satisfaction	1-9	0-10	1-7
	Happiness at the Present	1-7	1-7	0-10
	Happiness One Year Ago	--	1-7	0-10
Values	Importance of Particular Ambits in one's Life	--	1-7	0-10
Individual Traits and Dispositions	Self-esteem	1-4	1-5	1-7
	Motivation	1-5	1-4	1-4

Table 14.6 allows us to summarize the experimental design showing comparison among scales we used in paper-questionnaire and CATI-questionnaires. For each variable, tables show:

- number of used items
- used reference (agreement, judgment, etc.)
- scale type
- scale range.

Table 14.6. Different Scale Reference, Type, and Range for Paper- and CATI-questionnaire.

Areas	Variables	Paper-Questionnaire				Cati-Questionnaire							
						A				B			
		N. of items	Reference	Type	Range	N. of items	Reference	Type	Range	N. of items	Reference	Type	Range
UNIVERSITY EVALUATION	Faculty Evaluations	23	Image	Graphical (no numerical reference)	1-7	9	Agreement (Positive adjectives)	Numerical*	**1-7**	9	Agreement (Negative adjectives)	Numerical*	1-7
SATISFACTION AND WELL-BEING PERCEPTION	General Life Satisfaction	1	Evaluation	Numerical	0-10	1	Evaluation	Numerical*	0-10	1	Evaluation	Numerical*	1-7
	Subjective Well-Being in Particular Ambits	10	Evaluation	Numerical	0-10	10	Evaluation	Numerical*	0-10	10	Evaluation	Numerical*	1-7
	Student Life Satisfaction	1	Judgment	Graphical (Self Anchoring Ladder Scale)	1-9	1	Agreement	Numerical*	0-10	1	Agreement	Numerical*	1-7
	Happiness at the Present	1	Judgment	Graphical (Face Scale)	1-7	1	Evaluation	Numerical*	1-7	1	Evaluation	Numerical*	0-10
	Happiness One Year Ago					1	Evaluation	Numerical*	1-7	1	Evaluation	Numerical*	0-10
VALUES	Importance of Particular Ambits in one's Life					16	Judgment	Numerical*	1-7	16	Judgment	Numerical*	0-10
INDIVIDUAL TRAITS AND DISPOSITIONS	Self-esteem	10	Agreement	Verbal	1-4	10	Agreement	Numerical*	1-5	10	Agreement	Numerical*	1-7
	Motivation	10	Agreement	Verbal	1-5	10	Agreement	Verbal	1-4	10	Agreement	Verbal	1-4

Items marked by (*) are anchored verbally.

Number of items with the same scale amplitude differs among three groups because of the different number of items for questionnaire areas.

14.3. DATA ANALYSIS

The goals of data analysis, presented here, are to:

- Compare different performances of positive and negative references in individual evaluations. The analysis of distributions by graphical representations and statistical moments for quantitative data (from first moment to skewness index) allowed us to make these comparisons.
- Compare different scales for single items to evaluate different discriminate capacities. The graphical representations and statistical moments for quantitative data (from first moment to skewness and kurtosis indexes) of standardized scores allowed us to make these comparisons.
- Compare the impact of items presented in the different scales in selection of indicators. The Principal Component Analysis and the Additive Trees approaches have allowed us to explore, respectively, aggregations of items and aggregation process.
- Compare reliability of multi-item indicators with different scale types and scale ranges under different survey conditions; Internal Consistency Analysis allowed us to test reliability.

The analysis includes the areas and variables as reported in Table 14.7.

Table 14.7. Variables and Respective Number of Items Included in Our Analysis.

AREAS	VARIABLES	Number of defined Items		
		Paper	Cati (a)	Cati (b)
UNIVERSITY EVALUATION	Faculty Evaluations	23	9	9
SATISFACTION AND WELL-BEING PERCEPTION	General Life Satisfaction	1	1	1
	Subjective Well-Being in Particular Ambits	10	10	10
	Student Life Satisfaction	1	1	1
	Happiness at the Present	1	1	1
	Happiness One Year Ago		1	1
INDIVIDUAL TRAITS AND DISPOSITIONS	Self-esteem	10	10	10
	Motivation	10	10	10
VALUES	Importance of Particular Ambits in one's Life		16	16

14.3.1. *Comparability among Groups*

In order to verify the real comparability of our groups, we test statistical significance of difference between samples using external variables and applying the proper statistical test for independent samples (parametric or non-parametric test depends on measurement scale). None of the variables has registered a significant difference at the defined α-value (0.01).

Here, we show some outcomes yielded by exploring some consequences of using different survey condition and different rating scales in:

- individuation of subjective University Evaluation dimensions through Semantic Differential Scales;
- discrimination of individual Happiness and Satisfaction Perceptions and in pointing out well-being dimensions;
- validation of individual traits measures.

For each presented analysis we show tables showing, according to the goals of specific analysis, frequency distributions, descriptive indexes, graphical representations, factorial loading matrixes and/or reliability analysis indexes.

14.3.2. *Semantic Differential Scales in Different Survey Conditions*

One of the most useful tools for measuring individual images and evaluations is the Semantic Differential Scale (SDS). However, as we know, the identification of real bipolar adjectives represents one of its limits. In order to verify the bipolarity of suitable adjectives in our context and overcome the difficult application of SDS in telephonic interviews we defined three different approaches:

- 23 Semantic Differential Scales with graphical scales (0–6 points) in paper-questionnaire
- 9 Stapel scales defined by 'positive' adjectives with agreement rating scales (1–7 points) in CATI-questionnaire (a)
- 9 Stapel scales defined by 'negative' adjectives with agreement rating scales (1–7 points) CATI-questionnaire (b).

One of our goals is to validate an efficient shape for SDS in subjective university evaluation in different survey contexts. The traditional SDS approach (Osgood, 1957), which requires a large number of graphical items, is not suitable in telephonic contexts that require a different approach from that used in the paper questionnaire, e.g., the Stapel technique (Alreck and Settle, 1985). According to Stapel technique, each item requires only one adjective. This causes a change in scale references and requires a choice to be made between positive or negative adjectives. This choice is not trivial and needs to take into consideration the presence of a real semantic bipolarity between them. Our goal is to verify the appropriate item definition by testing the real bipolarity of defined and selected items.

Since efficiency in telephonic contexts is mostly related to brevity, we selected a smaller group of items from 23 items presented in paper-questionnaire. We were able to select items by taking Principal Component Analysis results into consideration in order to reject items that were clearly irrelevant in our context or with the same semantic content of others, and to introduce selected items in CATI-questionnaires.

In our experimental design, we defined two different groups of adjectives for CATI-questionnaires: positive ones for a-questionnaire and negative ones for b-questionnaire (Table 14.8). We first tested the hypothesis of bipolarity for these adjectives and then we compared the factorial composition of student evaluations between samples.

Table 14.8. Positive and Negative Adjectives for the Two CATI-questionaires.

CATI-Questionnaires		
a	Item number	*b*
stimulating	1	boring
useful	2	Useless
organized	3	Disorganized
encouraging	4	Discouraging
dynamic	5	Inactive
innovator	6	Traditional
simple	7	Difficult
easy	8	Hard
rewarding	9	Disappointing

Testing Bipolarity of Adjectives

Bipolarity evidence for two adjectives can be derived from the observation of two specula distributions for each pair of adjectives. For this purpose, we observed both graphical representations and skew ness values (Table 14.9).[1] In this context, we use these statistical tools as bipolarity indexes.

Table 14.9. Positive and negative Adjectives for the Two CATI-questionnaires: Statistical Indexes.

		median	mean	standard dev	skewness
a	stimulating	5.0	4.6	1.4	-0.4
	Useful	6.0	5.6	1.3	-1.0
	organized	4.0	3.8	1.5	-0.1
	encouraging	4.0	3.5	1.4	-0.1
	Dynamic	4.0	4.0	1.5	-0.2
	innovator	4.0	4.2	1.6	-0.2
	Simple	3.0	3.1	1.5	-0.2
	Easy	3.0	2.9	1.5	0.4
	rewarding	5.0	4.6	1.5	-0.6
b	Boring	3.0	3.0	1.7	0.5
	Useless	1.0	2.0	1.5	1.8
	disorganized	4.0	4.3	1.8	-0.2
	discouraging	4.0	4.1	1.8	-0.1
	Inactive	4.0	3.9	1.8	0.1
	traditional	4.0	4.8	1.8	-0.2
	Difficult	5.0	4.8	1.5	-0.5
	Hard	6.0	5.3	1.3	-0.7
	disappointing	3.0	3.0	1.8	0.7

The analysis reveals three different groups of items. A first group is composed of adjectives whose bipolarity is guaranteed by showing symmetrical distributions (Figure 14.1) and, as a result, skew ness values near zero (normal tendencies). We may notice that the opposite for two of these adjectives is obtained by the prefix "dis" in the Italian language, as well ("organized/disorganized" = "organizzata/disorganizzata"). This kind of adjective seems to assure perfect bipolarity.

A second group is composed of adjectives whose bipolarity is indicated by

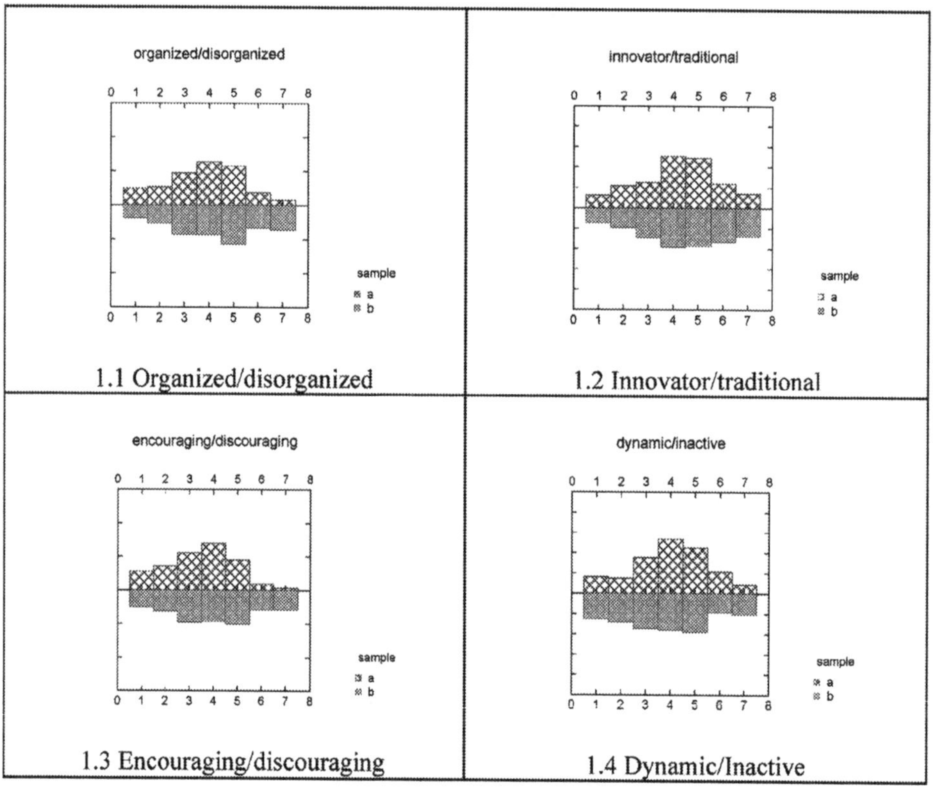

Figure 14.1. Bipolar Adjectives with Symmetrical Distributions.

showing opposite asymmetrical distributions (almost same skew ness values but of opposite signs). We can, however, also see that graphical representations (Figure 14.2) suggest a more prudent evaluation of students by negative adjectives (decreasing frequency values towards high scores) especially by 'useless' adjective.

A third group is composed of adjectives with a uncertain bipolarity (Figure 14.3). It may be interesting to verify, in the context of applying our questionnaires in other cultural contexts, to examine if the observed pondered use of negative adjectives represents a cultural and linguistic component only of Italian students.

3.1.2. *Comparing Component Structures in Positive and Negative Adjectives*

Comparing the factorial structures yielded by Principal Component Analysis (Table 14.10), we find an interesting difference between the two adjective groups: two components for positive adjectives, three components for negative adjectives, with almost the same level of total explained variance.

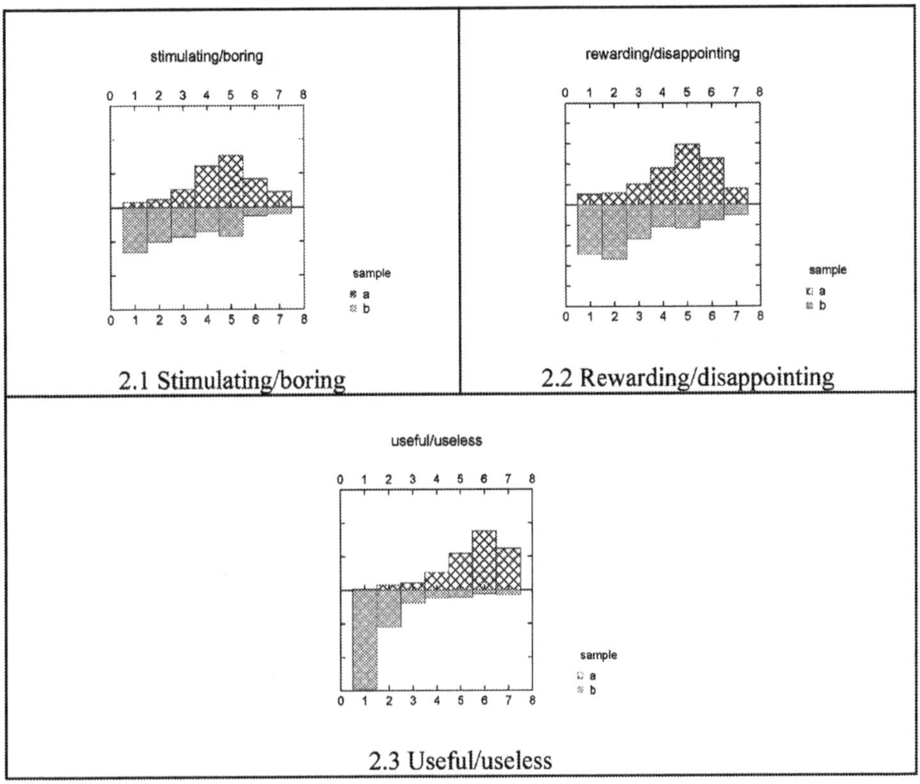

Figure 14.2. Bipolar Adjectives with Asymmetrical Distributions.

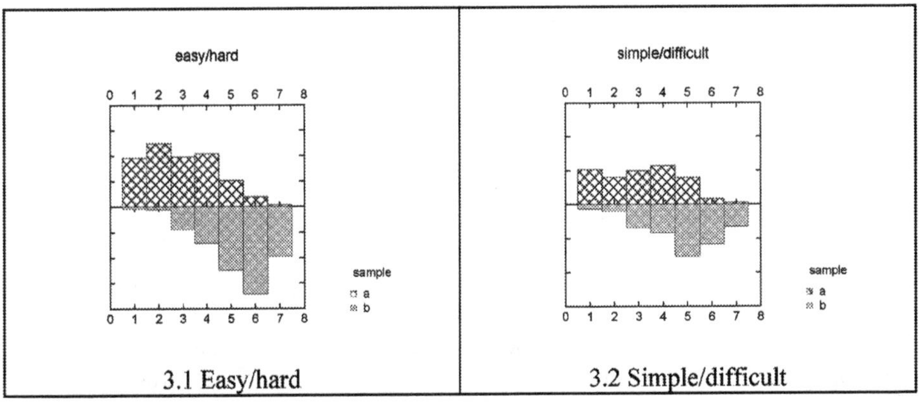

Figure 14.3. Adjectives without Bipolarity.

Table 14.10. Factorial Structures in Positive and Negative Adjectives.

Rotated Loading Matrixes (VARIMAX)						
CATI-Questionnaire						
a Sample				*b* Sample		
1	2			1	2	3
0.780	0.034	Stimulating	Boring	0.236	-0.014	***0.721***
0.701	-0.030	Useful	Useless	0.032	0.012	***0.798***
0.684	0.080	Organized	Disorganized	***0.823***	-0.131	0.009
0.684	0.297	Encouraging	Discouraging	***0.639***	0.302	0.207
0.731	0.174	Dynamic	Inactive	***0.699***	0.070	0.324
0.741	0.038	Innovator	Traditional	***0.681***	0.165	0.232
0.066	***0.914***	Simple	Difficult	0.097	***0.909***	0.071
0.109	***0.910***	Easy	Hard	0.074	***0.908***	-0.048
0.691	0.078	Rewarding	Disappointing	0.360	0.059	***0.655***
3.612	1.799	"Variance" Explained by Rotated Components		2.239	1.795	1.795
40.133	19.985	%		24.883	19.949	19.948

The observation of component compositions allows us to say that the first component for positive adjectives corresponds to two dimensions for the negative adjectives; this distinction seems to be related with bipolar typologies (first dimension for negative adjectives is composed of all adjectives with symmetrical distributions).

Moreover, the negative adjective solution seems to be more interpretable by showing a better discrimination among evaluation dimensions. We may label the three components respectively organizational environment (1), study (2) and psychological environment (3).

The application of the same analysis to the same adjectives in the paper-questionnaire yields same component solution of *a* group (63% of total explained variance).

This analysis seems to confirm the importance of using adjectives with a perfect bipolarity. Regarding Stapel scales (CATI-SDS), it is more useful, in order to meet individual evaluations, to apply negative adjectives. These negative adjectives seem to be used in a more meditated way. This observation needs a further investigation in order to verify its relation to cultural attitudes.

Moreover, we need to take into consideration the difficulty that occurs in converting these tools for cross-cultural surveys. The question is whether there is some relation between the cultural context and bipolarity of adjectives. Since in some cultural contexts, e.g. the Italian one, individual judgments are unlikely to be extremely positive or negative, it could be important to test the influence of cultural and linguistic factors of the respondent as regards bipolarity. This observation, also applicable to other subjective survey techniques, highlights a situation that might introduce a distortion (bias) that is difficult to evaluate, especially in cross-cultural comparisons. We come across this factor in the current research as well. The literal translation of our questionnaires into English does not always ensure a perfect semantic translation. Our intention is to plan new surveys involving different linguistic contexts.

14.3.3. *Life Satisfaction and Well-Being Perception Measures and Different Scale Ranges*

Variables defined in the conceptual model of our questionnaires, for the life satisfaction and well-being perception area, allow us to test the influence of different scale ranges in discriminating individual perceptions in single-item (general life satisfaction, student life satisfaction and happiness) and in highlighting well-being dimensions in multi-item scales.

Discriminate Capacity of Single-item Measures: General Life Satisfaction
Students referred their agreement on assertion concerning their general life satisfaction on a rating scale with different ranges

- 11 points agreement rating scale (from 0, *at all*, to 10, *completely satisfied*) in CATI-questionnaire, *a* (question 44), and paper-questionnaire (question 72)
- 7 points agreement rating scale (from 1, *at all*, to 10, *completely satisfied*) CATI-questionnaire, *b* (question 44)

Analyzing frequency distributions (Table 14.11) and descriptive statistical indexes (Table 14.12) we can observe, besides the high satisfaction levels expressed by almost all students, that

- Students with the longer rating scale did not use low score points
- Groups using the longer rating scale (paper-questionnaire and CATI-questionnaire, a) registered the same distribution shape (low concentration, long tails, revealed by low skew ness values)
- Different kurtosis values between groups using the longer rating scale (paper-questionnaire and CATI-questionnaire, *a*) may be attributed to survey effect

Table 14.11. Frequency Distribution of General Life Satisfaction Rating Scales.

FREQUENCY DISTRIBUTIONS					
CATI-Questionnaire				Paper-Questionnaire	
a		b			
RATING SCALE	PCT	RATING SCALE	PCT	RATING SCALE	PCT
0				0	
1		1	0.8	1	
2	0.2	2	1.5	2	0.7
3	1.2	3	2.3	3	2.0
4	1.2	4	6.6	4	2.4
5	3.0	5	23.2	5	7.1
6	8.7	6	38.7	6	13.9
7	25.7	7	26.9	7	30.4
8	35.4			8	22.0
9	15.8			9	14.5
10	8.9			10	7.1

Table 14.12. Descriptive Statistical Indexes for General Life Satisfaction Rating Scales (Standardized Data).

DESCRIPTIVE INDEXES	CATI-Questionnaire		Paper-Questionnaire
	a	b	
Mimimum	-4.2	-4.1	-3.3
Maximum	1.7	1.1	1.7
Median	0.2	0.2	-0.2
Skewness	-0.7	-1.3	-0.5
Kurtosis	1.5	2.3	0.6

- Group using the shorter rating scale (CATI-questionnaire, *b*) registered a compression of extremely high scores (high skew ness and kurtosis values).

These outcomes allow us to interpret the lack of extremely low values in longer rating scales as a clear positive group trend (nobody expressed a very low life satisfaction); the shorter rating scale does not allow us to reach the same conclusion even if students, using shorter rating, show the same trend.

In other words, longer rating scales are more useful in individual evaluation than the shorter rating scale, which seems unable to discriminate among extreme levels of satisfaction.

Discriminate Capacity of Single-item Measures: Student Life Satisfaction
In exploring respondent judgments about their student life satisfaction we used:

- Self Anchoring Ladder Scale by Cantril (9 steps), in paper-questionnaire (question 71)
- 11 points agreement rating scale, in CATI-questionnaire *a* (question 43)
- 7 points agreement rating scale, in CATI-questionnaire *b* (question 43).

Descriptive analysis (Tables 14.13 and 14.14) allows us to highlights, once again,

Table 14.13. Frequency Distribution of Student Life Satisfaction Rating Scales.

CATI-Questionnaire				Paper-Questionnaire	
a		b			
RATING SCALE	PCT	RATING SCALE	PCT	LADDER SCALE	PCT
0	3.6				
1	0.4	1	7.0	Step 1	0.7
2	2.3	2	10.8	Step 2	1.3
3	5.2	3	18.8	Step 3	4.0
4	8.2	4	21.7	Step 4	9.3
5	20.1	5	26.2	Step 5	24.3
6	17.4	6	9.0	Step 6	20.7
7	20.9	7	6.5	Step 7	26.3
8	14.2			Step 8	9.3
9	4.0			Step 9	4.0
10	3.8				

Table 14.14. Descriptive Statistical Indexes for Student Life Satisfaction Rating Scales (Standardized Data).

DESCRIPTIVE INDICES	CATI-Questionnaire		Paper-Questionnaire
	a	b	Ladder Scale
Mimimum	-2.8	-1.9	-3.2
Maximum	1.9	1.9	2.0
Median	0.04	-0.01	0.04
Skewness	-0.6	-0.1	-0.3
Kurtosis	0.7	-0.6	0.1

the better capacity of longer scales in discriminating extreme agreement/disagreement levels.

As we can see, the extreme quartile group using the longer scale shows a greater dispersion among extreme scores; this could mean that students of the group using the shorter scale had to compress their attitude expressions, especially in low scores (higher frequency values for this group compared with low frequency values for other two groups).

Discriminate Capacity of Single-item Measures: Happiness
Students expressed their happiness level by one of the following approaches:

- Face Scale (7 expressions), in paper-questionnaire[2] (question 102)
- 7 points agreement rating scale, in CATI-questionnaire, *a* (question 65)
- 11 points agreement rating scale, in CATI-questionnaire, *b* (question 65)

In CATI-questionnaires students expressed their happiness level regarding both the present and past years.

Once more, a long-range scale reveals a better discriminate capacity; here this is more evident in low levels because of the strong concentration along high happiness levels registered for all students (Table 14.15). As we can see, *b* group distribution appears more concentrated (high kurtosis value) and with a long tail in correspondence with low happiness levels.

It is interesting to compare paper-questionnaire and a group distributions since they have the same range scale but different scale type (graphical vs. rating). They registered different kurtosis and very similar skew ness values (Table 14.16), revealing a less concentrated distribution for the *face-scale*. Since we cannot assume different psychological conditions between two groups, the *face-scale* seems to allow a better individual 'identification' of happiness perceptions. In other words, longer scales reveal a better discriminate capacity than shorter ones (scale-effect) and graphical scale outcomes suggest a better discriminate capacity than rating scales (survey-effect).

The better discriminate capacity of long-range scales is confirmed by observing distributions regarding happiness in the past year for CATI-questionnaires (Tables 14.17 and 14.18).[3]

Table 14.15. Frequency Distribution of Happiness Rating Scales.

Happiness level at the present					
CATI-Questionnaire				Paper-Questionnaire	
a		b			
RATING SCALE	PCT	RATING SCALE	PCT	FACE SCALE	PCT
		0	0.6		
1	0.6	1	0.4	Face 7	1.7
2	0.6	2	0.8	Face 6	2.7
3	3.0	3	0.8	Face 5	8.8
4	9.9	4	1.5	Face 4	18.6
5	29.1	5	6.0	Face 3	34.6
6	39.9	6	10.1	Face 2	25.4
7	16.8	7	27.1	Face 1	8.1
		8	36.9		
		9	8.3		
		10	7.5		

Table 14.16. Descriptive Statistical Indexes for Happiness Rating Scales.

Happiness level at the present			
DESCRIPTIVE INDICES	CATI-Questionnaire		**Paper-Questionnaire**
	a	b	
Mimimum	-4.2	-4.7	-3.1
Maximum	1.4	1.7	1.6
Median	0.4	0.4	0.1
Skewness	-0.9	-1.3	-0.7
Kurtosis	1.6	3.8	0.5

Table 14.17. Frequency Distribution of Past Year Happiness Rating Scales.

Happiness level one year ago				
CATI-Questionnaire				Paper-Questionnaire
a		B		
RATING SCALE	PCT	RATING SCALE	PCT	
		0	0.6	Not Presented
1	1.8	1	0.8	
2	6.3	2	1.9	
3	6.9	3	3.1	
4	13.6	4	4.3	
5	25.9	5	9.1	
6	30.1	6	17.7	
7	15.3	7	23.2	
		8	24.1	
		9	8.4	
		10	6.8	

Table 14.18. Descriptive Statistical Indexes for Past Year Happiness Rating Scales (Standarized Data).

Happiness level one year ago			
DESCRIPTIVE INDICES	CATI-Questionnaire		Paper-Questionnaire
	a	b	
Mimimum	-2.8	-3.6	Not presented
Maximum	1.3	1.7	
Median	-0.1	0.1	
Skewness	-0.8	-0.8	
Kurtosis	0.1	0.9	

Well-being Dimensions of Multi-item Measures with Different Rating Scales

The above analysis allows us to show the importance of scale length in individual evaluation; now we need to consider in what way scale length influences the construction of synthetic subjective indicators of well being.

In our surveys, students related their agreement on assertions concerning subjective well being in 10 particular ambits on the same rating scale as they used before for general life satisfaction:

- 11 points agreement rating scale in CATI-questionnaire, *a* (questions from 45 to 54), and paper-questionnaire (questions from 73 to 82, except 80)
- 7 points agreement rating scale in CATI-questionnaire, *b* (questions from 45 to 54)

The investigated ambits are:

- *friendship*
- *free-time*
- *family relationship*
- *personal health*
- *family health*
- *faculty*
- *family financial situation*
- *university career*
- *personal financial situation*
- *university friendship*

For the sake of brevity, we will not to show all the outcomes regarding descriptive indexes. This is because we observed the same results for each item, as pointed out for the general life satisfaction single item.

In exploring and testing the influence of different scale ranges in the construction of synthetic well-being indicators, we applied Principal Component Analysis (Table 14.19).

We can very clearly observe three dimensions of life satisfaction for all groups, even if each dimension accounts for a different proportion of variance in each group. We can define dimensions by the following labels (in brackets component number for each group):

Table 14.19. Well-being Ambits: Factorial Structures for the Three Questionnaires.

		Rotated Loading Matrix (VARIMAX)								
		CATI-Questionnaire *a*			**CATI-Questionnaire *b***			**Paper-Questionnaire**		
		1	2	3	1	2	3	1	2	3
items	1	0.39	0.14	0.45	0.28	0.33	0.35	***0.64***	0.43	0.01
	2	0.18	0.11	***0.73***	0.11	0.22	***0.67***	***0.57***	0.04	0.26
	3	0.11	0.12	***0.78***	0.21	-0.03	***0.80***	***0.52***	-0.18	***0.52***
	4	0.11	***0.77***	0.27	***0.79***	0.02	0.32	0.31	0.05	***0.81***
	5	0.01	***0.88***	-0.00	***0.83***	0.00	0.08	-0.01	0.27	***0.86***
	6	0.13	***0.56***	0.15	***0.51***	0.35	-0.10	***0.61***	0.21	0.12
	7	0.06	0.13	***0.70***	-0.05	0.12	***0.63***	***0.75***	0.06	0.07
	8	***0.75***	0.18	0.07	0.03	***0.71***	0.17	0.10	***0.85***	-0.02
	9	***0.75***	0.17	0.14	0.03	***0.74***	0.11	0.18	***0.75***	0.28
	10	***0.70***	-0.11	0.16	0.13	***0.74***	0.08	Not presented		
Indexes	*	1.84	1.81	1.99	1.72	1.90	1.77	2.08	1.63	1.83
	**	18.37	18.06	19.86	17.15	19.03	17.65	23.06	18.14	20.37
	***	***0.60***	***0.62***	***0.68***	***0.56***	***0.66***	***0.59***	***0.64***	***0.65***	***0.70***

* *Variance explained by rotated components*
** *Variance explained by rotated components (%)*
*** *ALPHA only for marked items (with reference to items with high factor loadings)*

- university satisfaction (1: *a* group, 2: *b* group, 2: *paper-questionnaire* group)
- money satisfaction (2: *a* group, 1: *b* group, 3: *paper-questionnaire* group)
- satisfaction in relationships (3: *a* group, 3: *b* group, 1: *paper-questionnaire* group)

Free time is related with financial satisfaction (personal and family) in both CATI-questionnaires and with relationships in paper-questionnaire; in paper-questionnaire we also observed a relation between financial situation (family and personal) and family health that disappears in the component structure of CATI-questionnaires. Item concerning friendship satisfaction shows low component loadings in each dimension for *a* and *b* groups.

Furthermore, calculating the *alpha* values for each sub-dimension, taking into account only high factor loadings items for each component,[4] we can see that the paper-questionnaire and *a* questionnaire registered better values than the other one.

The outcomes of principal component analysis can be integrated by exploring the items aggregation process through the Additive Trees clustering method,[5] which yielded for each group a solution confirming preceding outcomes. The explained variance for three groups is, respectively, 87, 74 and 77 per cent. For the sake of brevity, we present only the graphical outcomes (tree diagrams – Figure 14.4).

In Figure 14.4, we also show the corresponding labels for each item for each questionnaire in order to appreciate three tree diagrams.

The Additive Tree analysis confirms the component structures of the a and b groups: the item aggregation process allows the identification of the same three dimensions. The item concerning friendship satisfaction (question 45) reveals its extraneousness as regards chosen variables.

In the paper-questionnaire group, Principal Component Analysis revealed some superimposition in two satisfaction dimensions (university satisfaction and relationship satisfaction); observing the tree diagram, the superimposition can be seen

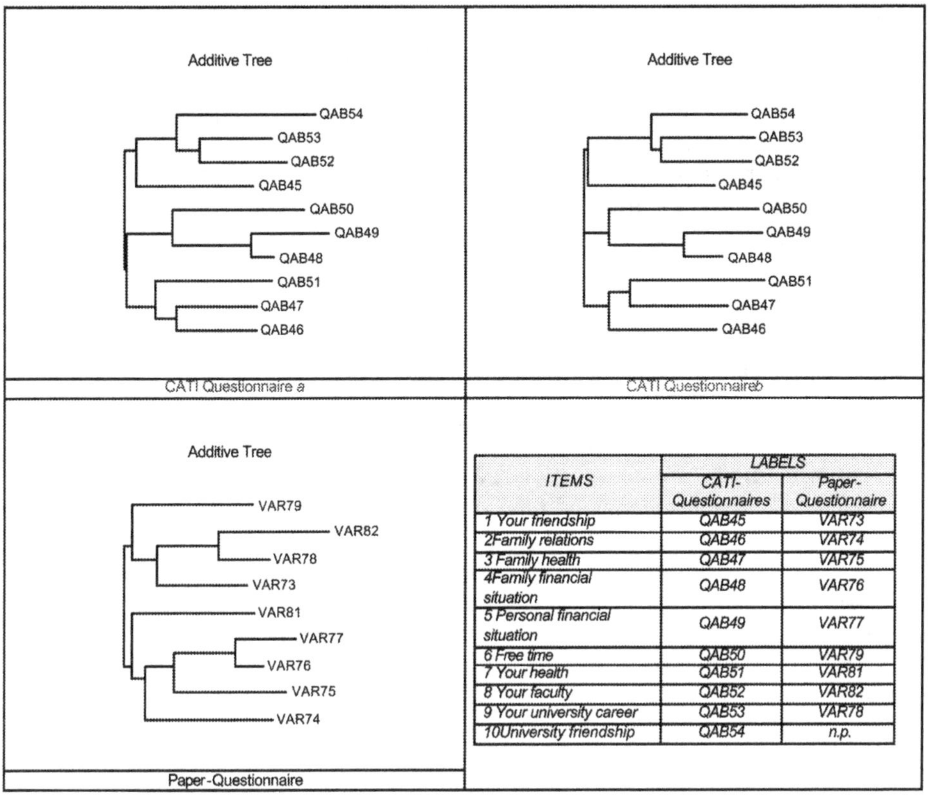

ITEMS	LABELS	
	CATI-Questionnaires	Paper-Questionnaire
1 Your friendship	QAB45	VAR73
2Family relations	QAB46	VAR74
3 Family health	QAB47	VAR75
4Family financial situation	QAB48	VAR76
5 Personal financial situation	QAB49	VAR77
6 Free time	QAB50	VAR79
7 Your health	QAB51	VAR81
8 Your faculty	QAB52	VAR82
9 Your university career	QAB53	VAR78
10University friendship	QAB54	n.p.

Figure 14.19. Tree Diangrams for Well-being Ambits.

more clearly; in particular, the items related with the first component join with items of the other two dimensions, which, on the other hand, can be clearly identified. The better appreciation of relations among variables, in terms of distances, allowed by additive tree analysis, highlights the potential insufficiency of Principal Component Analysis in the selection of variables for the construction of synthetic indicators purpose.

At this point, the registered differences between CATI outcomes and paper-questionnaire outcomes reveal a survey-effect rather than a scale-effect.

On the other hand, the outcomes obtained seem to suggest that the use of different scale ranges has no direct influence on the identification or construction of synthetic well-being indicators, but a partial impact related to reliability outcomes. The presence of a superimposition of both effects needs a follow-up analysis and evaluation.

Finally, the use of statistical multidimensional methods in selecting variables to construct synthetic indicators needs special attention. Even if all the methods can yield consistent and comparable results on the same data, each approach can produce and reveal original images and representations of data. This suggests, and makes desirable, integration among different approaches.

14.3.4. *ScaleRreliability in Different Survey Conditions*

The measurement of self-esteem and motivation towards study dimensions by different scale approaches allows us to evaluate the influence of different survey conditions (different survey techniques and different type and range scales) on scale reliability.

Self-Esteem
The 10 items Rosemberg Scale was chosen to measure self-esteem. These Rosemberg Scale items were expressed in the following manner:

- *On the whole, I am satisfied with myself.*
- *At times, I think I am no good at all.*
- *I feel that I have a number of good qualities.*
- *I feel I do not have much to be proud of.*
- *I am able to do things as well as most other people.*
- *I certainly feel useless at times.*
- *I feel I'm a person of worth, at least on an equal plane with others.*
- *I wish I could have more respect for myself.*
- *I take a positive attitude toward myself.*
- *All in all, I am inclined to feel that I am a failure.*

We decided to define and adopt three different scales approaches:

- 4 labeled agreement levels, in paper-questionnaire (questions from 83 to 92)
- 5 points agreement rating scale, in *a* CATI-questionnaire (questions from 55 to 64)
- 7 points agreement rating scale, in *b* CATI-questionnaire (questions from 55 to 64)

Before observing the reliability of the Rosemberg scale under different survey conditions we can point out that, independently of survey conditions, we have observed the same kind of distribution in regards to each item.

Motivation Towards Study
In order to explore one particular aspect of student life, motivation towards study, related with other dimensions (students' performances, evaluations, and so on) we adopted a scale whose items were expressed in the following way:

- *I would go on with studying even if I would receive an offer of work of my liking.*
- *In the future I look forward to get a work consistent with my study.*
- *I believe I have the ideal characteristics to attend this degree.*
- *In the future I look forward to get a work which could be fulfilled.*

- At this moment study represents one of the most important thing for me.
- *My final preparation will be my main strength point.*
- *All exams in my curriculum are important for the aspiring career.*
- *I am up to any exam's level I prepare.*
- *Exam mark depends especially on me.*
- *I always have an interest in subjects I study.*

In the paper-questionnaire (questions from 61 to 70), we used five labeled levels: (5) strongly agree, (4) quite agree, (3) neither agree nor disagree, (2) quite disagree, and (1) strongly disagree.

In CATI survey (*a* and *b* questionnaires, questions from 33 to 42), we used the same scales, but eliminated the median-labeled level in order to verify the influence of the lack of the neutral position. This additionally allowed us to avoid the difficult presentation of a great number of labels in telephonic interviews.

Reliability Analysis of Self-esteem and Motivation towards Study Scales

Comparing Rosemberg scale items, we can observe that items of the *b* questionnaire generally show better performances than those of the *a* questionnaire and that paper-questionnaire items reach better performances than CATI-questionnaires items (Table 14.20). These outcomes are confirmed by total scale performance: the Rosemberg scale reaches a better internal consistency in paper-questionnaire than in other questionnaires. These outcomes allow us to conclude that whereas different results between CATI groups can be imputed to scale-effect, better paper-questionnaire performances can be explained by survey-effect.

Following the reliability analysis of motivation towards the study scale allows us to test the existence of survey-effect in the presence of the same scale type. Outcomes confirm the observed difference between paper-questionnaire and CATI-questionnaire (Table 14.21). In particular, it is very important to observe the low performance levels of CATI-questionnaire.

The low level of internal consistency for the CATI-group could be evaluated in

Table 14.20. Reliability Item Analysis of Rosemberg Scale for the Three Questionnaires.

	Paper-Questionnaire Labeled scores (4)				CATI-Questionnaire *a* Rating scales (1-5)				CATI-Questionnaire *b* Rating scales (1-7)			
	*	**	***	****	*	**	***	****	*	**	***	****
1	0.70	0.47	0.62	0.84	0.52	0.44	0.39	0.71	0.61	0.70	0.50	0.72
2	0.70	0.67	0.59	0.84	0.63	0.72	0.47	0.67	0.66	1.13	0.50	0.72
3	0.65	0.45	0.56	0.84	0.43	0.32	0.30	0.72	0.47	0.46	0.37	0.74
4	0.71	0.50	0.64	0.84	0.45	0.38	0.31	0.72	0.52	0.55	0.41	0.74
5	0.52	0.43	0.40	0.85	0.33	0.29	0.17	0.74	0.40	0.49	0.25	0.75
6	0.77	0.73	0.68	0.83	0.66	0.73	0.52	0.69	0.63	0.95	0.49	0.72
7	0.54	0.41	0.43	0.85	0.48	0.38	0.35	0.72	0.48	0.54	0.35	0.74
8	0.59	0.60	0.45	0.85	0.67	0.99	0.46	0.71	0.62	1.37	0.39	0.75
9	0.73	0.60	0.64	0.83	0.65	0.68	0.51	0.69	0.68	0.95	0.56	0.71
10	0.72	0.59	0.64	0.83	0.58	0.40	0.49	0.70	0.59	0.57	0.50	0.73
alpha	0.85				0.73				0.75			

* *item-total r*
** *item-reliability index*
*** *item-total r excluding the item*
**** *alpha value excluding the item*

Table 14.21. Reliability Item Analysis of Motivation towards Study Scale for the Three Questionnaires.

	Paper-Questionnaire Labeled scores (5)				CATI-Questionnaires Labeled scores (4)			
	*	**	***	****	*	**	***	****
1	0.72	0.95	0.60	0.79	0.43	0.45	0.18	0.55
2	0.67	0.68	0.58	0.79	0.45	0.33	0.29	0.52
3	0.67	0.66	0.58	0.79	0.45	0.33	0.29	0.52
4	0.58	0.59	0.47	0.80	0.38	0.21	0.25	0.53
5	0.59	0.62	0.47	0.80	0.53	0.52	0.32	0.51
6	0.73	0.80	0.64	0.79	0.51	0.48	0.31	0.51
7	0.54	0.64	0.40	0.81	0.51	0.52	0.28	0.52
8	0.57	0.62	0.46	0.80	0.39	0.36	0.18	0.55
9	0.55	0.74	0.40	0.81	0.36	0.36	0.12	0.57
10	0.57	0.65	0.44	0.79	0.49	0.46	0.28	0.52
alpha	0.82				0.56			

* *item-total r* *** *item-total r excluding the item*
** *item-reliability index* **** *alpha value excluding the item*

the context of the difficulty of use of the verbal scales in telephonic situations (survey-effect). It could thus be interesting to verify the possible superimposition of the scale-effect on survey-effect through supplementary studies.

14.4. CONCLUSIONS

The goal of the study essentially concerned methodological aspects involved in surveys. The presented analyses and outcomes show the importance of the choice of the scale under different survey methods. In fact, the outcomes show the different influence of survey-effect and scale-effect on quality of data.

A scale-range-effect exists independently from survey-effect. In particular, we can say that it is possible to reach better individual measurement and evaluation by wide-range scales. Longer scales reveal a better discriminate capacity than shorter ones (scale-effect). On the other hand, graphical scales suggest a better discriminate capacity than rating scales aside from scale range (survey-effect).

The formation of satisfaction dimensions and the aggregation processes of single-items in the construction of synthetic indicators seem not to be directly influenced by scale-range.

We also observed partial scale-effect and survey-effect in each scale item in regards to reliability and a combined scale- and survey-effect in whole multi-item scale reliability. In particular, labeled-scales do not seem to fit telephonic questionnaires; in fact, labeled-scale items in paper-questionnaire show better reliability performances than labeled-scale items in CATI-questionnaires.

Further study, such as a WEB-survey combining paper and CATI-questionnaires characteristics, are needed in order to evaluate the superimposition of both effects on reliability levels.

The reference-scale effect must be considered as it relates with item definition and cultural factors. In our experience, this effect allowed us to identify a particular outcome in judgments expressed by positive and negative references. This cultural-effect needs to be tested further in comparison with other cultural contexts.

These tests could be of great interest and could introduce important observations and considerations about the use of international comparison analyses.

Outcomes confirm our hypothesis about the importance of the measurement instrument under different survey conditions. This is especially true for the telephonic approach, frequently considered, erroneously, a simple survey method, for which the definition of the measurement instrument is less important. Unfortunately, in many cases, CATI-questionnaires are derived from a simple and direct adaptation of a paper-questionnaire, i.e. following the same criterion in expression and wording of the questions.

In our opinion, the theme is very delicate and complex since it also involves cultural components. In such cases, the generalization of individual experiences to other cultural contexts may not be allowed, in trying to provide a truly accurate data analysis.

14.5. NOTES

[1] Kurtosis values are not considered crucial to identify bipolar adjectives.

[2] Notice that *face scale* expressions show an inverted direction as regards the rating scales of CATI-questionnaires. In order to compare distributions, we reversed the *face-scale* codes.

[3] We cannot compare the three groups since this item was not presented in the paper-questionnaire.

[4] A follow-up analysis will define component scores by using factor scores.

[5] As we know the Additive Trees Clustering Method, unlike Hierarchical Clustering methods, uses tree branch length to represent distances between objects. Objects within a cluster can thus be compared by focusing on the horizontal distance along the branches connecting them.

14.6 REFERENCES

Alreck, P. L. and Settle, R. B. (1985). *The Survey Research Handbook.* Homewood Illinois: Richard D.Irwing Inc.

Andrews, F. M. and McKennel, A. C. (1980). Measures of self-reported Well-Being: their affective, cognitive, and other components. *Social Indicators Research*, **8**.

Arcuri, L. and Flores D'Arcais, G. B. (1974). *La misura degli atteggiamenti.* Firenze: Martello – Giunti.

Baker, T. L. (1994, 2nd ed.). *Doing Social Research.* New York-London: McGraw-Hill.

Bolasco, S. (1999). *Analisi multidimensionali dei dati. Metodi, strategie e criteri di interpretazione.* Roma: Carocci.

Carmines, E. C. and Zeller, R. A. (1992). *Reliability and Validity Assessment.* Sage University Paper Series on Quantitative Applications in the Social Sciences, series no. 07-017. Newbury Park, CA: Sage.

Converse, J. M. and Presser, S. (1991). *Survey Questions: Handcrafting the Standardized Questionnaire.* Sage University Paper Series on Quantitative Applications in the Social Sciences, series no. 07-063. Newbury Park, CA: Sage.

Dautriat, H. (1988, 6th ital. ed.). *Il questionario.* Milano: Franco Angeli Editore.

Del Vecchio, F. (1995). *Scale di misura e indicatori sociali.* Bari: Caccucci.

De Sandre, P. (1972). *Classificazione e misura nella ricerca sociale.* Padova: CLEUP.

De Vellis, R. (1991). *Scale devolopment. Theory and Applications.* Applied Social Research Methods Series, vol. 26. London: SAGE.

Edward, A. (1957). *Techniques of Attitude Scale Construction.* Englewood Cliffs, NJ: Prentice-Hall.

Edward, W. and Newman J. R. (1982). *Multiattribute Evalutation.* Sage University Paper Series on Quantitative Applications in the Social Sciences, series no. 07-026. Newbury Park, CA: Sage.

Flament, C. (1976). *L'analyse booléenne de questionnaire.* Paris-La Haye: Mouton Editeur.
Fordyce, M. W. (1988). A review of research on the happiness measures: a sixty seconds index of happiness and mental health. *Social Indicators Research*, **4**.
Ghiselli, E. E. (1964). *Theory of Psychological Measurement.* New York-London: McGraw-Hill.
Gilbert, N. (1993). *Researching Social Life.* London: Sage.
Guilford, J. P. (1936). *Psychometric Methods.* New York-London: McGraw-Hill.
Jacoby, W. G. (1991). *Data Theory and Dimensional Analysis.* Sage University Paper Series on Quantitative Applications in the Social Sciences, series no. 07-078. Newbury Park, CA: Sage.
Larsen, E. R., Diener, J., and Emmons, R. A. (1985). An Evaluation of Subjective Well-Being Measures. *Social Indicators Research*, **17**(4).
Lyubomirsky, S. and Lepper, H. S. (1999). A Measure of Subjective Happiness: Preliminary Reliability and Construct Validation. *Social Indicators Research*, **46**(2).
Maggino, F. (2000, 2nd ed.). *Il questionario. Aspetti metodologici, informatici e statistici.* Firenze: C.E.T.
Maggino, F. (1999). Metodi di validazione di strumenti soggettivi. In E. Aureli, F. Buratto, L. Carli Sardi, A. Franci, A. Ponti Sgargi, and S. Schifini D'Andrea (eds.), *Contesti di qualità della vita* (pp. 185–213). Milano: F. Angeli.
McIver, J. P., and Carmines, E. G. (1979). *Unidimensional Scaling.* Sage University Paper Series on Quantitative Applications in the Social Sciences, series no. 07-024. Newbury Park, CA: Sage.
Nunnally, J. C. (1978). *Psychometric Theory.* New York-London: McGraw-Hill
Oppenheim, A. N. (1966). *Questionnaire Design and Attitude Measurement.* London: Heinemann.
Osgood, C. E., Suci G. J., and Tannenbaum, P. H. (1957). *The Measurement of Meaning.* Urbana: University of Illinois Press.
Osterlind, S. J. (1983). *Test Item Bias.* Sage University Paper Series on Quantitative Applications in the Social Sciences, series no. 07-030. Newbury Park, CA: Sage.
Saris, W. E. (1990). *Computer-Assisted Interviewing.* Sage University Paper Series on Quantitative Applications in the Social Sciences, series no. 07-080. Newbury Park, CA: Sage.
Schifini, D'Andrea S. (1999). Qualità della vita: misure, teorie e modelli. In E. Aureli, F. Buratto, L. Carli Sardi, A. Franci, A. Ponti Sgargi, and S. Schifini D'Andrea (ed.), *Contesti di qualità della vita* (pp. 15–66). Milano: F. Angeli.
Schifini D'Andrea, S. and Maggino, F. (1999). Qualità della vita universitaria: validazione di strumenti soggettivi. In E. Aureli, F. Buratto, L. Carli Sardi, A. Franci, A. Ponti Sgargi, and S. Schifini D'Andrea (eds.), *Contesti di qualità della vita* (pp. 155–184). Milano: F. Angeli.
Spector, P. E. (1990). *Research Designs.* Sage University Paper Series on Quantitative Applications in the Social Sciences, series no. 07-023. Newbury Park, CA: Sage.
Spector, P. E. (1992). *Summated Rating Scale Construction. An Introduction.* Sage University Paper Series on Quantitative Applications in the Social Sciences, series no. 07-082. Newbury Park, CA: Sage.
Sullivan, J. L. and Feldman S. (1981). *Multiple Indicators. An Introduction.* Sage University Paper Series on Quantitative Applications in the Social Sciences, series no. 07-015. Newbury Park: CA:Sage.
Tesi, G. (1983). *Note per la ricerca mediante questionario.* Firenze: Università degli Studi.
Torgerson, W. S. (1958). *Theory and Methods of Scaling.* New York, London, Sydney: John Wiley & Sons, Inc.
Traub, R. E. (1994). *Reliability for the Social Sciences – Theory and Applications.* Measurement Methods for the Social Sciences series, vol. 3. London: SAGE Publications.
Zumbo, B. D. (ed.) (1999). Validity Theory and the Methods used in Validation: Perspectives from Social and Behavioural Sciences. *Social Indicators Research*, **45**(1–3).

14.7. AFFILIATIONS

Filomena Maggino, Università di Firenze – Italy
Silvana Schifini D'Andrea, Università di Firenze – Italy

Index

www.ingramcontent.com/pod-product-compliance
Lightning Source LLC
LaVergne TN
LVHW011751200926
848484LV00003B/678

* 9 7 8 1 4 0 2 0 1 4 7 4 1 *